HIGHER EDUCATION
An International Perspective

About the Editor

Dr. Mujibul Hasan Siddiqui, M.A. (Economics), B.Ed., M.Ed., M.Phill. (Education), Ph.D. (Education) PGDHE, PGDDE, MADE, CCCA, CCPALA is working as Associate Professor in the Department of Education, Aligarh Muslim University, Aligarh. He has authored and edited several books, encyclopaedias in the area education, research and innovative teaching, published more than fifty research papers, reviewed eighty national and international research papers.

He is a member of editorial board of several national and international journal of research. He has guided several Ph.D. research scholars and research projects of M.Ed. students. He has received several academic and research excellence awards in India like Life Time Education Achievement Award, Bharat Gaurav Ratan Award, Best Educationist Award, Bharat Shiksha Ratan Award, Eminent Educationist Award, Rashtriya Vidya Saraswati Purashkar.

His area of interest in Curriculum, Evaluation, Management of Education, Planning and Finance of Education, ICT, Models of Teaching, Guidance and Counselling, Value Education, Higher Education, Distance Education, Pedagogy of Economics, Social Studies, Indian Education and Problems, Educational Technology, Education of Children with Special Needs.

HIGHER EDUCATION
An International Perspective

Edited by
Mujibul Hasan Siddiqui
Associate Professor
Department of Education
Aligarh Muslim University
Aligarh-202002, Uttar Pradesh

CONCEPT PUBLISHING COMPANY PVT. LTD.
NEW DELHI-110059

ISBN-13: 978-93-86682-39-0

First Published 2019

Published and Printed by

Concept Since 1974

Concept Publishing Company Pvt. Ltd.
A/15-16, Commercial Block, Mohan Garden,
New Delhi-110059 (India)
T: +91 11 25351460, +91 11 25351794
E: publishing@conceptpub.com, *W*: www.conceptpub.com

Cataloging in Publication Data--Courtesy: D.K. Agencies (P) Ltd. <docinfo@dkagencies.com>

Higher education : an international perspective / edited by Mujibul Hasan Siddiqui.
pages cm
Contributed articles.
Includes bibliographical references and index.
ISBN 9789386682390

1. Education, Higher. 2. Education, Higher—India. I. Siddiqui, Mujibul Hasan, editor.

LCC LB2325.H54 2018 DDC 378 23

Preface

This book includes 22 chapters highlighting a collection of "Higher Education: An International Perspective" of USA, Thailand, Saudia Arabia, Canada, Japan, China, South Africa, Brazil, UK, Australia, Bangladesh and India. The perspectives were presented in the form of conceptual, historical, aims and objective, curriculum management, quality, values, examination, administration, research, teaching, pedagogical aspects of higher education of various countries of the world. This book makes good comparative study of higher education of different countries.

This book is very useful for the researchers, thinkers, teacher, philosopher and who have interest in comparative study of higher education in an international perspectives.

Dr. Mujibul Hasan Siddiqui
M.A. (Economics), M.Ed., M.Phil. (Education), Ph.D. (Education),
PGDHE, PGDDE, MADE, CCIPALA, CCCA
Associate Professor
Department of Education
Aligarh Muslim University
Aligarh, U.P.
INDIA

Acknowledgements

I would like to express my sincere gratitude to my contributors of this book who sent book chapters with their great efforts. I am also very grateful to my wife Professor Dr. (Mrs.) Nasreen, Department of Education, Aligarh Muslim University, Aligarh for her best cooperation and encouragement for the completion of this book.

I am also thankful to my colleagues and friends who cooperated me in completing this work.

I am very thankful to the Concept Publishing Co. Pvt. Ltd., New Delhi to publish my book within short time.

Dr. Mujibul Hasan Siddiqui
M.A. (Economics), M.Ed., M.Phil. (Education), Ph.D. (Education),
PGDHE, PGDDE, MADE, CCIPALA, CCCA
Associate Professor
Department of Education
Aligarh Muslim University
Aligarh, U.P. (India)

Acknowledgements

Contents

Section-IV
Emerging Trends and Future Prospects

List of Contributors

Dr. Anjum Ahmed, Assistant Professor, Department of Education, Aligarh Muslim University, Aligarh, Uttar Pradesh, India.
E-mail: *anjum.amu1312@gmail.com*

Anu Jose Vengal, Assistant Professor, Titus II Teachers College, Thiruvalla, Kerala, India. E-mail: *annuvengal@gmail.com*

Bilal Ahmad Bhat, Lecturer, Faculty of Education, University of Kashmir, Srinagar, Jammu & Kashmir. E-mail: *bilalbhat.amu@gmail.com*

Dr. Ismail Thamarasseri, Assistant Professor, Departmenc of Education, Central University of Kashmir, Wanabal, Nowgam Bypass, Srinagar-190015, Jammu & Kashmir, India. E-mail: *ismailktkl@gmail.com*

Dr. Kauser Tasneem, Department of Psychology, Mother Teresa Women's University, Kodaikanal, Chennai, Tamil Nadu, India.
E-mail: *kauser_k@hotmail.com*

Micheal M. Van Wyk, Department of Curriculum and Instructional Studies, School of Teacher Education, University of South Africa, South Africa.
E-mail: *vwykmm@unisa.ac.za*

Dr. Mujibul Hasan Siddiqui, Associate Professor, Department of Education, Aligarh Muslim University, Aligarh-2022002, Uttar Pradesh, India.
E-mail: *mhsiddiqui50@gmail.com, mhsiddiqui50@rediffmail.com*

Dr. Neena Sawhney, Principal, Chandigarh College of Education, Landran, Sector 112, Greater Mohali, Punjab, India.
E-mail: *principal_ccemohali@yahoo.com*

Nitika Goyal, Department of Mechanical Engineering, National Institute of Technical Teachers' Training & Research, Chandigarh-160019, India.
Email: *goyalniti@rediffmail.com*

Dr. Priti Banerjee, Associate Professor, Matushri Ahilya Devi Teachers' Education Institute, Indore, Madhya Pradesh, India.
E-mail: *pritijeet@gmail.com*

Dr. R. Uma Rani, M.C.A., M.Phil., Ph.D., Associate Professor of Computer Science, Sri Sarada College for Women (Autonomous), Salem-16, Tamil Nadu. E-mail: *umainweb@gmail.com*

Dr. Sadia Mahmood, Assistant Professor, Department of Education, Aligarh Muslim University, Aligarh, Uttar Pradesh, India.
E-mail: *sadia.mahmood84@gmail.com*

Dr. Sanjeev Kumar Dey, Assistant Professor in History, Government Kamalanagar College, Chawngte, Mizoram-796772, India.
E-mail: *sanjeev.knc@gmail.com*

Dr. Shabana A. Memon, M.Com., MBA, M.Phil., NET, Ph.D., Bharati Vidyapeeth, (Deemed University) Institute of Management, Kolhapur, Kadamwadi, Kolhapur-416003, Maharashtra, India.
E-mail: *memon.shabana@gmail.com*

Dr. Shah Raziq Khalid, Assistant Professor, Department of Law, SV College, Aligarh-202002, Uttar Pradesh, India.
E-mail: *srksvc70@gmail.com*

Dr. Shahnawaz Ahmad, Assistant Professor, Department of Physical Education, Shri Varshney College, Aligarh, Uttar Pradesh.
E-mail: *shahanawazkhan@gmail.com*

Dr. Shazli Hasan Khan, Assistant Professor, MANUU, CTE, Sambhal, Uttar Pradesh, India. E-mail: *drshazlikhan@gmail.com*

Dr. Sheeba, Assistant Professor, Majmaah University, Majmaah Kingdom of Saudi Arab. Email: *parvez@gmail.com*

Dr. Subhankar Ghosh, Department of Education, Visva-Bharati (A Central University), Santiniketan-731235, West Bengal.
E-mail: *sghosh.edu.vb@gmail.com*

Dr. V. Vijaya Lakshmi, Associate Professor, Department of Resource Management and Consumer Sciences, Professor Jayashankar Telangana State Agricultural University, Hyderabad, Telangana, India.

Dr. Vibha Singh Kushwaha, Assistant Professor, Matushri Ahilyadevi Teacher's Education Institute, Indore, Madhya Pradesh, India.
E-mail: *vibhavishnusingh@gmail.com*

Vivek N., MBA, MISTE, UGC NET, RBP, Teaching Fellow, Department of Management Studies, Anna University Regional Campus, Madurai-19, Tamil Nadu. E-mail: *vivekautcbe@gmail.com*

Zaffar Ahmad Nadaf, Research Scholar, Department of Education, Aligarh Muslim University, Aligarh-202002, Uttar Pradesh, India.
E-mail: *ali.zafar000324@gmail.com*

Introduction

"Higher Education: An International Perspective" is a broad and global concept of education which focuses on different aspects of higher education, which is suitable for all countries of the world and fulfil the needs of the people consists of aims and objectives, quality assurance, quantity, equity, content, curriculum structure, pedagogical practices, management, administration, admission policies, examination pattern, employability, social reforms, youth development, skill development, creativity, reasoning power, critical thinking, adopting standardization approach, maintaining sufficient financial resources with incorporation of efficient budgeting system are essentials for the advancement of higher education and ultimately equip the students with technical, vocational and professional skills to become internationally competent and making the whole world enlightened with help of higher education. This book gives an international vision of higher education of different countries such as Thailand higher education system was reformed after coming its "The National Education Act of 1999" on the other hand the ultimate and higher priority of universities in Canada is teaching, search and community service. Japan maintains world-class centres of excellence, foster professionals with advanced specialized skills, develop comprehensive liberal arts education, advancement of research in specialized areas. The China system of higher education gives more stress on vocational and technical skill development suitable for the youth. A very good comparison is made of higher education of Brazil, UK and USA in this text. Legal comparative studies in India and Bangladesh and other countries develop excellent insight for the comparison of higher education at international perspectives.

This text is broadly divided into twenty two chapters, four sections, which focuses on international perspective, comparative perspective, development perspective and emerging trends and future prospects.

SECTION-I: INTERNATIONAL PERSPECTIVE

There are ten chapters in this section. The first chapter is on "Higher Education in Thailand". This chapter shows that Thailand is the only South-east Asian country that was never colonized by a European country. There are 35,000 temples in Thailand. About sixteen million tourist, fly into Thailand each year. The modern education system in Thailand started during the reign of King Rama V. (1868-1910), where the first "National Education Plan" proclaimed. The Ministry of Education (MOE) is responsible for higher education at the undergraduate and graduate-level at both public and private universities. The expectation of universal basic education to their people implies a large increase in demand for higher education in near future. The admission at each level depends on the competitive test. This chapter also depicts the present condition of higher education in Thailand. At present, there is a high increase in social demand for higher education due to the expansion of basic education. Advancement in information technology makes higher education more flexible. The National Education Act of 1999 was made for the reform of the Thai higher education system. Perceiving Globalization Thailand is a founding member of "The Association of South-East Asian Nations (ASEAN)". The Commission on Higher Education has adapted the Q S.Com Asian University Ranking System. This gives weight to research quality (60%), teaching quality based on teacher/student ratio (20%), graduate employment (10%) and internationalization (10%).

The chapter second in this section is on "Trends in Canadian Higher Education". It is observed from this chapter that the most important function of universities is teaching, search and community service. There are 128 colleges affiliated to the Association of Canadian Community Colleges. Full-time students in universities and colleges are estimated at around 1.4 million. The education quality in Canada is one of the major factors in attracting foreign students to their shores. Under the Canadian constitutional arrangements, the 10 provinces and 3 territories have legislative authority for all public policy relating to the organization and delivery of formal education services within their jurisdiction including higher education. The cost of living and study in Canada at all levels, right from schooling to university, is lower than the United States, UK, Australia and other countries. In Canada, both government and Industry support research, which includes all areas of telecommunication, medicines, agriculture, computer technology and environmental science. Canada is an international computer and information technology leader and enjoys an excellent reputation in communications, transportation and engineering. The Conference Board of Canada estimates that over $ 40 billion is spending flows through Canada's colleges and universities each year through government funding, enrolment tuition and additional research funding.

The chapter three in this section presents "Monbusho and Higher Education in Japan". This chapter shows that the main functions of universities in Japan are to maintain world-class centres of excellence, foster professionals with advanced specialised skills, develop comprehensive liberal arts education, advancement of research in specialized areas such as arts or sports; development of centers for lifelong learning in the community and making contributions to society such as industry-academia cooperation, international exchanges and so forth. There is a strict entrance examination in the universities of Japan. For the sake of raising global competitiveness and securing international validity and reliability, the Ministry of Education of Japan recently tried to enhance the functions of education and research of graduate programmes. The Ministry of Education, Japan recently makes certain reforms in education such as course orientation, clear definitions, goals, terms of study, curriculum and the process of degree earning as course work, guidance in thesis writing and examination of academic dissertations to overcome systematic failure and to encourage professors. The educational ladder of Japan is 6+3+3+4 system, i.e. 6 years elementary school, 3 years of junior high school, 3 years of senior high school and 4 years at the university. There are 783 universities, 372 junior colleges, 57 colleges of technology. One of the most important features of higher education system of Japan is that the private sector quantitatively occupies a large part than the public sector; more than 75 per cent students are enrolled in private colleges and universities. The main functions of the National Institute for the Educational Policy are covering wide range of activities such as educational and research studies in conjunction with schools, pursuing practical research into school education and organising joint international initiations in the area of education. The Ministry of Education of Japan made an excellent improvement in classroom management teaching, methods and materials.

The chapter 4th in this section is on "Higher Education in China: The Conceptual Framework". It is shown from this chapter that the Asian region are more integrated through economic and social exchanges. Higher education across Asia plays significant role in human resource development. The modern universities in China were founded in the late nineteenth and early twentieth century. In 2016, the number of graduates to raise China's labour market each year is seven million. In 1914, the numbers of private higher education institutions were 727; however, their quality is highly variable. The medium of instruction in elementary, secondary schools is Mandarin, the official language in China. However, for students belong to minorities is dominant Local Language. There are three programmes for higher education such as Regular Higher Education, Adult Higher Education and Self-study programmes. Admission in higher education depends on high school graduation and Gaokao scores, National Adult College Entrance Examination and Provincial self-taught "Higher Education Examination Committee (HEEC)." The main task of Higher Education Centre funded in 2004 is the systematic evaluation of higher education institutions and their programmes.

In this section, the chapter 5th focuses on "Higher Education in China: An Existing Scenario". This chapter highlights that China, the largest populated country in the world has the largest higher education system in the world. Higher education is given different types of universities such as general and technical, medicine, agriculture, foreign language, vocational universities such as teacher training and specialised colleges. There are also administrative colleges known as "In-Service Management Cadre Colleges". Other description is more or less is the same as described in earlier chapter.

The chapter 6th in this section is on "Higher Education in USA". This chapter presents that the United States, a federal republic, constitutes 56 states. In USA Central Government does not control the educational system. The whole higher education system is controlled either by independent groups of people or trustees and shared between local and State Governments. This chapter further highlights about the description of colleges, universities, institutes, Bachelor's and Associate degrees, the liberal arts, philosophy professional education state and private universities, community technical and vocational colleges, distance education and accreditations, and the curriculum and degree of higher education in the United States of America.

In this section chapter 7th poses "The System of Education in Brazil, UK and USA". This chapter shows that Brazil the largest country in the whole of South America was formally a federation of states, but later divided into many municipalities as well as local districts. The education system of Brazil is divided into different stages as the other countries have such as pre-primary education, secondary education, higher education and teacher education etc. The Brazilian Government constructed a new Constitution in 1488. The provision of free tuition for all public schools was incorporated. Education in English at the initial stage was provided by voluntary agencies including the Churches in England. There are elementary, secondary, preparatory and public school. The stages of education are nursery education, primary education, and secondary education. Technical or further educations in England are to develop various aptitudes and train the generation to become responsible adult in life. The first Teacher's college for training of secondary school teachers was the college of Preceptors, which was founded in the year 1846. There was also a provision of adult education. In the field of higher education, the most popular universities are Oxford University founded in 1185, Cambridge University in 1230 and London University in 1828. However, this chapter further shows the system of higher education in USA as it was presented in earlier chapters.

In this section, the chapter 8th is on "Understanding the Australian Higher Education System". It has been seen from this chapter that the Australian university system is made up of 41 universities. Domestic students receive scholarships and financial aids from the common wealth. However, international students are not eligible for these awards. Bachelor degrees in Australia require three years of study. The academic culture in Australia is very much based on student involvement with the higher level of participation. Australia offers excellent education system in the world.

The chapter 9th in this selection is on "United States Higher Education: An Overview". This chapter presents that American higher education is so diverse and complex. The US Department of Education counts 6500 post-secondary institutions that participate in its student financial aid programmes including 4200 colleges and universities that award degrees and 2300 institutions that award vocational certification. Some institutions such as the University of California and the University of Michigan enjoy constitutional autonomy as separate branches of state government. Some public universities are part of state-wide multi campus systems in which an additional layer of oversight exists between the campus and the State Government. The federal government generally does not provide direct operational support to colleges and universities; this special purpose funding is an extremely important revenue source and, in turn, has increased the ability of federal government to influence colleges and universities in areas outside research and financial aid. This chapter has very analytical and systematized presentation of higher education of USA. Many US colleges and universities are making concerted efforts to make their institutions and curricula more international and to provide experiences for students that broader and deepen their understanding of other cultures.

The chapter 10th in this section is on "Higher Education in the United States of America". It covers strength of US higher education, authority and responsibility for US higher education, types of US higher education institutions, accreditation, quality, and standards and Internationalization.

SECTION-II: COMPARATIVE PERSPECTIVE

The 11th chapter in this section is on "Higher Education in India and Abroad Comparatively". It includes higher education reform in India, a new breed of Indian University, private institutions with student support structures, higher education for the masses—innovations in distance learning, and partnership with foreign institutions. Progressive institutions of higher education in India are well on their way towards obtaining seals of approval from western institutions and international experts.

In this section chapter 12th presents "Status of Higher Education of World and India". This chapter shows that the University of Oxford become the first UK University to top the Times Higher Education World University Rankings in the 12-year history of the table. It knows the five times leader the California Institute of Technology, into second place in the World University Ranking 2016-17. However, The Indian Institute of Science is closer to the top 200, claiming a spot in the 201-250 band edging its highest ever position. This chapter consists of some big challenges of higher education, implications, global challenges and issues etc. This chapter further aims at analysing the current scenario of Higher Education system in India, identifying on the emerging challenges and issues of higher education in India and suggestions for improving quality of higher education. In this direction, some effective strategies for higher education reform are required to make the scientific and technological development and raise the level of employment in India.

SECTION-III: DEVELOPMENT PERSPECTIVE

In this section, the chapter 13th is on "Higher Education and Industrial Development: A Comparison Between India and Other Countries". This chapter presents very good comparative study of higher education with the inclusion of market size, regulatory framework of higher education on investment, government initiatives' progress, role of industry in higher education, quantitative & qualitative development, mixing traditional education & MOOCs, teaching focused institutions, research role & brain drain.

The chapter 14th keeps "Physical Health Education: A Comparative Study". It studied health code of ethics, trends, technology use in physical education, health education career opportunities, work site health promotion, independent consulting and government contracting.

The 15th chapter poses "e-Governance in India: A Focus on Higher Education" discussed the integration of ICT helps to reduce the intricacy and enhance the overall administration of higher education and how E-Governance is deliver cost-effective and easy-to-access citizen services, and improve processing of transactions both within the government, and between the government and other agencies. E-Governance is understood as a set of activities involving the effective contribution of ICT for strengthening administration and management in higher education system.

The chapter sixteen in this section presents "Information Technology: A Development within the Space of Post-Colonial Era". This chapter highlights the importance of information technology as an aid to teaching and learning and focuses the post-colonial era as a boom of information technology. This chapter further gives more emphasis on skills and understanding of information technology.

The 17th fourth is on "Role of Educational Institutions in the Entrepreneurial Ecosystem". This chapter shows that Entrepreneurship is a critical aspect of the knowledge economy. This chapter highlights the four important aspects for the promotion of a favourable entrepreneurship education ecosystem such as importance of entrepreneurship education, the strategic role of Educational Institutions, a tentative curriculum for Embedding Entrepreneurship in formal education and the teacher's role in creation of a healthy Entrepreneurship education ecosystem. A critical review of literature is given in this chapter.

SECTION-IV: EMERGING TRENDS AND FUTURE PROSPECTS

The chapter 18th in this section is on "Role of Women Education in Saudi Arabia: Challenges and Achievements". This chapter depicts that the education of women in Saudi Arabia is administered according to the principles of Islam: An official religion of Saudi Arab. It comprised the norms of education, enrolment and segregation in education, political participation, social status, the struggle for women's education, list of universities that enrol women, women and education in Islamic teaching and progress achieved in social change for women.

The chapter 19th made a study on "Pedagogy in Teacher Education

Course". This is seen from this chapter that in order for the higher education sector to be relevant and compatible in this challenging society, universities need to commit to the process of continuous change or become redundant. The current debate at colleges and teacher education about introducing and redesigning learning programmes by including Flipped Classroom Pedagogy (FCP) emerged as a technology—integrated teaching strategy as a means to support students in an open distance learning approach. It is concluded further from this study that FCP approach is on-line e-learning tool created through an online learning management system by lecture to support student teachers to demonstrate authentic learning experiences, performances, and achievements as evidence of achieved learning outcomes over time. Mixed method approach of teaching is quite suitable for the enhancement of learning.

In this section chapter 20th is on "Towards Quality in Higher Education for Sustainable Development in India: An Overview". This chapter presents an elaborative study on quality of higher education consisting of historical perspective, quality concern, quality indicators, good presentation of data on higher education, notable education policies and different higher education statutory bodies, various five year education plans highlighting thrust areas of higher education, some challenges and measures of higher education of India.

The chapter 21st in this section stresses on "Transformation of Higher Education System of India: A Critical Appraisal". This chapter makes a critical presentation of higher education. It includes need and impotence of the study, National Knowledge Commission Recommendation in context of higher education, growth and trends in higher education in India, growth of enrolment ratio (GER) in higher education, status of women education in higher education, challenges in contemporary Indian higher education, staff development, financing higher education, curriculum development, research and some other important issues of Higher education in India.

The chapter 22nd in this section highlights Value Based Education: A Step Towards Humanitarian Society. Value based education always helps human beings to boost up morality, honesty, ethics, spirituality, responsibility, a good sense of respects, maintain internal identity, higher appearance of innovation, personal beliefs, optimism and commitment, scientific tempers, professionalisms, economic , political, and ultimately societal development with its highest cultural values. This chapter further highlights about the best character of Eklavya in *Mahabharata*.

Section-I
International Perspective

1

Higher Education in Thailand

Anjum Ahmed

Introduction

Getting to Know Thailand

Thailand is the only Southeast Asian country that was never colonized by a European country. In fact, in the Thai language, the name of the country is Prathet Thai which means "land of the free". Thailand is a constitutional monarchy much like England. Thailand loves its King, and shows great respect for the monarchy. It has 1,430 islands, among the most famous of which is Koh Phi Phi Lee. One-tenth of the entire population of Thailand lives in Bangkok. It is the capital of this great nation, and, of course, the largest city. We are lucky that we know Bangkok as "Bangkok". Its real name is one of the longest names of a place in the world, made up of Pali and Sanskrit root words:

> *Krungthepmahanakhon Amonrattanakosin Mahintharayutthaya Mahadilokphop Noppharatratchathaniburirom Udomratchani wetmahasathan Amonphimanawatansathit Sakkathatti yawitsanukamprasit.*

It means "City of Angels, Great City of Immortals, Magnificent City of the Nine Gems, Seat of the King, City of Royal Palaces, Home of Gods Incarnate, Erected by Visvakarman at Indra's Behest." There are about 35,000 temples in Thailand. Thailand is truly a land of temples. Visiting them requires modest clothing, meaning no shorts or sleeveless shirts. Showing respect for another person's head is imperative in Thailand. The head is considered to be the most important part of the body, and so

Thai culture forbids touching anyone on the head (even a child). Should you meet someone who is older or more important than you, it is best to lower your head in deference to show proper respect. Thailand is home to many, many animals. About a tenth of all of the animal species on the planet call Thailand home, and a tenth of all bird species. Thailand used to be known as Siam, and it is the country where Siamese cats originated from.

Sixteen million tourists fly into Thailand each year, and despite the influx of visitors, this country's cultural integrity remains relatively intact. A smile can go a long way, and one will find more smiles in Thailand than just about anywhere else. In fact, it is sometimes known as the "land of smiles" because the people of Thailand seem to be always ready with a smile. They are a peace-loving culture, desiring harmony over conflict. Thailand was voted as the world's fifth friendliest country by Rough Guides readers.

The Thai Education System

The modern education system in Thailand started during the reign of King Rama V (1868-1910), when the first "*National Education Plan*" was proclaimed. However, the promulgation of compulsory education, which required every 7-year-old child to receive free primary education until the age of 14, started in 1921. Primary education at that time consisted of 4 years. It was revised many times to 5 and 7 years and has been finally set at 6 years since 1978. Since the education reform in 1974, after the event of the student uprising in October 1973, education has been viewed as a lifelong process. Two kinds of education; namely a way-of-life learning process (non-formal education), and classroom system education (formal education), were presented side by side in the National Education Scheme of 1991.

The current formal education system is a 6-3-3-4 system. Beyond the six-year compulsory primary education is secondary education, which is divided into two levels, lower and upper secondary. Each level requires three years of study. Higher education is the level of education beyond upper secondary. It is divided into three levels; lower than bachelor's degree, bachelor's degree, and graduate. The educational management in Thailand falls under the responsibility of many ministries and agencies. The Ministry of Education (MOE) is responsible for preprimary up to the higher education levels. It also provides non-formal education or out-of-school programmes and supervises private schools at all levels except

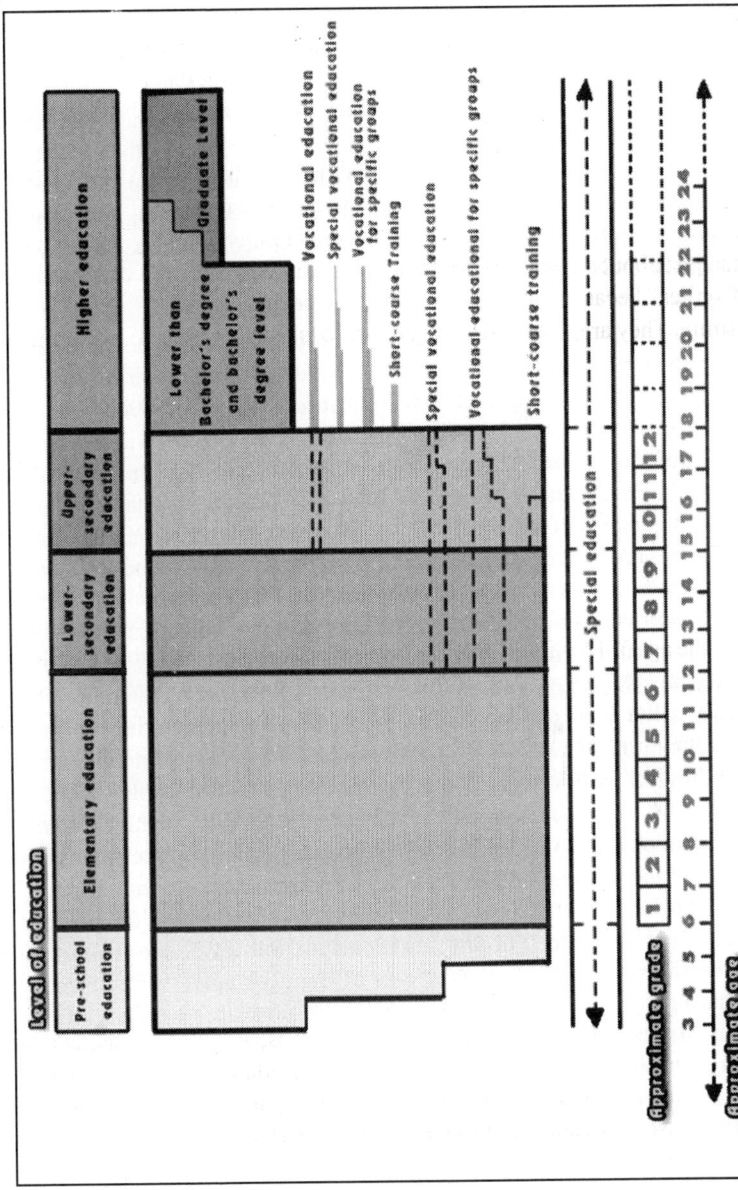

Fig. 1.1: Thailand Formal Education System
Source: UNESCO IBE-World data on Eduation, 6th Edition, Thailand.

the degree level. The Ministry of University Affairs (MUA) is responsible for higher education at the undergraduate and graduate levels at both public and private universities. The Ministry of Interior is in charge of administering and managing primary education in the municipalities of each province whereas the Bangkok Metropolitan Administration and the Pattaya City Administration are responsible for the management of primary education in their own jurisdictions. There are six other ministries that provide education in specialized fields for their own specific needs, namely Ministry of Defence, Ministry of Public Health, Ministry of Transport and Communications, Ministry of Agriculture and Cooperatives, Ministry of Justice, and Ministry of Labour and Social Welfare (*see* Fig. 1.1).

The extension of universal basic education to the Thai people implies a large increase in demand for higher education in the near future. It is estimated in the Ninth National Education Plan (2002-2006) that the number of students at the higher education level in 2006 will be around 1,942,000 or about 25 per cent of the population (age group 18-24). According to the Office of National Education Commission, the enrolment ratio of higher education in 1997 was 19.4 per cent, which includes those in the two open-admission universities. Hence, the higher education sector needs to be reformed tremendously in order to be able to meet such a large increase in the expected enrolment ratio in the future.

Admission Process: It is generally known that the system of selection based on competitive entrance examination for each articulated level has essentially a barring effect on the opportunity to continue to higher levels of education, particularly for the children of lower economic status families. All public schools that have higher educational standards, or charge low tuition fees normally require some kind of competitive entrance examinations. Various methods have been introduced to reduce the adverse effect of these examinations such as assigning a quota system, or giving higher priority to students whose houses are located within the schools' catchment area etc. For the higher education level, the provincial universities and provincial campuses of Bangkok universities normally retain a quota system to fill 50 per cent of seats available in each academic year with upper secondary school graduates from their respective regions. Some universities set up a special quota for secondary school graduates from remote rural areas or from low-income families in the cities who meet their specification. In general schools of high quality are concentrated in urban areas or big cities. Students in rural areas who have a strong determination for higher education have to migrate to these areas to get better secondary education in order to increase their chances of getting admission into state closed-admission universities. This process requires large expenses if their families do not have relatives or friends living in the areas where the schools are located. It was reported that the chance of entering a public university of children from professional families was about 54 times that of the children of farmer families, and about 31 times that of children of worker families (Vichai and Phitsanes, 1994: 24). The same report also revealed that the chances of being selected into public schools of children from professional and business families are found to increase as they climbed up the educational ladder, comparing to those of the farmers' children.

Present Condition of Higher Education Provision in Thailand

The provision of education above the upper secondary level or the higher education level in Thailand is mainly under the responsibility of two ministries—the Ministry of Education and the Ministry of University Affairs. The Ministry of Education is responsible for public educational institutions providing education both at lower than bachelor's degree and the bachelor's degree levels. These institutions are Rajabhat Institutes, formerly teachers' colleges, Rajamangala Institutes of Technology,

Colleges of Physical Education, Dramatic Arts and Fine Arts Colleges, Buddhist Universities, and formal public vocational education colleges. Currently, the Rajabhat Institutes (totally 36 institutes) have extended their curriculum to cover three areas: education, sciences and liberal arts. Some Rajabhat Institutes are capable of offering master's degree programmes. The role of the Rajamangala Institutes of Technology is to produce teachers for vocational schools.

According to the Office of National Education Commission (Thailand, ONEC, 1997: 10-11), the Ministry of Education has under its supervision 294 public colleges and public higher schools, plus 208 private vocational schools providing lower than bachelor's degrees. The Ministry of University Affairs is in charge of supervising and coordinating public and private higher educational institutions that offer programmes leading to bachelor's degree and higher level. There are totally 60 universities: 21 public universities (30 campuses), 37 private universities (39 campuses), and 2 autonomous universities. The two open-admission universities, Ramkamheng and Sukhothai are included in the public universities [*ibid.*: 10]. There are other ministries and agencies which also provide higher education for their specific needs. For example the education and training of professional soldiers and police, specific technician training for the armed forces and for irrigation, railways, merchant marines, cooperatives, postal service, civil aviation, nurses etc., are under the respective organizations. The number of these institutions is 68. The expansion of higher education in the past decade in the public sector has been in the direction of increasing the number of higher educational institutions in the provincial areas outside Bangkok. Most of the increase in the demand for higher education in Bangkok has been met by private institutions, either by expanding the existing institutions or by the establishing new ones. The expansion of private institutions has been encouraged by an increasing relaxation of the Ministry of University Affairs in the control of tuition and fees. The increase in the demand for higher education was a consequence of the continuous economic boom prior to the 1997 crisis, which enlarged the job market for university graduates as well as increased parents' income. Another recent development in the higher education system relates to changes in university entrance examination requirements. The national entrance examination, which used to be based on the result of a once-a-year exam, is being modified to a system that organizes entrance exams twice a year. Students can choose the best result. In addition, the average GPA of the last three years in upper secondary education will be counted for around 10 per cent of total scores for admission. The intention of the change is to draw students' attention to the importance of the last three years of study in upper secondary school. This procedure is expected to solve the problems that have occurred in the past two decades where a large number of upper secondary students in the formal education system have left schools after getting a secondary education certificate from the Department of Non-Formal Education, which is equivalent to the certificate of formal higher secondary education. This certificate, which normally could be obtained within one year of enrolling in a non-formal education programme, provides the right for the holder to sit for the university entrance examination. Many upper secondary students take this loophole as a short-cut route to finish the three years of formal upper secondary school and concentrate in tutorial schools for university entrance examination.

Graduates often lack information about jobs until they graduate and may not understand what they are equipped to do after graduation. Thai graduates in 2008 reported difficulties encountered in their search for employment (Figure 1.2). A recent examination of the state of the Asian labour market for graduates of higher education reveals some troubling trends: "In countries like Thailand, Indonesia, and the People's Republic of China (PRC), the per cent of tertiary level graduates in the workforce is now about 20 per cent, double from what it was 15 to 20 years ago. At the same time, employers fret that they are not getting the skilled workers they need to compete in a global economy. Investment climate assessments report that 20 per cent of employers feel that skills availabilities are a major impediment to business, as much as, if not more than, meeting onerous regulations.

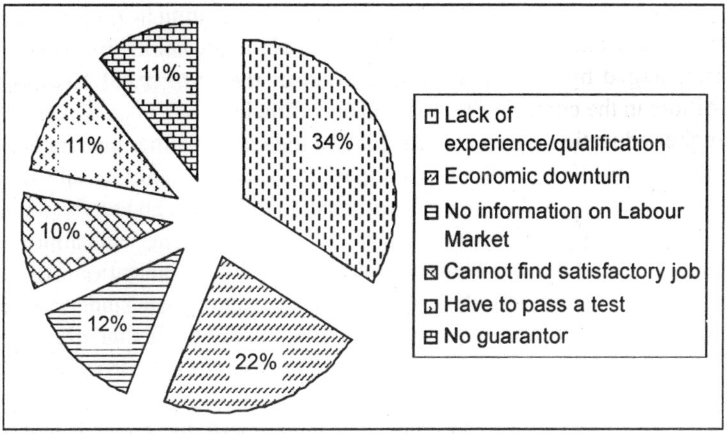

Fig. 1.2: Problems Encountered in Job Searching by Thai Students
Source: World Bank (2010).

Trends that Lead to Higher Education Reforms

Currently many forces, both external and internal, have played important roles in signifying the need for education reform at the higher level all over the world as well as in Thailand. They may be put together as follows:

Increase in social demand for higher education due to the expansion of basic education, economic growth and institutional factors. Higher education is no longer confined to a specific selected group in the society, but must be made available to the masses. Higher education is being considered as an instrument to obtain better employment as well as a means for upward social mobility. As to the institutional factor, many jobs require that the holders have a minimum of university degree; for example the Members of Parliament and the Senate.

Advancement in information technology has created the need to restructure and reform higher education to be more flexible and more open in dealing with lifelong education. In an era of an increasingly aging population, the new generation of students who will enroll in higher educational institutions will be less homogeneous in their age, needs, time requirements, and places of study. Higher educational institutions must be able to adjust themselves to the new circumstances.

The globalization movement intensifies competition and cooperation among nations. Higher education must be reformed in order to be able to compete in the international environment. Participation in globalization of international activities and exchange programmes requires the development of networks and updating of higher education programmes. Hence, higher education needs to be reformed in order to be able to benefit from the globalization movement (Japan, NIER/UNESCO-APEID, 1998).

The economic crisis and other alternative programmes that compete for public resources, such as welfare for the aged and other social safety net programmes, will force the government to reduce the budget for higher education, or not at least increase spending on the higher education. At the same time, an increase in social demand for higher education will put pressure on higher educational institutions to admit more students. The need to look for other sources of funding will force the higher education sector to reevaluate the situation and adjust to the new environment.

In order to be able to respond effectively and efficiently to the changing global as well as domestic environment, the management of resources available to higher educational institutions must be flexible. There is an increasing trend for higher educational institutions to be more autonomous in managing their resources, personnel, curricula, and admission policy. This trend started in the United Kingdom in the early 1908 and is now spreading all over the world. There is also an increasing requirement from all parties concerned for higher education management to be accountable for their financial performance as well as for the quality of their education programmes. Hence, management in higher educational institutions needs to be reformed in order to be able to meet these requirements.

Reform of the Thai Higher Education System

Reform of the Thai Higher Education System came in the form of the National Education Act of 1999, and subsequent acts under this legislation. The major features related to globalization were the granting of autonomy to some institutes and the designation of research universities. King Mongkut's University of Technology, Thonburi (KMUTT) was the first institute to become autonomous and is also one of the nine designated research universities. The roadmap for this reform specifically mentions globalization and the increased dependence on technology, especially IT. According to the roadmap this, and the desire for a knowledge-based society, has changed the human resource needs of the nation, requiring education to adapt accordingly. This major reform of the Thai education sector has resulted in significant changes in the way education and research is managed. With greater autonomy comes greater accountability. This new "managerialism" is a direct consequence of globalization. It is seen as the means to implement reform and achieve recognition through ranking. Standards, accountability and quality assurance are the new higher education tools of the globalized era. For Thailand at least, the responsibility of higher education institutes, even those designated as research universities, to serve communities at the national level is also given emphasis. This includes preservation and enhancement of local culture and the recognition and application of local wisdom. While responding to globalization, the "have-nots" cannot be forgotten and a balance must be sought.

Globalization at the Regional Level

The Association of South East Asian Nations (ASEAN), of which Thailand is a founding member, aims to achieve full integration in 2015. English is the common language of ASEAN. The implications for higher education in the region are profound. Countries such as Thailand, Indonesia and Vietnam will have to quickly develop more degree programmes in English or "international" courses. The short term solution may be to engage more foreign staff. However, the major implication for higher education arising from an integrated community will be in the area of common standards. ASEAN has already developed a policy framework for Science, Technology and Innovation (STI) and is exploring benchmarking for both research and education. While Singapore is pre-eminent in both areas, Thailand ranks as either second or third in the region. Benchmarking for ASEAN universities will require careful consideration. Due to an emphasis on proprietary work with industry and specific programmes to assist marginalized societies, it has been found that the world ranking methods have severe limitations when applied to Thai universities. The Thai Commission on Higher Education has adopted the QS.com Asian University Ranking System. This gives weight to research quality (60%), teaching quality, based on teacher/student ratio (20%), graduate employment (10%) and internationalization (10%).

Due to strong capability in English, universities from Singapore, Malaysia and the Philippines tend to rank better in internationalization. Will ASEAN be simply bypassed on the globalization highway, being deemed as not relevant? Universities are now standards driven and many in ASEAN would be reluctant to see any lowering of existing standards they have fought to achieve as the price for accommodating universities in the still developing member countries of the group. National education priorities will not change dramatically as a result of integration and already some universities are preparing for a windfall of regional students. Nations may speak regionally, but will continue to service their own interests first. This is natural. In reality it could mean that nations will participate regionally, while at the same time striving to achieve globally. In the field of research, however, there is good reason for collabouration at the regional level, pooling resources towards solving common problems due to climate, environment, agricultural systems etc. ASEAN has quite a good history in this area, particularly in science and technology. This collabouration was reliant on external funding and it involved individual research groups in each country doing their own work under a common umbrella or theme. Nonetheless, these could be viewed as the first tentative steps towards regional collabouration on research, which in turn could lead to bilateral or trilateral partnerships within the region.

Conclusion

Education reform in Thailand is moving in the right direction in the sense that it attaches higher importance to the basic education of the masses. The expansion of basic education to the masses in both quantity and quality should have been done decades ago. Resources for higher education should be diverted into the basic education level for the masses, and those who receive the benefits of higher education should bear a higher share of the cost than at the present time. This will reduce the inequity problem existing in the Thai education system. According to the World Trade Organization Agreement, education is being considered as a public service. As a result, foreign educational institutions will be allowed to set up their branches at their own discretion in any member countries. Hence, it is essential that the quality of Thai educational institutions at all levels must be improved in order to be able to compete effectively with those of the foreigners. At the basic level of education, competition may not be as strong as the higher levels. In addition, at the basic level of education, emphasis should be on the national cultural value which should be carried out by domestic educational institutions rather than by foreign institutions. At the higher levels of education, however, academic and technical skills will be more emphasized since they are related to employment opportunities. In this respect, foreign educational institutions will have an advantage over the domestic ones. Competition for students and faculty members may be severe in the future. Autonomy of public higher education by transferring decision making for resources and personnel management to the organization level is one way to improve flexibility in management. The system of the civil service and the government budget bureau are too rigid to be able to cope with changes that take place so quickly in the educational world. Without autonomous decision making in personnel matters, higher educational institutions could not attract new competent faculty members, but would continue losing their good ones to the business sector due to wide difference in salary scales. However, in order to make sure that the flexibility in management would improve the efficiency of performance of the organization, accountability of management is required. Since state autonomous higher educational institutions also receive resources from other sources beside the government budget, funding agencies need to have some assurance that the scarce resources handed over to higher educational institutions be maximally utilized. Society needs to know that not only are the higher educational institutions producing quality graduates required in the system but that the process of doing this is effective and efficient (Woodhouse, 1996). The problem is how to evaluate the effectiveness and the efficiency of higher educational institutions. In order to evaluate a programme of study, not to mention the whole institution, we should take into account the whole educational process starting with the input, e.g. quality of those entering and qualifying in such programme; the process of educating or training them, e.g. teachers, teaching method, facilities and equipment etc.; the final output—the graduates, e.g. their knowledge in the field of study compared to their entry point, their ability to get appropriate job within an appropriate length of time etc. (Olmesdahl, 1999).

The whole process should be evaluated systematically. Performance indicators have been widely used to indicate the efficiency or cost effectiveness of institutions concerned. To their many proponents, performance indicators are dearly needed by governments and by institutional managers. They are intended to be useful, simple, reliable, and objective. However, they must be used with great care, otherwise they could be harmful to the institution's programme and the system that used these indicators. The use of indicators across institutional and country boundaries is fraught with difficulties. The major reasons relate to the nature of the organization(s) and the data *per se*. The nature of the organization(s) relates to the characteristics of institutions of higher education, variables representing their goals, and differences in their programme structure and composition. The data problem relates to difference in the basic definition of the data elements concerned, verifiability of the data, aggregation level and dispersion of the data (Kells, 1994). Hence the assessment of effectiveness and efficiency of institutions' performance using performance indicators should be carried out carefully, particularly in making comparisons across institutions. If we are going to apply private business concepts to quality assurance, the centre of interest should be the customers of the higher educational institutions; namely the students or recent alumni, the employers of the graduates, and the sponsors of research projects. They should be allowed to express their opinions regarding the academic content of the curriculum, whether it is up-to-date and relevant, whether the academic training prepares students for lifelong learning and whether the research work produced is of high academic quality? Their views should be included in the evaluation of the higher educational institutions. If quality improvement of educational institutions is to be actualized, it must be a continuing and repeating process (Thailand, ONEC, 1998).

It is a good thing that educational institutions are starting self-assessment process, and are preparing to be assessed by outsiders. In the process they will learn to find out their weakness and ways to improve their performance and outputs. The public university system has long been secure and stable, which causes the system to tend to resist change, just like any bureaucratic organizations. However, due to resource and time limitation of administrators and faculty members, various aspects of quality assessment should be ranked according to their urgency. Top priority should be given to the teaching and learning aspect, and extend to research and social academic service later. It should not cover too many aspects at the same time. The Ministry of University Affairs should be realistic regarding resources, time, and institutional culture. Besides, we have to be aware that the process of quality assessment itself takes time and resources of the institution away from delivering high quality education or research.

References

Bhumiratana, Sakarindr and Commins, Terry (2012). Cultural and Historical Factors and their Influence on the Development of Higher Education in Thailand. *Asian Journal on Education and Learning*, 3(1): 1-9.

Japan, National Institute for Educational Research (NIER)/UNESCO-APEID. (1998). *Recent Reform and Perspectives in Higher Education: Report of the Seminar Including a Range of Countries from Asia-Pacific and Europe.* Tokyo: National Institute for Educational Research.

Kells, H.R. (1994). Performance Indicators for Higher Education: A Critical Review with Policy Recommendations. In *Revitalizing Higher Education*, Edited by J. Salmi and A M. Verspoor. Washington, D.C.: The World Bank.

Olmesdahl, P. (1999). Preoccupation with Quality. *Teaching in Higher Education* 4(3): 419-424.

Sarakadee, (2000). Cost and Sources of Financing of Higher Education, *The Long-Range Planning of Higher Education*. Bangkok: Ministry of University Affairs.

Thailand, Ministry of University Affairs (MUA) (2000). Quality Assurance Policy. www.ga.mua.go.th/English/policy1.html. www.mua.go.th/data/mis/main2.html

Thailand, Office of the National Education Commission (ONEC). (1997). *Report on the 1997 Educational Condition in Thailand.* www.onec.go.th-pub/rtec2540/chapter

Varaporn Bovornsiri (1998). Country Report: Thailand. In *Recent Reform and Perspectives in Higher Education: Report of the Seminar Including a Range of Countries from Asia-Pacific and Europe.* Tokyo: National Institute for Educational Research.

Vichai Tunsiri and Phitsanes Jessadachatr (1994). Financing of Education and Allocation of Public Resources to Education: A Case Study of Thailand. Paper prepared for *International Symposium on Market Economy and Education Reform*, 3-7 November, 1994, Beijing: The People's Republic of China.

Woodhouse, D. (1996). Quality Assurance: International Trends, Preoccupations and Features. *Assessment and Evaluation in Higher Education*, 21: 347-356.

Ziderman, A. and Albrecht, D. (1995). *Financing University in Developing Countries*. Washington, D.C.: The Falmer Press.

2

Trends in Canadian Higher Education

Kauser Tasneem

Introduction

A Brief History of Higher Education in Canada

Higher education usually refers to education and training in universities, colleges and institutes of technology or art. Today at least eight universities offer degrees and other credentials in higher education. Operating at the graduate level, higher education programmes typically offer preparation for academic, administrative, policy, and leadership careers.

What would now be called higher education was first organized by the churches in the 17th century but it was not until 1789 that the first "church-sponsored" University, University of King's College (NS), was founded in Canada.

Mcgill University (founded in 1821) was the first private non-denominational university to receive a charter. The establishment of provincial universities began with the University of Toronto in 1850. The Royal Military College of Canada operated by the Federal Government, opened in 1876.

The universities' chief functions are teaching, research and community service. Programmes of study leading to bachelor's, master's and doctoral degrees are offered in the arts and sciences and in the professions. There are 95 degree-granting institutions of higher education, mostly universities, affiliated to the Association of Universities and Colleges of Canada.

Until the mid-1960s, post-secondary vocational education was provided by a variety of specialized institutions. At that time, systems of colleges were introduced, mostly by provincial governments. In some cases the colleges absorbed former institutions of post-secondary education (PSE). Such non-university institutions are called by a variety of names including college, community college, regional college, college of applied arts and technology, collège d'enseignement général et professionnel (CEGEP), institute of technology, and polytechnics. These colleges for the most part offer programmes leading to diplomas rather than degrees. Some provide academic education for transfer to university and almost all provide vocational training, covering a vast array of occupations, while others offer both academic and vocational programmes; most provide a wealth of community services. There are 128 colleges affiliated to the Association of Canadian Community Colleges.

Enrolment in PSE has risen steadily since the Second World War and the participation rate is over 35 per cent (the participation rate is defined as the total of full-time students in PSE as a percentage of the population 18-24 years old). Full-time students in universities and colleges are estimated at around 1.4 million; of these, 8,82,000 attend university. An additional 3,21,000 and 191,000 part-time students attend university and college, respectively. According to Statistics Canada, about 25 per cent of the population aged 25-64 has a university degree and another 25 per cent has a college or trade school certificate or diploma.

PSE is funded primarily by governments, but private sources of funding, including tuition, have steadily increased in recent decades. Both the provincial and federal governments contribute, but in the context of overall federal-provincial fiscal arrangements the federal share is being constantly renegotiated.

Comparing the Higher Education Systems of America and Canada

The two systems may stratify students in quite different ways. For instance, both Canadian and American students face similar competitive pressures but are responding to these demands in different ways. Brought about by the highly stratified post-secondary structure, much more inter-institutional competition exists in the US. In Canada, the transition from high school to post-secondary education usually occurs locally, placing a premium on entry into the most lucrative fields rather than selective institutions (Davies and Hammack, 2005). American higher education has long been marked by a steep hierarchy of institutions. Since the emergence of a distinct prestige hierarchy in the late 1800s, American colleges and universities have been preoccupied with conveying status (Collins, 1979).

As such, US colleges and universities differ greatly in their selectivity and resources (Davies and Guppy, 1997). Famous and elite universities and colleges greatly overshadow less renowned entities in a system composed of several segments of highly unequal public and private institutions (Brint, 2002).

Prestigious universities enjoy a "halo effect" as past accomplishments resonate in subsequent ratings (Geiger, 2004). In contrast, the Canadian system is composed of formally equal, academically oriented public universities. Differences among universities in budgets, expenditures, resources, and selection are relatively small compared to the American case. As a result, Canada lacks a national market for undergraduate credentials (Davies and Hammack, 2005).

Applications to Canadian universities are mainly at the local level, with only small numbers of undergraduates crossing provincial borders. The practice of ranking colleges, so established in the US, is relatively new to Canada (Dill and Soo, 2005). A decline in public funding and increasing pressures to secure external grants may cause more stratification, as the market expands to encourage non-public monies from corporations and other private enterprises (Geiger, 2002). Alternatively, the apparent 'flatness' of the Canadian higher education hierarchy may lead to more pronounced inter-disciplinary inequalities rather than a vast inter-institutional hierarchy that exists in the US, as only some disciplines successfully manage a changing institutional environment (McLaughlin, 2005). Recent growth in institutional stratification has been paralleled by a new form of stratification among college and university students. While many European nations stream students at the secondary and often elementary levels (Kerckhoff, 2001), finding one's way in North American systems of higher education is more likely to occur with one's choice of programme. Where students enter into the post-secondary system may be becoming increasingly important. That is, choosing the right school or right programme may have greater implications for students than simply making the transition from high school to post-secondary education. It is plausible that this new form of sorting and selecting characterizes systems of higher education that have once confronted issues of access.

The Canadian Context

Various economic and social phenomena have made post-secondary education (PSE) very valuable for both current students and graduates—for all levels of Canadian society. Globalization and technological change are influencing Canada's industrial and occupational structure, making higher order skills increasingly important not only for individual success but also for national economic growth and social development.

Post-secondary participation rates for youth in their late teens and early twenties and attainment rates for prime age workers, are high in Canada by international standards. The education quality in Canada is one of the major factors in attracting foreign students to their shores. Canada's high academic standards and rigorous quality controls reflect the high-quality education provided which helps in successful future and benefits one's career in the long term.

The higher education policy landscape in Canada is highly decentralized, as the provinces (Alberta, British Columbia, Manitoba, New Brunswick, Newfoundland and Labrador, Nova Scotia, Ontario, Prince Edward Island, Quebec, and Saskatchewan), and territories (Northwest Territories, Nunavut, and Yukon) govern the educational systems within their respective jurisdictions. Under the Canadian Constitutional arrangement, the 10 provinces and 3 territories have legislative authority for all public policy relating to the organization and delivery of formal educational services within their jurisdictions, including higher education.

There is no national ministry or binding policy lever for higher education. Universities function under provincial legislation, and most were created as autonomous not for profit corporations that receive public support through provincial operating grants. There is considerable variation in the funding arrangements and governance structures for higher education in each province and territory (Shanahan & Jones, 2007). Despite this variation, Canadian universities on the whole comprise a mature higher education sector with a global reputation for high quality and internationally leading levels of post-secondary educational attainment (Organisation for Economic Co-operation and Development, OECD, 2012).

Trends Impacting Academic Work in Canadian Universities

In 2010, there were almost 1.2 million students in degree programmes on Canadian campuses: 7,55,000 undergraduates, 1,43,400 graduate students studying full-time, and an additional 2,75,800 students studying part-time. Fifty six per cent of university students were women, and 10 per cent were international students. The number of full-time university students has more than doubled since 1980, and part-time enrolment is up to 16 per cent. In 1980, there were 5,50,000 full-time and 2,18,000 part-time university students on Canadian campuses. Clearly, universities have experienced tremendous growth over the last 30 years.

The fastest growing occupations are now in Canada's service sector, which grew from 6 million jobs in 1975 to more than 13 million jobs in 2010. In the last 20 years alone, there were 1.5 million new jobs for professional and management occupations in Canada, of which 1.3 million were filled by university graduates. This shift to a service sector economy has created high-paying, quality jobs. The growth in university enrolment is evidence that students are responding to changes in the labour market, and that universities, in turn, are responding to students.

Field of Study

Between 1992 and 2008, full-time master's enrolment grew by 80 per cent overall, with strong growth in all major fields of study. Enrolment in health-related disciplines grew the fastest, tripling between 1992 and 2008. Health-related disciplines now represent 12 per cent of full-time master's students.

International Students

Canadian universities are becoming increasingly internationalized. Over the last 30 years, the proportion of visible minorities, international students and even faculty from other countries has grown significantly. More universities are engaging in international research collabourations; more international students are coming from a larger number of countries; and more Canadian students are taking advantage of international learning and research opportunities abroad.

An additional 13,000 international students were studying part-time in 2010. In 2010, international students represented approximately eight per cent of full-time undergraduate students in Canada, approximately 18 per cent of full-time master's students and 23 per cent of full-time Ph.D. students. Greater representation of international students at the graduate level is not unique to Canada.

In 1980, there were only 650 Indian students enrolled at Canadian institutions. Indian students enrolment fluctuated between 1980 and 1997 when it began to grow rapidly. By 2008, there were almost 3,000 Indian students registered at Canadian universities—an approximate five-fold increase since 1997. Enrolment of Indian students is also likely to continue to grow in future years because the population in India is growing very rapidly, and because there has been a concerted effort on the part of the Canadian higher education sector to attract students from India.

Over the past decade, the number of visa students and new immigrants coming to Canada with a university degree has grown strongly.

India is also expanding rapidly, growing from 9.4 million students in 1999 to more than 15 million in 2007.

In spite of being one of the largest and fastest-growing economies in the world, India does not have enough university capacity to meet student demand. As a result, many Indian students seek university education abroad. For example, in 2008 more than half (86,000) of the approximately 1,60,000 Indian students who studied abroad went to the US. Approximately 30,000 registered to study in the UK. and more than 27,000 went to Australia. Only about 3,000 came to Canada. Moreover, the Indian Minister of Human Resource Development recently announced that the Indian Central Government is looking to add approximately 30 million more university student places by 2020. Another major attraction for Indian students is the possibility of immigration. After studies, people with Canadian credentials and Canadian work experience may apply for permanent residency without leaving Canada.

Affordable Education: The unique advantage Canada enjoys is that while it is Western developed world, it offers education at comparatively less cost than its other Western counterparts. Though the education costs may vary based on the courses, for most of the general courses, the tuition fees is less than other major countries. Cost of living and study in Canada at all levels right from schooling to university is lower than the United States, Britain, Australia and other countries. On comparing the standard of living and the high quality education facilities that are provided in Canada with the other developed countries, we realize that students get all the benefits at a lower cost.

Internationally Recognized: A Canadian degree, diploma or certificate is globally recognized as being equivalent to those obtained from the United States or Commonwealth countries. University of Toronto, University of British Columbia, McGill University, University of Waterloo all feature in top 50 engineering and technology institutes in the world.

Long Term Advantage: There are major long term benefits to studying in Canada as one would get points for permanent residency in Canada if they have graduated from a Canadian University.

Campus Lifestyle: Canada's post-secondary campuses are not only wired with the latest in sophisticated technology, but also offer countless other modern amenities for the students to enjoy. From Olympic-quality sports facilities to public concert halls and art galleries, Canada's post-secondary campuses offer enormous possibilities for learning and leisure.

Pioneering and Abundant Research Opportunities: Since research is one of the key components of a Canadian post-secondary education, one will have ample opportunities to become a part of this aspect of education. In Canada, both government and industry support research which includes all areas of telecommunications, medicine, agriculture, computer technology, and environmental science. According to Gopaul *et al.* (2016) the findings of the Canadian component of an international survey that was administered in 19 different jurisdictions to understand the perceptions of faculty members about the nature and scope of changes to academic work explored the perceptions on research and teaching of full-time faculty members affiliated with Canadian universities. Overall, faculty members revealed that Canadian universities have strong, engaging, and vibrant research and teaching environments, yet there are also areas for improvement. Specifically, findings showed that faculty members perceived considerable autonomy with respect to research activities, despite the increasing need to secure external funding for research. Also, faculty expressed substantial commitment to teaching undergraduate students but a lack of clarity about some issues related to graduate teaching.

Canada is an international computer and information technology leader, and enjoys an excellent reputation in communications, transportation and engineering. Aviation, urban transport, micro-electronics, medical devices, advanced software, hydroelectric and nuclear power, lasers and optoelectronics, biotechnology, food and beverage processing, geometrics and ocean and environmental industries are more prominent.

Career Prospects

In recent years, Canada's foreign trade, marketing professional, commercial and financial expertise will continue to take the heat. The financial services industry is an important pillar of the Canadian economy, which employs 550,000 employees. In terms of employment for the majority of students, Canada provides a broad platform.

Canada's universities and colleges generate over $55 billion of economic activity. Off-campus student spending could generate as much as $17 billion in benefits to surrounding communities. The sector supports close to 680,000 direct and indirect jobs across Canada. University degree holders earn $138 for every $100 earned by a person who has a high school diploma.

The Conference Board of Canada estimates that over $40 billion in spending flows through Canada's colleges and universities each year through government funding, enrolment tuition, and additional research funding. This spending produces over $55 billion annually in economic activity and supports close to 6,80,000 direct and indirect jobs. Of note, approximately half of the economic benefits can be attributed to government funding of post-secondary education institutions.

Secondary Education in Ontario

High School

Education in Canada falls under provincial jurisdiction, which means that each of the 10 Canadian provinces and three territories have their own education regulations and curriculum.

Generally speaking, Ontario's education system has three stages:

- Elementary (sometimes called primary school).
- Secondary (also called high school, Grades 9 through 12).
- Post-secondary (university, college, apprenticeships).

During high school, students take courses that prepare them for higher level, post-secondary education. For example, in Ontario, "U" courses prepare students for university studies while "C" courses prepare students for studies in a college of applied arts and technology, commonly referred to as "community colleges".

Typically, students start taking U or C classes in Grade 11 and into Grade 12. The marks they earn in these courses determine whether or not they will be able to enter a post-secondary institution or programme.

Normally, students apply to the university or college of their choice in the fall/winter of Grade 12.

Sample of Courses for Entry into Degree-Level Programmes

- ENG4U — English
- MCV4U — Calculus and Vectors
- CGW4U — World Issues

- HHG4U — Human Growth and Development
- SCH4U — Chemistry
- BAT4M — Accounting

Sample of Courses for Entry into Diploma, Certificate or Applied Programmes

- ENG4C — English
- MCT — Math for College Technology
- CGU4C — World Geography
- HHS4M — Individuals and Families
- PLF4C — Recreation and Fitness Leadership
- TCJ4C — Construction Technology

Options after Completing High School

Students have several options after completing high school:

- University
- Colleges of Applied Arts and Technology (CAATs or community colleges)
- Apprenticeship
- Private Career Colleges

These options differ from each other in the types of programmes they offer and the credentials a student will earn upon completion. This is important to know because different career paths may require specific credentials.

Unlike elementary school and high school, students are not required to attend a university, college or apprenticeship programme, but in today's highly-demanding job market, further education or training after high school is common-place.

Universities

Universities are institutions that place emphasis not only on teaching, but research as well. Many university professors conduct their own research and publish academic papers in addition to teaching classes.

Students entering universities from high school enrol in a programme at the undergraduate level and earn a Bachelor's degree upon graduation (for example, a Bachelor of Arts, Bachelor of Science or Bachelor of Commerce). A Bachelor's degree normally requires three to four years of full-time study to complete.

After earning a Bachelor's degree, students may choose to continue their university education at the graduate level. Graduate studies can involve earning a Master's degree (for example, a Master of Arts or Master of Science) or a Doctorate (for example, a Ph.D.—Doctor of Philosophy).

Colleges of Applied Arts and Technology (CAATS)

Colleges of applied arts and technology (CAATs) are institutions that focus not only academic learning, but also on skills training. Generally speaking, university programmes take more of a theoretical approach to learning, while CAAT programmes involve more practical, or hands-on, methods. College instructors often have current or recent work experience in the field they teach.

CAATs offer certificate programmes (usually one year of study or less), diploma programmes (usually two to three years of study), and applied degrees leading to a four-year Bachelor's degree. Some universities and CAATs offer joint programmes where students get both a university degree and a college diploma.

Many universities and CAATs have more than one campus so students can study in different locations. Most have on-campus housing for students who do not live nearby. Some universities and CAATs offer distance education (sometimes called correspondence) so students can earn course credits without leaving home.

Apprenticeships

An apprenticeship programme involves work-based training for students who want a career in a skilled trade. Examples of skilled trades include: auto mechanic, carpenter, chef, electrician, hairstylist, painter, plumber, and welder. With apprenticeships, experienced tradespersons pass their knowledge and skills onto the apprentice.

Apprentices receive formal classroom training to compliment their paid, on-the-job training. Most apprenticeships in Canada run between two and five years, over which time the apprentice must complete a list of certain work-related tasks. The apprentice must then pass a provincial qualification examination to earn a Certificate of Qualification, which is required to work in some skilled trades.

Each province and territory in Canada manages its own apprenticeship programmes, for example in Ontario the Career pathways roadmaps fall under the Peel district school board; however the Canadian Federal Government established the Interprovincial Standards Red Seal Programme to standardize trade certification requirements. This gives skilled tradespeople across the country the ability to work in any province or territory.

Private Career Colleges

There are also private career colleges in Canada that offer training geared toward a specific career (also known as vocational training). Private career colleges vary from CAATs in that they are private organizations that are not funded by the government. Private career college classes may be more intensive, more expensive, run over a shorter period of time and may offer smaller class sizes.

Professional Programmes

A professional programme is a programme of advanced learning that leads to an occupation—such as doctor, lawyer, pharmacist—governed by a mandatory regulatory body. Practicing members of the profession must complete a licensing examination before they can actively practice and must keep their credentials current, through additional education mandated by the regulatory body.

There are some professional programmes that students can enter directly from high school, but there are many where some university undergraduate preparation is necessary. In some cases, there are multiple choices of pathways a student can pursue. It is also important to know that not all of these programmes are available at all universities and that competition for entry is intense.

Some examples of professional programmes include:

Programme	*Undergraduate Entry Available*	*Entry After Some Undergraduate Work*
Architecture	Yes	Yes
Chiropractic Medicine		Yes
Dentistry		Yes
Education	Yes	Yes

(*Contd.*)

Programme	*Undergraduate Entry Available*	*Entry After Some Undergraduate Work*
Engineering	Yes	
Law		Yes
Massage Therapy	Yes	Yes
Medicine		Yes
Midwifery	Yes	
Nursing	Yes	Yes
Occupational Therapy		Yes
Optometry		Yes
Pharmacy		Yes
Physiotherapy		Yes
Speech Language Pathology/ Audiology		Yes
Social Work	Yes	Yes
Veterinary Medicine		Yes

Many of these particular areas of study also require standardized aptitude tests for admissions in addition to stringent academic requirements. Some of these tests include:

DAT – Dental Admissions Test
GMAT – Graduate Management Admission Test
GRE – Graduate Record Examination
LSAT – Law Schools Admissions Test
MCAT – Medical College Admissions Test
OAT – Optometry Admissions Test
PCAT – Pharmacy College Admissions Test

Graduate Programmes

Graduate studies programmes (i.e. Master of Arts, Ph.D., Master of Business Administration) require students to first obtain an undegraduate bachelor's degree before they can be admitted. Aside from the professional programmes, there are endless possibilities for post-graduate work as well. Universities in Canada and throughout the world offer Masters and Doctorate degrees among other available types of post-graduate credentials.

College or University

There are many areas of study that are available through both the college and university systems, and each provides its own unique preparation for careers in areas such as medicine, architecture, accounting, dentistry, engineering and nursing. Entry into these programmes depends upon a number of factors, including the student's area of interest, his or her academic ability, the number of years that can be devoted to a programme and financial resources.

Some examples of these types of programmes include:

Area of study	*Examples of College Diplomas/Certificates*	*Examples of University Degrees*
Accounting	Various Diplomas/Advanced Diplomas in Accounting	Bachelor of Commerce (B.Com.)
Architecture/ Landscape Design	Architectural Technician Architectural Technology	Bachelor of Arts in Architecture (BAAR, BA) Masters of Architecture (M.Arch.) Masters of Architectural Science (MAsc)
Business Administration	Various Diplomas or Applied Degrees	Bachelor of Arts/Science (BA, BSc) Bachelor of Business Administration (BBA)
Early Childhood Education	Early Childhood Education Diploma Child and Youth Worker Graduate Certificates	Bachelor of Applied Science (BASc) Bachelor of Arts (BA)
Engineering	Various Diplomas or Applied Degrees	Bachelor of Engineering (BEng) Bachelor of Applied Science (BApSc)
Dentistry	Dental Hygienist Dental Assistant Dental Technician	Doctor of Dental Surgery (DDS)

(*Contd.*)

Area of study	*Examples of College Diplomas/Certificates*	*Examples of University Degrees*
Marketing	Various Diplomas or Applied Degrees	Bachelor of Commerce (BCom) Bachelor of Business Administration (BBA)
Occupational Therapy	Occupational Therapy Assistant	Master of Science Occupational Therapy (MScOT)
Pharmacy	Pharmacy Technician	Bachelor of Pharmacy (BscPhm)
Physical Therapy	Physical Therapy Assistant	Master of Science Physical Therapy (MScPT)
Veterinary Medicine	Veterinary Technician Veterinary Assistant Animal Care Certificate	Doctor of Veterinary Medicine (DVM)

Choosing the Right College or University

Once a student decides which programme to take, the next step is to determine which school to apply to. There are many choices, and there are a lot of reasons to choose one school over another. Some of those factors include:

- Size
- Location
- Reputation
- Programme Availability
- Academic Requirements and Preparation
- Cost
- Family goals, values and obligations
- Instinct

Students and their parents identify two, three or even four potential colleges or universities and, where possible, visit each campus. Colleges and universities often hold open houses throughout the year, particularly in the fall and over March Break. Additionally, campus tours are generally available year round.

Size

Colleges and universities come in all sizes, from small, more intimate campuses with 2,000 or fewer students, to large, research-intensive schools in big cities with a student population of 50,000. There are advantages to each. A smaller college may seem to have a more closely-knit student body, while a larger university will be able to offer a greater variety of programmes, resources and facilities.

Location

College and university students fall into three broad categories:

- Students who live on-campus in a residence;
- Those who commute from the family home; and
- Those who live on their own or with roommates in off-campus housing.

Each situation has advantages and challenges. Living away from the family home tends to encourage a greater sense of independence and personal responsibility, while staying in the family home is usually less expensive, but may not be as conducive to studying.

A university education has a great deal to offer. Students who combine the right degrees with work experience and an impressive work ethic can do extremely well in today's job market.

Those who select a non-career-oriented degree, have little work experience, or are not really given to hard and high quality work can find themselves in the growing ranks of underemployed or unemployed university graduates. And those without the right ability or motivation can easily join the 30 per cent or more of university students who fail to complete their studies.

For some Canadian high school graduates, going to university is an impressive and valuable option. For others, it is an expensive and time-consuming exercise in self-discovery and, often, failure.

Despite these realities, parents, guidance counsellors and politicians continue to over-promote universities, leaving the impression across the country that universities offer the only realistic and reliable paths to middle-class job security and a productive and rewarding career. This is a serious misunderstanding, one that is not connected to the realities of the Canadian job market and the nature of work in the 21st century.

Canadian university graduates move into a college or polytech programme shortly after graduating is but one sign of the mismatch between a university education and the contemporary job market.

Canada has one of the highest quality and most comprehensive post-secondary systems in the world. Just as Canadian universities rank well internationally, other institutions perform at a high level.

This country's polytechs, like Red River College in Manitoba, Sheridan, Seneca and Humber College (Ontario), NAIT and SAIT (Alberta) and BCIT (British Columbia), are world leaders in the development of practical, applied and career-ready diplomas and degrees.

Universities focus on academic and professional programmes. Colleges focus more on career training and trades.

The words "college" and "university" have different meanings in different English-speaking countries. In Canada, colleges and universities are different institutions—usually, colleges have different kinds of programmes than universities do.

Colleges of applied arts and technology have full-time and part-time diploma and certificate programmes. Many also offer Bachelor degrees in applied areas of study.

Colleges tend to be more directly career-oriented than universities. This means they offer practical or hands-on training. Generally, a certificate programme is 1 year or less, and a diploma programme is 2 or 3 years.

Colleges also have pre-trades and apprenticeship training, language training and skills upgrading. Some Ontario colleges focus on agriculture, health science, art or military programmes.

Universities are institutions that can grant degrees. All universities have undergraduate (bachelor's) degrees, and many have graduate (Master's and doctoral) programmes. Universities in Ontario are independent. Although they receive funding from the Ministry of Advanced Education and Skills Development, each institution is self-governing and regulates its own programmes, admissions and faculty.

Many universities also offer professional programmes, such as medicine, dentistry and law. In some cases, these programmes begin after 2 or 3 years of undergraduate study.

An educational institution cannot grant a degree in Ontario unless the provincial government has given it this right. There are private institutions in Ontario that have been given partial degree-granting authority. All of these schools are denominational, which means that they have a religious affiliation.

In Ontario alone there are 20 public universities, 24 colleges, 400+ registered private career colleges and over 1,000 online and distance education programmes.

Colleges are more practical, hands-on training institutions that tend to be more directly career-focused than their counterparts. They offer pre-trades and apprenticeship training, language training, and skills upgrading. Their programmes, including Bachelor's Degrees, are as follows:

Certificate Programmes: Involves the student taking courses in a particular subject, and is finished in two semesters (one year) of study. Usually people get certificates in order to get ahead in their field, and some jobs actually require certificates.

Diploma Programmes: Require completion of four semesters (two years) of study, with advanced diplomas granted after six semesters (three years) of study. They're slightly more general than certificates, often earned through community or technical schools.

Associate Degrees: Typically, a 2- or 3-year programme that provides training necessary to get students ready for entry-level positions in areas like nursing, graphic design, and additional vocational fields. These degrees are usually available through community colleges and technical schools, and qualify graduates for the workplace. Some courses taken under an associate degree may be considered as part of the requirements for a 4-year education at a university.

Bachelor's Degrees: An undergraduate programme tends to take four years to complete. It involves students choosing a major field of study, and gives them the qualifications for entry-level or management positions in their respective fields. An "honours degree" (the fourth year) is usually required to go to a graduate programme (Master's degree). Many universities allow students to combine subject areas (e.g., a Bachelor of Science in Chemistry and Biology) into a "double major".

Master's Degrees: Graduate programmes allow students to specialize in fields of study, which usually take 1-2 years to complete. To enrol in a master's degree programme, students require a minimum GPA and an acceptable score on a graduate entrance examination. In addition, many master's programmes require a thesis (research project) or capstone project (a culmination of everything learned) for graduation.

Doctoral Degrees: The most advanced type of degree programme. Upon completion a student becomes qualified to work as an expert in their field of business or research. A doctoral degree can take several years, requiring a master's degree and the completion of a major research project.

Polytechnic Schools

Polytechnic schools offer instruction in a wide variety of industrial arts, applied sciences, and technical subjects. There are over 220,000 full-time Canadian students in polytechnic institutions. They focus on applied research and industry innovation, enabling college applied research, and taking on issues that affect the businesses they are partnered with. In Canada, they offer bachelor's degrees, joint bachelor's degrees with universities, diploma programmes, certificate programmes, apprenticeships, and graduate certificate programmes. Their members include Algonquin College, Red River College, British Columbia Institute of Technology and Seneca College.

Current State of Work-Integrated Learning in Canada

Universities: According to Universities Canada, 55 per cent of undergraduate students benefit from some form of work-integrated learning during their studies. A 2011 survey by Higher Education Strategy Associates found that among university undergraduates, 16 per cent had participated in a co-op and 18 per cent participated in internships, placements, or practicum programmes.

Colleges and Polytechnics: According to the Higher Education Quality Council of Ontario (HEQCO), 70 per cent of college students participate in some form of work-integrated learning during their studies.

The Business/Higher Education Roundtable

Launched in 2015 by the Business Council of Canada, the Business/Higher Education Roundtable represents some of Canada's largest companies and leading post-secondary institutions. Composed of leaders from the private sector, universities, colleges and polytechnics, the Roundtable works to support young Canadians as they transition from education to the workplace, strengthen research collabouration between industry and institutions, and help Canadian employers as they adapt to the economy of the future. His Excellency the Right Honourable David Johnston, Canada's Governor General, serves as the Roundtable's Honorary Patron.

More than ever before, Canadian colleges and universities are collabourating to deliver these opportunities, and to ensure students are getting a relevant education. In fact, in 2014, the Organization for Economic Cooperation and Development (OECD) reported that one of

Canada's greatest strengths was our high degree of mobility between post-secondaries.

The same year, both Universities Canada, and Colleges and Institutes Canada signed an agreement to further enhance innovative programmes and partnerships that elevate student success. Most recently, that initiative has led the creation of a new web resource showcasing the wide variety of university-college partnerships across Canada.

Calgary welcomed an exciting model of how post-secondaries and business can work together to tackle the challenges facing industry and the community. The federal government committed almost $300,000 in funding for the Kinetica Innovation Centre, housed at SAIT (Southern Alberta Institute of Technology) in Calgary. By providing much-needed wet lab space for researchers and entrepreneurs the centre will harnesses the combined strength of SAIT, the University of Calgary, Innovate Calgary, and its energy technology accelerator, Kinetica Ventures, to fast-track technology development for the energy sector.

The Campus Alberta South partnership between the University of Lethbridge, Bow Valley College, Olds College and Athabasca University provides campus space in downtown Calgary for all four institutions. This campus gives students access to a more complete learning experience through shared services and integrated pathways.

An important aspect of collabouration is increasing opportunities for Indigenous students and other under-represented groups. The University of Lethbridge has a longstanding partnership with nearby Red Crow Community College, located on the Kainai Nation Reserve. Recently, they signed a memorandum of understanding to deepen the collabouration between the two institutions, which provides expanded opportunities for RCCC's Blackfoot students and cross-cultural opportunities for all students.

Partnerships like these create more freedom for students to choose the institution and pathway that works best for them, and they also help students prepare for the realities of the workplace. For example, SAIT (Southern Alberta Institute of Technology) healthcare students and University of Calgary medical students learn alongside each other in simulated real-world medical scenarios, offering them a taste of what it is like to work in an integrated healthcare team. Programmes like these not only help students develop essential interdisciplinary teamwork skills, but they ultimately benefit all who use the healthcare system.

Sharing resources and leveraging other institutions' expertise is good for students helps provide the very best in education and support to students, communities and businesses.

Recent polling across the country shows Canadians support this collabourative spirit. An opinion poll conducted in 2015 by Abacus Data revealed that Canadians believe the governments should invest in all types of post-secondary education.

"Together, Canada's colleges and universities are building the human capital Canada needs to succeed in the global knowledge economy," says Paul Davidson, president of Universities Canada. "Through partnerships and collabouration, students have more course and programme choices than ever before. They're increasingly able to customize their education and career paths."

Students today have access to an increasingly multi-dimensional educational path that includes joint and collabourative academic programmes and research projects, block credit transfers, shared campus space and flexible learning plans. More student choice in post-secondary education leads to greater student satisfaction and improved career preparation.

College, institute and university collabouration is a growing trend in Canada. In Ontario, almost 60 per cent of diploma programmes have a pathway to a degree. Provincial credit transfer councils in Alberta, British Columbia, New Brunswick and Ontario agreed in 2014 to enhance higher education credit transfer and student mobility across their jurisdictions and on a pan-Canadian basis.

Challenges in the Canadian System of Higher Education

Across Canada, post-secondary leaders and policy makers recognize a range of challenges from the technical (mechanisms of credit transfer, reciprocity of quality assurance) to the strategic.

Recruitment, Revenue and Retention

Revenue and cost management are an issue, with a growing number of institutions facing financial difficulty. This leads to pressure on all to increase recruitment and retention but also to lower programme delivery costs.

Competitive Position of Canadian Universities Internationally

Canada has some flagship institutions highly regarded around the world for their research, teaching and scholarship. These include McGill University, the University of Toronto, University of British Columbia and the University of Alberta. But their position is constantly challenged by strong performance by other institutions world-wide, especially emerging Asian institutions and institutions across Europe. Canada has 4 universities in the top 100 of the Times Higher Education World Ranking—University of Toronto (20), University of British Columbia (32), McGill University (39) and McMaster University (94). It has an additional 4 in the top 200—University of Montréal (113), University of Alberta (124), University of Victoria (173) and University of Ottawa (188).

Liberal Education

Student organizations, are concerned about the employability of graduates from colleges and universities. They are raising the issue of the relevance and focus of programmes and the link between education and employment. The ideal of a "liberal education" is taking second place to a focus on skills, competencies and relevant programming, although this idea is being challenged. Community colleges/CEGPs (Collège d'enseignement général et professionnel) have always had employability as a focus, but there is growing pressure on universities (linked to financial pressure and reputation) to reduce the number of programmes which are not work-related and to focus more on programmes that are.

Changing Student Demographics and Expectations

Throughout the review of higher education in Canada, especially in the Maritime provinces, demographic shifts found their way into the narrative. These shifts are very real and affect all institutions. The implication, especially as students are generally paying for more of their own education, is that there is a growing demand for flexibility in delivery, for learner mobility, prior learning recognition and transfer credit. While some have seen this as a demand for more online learning, this is only part of the response. The real shift is in student expectations about flexible and affordable access to quality courses and programmes and varied completion pathways—a more personalized pathway for learning. The adaptive capacity of universities and colleges to respond to these opportunities and new set of expectations requires varies significantly.

Online and Distance Education

Some schools offer online education, if direct attendance is not possible. These schools include Laurentian University, Athabasca University, Carleton University, and University of Manitoba. Usually, this kind of post-secondary education is utilized by those who are constantly moving or would not be able to keep up with direct schooling.

A number of college and university business programmes offer co-op or apprenticeship programmes which allow students to work in-field to gain valuable hands-on experience. Students who enrol in an undergraduate degree programme often pursue a college diploma or certificate in a particular discipline upon graduation (such as marketing, public relations) or apply for acceptance into an MBA programme.

Two of the leading learning management systems (LMS) platforms in the world were developed in Canada—Blackboard Web CT and Desire2Learn.

- Smart Boards—now present in classrooms around the world—were pioneered and developed by a Canadian company (SMART Technologies was founded in 1987 by David Martin and Nancy Knowlton as a Canadian company).
- Massive Open Online Courses (MOOCs) began in Canada with the work of Stephen Downes and George Siemens at the University of Manitoba in 2008.

Both the University of British Columbia and the University of Toronto were amongst the first Provinces have established coordinating mechanisms for online and distance learning and related infrastructure—BC campus, e-Campus Alberta, e-Campus Manitoba, Ontario Learn, Ontario Online Learning Consortium, and Contact North.

All universities and colleges in Canada offer blended learning, with a growing focus on the use of open education resources especially in Western Canada. The University of Laval offers more blended learning courses in French than any other institution in the world. Canada is home to a number of centres of excellence in online and distance education and is also home to the most read journal in the field—the International Review of Research in Open and Distance Learning. The National Research Council supports a programme focused on Learning and Performance Support Systems. institutions to offer MOOCs through Coursera.

Together, Universities Canada and Colleges and Institutes Canada represent over 230 post-secondary institutions serving more than three million students. Canada has developed a robust, innovative and successful post-secondary education system which has many institutions with a global reputation for teaching, research and community service.

Enhancing Collabourative Programmes

There are a growing number of collabourative programmes between institutions, often between institutions in different provinces or in different parts of the world. These range from the Kellogg-Schulich MBA at York University to a collabourative Nurse Practitioner programme between the Saskatchewan Polytechnic and the University of Regina or a joint PhD at 3 Ontario universities or joint MA programmes in history between the University of Manitoba and the University of Winnipeg. Students at the Canadian University of Dubai can complete their first 2 years of study in Dubai and complete their degree at one of several Canadian universities—similar arrangements are made with many other accredited institutions around the world. British Columbia recently announced a series of joint programmes between its post-secondary institutions and partner institutions in China.

Canada's post-secondary institutions can build on a history of responsive, innovative and collabourative approaches supported by government and communities across Canada. To sum, Canada prides itself on significant expansion of access to post-secondary education coupled with growing satisfaction and completion rates, with a strong focus on women in higher education, contributing significantly to Canada's commitment to gender equity. Investments in network centres of excellence—the Canadian Water Network, Stem Cell Network, BioFuel Network—has enabled researchers from across Canada to work together on grand challenges that impact social and economic fabric of Canada. Rather than compete, universities and research centres collabourate for greater social impact.

References

Dennison, J.D. and Gallagher, P. (1986). Canada's Community Colleges; Edward Sheffield *et al.*, (1982) *Systems of Higher Education: Canada*; Robin S. Harris, (1976) *A History of Higher Education in Canada*, 1663-1960.

Gopaul, B.; Jones, Glen. A., *et al.* (2016). The Academic Profession in Canada: Perceptions of Canadian University Faculty about Research and Teaching.

Canadian Journal of Higher Education, Volume 46, No. 2, pp. 55-77.

Maxim, J.L. (2015). Briefing Notes UK Top Management Programme for Higher Education Toronto.

Ross Finnie (2010). *Pursuing Higher Education in Canada: Economic, Social, and Policy Dimensions*. McGill-Queen's University Press.

Zarif, A. (2008). Emerging forms of stratification in higher education: Comparing Canada and the United States, Disseratation Abstract, McMaster University, Hamilton, Ontario, Canada.

3
Monbusho and Higher Education in Japan

Priti Banerjee

Introduction

The Japanese higher education structure is a very potent instrument for their national politics, culture and way of life. The educational accomplishments of the students studying in Japan are advanced and befitted the international criteria and principles. The general strategy, management and supervision are under the influence of the Ministry of Education.

The Japanese Government has the authority to support and approve the composition of all new higher education institutions, both private and public. The finances of Universities, Junior Colleges, Specialised Colleges, Graduate Schools and College of Technology come in the power of the Ministry of Education or Monbusho. It also frames the minimum standards for universities with regard to curriculum, facilities, qualification and number of teachers. A number of institutions can use autonomy in many issues, but the Ministry of Education (Monbusho) keeps hold of the main power over the expansion and progress of higher education in Japan. Higher education in Japan is given at universities (*daigaku*), junior colleges (*tanki-daigaku*), colleges of technology (*koto-senmongakko*) and special training schools and community colleges (*senshu gakko*) and miscellaneous schools offering advanced courses may be counted as institutions of higher education. A college of technology usually offers several courses in engineering and mercantile marine studies. There are a variety of main courses, including those in mechanical engineering, electric engineering, electronic control, information technology, material/ bio-engineering, civil engineering, mercantile marine and management information. The duration of the course is five years (five and a half years for mercantile marine course).

Miscellaneous schools are intended to give adults and young people a wide range of educational opportunities similar to the formal educational offered in secondary schools or institutions of higher education. They provide students of varied ages with knowledge and skills required for their vocational and daily life. Special training schools are a new type of educational institution created in 1976 which offer systematic educational activities, aiming to help students develop the abilities required for vocational and daily life and also to help improve their cultural standards. These have to maintain an enrolment of at least forty students and have to offer instruction for 800 hours or more per each year for each course.

According to Clark, of these four types of institutions, only universities and junior colleges are strictly considered post-secondary education providers. Although stimulated by countries like the United States and the United Kingdom, the Japanese higher education system differs from higher education in most other developed countries in many significant ways. The main differences comprise the method of getting, which relies almost entirely on one or two tests, as opposed to GPAs (Grade Point Average) or other methods of assessment used in Western countries. Since the students only have single opportunity to appear for this examination every year, there is a huge amount of pressure to do well on this test, and the greater part of senior high school education is devoted to do well on this single test. Unlike higher education in some other countries, public universities are generally regarded as more prestigious than private universities, especially the National Seven Universities (University of Tokyo, Kyoto University, Tohoku University, Kyushu University, Hokkaido University, Osaka University, and Nagoya University).

As the Japanese economy is largely scientific and technological based, the labour market demands people who have achieved some form of higher education, particularly related to science and engineering in order to gain a competitive edge when searching for employment. According to the MEXT in *School of Education*, about 75.9 per cent of high school graduates attended a university, junior college, trade school, or other higher education institution.

Administration

The broad-spectrum of policy, administration and supervision are under the influence of the Ministry of Education. Monbusho has the right to approve the establishment of all novel institutions, both private and public. It controls directly over the budgets of all national universities, colleges, junior colleges, and any connected research institutes; provides subsidies to private and prefectural institutions; prescribes minimum standards for universities with respect to curricula, number and qualifications of teachers, and size of buildings and grounds; and provides research and foreign travel support to individual scholars. While individual universities can exercise autonomy in many matters, particularly if they are very prestigious, private or both, the Ministry retains primary influence over the development of higher education in Japan.

Teaching Staff

There is no official recognition system for teachers at Higher Education Institutions. Credentials for teaching staff at universities (including graduate schools), junior colleges and colleges of technology are precise and specified in the ordinance of the Ministry of Education entitled *standards for the establishment of Universities, standards for the establishment of graduate schools, standards for the establishment of junior colleges, standards for the establishment of colleges of technology.*

There are four scales for teachers: the first for teachers at Kindergartens, elementary schools and lower secondary schools; the second for those at upper secondary schools; the third for those at colleges of technology; and the fourth for those at universities and junior colleges.

Academic Year

The majority of the higher educational institutions in Japan lay down its academic year to commence from April to March of the next year. *Ea*ch academic year is divided into two semesters—

1. First semester runs from April till September.
2. Second semester starts in October and ends in March.

Nevertheless, there are certain higher education institutions in Japan that commences its academic session in September or October, referred as an autumn-term. In broad, it can be said that closed on Sundays and on national holidays the educational institutions are closed. Moreover, a five-day school week was introduced in a phased manner by implementing such a week once a month from September1992 and twice a month from April 1995. The system has been implemented in a full-fledged manner since April 2002, making every Saturday a no-school day.

Entrance of Higher Education

University entry is the conventional way taken by Japanese students to go into the entrance of higher education as it is by far the most exalted and prestigious form of higher education in Japan. Unlike the usage of grade point averages and test scores used in Western countries as a yardstick for eligibility, entry to universities based mainly on the scores that students achieved in entrance examinations. Private institutions accounted for nearly 80 per cent of all university enrolments in 1991, but with a few exceptions such as Waseda University and Keio University, the public national universities are more extremely regarded. Especially, National Seven Universities are the most prestigious. This dissimilarity had its origins in historical factors—the long years of supremacy of the top quality imperial universities, such as Tokyo and Kyoto universities, which educated Japan's leaders before the war—and also in differences in quality, particularly in facilities and faculty ratios.

Undergraduate and Graduate Education

The universities used to function as training grounds for national leaders in areas such as politics, economics, academia, and administration when only a small number of students had opportunities to enter higher education. Universities are now expected to respond to the various needs of students in an age when half of the same age group is enrolled in higher education institutions. Each university is expected to have a distinct institutional identity and the system as a whole should be diversified. The government expects universities to attain functions such as: (1) world-class centres of excellence; (2) fostering professionals with advanced specialized skills; (3) fostering professionals in various fields; (4) comprehensive liberal arts education; (5) education/research in specialized areas such as arts or sports; (6) centres for lifelong learning in the community; and (7) contributions to society, such as industry-academia cooperation, international exchanges, and so forth.

The strict entrance examinations have compelled students to engage in time consuming preparation and have led to the enrolment of highly able students, making it easier to educate them and for them to learn independently. The universities and university professors have lost eagerness for teaching and have become oriented towards research (although it does not hold they are all first-rate researchers either) because of the current sellers' market which led the academic staff both in national and private universities tend to regard themselves as researchers rather than teachers. This is building displeasure among students, educational reformers, and policy makers. New university reforms emphasize teaching at the undergraduate level as well as institutional research activities.

Most students go to university at age 18 and most graduates four years later. The dropout rate is not so high, about 10 to 20 per cent at most. After undergraduate education, some students continue to study at graduate school, which involves two years for a master's course and then three years more for a doctoral course. This structure of graduate programme is similar to that of the United States, although there are far fewer Japanese graduate students; 8.6 per cent of students in Japan are under-graduate students compared with 13.6 per cent in the US. There were about 100,000 graduate students in 1991, but this number has grown steadily to more than 250,000 students enrolled in master's and doctoral programme in 2005.

A university has one or more undergraduate faculties or other basic units for educational activities, which offer courses usually lasting four years (six years for medical, dental and veterinary courses) leading to a bachelor's degree.

A university may set up a graduate school aiming to give graduate students opportunities to pursue in-depth study and research concerning academic theories and their application. Graduate schools require the completion of an Undergraduate course or its equivalent for admission. A graduate school offers master's degree courses (usually two years of study) and doctoral degree courses (the standard duration of course is five years, except for medical, dental or veterinary courses, which last four years) and professional degree courses (standard two-year term of study; however, three years in the case of law schools).

To promote global competitiveness and to secure international validity and reliability the Ministry of Education recently tried to enhance the functions of education and research of graduate programmes. However, recent reform initiated by the Ministry emphasizes that graduate education should be course-oriented, providing clear definitions of educational goals, terms of study, structure of curricula, and the process of degree earning such as course work, guidance in theses writing, and examination of academic dissertations to overcome systemic failure and to encourage Professors.

Admission Requirements for Higher Education in Japan

The students who have completed upper secondary courses on a competitive basis admission to universities and junior colleges is granted to them. The students selected in entrants by means of scholastics achievement tests (including the nationwide examination administered by the National Centre for University Entrance Examinations through national, local public and private universities) and other tests assessing students' abilities and aptitudes. Assessments submitted by upper secondary schools are also taken into account. Lately, however the number of universities admitting a certain number of students merely on the basis of the recommendation from upper secondary school principals has been increasing or junior colleges, colleges of technology require for admission the completion of lower secondary schooling.

Students in universities, junior colleges and colleges of technology are required to meet certain credit requirements for the completion of a specific course. The optimum standard requirements for credits are specified in the respective ordinances of the MEXT providing for optimum national standards for the structure, teacher staffing, content of education, physical facilities etc., for different types of higher education institutions. Content and methods of teaching are at the discretion of individual institutions of higher education.

In 1989, the Ministry introduced the following reforms in the graduate school system: (i) the authorization of graduate school evening courses; (ii) the revision of the National Standards for the Establishment of Universities, so as to authorize the establishment of universities providing a graduate school only (i.e. "graduate universities"); (iii) the introduction of flexible provisions which will enable students to obtain a master's degree in one year after completion of an undergraduate course, and which will enable students to earn a doctoral degree in three years after completion of undergraduate course; and (iv) the introduction of flexible provisions regarding qualifications of graduate school after completing the third year of an undergraduate course.

In 1991, the Ministry introduced a thorough reform of the academic degree system. Under this reform, some consolidation was made of, and more flexibility was given to, the categories of degrees. It was made possible for those who have not graduated from university to obtain a bachelor's degree, under certain requirements and subject to the screening by the National Institutions for Academic Degrees.

In 2000, the total number of universities was 649, with 2,740,023 students enrolled and 1,50,563 teachers. The total number of junior colleges was 572, with 3,27,680 students enrolled and 16,752 teachers. The total number of colleges of technology was 62, with 56,714 students enrolled and 4,459 teachers. In addition, there were 3,551 specialized training colleges (7,50,824 students enrolled and 37,656 teachers) and 2,278 miscellaneous schools (2,22,961 students enrolled and 13,412 teachers).

The qualifications for admissions in higher education in Japan differ according to the type of higher educational institution you wish to apply.

General Requirements

Admissions in Japanese Higher Education Institutions—Universities, Junior Colleges, Specialized Training Colleges and Colleges of Technology, one must hold an upper secondary school certificate. It is mandatory to have 12 years of school education (elementary and secondary education) completion for entry into Japanese institutions. This hierarchy is well projected in educational ladder:

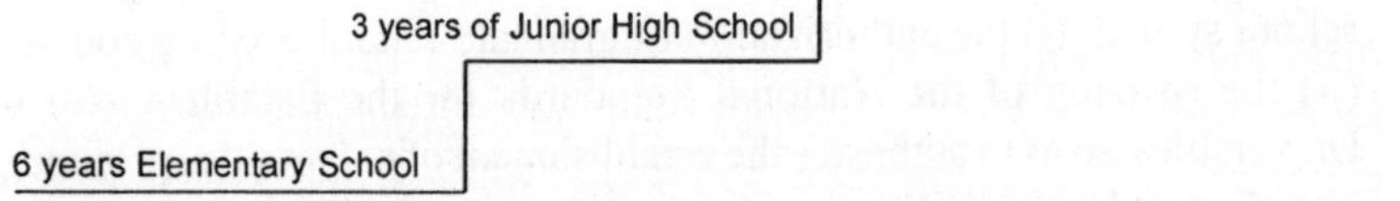

Fig. 3.1: Educational Ladder (6-3-3-4 System)
Source: Self Constructed

Japan has 100 per cent literacy and it is based on age, grade and available educational facilities. Students without 12 years of Education are eligible to apply to higher education institutions in Japan, but subject to a precondition—they must have passed the entrance examination—the national examination of the relevant country (like Baccalaureate in France, Abitur in Germany etc.), that confirms that the students have the achievements equal or higher than those who have completed 12 years of school education.

Higher Educational Facts and Figures

Japan's educational system is in a top position in terms of quality and performance. The average student scored 540 in reading literacy, maths and science in the OECD's Programme for International Student Assessment (PISA), which is higher than the OECD average of 497, making Japan one of the top OECD country in students' ability and skills. Approximately 70 per cent of students who graduate from high school go for higher education studies, thereby making Japan one of the most educated nation in the globe.

Total Number of Higher Education Institutions

- *Universities*—783 (Out of which 86 are National, 92 are Local, and 605 are Private Universities).
- *Junior Colleges*—372 (Out of which 22- are Local and 350 are Private Junior Colleges).
- *Colleges of Technology*—57 (Out of which 51 are National, 3 are Local, and 3 are Private Colleges of Technology).
  Source: MEXT, School Basic Survey (2012).

Japan Higher Education: Timeline

The Japanese altered their higher education structure by adapting and acquiring constructive and precious information and technology from different education systems. The educational culture of Japan is established on the Shinto, Buddhism and Confucianism philosophy. Three major reforms were introduced during the 19th-20th century in the area of education in Japan, which contributed to individual work of students, as well as originality, individuality and internationalization of education. Equality in education is one of the modern educational norms of Japan.

Equality of opportunity: The significant measure of equality of opportunity is due to the extensive size of the Japanese higher education system. Children from families in the lowest 20 per cent income bracket have a 1 in 3 chance of attending a university compared with a 9 in 10 chance for those from the top 20 per cent income bracket. This state of affairs does not match up to unfavourably with the state in most other major nations.

Yet the class differentials at leading institutions are much greater. Four of every 5 students at the University of Tokyo come from professional or executive homes. A small number of working class youth are represented. Special treatment for students from poor families or other disadvantaged groups is not a matter of national policy.

Status of Women: The women in Japan are almost like men to enter a higher education institution. However, the enrolment pattern of women differs significantly, reflecting societal expectations and occupational realities. For example, women comprise less than 10 per cent of the enrolment at the University of Tokyo. Nationally, there is a strong tendency for them to major in home economics, the arts, or social sciences. Only 3 per cent of the engineering students in universities are female, compared to about 14.5 per cent in the United States.

Urban-rural differential: The urbanized prefectures are more likely to send students to higher education, but this differential is accounted for by their families' occupational and income distribution, as well as by more extensive secondary school opportunities and the geographic distribution of post-secondary institutions. Indeed, the Tokyo metropolitan area alone accounts for 30 per cent of the students and at least15 per cent of the nation's total population, depending upon how the metropolitan area is defined.

All things considered, the Japanese higher education system has made important progress towards equality of opportunity in a relatively brief span of years. However, there is a potentially serious problem in the apparent trend towards monopolization of the most prestigious universities by children from the highest socio-economic levels. While these young people gain admission on the basis of their outstanding performance in the examinations, some Japanese social critics worry that the related phenomena of elite high schools, family tutors, and the best *juku* which help make such performance possible are more accessible to affluent families. They foresee the possibility that if such a trend were to continue, it could undermine the legitimacy of the entrance examinations as an objective, meritocratic filter for entry into higher education.

Higher Education Institutions: Snapshot

Universities are higher education institutions that, as centres of learning, conduct teaching and in-depth research in specialized academic disciplines and provide students with broad knowledge. Junior colleges offer courses lasting two or three years, mainly in the fields of humanities, home sciences, education and social sciences. In Japan, there are five types of higher education institutions. These higher educational institutions are classified as—national, local, public and private.

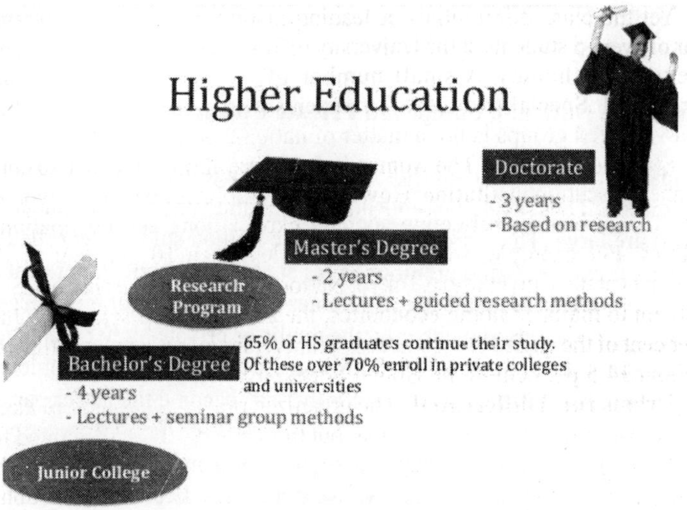

Fig. 7.2: Bird's eyeview of Higher Education
Source: www.japaneducation.info/Higher-Education/index.html

Universities (Undergraduate): There are national, public and private universities in Japan. The duration of studies in an undergraduate university is 4 years with the exception of medical specialty, dental medicine, pharmacy, and veterinary science department, which needs six years of study.

Junior Colleges: The duration of studies at a Junior College is two years or three years depending on the department. The Junior Colleges mainly focus on the following departments—home economics, education, nursing, humanities and sociology.

Specialised/Professional Training Colleges: Specialised training colleges provide vocational and technology-related education as well as education in the enhancement of skills and knowledge required in life. These colleges mainly provide specialized training in a particular industry or career. The duration of studies is 1 year or more, but most courses lasts for two years.

Colleges of Technology: Colleges of technology provide courses in engineering field, merchant shipping and other related areas of study, which lasts for 5 years (five and half for the mercantile marine course). Students who have passed junior high school are eligible for courses/ programmes offered by Colleges of Technology.

Graduate Schools: The duration of studies in graduate schools in Japan depends on whether you are enrolled in a master's or a doctoral course of study. A Master's programme lasts for two years and the doctoral course of study lasts for five years.

Scenario of National, Public and Private Universities

Compared to European countries, Japan has a huge population of around 120 million. Thus, its higher education population and higher education system are large. There are more than three million students enrolled at Japanese universities and junior colleges at present. About 50 per cent of high school graduates at the age of 18 enter universities or junior colleges. These institutions are run either by the public or private higher education sector. The public sector institutions consist of national and municipal institutions, but it is the private sector that has become the larger part of the system.

Since the late 19th century, Japan's government has established and supported national universities whose aims have been to train senior bureaucrats, engineers, academics, medical professionals, and lawyers destined to become leaders in their respective fields. Among the seven flagship national universities in the regions, the most prestigious and largest has been the Imperial University of Tokyo, now the University of Tokyo.

The equally long history of the private universities has also produced political, commercial, and social leaders, with some private institutions initially established by ambitious individuals, social reformers, entrepreneurs, and religious groups. While private institutions cover all areas of study, they have traditionally focused on the humanities, social sciences, business and law because they have had insufficient resources to provide higher cost education in, for example, natural sciences, engineering and medical sciences. From the beginning, private institutions have not received government subsidies and their main source of revenue has been tuition fees. They have always suffered financial difficulties, which has resulted in a poorer quality of teaching in private universities compared to national universities. This has continued until the present and is reflected in the statistics on the number of academic staff in each sector: there are 60,000 teachers in national universities and 92,000 teachers in private universities, despite the fact that three quarters of all students are in private institutions.

It is traditionally recognized that the government should be responsible for providing higher education opportunities. The government has, therefore, opened national universities in everyone of the 47 prefectures to train primary and secondary school teachers, medical doctors, and other professionals. Until the early 1970s, the tuition fees for national universities were low at about eight Euros per year. But the tuition fees for private universities have always been relatively high. In Japan, private universities have played a role to provide higher education opportunities for the masses while national universities with lower tuition fees have been functioning as elite training schools for nation building. This is one of the contradictory aspects of the Japanese higher education system. To compensate for tuition fee hikes in both national and private universities, the government has recently begun to provide more student loans.

Quality Assurance and Evaluation

The Ministry of Education has controlled the establishment of universities since the 1950s. This control has a quality assurance function in higher education institutions. Before opening a new private university, the Ministry examines the application for establishment with regards to the quality of teaching, facilities and equipment, and other conditions of education. If the Ministry judges the level of quality unsatisfactory, it can refuse to grant approval to open. The quality assurance of universities has depended on Ministry control for a long time, but once open, private universities have some considerable freedom to manage the provision of their higher education opportunities. Thus, to assure the continuation of quality after establishment, in the 2000s quality assurance is now determined by evaluation.

Quality assurance of higher education and evaluation as a means to achieve higher quality are important issues in the recent university reforms. Until recently, there has been more demand (applicants) than supply (the capacity of universities and junior colleges) in the higher education market, so the quality of students has, to some extent, been assured by implementing selective entrance examinations. However, now that the supply exceeds the demand in this market, some students are being allowed to enroll without sufficient basic knowledge and learning skills to study there effectively. The quality assurance of higher education is also an important issue for institutions to manage as international cooperation and competition continues to increase, such as increases in the number of foreign students studying in Japan, Japanese who study abroad and students on exchange programmes.

The Ministry of Education well acknowledges that it has responsibility for arranging the higher education system of quality assurance and operating it effectively in order to provide higher quality education for students and to secure international validity for Japan's higher education. In the present system, all universities, both national and private, should carry out self-monitoring and self-evaluation, and should make the results public in efforts to improve and enrich their levels of education and research activities. This should go hand-in-hand with the efforts they make in their evaluations by the Organization for University Evaluation which is certified by the Ministry of Education. Mainly three organizations are engaged in the evaluation of universities: one is national institute and the others are private or voluntary ones.

The achievement by national universities of a mid-term target and plan must also be evaluated at the end of a six-year mid-term period. This evaluation is very comprehensive; including both self-evaluation and third-party evaluation, and it covers the evaluation of achievement not only for mid-term goals and targets, but also the level of education and research activities, and individual research outcomes. This evaluation system requires tremendous energy and time from the academic and administrative staff involved, and it is often pointed out that the system ironically deteriorates the level of education and research activities in universities. Tradition and experience of self-evaluation and third-party evaluation have been relatively lacking in the world of Japanese higher education, and the new emphasis on quality assurance will place a heavy burden on higher education institutions.

The introduction of quality assurance in higher education follows the government's plan for deregulation in various areas, from *ex-ante* regulations to *ex-post-facto* checks. However, in light of a recent case of misconduct at a private for-profit university, the Ministry considers that regular evaluation is not sufficient and that the examination before establishment should still be done in order to maintain the quality of higher education. Since the spring of 2004, each of Japan's 87 national universities has been given an independent corporation status. Before that, national universities were state-owned institutions controlled by the government for over a hundred years. Both faculty members and administrative staff were civil servants, although the former were mainly chosen by peer faculty members. The universities' assets were owned by the State and the Ministry of Education allocated to each national university its earmarked budget which had to be spent by the end of the fiscal year.

One of the characteristics of the Japanese higher education system is that the private sector quantitatively occupies a larger part than does the public sector; more than 75 per cent of students are enrolled in private colleges and universities. The vastness of the private sector is partly attributable to the higher education policy implemented by the Ministry of Education in the era of expansion in the 1960s and 70s. Facing the tremendous demand for higher education, the Ministry, which had insufficient resources to provide higher education opportunities through public institutions, permitted the establishment of private institutions or allowed the expansion of existing ones by adopting less strict regulations. This thrifty model of higher education expansion is a double-edged sword however. While it certainly helped lessen public spending, it placed a heavy cost burden on households and the quality of education has not necessarily been assured. In this chapter, after describing the expansion of higher education in the 1960s and 70s, it is pointed out that teaching has become emphasized on both undergraduate and graduate education reform. It is also shown that quality assurance is an important issue in Japanese higher education. Finally, recent developments in the financing of higher education are discussed.

Educational Research and Information

The National Institute for Educational Policy Research (NIER) started out as the National Institute for Educational Research, founded in 1949. The name was changed as part of the reorganization of central government ministries that took place in January 2001. The functions and responsibilities of the organization structure was overhauled and reconfigured to enable it to provide improved assistance with the planning, formulation, and implementation of educational policy. The NIER also pursues a wide range of activities such as providing academic sectors with information about educational studies, conducting research studies in conjunction with schools, pursuing practical research into social education, and conducting joint international initiatives (including research studies) in the educational field.

NIER serves as the Secretariat for the National Federation of Educational Research Institutes, and consists of prefectural, municipal, and private sector education research institutes throughout Japan. As much, the Institute works together with individual education research institutes from the Federation collabourative symposiums designed to promote the dissemination of research outcomes and enhance the standard of education in schools.

The Ministry of Education and the local boards of education encourage school-based research by classroom teachers for the improvement of teaching methods and materials. Universities faculties in educational institutes or centres (Kanaya, 1995: 488).

References

Clark, Nick (1 May, 2005). "Education in Japan." Retrieved 28 October, 2016.

Kanaya, T. Japan. In: T.N. Postlethwaite, (ed.) *International Encyclopedia of National Systems of Education*, pp. 482-89. Second edition, Oxford/New York/Tokyo, Elsevier Science, 1995.

Ministry of Education, Science, Sports and Culture. Development of Education in Japan 1992-1994. *International Conference on Education*, 44th session, Geneva, 1994.

Ministry of Education, Science, Sports and Culture. Development of Education in Japan 1994-1996. *International Conference on Education*, 45th session, Geneva, 1996.

Ministry of Education, Science, Sports and Culture. Development of Education in Japan 1997-2001. *International Conference on Education*, 46th session, Geneva, 2001.

Ministry of Education, Science, Sports and Culture. Development of Education in Japan 2002-2004. *International Conference on Education*, 47th session, Geneva, 2004.

Ministry of Education, Science, Sports and Culture. *FY2004 White Paper on Education, Culture, Sports, Science and Technology*. MEXT, Tokyo, 2005.

Ministry of Education, Science, Sports and Culture. *Japan's Education at a Glance 2005*. MEXT, Tokyo, 2005.

"School Education" (PDF). MEXT. Archived from the original (PDF) on 2 January, 2008. Retrieved 2 March, 2014.

Web Sources

Ministry of Education, Culture, Sports, Science & Technology: http://www.mext.go.jp/english/[In Japanese and English. Last Checked: October 2007.]

National Information Centre for Educational Resources: http://www.nicer.go.jp/index_en.html[In Japanese and English. Last checked: October 2007.]

National Institute for Educational Policy Research of Japan: http://nier.go.jp/homepage/kyoutsuu/English/index.html [In Japanese and English. Last Checked: October 2007.]

National institute of Special Education: http://www.nise.go.jp/[In Japanese and English. Last Checked: October 2007.]

For updated links, consult the web page of the International bureau of Educational of UNESCO: http://www.ibe.unesco.org/links.html

4

Higher Education in China

The Conceptual Framework

Anu Jose Vengal

Education is the most powerful force for human development. Over the centuries education is considered as an enabler. Among the different stages of education, Higher education is on the apex of the process. Moulding and mentoring of students is the focal theme of higher education which results in holistic personality development.

Higher education, Post-secondary education or Third level education is the one which succeeds secondary education. This is also known as Tertiary education. The quality of higher education institutions should be given utmost focus than mushrooming of higher education centres.

The right of access to higher education is mentioned in a number of international human rights instruments. The UN International Covenant on Economic, Social and Cultural Rights of 1966 declares, in Article 13, that **"higher education shall be made equally accessible to all, on the basis of capacity, by every appropriate means, and in particular by the progressive introduction of free education."**

Higher education includes teaching, research, exacting applied work (e.g. in medical schools and dental schools), and social services activities of universities. Within the realm of teaching, it includes both the undergraduate level, and beyond that, graduate-level (or post-graduate level).

Higher Education Across Asia

As economies in the Asian region have grown larger and more intricate, they have also become more integrated through economic and social exchange. Higher education is seem to have an ever more important role in human resource development and the movement of people, students, and the workforce in the region.

Higher education across much of Asia is a remarkable success story. It enjoys a high level of government support. Leaders understand that higher education is an important ingredient in the economic and social development of their countries. They recognize that the globalization of markets, the interdependency of international financial systems, the expanded role of technology, and high-speed communications have created an enormous need for highly skilled technical, professional, and managerial leaders. They understand that modern economies cannot be managed by only primary and secondary school graduates. Evidence of this support is quite concrete. Enrolments have grown, participation in higher education has diversified, new universities have been created, and universities are experimenting with new forms of instructional delivery.

At the same time, higher education across the Asian region faces a set of interwoven challenges. Many higher education institutions (HEIs) in Asia are coping with explosive enrolment growth, shortages of qualified instructional staff, widespread concern over instructional quality and in many cases, severe financial constraints. These issues are interwoven, and their solutions are interdependent. Efforts to address any one problem need to be undertaken with attention to the larger constellation of issues.

While the contribution of higher education to economic development is generally accepted, the mechanisms through which those benefits are achieved are less well understood. It is widely accepted that that higher education contributes to national development in three principal ways:

Higher education institutions prepare the primary and secondary teachers, who shape the dimensions and quality of the overall education system of a country: Low-quality primary and secondary education leads to huge inefficiencies in higher education, as incoming students lack essential prior preparation for post-secondary study (Hanushek and Woessmann 2007). This creates a tarnished cycle, as poorly prepared entering students combine in many institutions with low-quality instruction to yield poorly prepared graduates. One way to break that cycle is to raise the quality of post-secondary preparation that future teachers receive. Those individuals need solid content preparation in the subjects they will teach, preparation in modern pedagogical techniques, and training in the use of technology for instruction. To the extent that schools receive better prepared teachers, and to the extent that those teachers have the support they need to implement their new abilities once they are in the schools, future secondary graduates will be better equipped for either direct entry to the labour market or higher education (ADB, 2008).

HEIs train the high-level technical and administrative personnel needed in government, business, and industry: International finance, business management, and national governance increasingly depend on mechanization, high-speed communication, and complex information flows, which all require high levels of administrative sophistication, technical expertise, and analytic capacity. Secondary education alone cannot provide the managerial and technical leadership needed in modern business, industry, and government.

HEIs operate as incubators of innovation and creative thinking needed for an economically competitive society: Economic and social development increasingly depends on innovation. Universities have a potentially important role in driving innovation and development. They can do so both through their role in carrying out research and development and by training workers for the knowledge economy (LaRocque, 2007). The ability of higher education systems to accomplish these ends depends, to a significant extent, on how the systems are designed, financed, and managed; on how well equipped the instructional staff are to meet the changing demands being placed upon them; and on how good at planning and how realistic governments are in the demands they place on their universities.

A Brief Description of Higher Education in China

History

Although China's modern universities were founded in the late nineteenth and early twentieth century, the history of formal education in China predates the establishment of Western-style educational institutions by centuries. The imperial education and examination system developed as a meritocratic means to train and select civil servants during the Han dynasty (206 BCE to 220 CE).

In the second half of the twentieth century the Chinese higher-education scenario was chiseled by the Soviet-style reorganization. Starting in the 1950s, universities became primarily teaching institutions, affiliated with specific government bodies. They taught subjects, such as medicine, art or agriculture. The result was a high degree of specialization and lack of cross-fertilization between the disciplines. This changed in the 1980s and 1990s, when formerly specialized institutions were joined to form larger, more diverse universities. These institutions were granted increased autonomy over decisions about hiring, admissions, and the allocation of funds.

Over the last quarter century, China has seen a "massification" of its university system. The number of 18- to 22-year-olds in higher education has increased dramatically, from four per cent in 1990 to 6.5 per cent in 1999 to 37.5 per cent in 2014. As of 2016, the number of graduates to flood China's labour market each year is million. The factors behind this explosive growth are diverse, and include the demands of a growing middle class, economic expansion, and government policies that explicitly seek to boost participation in higher education. In terms of enrolment rates, those policies have been broadly successful, but critics charge that a focus on the country's most prestigious institutions, led by Peking University and Tsinghua University, has created an imbalance in quality. Well-known initiatives such as Project 211 and Project 985, for example, have allocated billions of dollars to a limited number of top-tier public schools in an effort to increase their international standing and support research output.

Public and Private Institutions

Many of the country's best and most generously funded universities are in Beijing, Shanghai, and the great cities of eastern China, and all of them are public. However, China has seen exponential growth in the number of private institutions of higher education since the 1980s, when laws governing the sector began to be relaxed. More recently, China has come to see private institutions as a key mechanism for addressing the scale of demand. The 2002 Law on the Promotion of Privately Run Schools, for example, states explicitly that private educational institutions are integral to the invigoration of the country through science, technology and education.

In the fifteen years leading up to 2014, the number of private higher education institutions in operation rose from 39 to 727. The quality of these institutions is highly variable, say observers, and their status and future are hotly debated. Recent enrolments have declined steeply for some schools, not least because internationalization has heightened competition for qualified students.

Programmes offered by private institutions are generally more practice-oriented than their counterparts in the public sector. Other differences between the two types of institution involve admission requirements, governance, and funding models. Public universities, which receive government funding as well as tuition fees (introduced in the 1990s), are generally more affordable than their private counterparts.

Government Improvement Initiatives

Institutions in the Chinese higher education sector are of totally differing quality, with a select few at the top. This stratification is the result of government policy. In the mid-1990s, the Central government launched two significant initiatives to improve the quality and international competitiveness of top-tier higher education institutions in China. These initiatives include:

> *Project 211:* The State Council, Department of Finance and the Ministry of Education of China co-issued the General Plan for Project 211 in 1995 to strengthen selected higher education institutions and key disciplines. The project started with 99 institutions. It currently includes 112 universities. Target areas of improvement are the overall infrastructure of institutions, key disciplines, and higher education public services system.
>
> *Project 985:* The State Council and the Ministry of Education of China launched Project 985 in 1998 with the explicit aim of building world-class universities. Thirty-nine elite institutions from Project 211 received a large earmark of US $ 40.4billion (264.9 billion CNY) from the Central government and US $ 28.4 billion (186.3 billion CNY) from local government to enhance their research capacity.

Education System

Education in mainland China (excluding Hong Kong and Macau) is governed on three levels—national, provincial, and local.

- At the national level, the Ministry of Education is the Central Governmental Agency responsible for formulating macro-education policies.
- Provincial education departments manage the local policy development and implementation under the guideline of the state regulations. Apart from 111 prestigious universities under the

direct jurisdiction of the Ministry of Education and other Central Government Authorities, and a few universities administered jointly by the Central and Provincial Governments, the majority of higher education institutions are affiliated with provincial authorities or lower local governments.

- The local education authorities have primary supervision responsibility over elementary education.

The most common language of instruction in elementary and secondary schools is Mandarin, the official language in China. In regions where the majority of students are ethnic minorities, instruction is offered in both Mandarin and the dominant local language.

Higher Education

China's higher education is highly stratified. Structurally, it is divided into two sectors: regular higher education and adult higher education. As of 2015, the Education reported a total of 2,845 Chinese higher education institutions (HEIs) in both the regular and adult higher education sectors. Tertiary education can also be obtained through a prescribed self-study programme.

Regular Higher Education

Ninety per cent of China's HEIs (2,553) are in the **regular higher education sector.** Over 70 per cent of undergraduate students are enrolled at regular higher education institutions.

Not all Chinese institutions of Higher Education, even in the regular sector, offer degrees; many offer only graduation certificates. Around 1,202 institutions in the regular higher education sector are academically oriented and grant degrees. The rest focus on practical and occupational skills and offer graduation certificates.

The regular higher education sector includes 447 private institutions, 275 independent colleges (quasi-private), and seven Chinese-foreign cooperative initiatives, set up as joint partnerships between Chinese and foreign education institutions.

Adult Higher Education

Adult education programmes follow the curriculum offered by regular institutions, but the teaching format is more flexible and diverse, including distance-learning and part-time study. Just fewer than 30 per cent of undergraduate students are enrolled in adult higher education institutions.

Self-Study Programmes

In addition to regular and adult education, higher education can be obtained through a *"self-study" programme.* Depending on the level of study (junior college or undergraduate), the programme consists of 12-20 subject examinations in a pre-determined discipline. Success is assessed by Self-taught Higher Education Examinations.

Admissions

Regular higher education: Admission to a regular higher education institution depends on high school graduation and Gaokao scores. The Gaokao is held on June 7 and 8 every year. (Some provinces extend the exam to the 9th.) Results are released by the end of June. Applicants are typically high school students in their senior year, however, there has been no age restriction since 2001. Nearly nine million students take the Gaokao annually.

Adult higher education: Admission to adult higher education institutions, or adult education programmes at regular universities, is based on the National Adult College Entrance Examination (also known as "the adult Gaokao"). Applicants are expected to have academic skills on par with high school graduates at the time of the examination, however, a high school diploma is not required for enrolment in adult higher education programmes.

Self-study: Self-taught Higher Education has an entirely open enrolment policy that accepts applications from all backgrounds and academic levels. Applicants register with the provincial Self-taught Higher Education Examinations Committee and complete the programme at their own pace. Depending on the level of study (junior college or undergraduate), the programme consists of 12-20 subject examinations in a pre-determined discipline. Students receive a graduation certificate, called the *biye zhengshu* when they obtain satisfactory test results in all subjects. Upon completion of a self-taught undergraduate programme and fulfillment of a handful of additional requirements, students can apply for a bachelor's degree certificate called a *xueshixuewei zhengshu.*

Degrees and Certificates

As of 2015, roughly 1,350 of China's HEIs offer two to three-year junior college programmes leading to a graduation certificate rather than a degree. Compared to academically oriented degree programmes, these non-degree programmes focus on practical and occupational skills. Graduates of these programmes either enter the workforce or opt to apply for "top-up" programmes, which are designed to allow them to study further in a bachelor's programme for an additional two to three years.

An estimated 1,200 institutions in the regular higher education sector grant degrees. There are three ladders of degrees in China—bachelor's, master's and doctorate.

Bachelor's Degrees

Bachelor's programmes normally require four years of full-time study in a traditional classroom setting. (Some programmes at the bachelor's level—for instance, architecture, medicine, and a few engineering programmes—require five-years of study.)

Upon successful fulfilment of these criteria, students are typically awarded two types of certification:

- A graduation certificate issued directly by the institution.
- A bachelor's degree certificate issued by the Academic Degrees Committee of the State Council.

The graduation certificate is the prerequisite of the awarding of degree. In cases where the student does not meet the requirements for a bachelor's degree, they may still receive the graduation certificate.

Master's Degrees

Students with a bachelor's degree can apply for admission to master's programmes. At master's level, there are two types of programme: academic and professional. Most full-time academic programmes are three years long. Professional programmes are typically two years long; there are 39 recognized professional degrees at master's level.

Upon successful completion of master's programmes, students receive a master's degree certificate, called a *shuoshi xuewei zhengshu.* The certificate should denote whether the programme was academic or professional.

Doctoral Degrees

Doctoral programmes, the highest-level degree programmes offered in China, normally require a minimum of three years to complete. During this period, students are expected to complete coursework, pass a final examination, and write and defend a dissertation. A doctoral degree certificate, called ***a boshi xuewei zhengshu*** is awarded upon successful completion of all requirements.

Curriculum

The curriculum in most disciplines consists of four major areas:

- General compulsory subjects such as computer basics, English, mathematics, ideology and politics, fundamentals of law, and physical education.
- General elective subjects in humanities and sciences.
- Specialty compulsory subjects in the chosen field of study.
- Specialty elective subjects in the student's focus of interest.

Students also have to complete other components of the graduation requirements, including short-term or long-term internships, social practice, external English tests, and a thesis.

Accreditation

Higher Education Evaluation Centre (HEEC)

The Higher Education Evaluation Centre was founded in 2004 and operates under the Ministry of Education. The HEEC is tasked with systematic evaluation of institutions of higher education and their programmes.

Academic Degrees and Graduate Education Development Centre (CDGDC)

The Academic Degrees and Graduate Education Development Centre was set up in 2003 and operates under the joint leadership of the Ministry of Education and the Academic Degrees Committee of the State Council.

The CDGDC evaluates academic degrees and graduate education, and verifies the authenticity of academic degree certificates.

Governance for China-Foreign Cooperative Programmes

The Regulations of the People's Republic of China on Chinese-Foreign Cooperation in Running Schools took effect in September 2003. These regulations standardise governance of jointly run Chinese-foreign schools, with the objective of fostering international educational exchange and enhancing development of China's education system. The regulations articulate the legal and procedural responsibilities of Chinese educational institutions and foreign partners involved in the establishment, administration, financing, and teaching at joint venture schools. All approved programmes can be observed on an authorized platform. The types of institutions eligible do not include compulsory education service or special education services such as military, police and political education.

Types of Colleges and Universities

In China, according to ownership-based categories of HEIs, the higher education can be divided into two categories—State-owned or government-owned HEIs, including Regular HEIs, Independent Institutions, Higher Vocational Colleges, Adult HEIs, and non-government or private universities. Due to the long-time influence by Soviet Union and late development of private universities, it has deeply rooted in Chinese heart that government-owned is much better than private ones. Regular HEIs is the cornerstone in China's higher education, while private universities development could not be ignored.

According to the latest data (2015) of People's Republic of China Ministry of Education, total number of Chinese National Higher Institutions is 2845, including 2,553 National General Colleges and Universities and 292 Adult Higher Institutions. Government-owned HEIs are likely to receive more policy and finance support from official level.

Due to the large population, Chinese public universities are impossible to satisfy everyone's needs. Under this condition, private universities of China come into being. The advantages of their professional setting that more in line with market requirements could not make up for the lack of financial funds and students. Actually, these two factors are equal. The source of funds for them depends largely on students' tuition fees.

Analysing the higher education in Asia and in particular China, which is the first populous country in the world, it can be said undoubtedly that

China promotes quality higher education. The pattern of educational framework with the number of institutions in the governmental and private sector gives clear evidence on the benchmark followed in the educational system of China. The curriculum in higher education also provides much scope for students to develop holistically. Self empowerment and societal empowerment are the two major goals emphasized in China through their Higher Education System. Thus the country serves as a role model in promoting quality education to the world.

References

Books and Articles

Hall Stanley G., (2006). *Prophets of Eduction*, Sarup & Sons, New Delhi.

Pucciarelli F., Kaplan Andreas, M. (2016). Competition and Strategy in Higher Education: Managing Complexity and Uncertainty, *Business Horizons*, Volume 59.

"2015 National College List", People's Republic of China Ministry of Education, May 21, 2015

Zhu, Hong Zhen and Lou Shiyan (2011). *Development and Reform of Higher Education in China*. Woodhead Publishing Limited, pp. 41-42. ISBN: 9781843346395.

Zhou, Guoping and Xie, Zuoyu (12 May, 2006). *Bankruptcy Analysis of China's Private Universities*. XiaMen University Press, pp. 46-53.

Private Education Promotion Law of the People's Republic of China, *Education Act No. IV of 28 December 2002* (in Chinese). Retrieved on 1 September, 2003.

Online Sources

http://blogs.economictimes.indiatimes.com/HigherEdChange/what-india-can-learn-from-china-s-higher-education/

http://www.sicas.cn/Students/Info/Content_110621144852564.shtml

https://www.adb.org/sites/default/files/publication/29407/higher-education-across-asia

http://wenr.wes.org/2016/03/education-in-china-2

5
Higher Education System in China

An Existing Scenario

V. Vijaya Lakshmi

China has the largest population and largest higher education system in the world. The Ministry of Education of the People's Republic of China is the supreme education administration body in China. It is responsible for carrying out related laws, regulations, guidelines and policies of the central government; the planning development of the education sector; integrating and coordinating educational initiatives and programmes nationwide; manoeuvring and guiding education reform countrywide. It controls all higher education institutions through policy-making, legislation, planning, funding, and evaluation. In each institution, the President works under the leadership of the Committee of Chinese Communist Party. The Committee of Academy and the Representative Conference of Faculty and Staff deal with faculty and staff issues.

Basic education system in China starts with compulsory education for all the children which lasts for nine years. Children enter primary school at the age of six. Before primary school the children may have attended preschool for a few years. Compulsory education is divided into six years of primary school and three years of lower middle school.

Upon completion of the nine-year compulsory education, students undertake entrance examinations towards senior secondary education which is provided by three different types of schools. The general senior secondary school (senior middle school) prepares students for the national university entrance examination and subsequently for admission to higher education. Specialised (sometimes translated as "technical") and vocational (sometimes translated as "professional") schools provide subject/occupation specific education and training. Graduates from these two types of schools enter the labour market. Although it is possible for graduates from a specialised secondary school to take the national university entrance examination and enter a vocational university, this is extremely rare in practice.

Types of Higher Education Institutions

Higher education is provided by institutions of various types including universities (general and technical), specialised institutions (medicine, agriculture, foreign languages etc.), vocational universities (e.g. teacher training) and specialised colleges. Entry to higher education in China is highly competitive.

The Bachelor's degree is granted by universities and specialised institutions. However, the right to grant the Bachelor's degree has also been given to some vocational universities. Vocational universities and specialised colleges provide non-university post-secondary studies and their graduates are awarded diplomas.

Higher education is also provided by adult higher education institutions of various types. The length of studies may vary from one month to three years. Some institutions have the right to award the Bachelor's degrees upon the completion of four-year studies.

Specialised offer higher education programmes which represent less than four years of full-time study, in the following fields: agriculture, animal husbandry, various areas of commerce (i.e. accounting and customs), engineering and technology, medical sciences, navigation, sericulture, teacher training, and tourism.

Admission to specialised colleges is generally based on graduation from senior middle school and scores on the unified national university entrance examinations. Diplomas may be earned upon completion of two- or three-year full time programmes, or three- to four-year part-time programmes. The most common length of an academic programme offered by specialised schools is three years of full-time study. After two years of study, successful students in specialised colleges can apply to the third year of a Bachelor's programme in a degree-granting higher education institution.

Vocational universities are part of the formal system of higher education. The purpose of vocational universities is to address the manpower requirements of the community in which they are located. Some of the institutions have grown out of employees' colleges and some out of the branch colleges of large universities, while some are entirely new establishments. The graduates are usually awarded diplomas, but very few vocational universities also have the right to offer the Bachelor's degree programme.

Universities and specialised institutions offer degree programmes in 11 different fields like agriculture, arts and culture, engineering, finance and economics, forestry, humanities, medicine and pharmacy, natural science, physical science, political science, law and teacher training. Each field is divided into sub-fields and then further into specialties.

In China, adult higher education is considered to be at tertiary level, but nevertheless to be at lower level than the formal programmes of higher education. In most cases the admission is based on the unified national entrance examination for adult higher education, which differs from the unified national college/university entrance examination. The graduates are not assigned employment by the government.

Administrative colleges are also known as "in-service management cadre colleges". They offer adult middle school and higher education programmes for "cadres", a term which designates all the levels of the staff members employed in government offices. Some training courses are also offered in separate departments or sections at colleges and universities.

Many colleges and universities offer part-time adult higher education programmes through correspondence and attached evening colleges. Diploma programmes, in-service courses, refresher courses, and other courses are offered on a tuition basis in order to supplement an institution's income. Bachelor's degree programmes may also be offered on a part-time basis by correspondence departments and evening colleges. Bachelor's degrees earned in this way are considered to be equivalent to Bachelor's degrees earned in formal higher education programmes and therefore approved by the Ministry of Education.

The employees' colleges award two types of credentials: specialty certificates which testify a certain level of specialised knowledge and single-subject certificates. There is some evidence that a few employees' colleges may offer Bachelor's degree programmes recognised by the Ministry of Education. Admission to an employees' college requires completion of a unified national entrance examination for adult higher education. This examination is required if the college is not registered and approved by the Ministry of Education.

Independent self-study examination is the only form of higher education in China with an entirely open admissions policy. In the self-study examination system, a regular university, under the supervision of the municipal or provincial Higher Education Self-Study Examinations

Guidance Committee, develops the study materials, conducts the examinations, as well as awards the Bachelor's degree.

Radio and television universities are open and distance education institutions which offer multi-media courses through radio, television, print, audio-visual materials and computer networks on a nationwide basis. The Central Radio and Television University (CRTVU) in Beijing controls the unified admission standards, teaching plans, level of education and examination criteria. It is also the national centre of teaching administration, programme production, course delivery and distance-education research. Spare-time universities offer sub-degree level programmes undertaken in the students' "spare-time".

Fee Structure

The tuition fee varies according to institution, programme and location. According to guidelines from the Minister of Education, tuition fee should reflect the per student operational costs of the institution, the appropriation from the government, local economic development and household income. Within an institution, students in different programmes are charged different tuition fees. For some majors such as software engineering, tuition levels in the 3rd and 4th year are doubled or even nearly tripled the tuition in the first two years.

Students in the six national normal (i.e. teacher education) universities (Peking Normal, East China Normal, Centre China Normal, East-North Normal, Shanxi Normal and West-South), which are affiliated to the Ministry of Education, have had their tuition fees waived since the fall semester of 2007. These students are required to work as teachers in the K-12 education system after graduation.

With the implementation of, and increase in, tuition and fees in higher education institutions, a student financial aid system was initiated in recent years. Financial aid to students includes grants and scholarships. Only a very limited number of needy students may get this kind of aid.

There are three types of student loan programmes in China: the General-Commercial Student Loans Scheme (GCSL) for which all students enrolled in higher education (public and private) are eligible, full time students from low income families enrolled in public regular higher education institutions are eligible for the Government-Subsidized Student Loans Scheme (GSSL), and the Government-subsidized Student Resident Loan (SRL) is for low income students enrolled in public and private higher education whose legal residence is in same region as the bank/financial institution offering the loan.

One of the biggest obstacles for the development of student loans in China has been the lack of a well-established credit system, which makes it very difficult to track borrowers after they leave school. In recent years progress has been made towards creating a more favourable borrowing environment.

Academic Calendar

The academic year of full-time universities is divided into two semesters (a few have three). The first semester begins in September and the second in February. Each semester consists of about 20 weeks and each week of six school days. In addition to mandatory winter and summer vacations, every May (International Labour Day, May 1st) and October (National Day) students have seven-day holidays. Also for the celebration of the Chinese New Year the students have a week-long holiday either in January or February. On other anniversaries and traditional festivals the universities operate normally.

Eligibility Criteria

Formal higher education has the following characteristics:

(1) Admission is based on scores obtained in the unified national university/college entrance examination:

- Applicants to Master's degree programmes have been obliged to hold a Bachelor's degree and be under the age of 35. Most Master's degree programmes involve three years of full-time study after the Bachelor's degree. It is, however, in some cases possible to earn a Master's degree in 2 to 2.5 years.
- Master's degree programme components include:
  - completion of basic theoretical and specialised courses.
  - reading and research ability in one foreign language.
  - study of Marxist theory.
  - thesis and its oral examination: A substantial portion of the degree involves research work and writing a thesis in preparation for the oral examination.

The Doctor's degree is offered at degree-granting universities, institutes and research institutes. Generally, candidates must hold a Master's degree and be 40 years of age or younger to gain admission. Candidates must take an entrance examination. A graduate from a Bachelor's programme with top grades can also be allowed to take the Doctor's entrance examination and gain admission, but this is extremely rare:

- Doctoral programmes usually take a minimum of three years to complete for persons with a Master's degree, or four to five years for persons with a Bachelor's degree.
- The required coursework includes advanced courses in one specialised area and the mastery of two foreign languages. The preparation and defence of a dissertation are also required.

Students may apply to university an unrestricted amount of times as long as they meet the following requirements:

- The applicant supports the "four cardinal principles" of China: love motherland, observe discipline, observe laws, and express determination to study hard for the socialist modernisation programme.
- The applicant is a graduate of senior middle school or its equivalent.

Admission to all formal higher education (Bachelor's degree programme) requires graduation from senior middle school and a passing grade on the annual national university entrance examination.

(2) Curriculum guidelines are prepared nationally, and the number of student places available in specific programmes at specific institutions is based on economic needs as determined through central government planning.

(3) Upon successful completion of the programme, in some cases the graduate is assigned a post of employment by the government. In the past most graduating students were assigned to employment by the government, but this is changing.

(4) Graduates from specialised (technical) upper secondary schools are allowed to take the national university/college entrance examinations in order to enter vocational universities. However, in reality they are not encouraged to do so because this kind of upper secondary education is labour market oriented. The purpose of this education and training is to prepare graduates for jobs for which academic degrees are not required.

Award of Degree

Degrees are regulated by the Academic Degrees Committee of the State Council together with the Ministry of Education. In principle, all degrees and examinations throughout the country are the same. However, the concept "credit" has not been defined nationally. This is why the required number of credits for graduation varies among colleges and universities. There is also a lot of variation in the names and contents of courses provided by different higher education institutions.

The Bachelor's degree is generally awarded after four years of full-time study. Programmes in medicine, dentistry, architecture and engineering in some universities, however, may take five to six years to complete. Students who successfully complete all requirements are awarded two certificates: the degree certificate and graduation certificate. Those students who do not pass all the requirements for a degree, by getting marks that are too low, failing courses or the National English Examination, for example, only receive the graduation certificate. Those students who enrol in non-degree programmes also only receive the graduation certificate. The requirement for the graduation certificate is lower than that for the degree certificate.

Students who complete the Master's curriculum without a thesis can only be awarded a diploma. The diploma states the completion of the courses but does not mention completion of the thesis examination. A thesis can be completed later, and the Master's degree can be earned upon the successful completion of the thesis examination. The graduates will be issued two diplomas: the graduation certificate and degree certificate.

References and Websites

Minister of Education. China. (2002). *Introduction of Higher Education Tuition Reform*. Retrieved May 13, 2009 from http://www.moe.gov.cn/edoas/website18/75/info6275.html

Minister of Education. China. (2006a). *Number of Higher Education Institutions*.

Shen, Hong and Wenli Li. (2003) *A Review of the Student Loans Scheme in China*. UNESCO Bankgkok, International Institute for Educational Planning. Retrieved July 4, 2009, from http://unesdoc.unesco.org/images/0013/001336/13367.pdf

Ministry of Education www.moe.edu.cn

Education Law of China

www.moe.edu.cn/english/laws_e.html
CERNET (China Education and Research Network)
www.cernet.edu.cn/HomePage/english/index.shtml
China Education Association for International Exchange (CEAIE)
www.ceaie.edu.cn

6
Higher Education in USA

Neena Sawhney

Introduction

The United States is a federal republic made up of 50 states, one district (the capital) and four territories. The National Department of Education sets guidelines relating to general education policy, collects data and awards subsidies and scholarships, but exerts limited influence on the content, learning outcomes or quality of education—these tasks have been delegated to the individual states, who are responsible for education at primary and secondary level, and partially at higher level. Each state has a State Board of Education responsible for education policy, funding for education, and quality assurance at primary and secondary level.

The education system in the United States is very diverse, with major differences in level, content and quality. None of the various phases of education conclude with a standardized final examination. For this reason, the concept of standardized entrance and outcome levels does not exist in the American system. This means that the content of the relevant programme must always be examined to determine how the course will be evaluated; the diploma itself indicates very little. Private and public institutions exist at all educational levels, from primary school to higher education. Although the number of private higher education institutions is much higher than that of public institutions, the number of students is the reverse: more students study at public institutions. The status of an institution (i.e. public or private) is no indication of level or quality, and all institutions must be accredited in the same fashion. The academic year runs from September to May/June, and education is compulsory until the age of 16 or 18, depending on the state. The language of education is English.

Role of U.S. Government in Education

Unlike in many other countries, the United States central government does not control the educational system. Rather, the higher education systems are either: (1) controlled by independent groups of people, or trustees (in the case of private schools); or (2) shared between local and state governments (in the case of public schools). A major difference between these two types of schools is the cost. Private schools are generally much more expensive to attend than their public school counterparts, mainly because the private schools must rely on sources outside of the government for their funding.

Higher Education

Higher education refers to study beyond secondary school level and

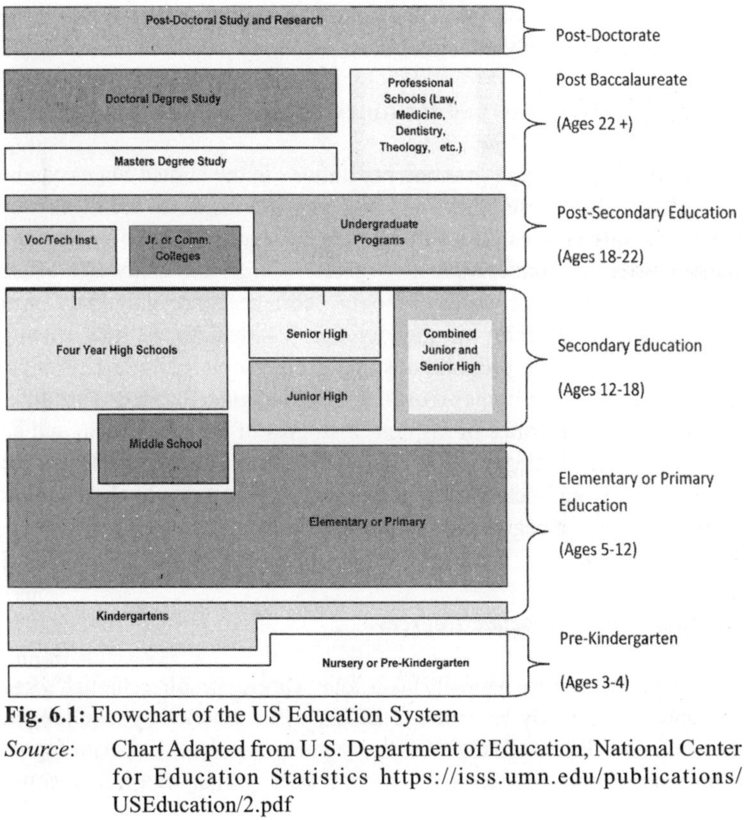

Fig. 6.1: Flowchart of the US Education System

Source: Chart Adapted from U.S. Department of Education, National Center for Education Statistics https://isss.umn.edu/publications/USEducation/2.pdf

usually assumes that a student has undertaken 13 years of study and has a high school diploma. There are three main levels of higher education in USA, Undergraduate studies (bachelor's degree), Graduate studies (master's degree) and Postgraduate studies (doctor's degree). The minimum age for enrolment at university is usually 18, and some 40 per cent of college students are 25 or over, many of them taking advanced degrees.

Degree level courses are offered by around 3,500 accredited colleges and universities, with a wide variety of admission requirements and programmes. Of the total college population of 15 million students (12 million in public colleges and 3 million in private), around 500,000 are overseas students, roughly half of which are working on graduate level degrees. Hundreds of American colleges recruit students in countries such as the UK, Hong Kong, Japan and Malaysia. Although the terms 'college' and 'university' are often used interchangeably, a college may be independent or part of a university (both colleges and universities are also referred to simply as schools).

Colleges, Universities, and Institutes

The Distinction Degree-granting institutions in the United States can be called by any of these terms, and colleges and institutes are in no way inferior to universities. As a general rule, colleges tend to be smaller and usually offer only undergraduate degrees, while a university also offers graduate degrees. The words "school," "college," and "university" will be used interchangeably throughout this booklet. An institute usually specializes in degree programmes in a group of closely related subject areas, so you will also come across degree programmes offered at institutes of technology, institutes of fashion, institutes of art and design, and so on. Within each college or university you will find schools, such as the school of arts and sciences or the school of business. Each school is responsible for the degree programmes offered by the college or university in that area of study.

Bachelor's and Associate Degrees

The bachelor's degree typically takes four years to complete, though some students take slightly less time to finish, while others may take longer. The associate degree usually takes two years to complete. Associate degree programmes may be "terminal" programmes, which lead into specific careers upon graduation, or "transfer" programmes, which correspond to the first two years of a bachelor's degree and tend to be more liberal arts based. Under the latter option you could then transfer into the third year of a four-year bachelor's degree programme. Associate degree programmes are offered at two-year colleges known as junior or community colleges (see below). Four-year colleges and universities offer bachelor's degree programmes, with a small number also offering associate degree programmes.

The Liberal Arts Philosophy

Liberal arts is a shortened form of the term "liberal arts and sciences," and the liberal arts philosophy is a unique feature of the US higher education system. US undergraduate education is based on this concept, which believes in providing a well-rounded academic education that develops the student's verbal, written, and reasoning skills. Students at a liberal arts college, or at a university with a strong liberal arts programme, begin their degree study by taking classes in a wide variety of courses in the arts, humanities, languages, and the social and physical sciences. They then choose a subject in which to specialize (called a "major") and take about 25 to 50 per cent of their classes in the major area. Even those who do not follow a liberal arts programme and instead plan to major in a specialized subject like engineering are usually required to take about 25 per cent of their classes in humanities and social sciences to complement their studies. Similarly, a student who wants to complete a major in history is required to take some classes in mathematics and, possibly, the sciences.

Professional Education

Professional (that is, career-oriented) education is included within the US university system. Large universities tend to be comprised a college of arts and sciences and several professional schools—usually business, agriculture, medicine, law, and journalism. Institutes of technology have a scientific emphasis in all the degrees they offer. More information on professional education can be found in Booklet Two of this series, Graduate and Professional Study and Research.

State Universities

State universities are founded and subsidized by US State Governments (for example, California, Michigan, or Texas) to provide low-cost education to residents of that state. They may also be called public universities to distinguish them from private institutions. Some include the words "state university" in their title or include a regional element such as "eastern" or "northern". State universities tend to be very large, with enrolments of 20,000 or more students, and generally admit a wider range of students than private universities. State university tuition costs are generally lower than those of private universities. Also, in-state residents (those who live and pay taxes in that particular state) pay much lower tuition than out-of-state residents. International students, as well as those from other states, are considered out-of-state residents and therefore, do not benefit from reduced tuition at state institutions. In addition, international students may have to fulfil higher admission requirements than in-state residents.

Private Universities

Private institutions are funded by a combination of endowments, tuition fees, research grants, and gifts from their alumni. Tuition fees tend to be higher at private universities than at state universities, but there is no distinction made between state and non-state residents. Colleges with a religious affiliation and single-sex colleges are private. In general, private universities have enrolments of fewer than 20,000 students, and private colleges may have 2,000 or fewer students on their campuses.

Community Colleges

Community colleges provide two-year associate degree programmes, usually called the associate of arts (A.A.) or associate of science (A.S.) degrees, as well as excellent technical and vocational programmes. As the name suggests, community colleges are community-based institutions with close links to secondary schools, community groups, and employers, and many US students live close to campus with their families. Community colleges can be public or private institutions and are sometimes called junior colleges or two-year colleges. A growing number of international students are choosing to study at community colleges, and this is discussed in further detail later in this booklet. Tuition costs are often lower at two-year than at four-year institutions, and many have agreements to allow students on transfer programmes to move easily into the third year of a bachelor's degree at the local state university.

Technical and Vocational Colleges

These institutions specialize in preparing students for entry into, or promotion within, the world of work. They offer certificate and other short-term programmes that train students in the theory behind a specific vocation or technology, as well as in how to work with the technology. Programmes usually last two years or less. There are several thousand technical and vocational colleges across the United States, and they may be private or public institutions.

Distance Education and Accreditation

Distance Education is an increasingly popular way to study for everything from a short professional course to a graduate degree in the United States, and there are numerous institutions offering undergraduate degree programmes using distance education teaching methods. Under the distance education model, students no longer attend classes in a classroom on a campus; instead, classes are delivered "from a distance" through the use of technologies such as the Internet, satellite television, video conferencing, and other means of electronic delivery. For international students this means that they can study for a US degree without leaving their home country, though they will almost certainly have to go to the United States for short periods of face-to-face contact and study on the campus. Studying for a degree using distance education requires students to have special qualities such as self-discipline and the ability to work on their own. If you are considering distance education, you should thoroughly research the quality of the programme, the accreditation of the institution in the United States, and its recognition in your home country to make sure this option is the appropriate one for your future goals. Further information on distance education is provided in the third booklet of this series.

Non-Degree Study at a US College

Do you want to study in the United States at a college or university, but not for a full degree? Perhaps you want to experience life on a US campus, while improving your knowledge of certain subjects. This is certainly a useful addition to your educational experience, and US colleges welcome students such as you. You should write to colleges, explain your situation, and request information on applying for "special student" or "non-degree student" status. See Booklet Three in this series for more information on short-term study opportunities in the United States, and refer to chapter 8 in this booklet for further details on requesting information from US universities.

Admission to a University

Although admission policies vary from one university to the next, most determine admission based on several criteria, including a student's high school course of study, high school Grade Point Average (GPA), participation in extracurricular activities, SAT or ACT exam scores, a written essay, and possibly a personal interview:

- The university admissions office considers whether a student has taken courses in high school that have prepared him/her for more difficult coursework. A student's high school GPA is also considered. A GPA is a quantitative figure representing a student's accumulated grades. Each letter grade is assigned a number of points: A = 4 points, B = 3, C = 2, D = 1 and F = 0 points. A GPA is calculated by adding all of the points earned for each course grade and dividing the total points by the total number of courses taken. For example, a GPA of 3.0 is a "B" average for all of the courses taken.
- University admissions officers like to see applications from high school students who have participated in extracurricular activities, such as scholastic clubs, athletic teams, student government, and philanthropic clubs. Voluntary participation in these kinds of activities is an indication that students have learned valuable life lessons, such as teamwork, leadership, or civic responsibility.
- Most students in the United States take the SAT Reasoning Text (formerly known as the Scholastic Aptitude Test) or the ACT (formerly known as American College Testing) during their final year of high school. Each university sets a minimum SAT or ACT score that a student must achieve in order to gain admission. These are standardized quantitative examinations. The SAT tests critical reading, mathematics, and writing skills. The ACT tests English, mathematics, reading, and science reasoning, and includes an optional writing test.
- Universities often require students to write an essay as part of

the application process. Each admissions office determines the length and content of the essay. The applicant also may be required to have a personal interview with a representative from the admissions office.

At the University

University students pursuing a Bachelor's degree are called "undergraduates," whereas students pursuing a Master's or Doctoral degree are called "graduate students". American undergraduate students will say they are "going to school" or "going to college," which means they are attending university. A common question one student asks another is, "What is your major?" This means, "What is your major field of study?"

Most universities give undergraduate students a liberal education, which means students are required to take courses across several disciplines before they specialize in a major field of study. Graduate and professional (such as medicine or law) programmes are specialized.

At the university level, most courses are only one semester long. Each course is assigned a number of credit hours. Credit hours are usually based on how much time is spent in class each week. Most courses are 3 credits. However, some courses may be 1, 2, 4 or 5 credits. All degree programmes require students to complete a minimum number of credit hours before graduation. Most Bachelor's degree programmes in the United States do not require students to write a final thesis.

Selection for admission to a graduate programme is based on several criteria. These include completion of a Bachelor's degree, the student's undergraduate coursework, and their GPA. Students are also expected to write an essay as part of their application or submit a writing sample. Most Master's programmes require students to have a minimum score on the Graduate Record Examination (GRE), which tests verbal reasoning, quantitative reasoning, critical thinking, and analytical writing skills.

Students continue to take courses at the graduate level. A final thesis is required for most Master's programmes. Doctoral students take courses until they have earned enough credit hours to attempt their qualifying examinations, which are usually taken over several days and often include both a written and oral component. After doctoral students pass their qualifying examinations, they are advanced to candidacy and can begin writing their dissertation. Before the degree is given, the completed dissertation must be orally defended before the candidate's faculty committee.

Because degree requirements can be very complex and vary from one university and department to another, all students should check with their university and department advisers to make sure they are meeting their educational requirements.

Educational Standards

An American college typically offers a blend of natural and social sciences and humanistic studies. Students are usually 18 to 22 and attend college for around four years to earn a bachelor's degree in arts or science. On the other hand, a university is usually composed of an undergraduate college of arts and sciences, plus graduate and professional schools and facilities. The four years of undergraduate study for a bachelor's degree are referred to as freshman, sophomore, junior and senior (also used in high schools).

One of the most surprising and unique aspects of the US education system is that many of the most prestigious universities are private foundations and receive no federal or state funds (their main source of income in addition to fees is endowments). The most famous universities include the Ivy League universities (so called because they have been sufficiently long established for ivy to have grown on the walls): Brown, Columbia, Cornell, Dartmouth, Harvard, Pennsylvania, Princeton and Yale. The Ivy League, together with the 'heavenly seven' or 'seven sisters' (Barnard, Bryn Mawr, Mount Holyoke, Radcliffe, Smith, Vassar and Wellesley) of once all female colleges, are the most prestigious American universities.

Although some people claim their fame rests more upon their social standing than their academic excellence, attending one of these colleges usually pays off in the job market, particularly at executive level. Other world-renowned American higher education institutions include the Massachusetts Institute of Technology (MIT) in Cambridge (Massachusetts), the California Institute of Technology (Caltech) and Stanford University in California, all of which have earned distinguished international reputations for their research and academic excellence.

The academic standards of American colleges and universities vary greatly, and some institutions are better known for the quality of their social life or sports teams than for their academic achievements. Establishments range from vast educational 'plants' (with as many as 50,000 students) offering the most advanced training available, to small private academies emphasising personal instruction and a preference for the humanities or experimentation. Major universities are like small cities with their own shops, banks, police and fire departments, and are usually renowned for the excellence of their teaching, research facilities, libraries and sports facilities.

Differences with the Others Countries

The main difference between higher education in the US and that in many other countries is that in the US, the system is designed to keep people in education rather than screen them out. Some 55 per cent of American high school graduates (55 per cent of whom are male and 45 per cent female) go on to some sort of higher education (a total of over 14 million). Many Americans look upon a bachelor's or master's degree, rather than high school graduation, as the natural completion of school life. With the exception of the top dozen or so, American colleges and universities are geared to the average rather than the brighter student.

The academic standards required to earn a bachelor's degree in the US are lower than in many other countries. Some colleges accept almost any high school graduate and are disparagingly referred to as 'diploma mills' (which has diminished the value of degrees). It is at the graduate schools (where students study for a master's degree) that American universities are seen at their best, where serious students receive an education rivalling that of any country.

Most universities have excellent professors, due in large part to paying vast salaries which enable them to attract the best brains (many from abroad). Professors have a much higher social standing than school teachers and are permitted a high degree of autonomy in their teaching methods (associate and assistant professors are fancy names for readers or lecturers).

Terms and Grades

Most colleges and universities have two terms (semesters) or sessions a year of around 14 weeks each: fall, from September to late December, and spring, which extends from late January to late May (some divide the academic year into three sessions: fall, spring and summer). Those who miss or fail a course can catch up by attending summer school, an intensive eight-week course offered between terms.

Most students complete ten courses per academic year and usually take four years (although it can be much longer) to complete a bachelor's degree requirement of around 40 three-hour courses or 120 credits. Those who achieve the highest grade point averages (GPAs) graduate (or 'are graduated') as Summa cum Laude (excellent), Magna cum Laude (very good) and Cum Laude (good).

All other successful students are awarded ungraded degrees. As bachelor's degrees have become commonplace, more students are pursuing postgraduate studies (almost always called 'graduate school'), particularly professional degrees in law (JD) and business (MBA), and PhDs.

The Curriculum and Degrees

Five types of degrees exist in the United States.

Two-year colleges (community colleges) and a small number of four-year institutions grant associate degrees, typically awarded after the completion of 60 credits. Associate degrees may represent a terminal degree in a vocational field or may prepare students to complete a bachelor's degree at a four-year institution.

The bachelor's degree is by far the most common type of degree awarded, preparing students for most jobs that require a college degree and for further graduate study. Three degrees exist at the graduate-level:

1. The master's degree is the most common type of graduate degree. About 75 per cent of graduate students are enrolled in master's degree programmes, divided roughly evenly among students in education, business administration, and all other fields (US Department of Education, 2002c). A master's degree may have either a professional or theoretical focus and usually requires a comprehensive examination and/or thesis or other original piece of work. The master's degree either prepares graduates for future advanced study at the doctoral level or is itself a terminal degree.

2. A professional degree provides access to advanced professions in fields such as law and medicine.

3. The doctoral degree is the highest academic award and recognizes the graduate's ability to conduct independent research. The most common degree of this type is the doctor of philosophy (Ph.D.), but it also includes the doctor of education (Ed.D.).

No national laws govern the titles of degrees, although each state typically regulates the level of degree that institutions located within its borders can award. Each institution has the autonomy to determine its own programme requirements, typically following broad degree guidelines set by the states or by specialized accrediting agencies.

The undergraduate curriculum typically consists of two components—general education and the major field of study (the major). The purpose of general education is to provide students with broad knowledge and prepare them to be engaged and informed citizens. General education is delivered predominantly through either a core curriculum, in which all undergraduate students take the same courses, or an elective or distributive format, in which students choose courses from a pre-specified list representing a range of topics (such as science, art and aesthetic appreciation, mathematics, humanities etc.). General education requirements typically constitute between one-quarter and one-half of a student's courses, depending upon the institution and the student's major. The other courses include those related to the major. Students choose their major either upon enrolling or after completing their second year of studies, depending upon institutional policy. Students may change their majors if their interests change and keep most of their credits earned towards their degree.

Although most institutions continue to rely on a traditional nine-month (two semesters) academic calendar, many colleges and universities are innovating with their academic calendars, and additionally offer short month-long courses, overlapping semesters, and courses in a condensed weekend format, as they try to create programmes that meet student needs and schedules.

Fees, Grants and Scholarships

Tuition fees vary widely among colleges and universities and no two institutions charge the same fees. Public state colleges and universities charge significantly lower fees for in-state residents (also applies to resident foreign students) and higher 'out-of-state' fees to non-residents. One year's residence in a state is usually necessary to qualify for the resident tuition rate. Higher fees may also apply to out-of-county students at a two-year community college.

Average tuition fees for public (state) four-year colleges and universities are around \$3,500 per year and for private institutions around \$15,000 per year, although you can pay twice as much for tuition at an Ivy League college. Fees for private universities have increased alarmingly in recent years and many colleges have reduced their entrance standards (called 'dumb-downscaling') to attract students who can afford the fees.

In addition to tuition fees, there are also fees for registration, health centre, sports centre and parking (all of which must be paid at the start of each semester). Room and board, books and supplies, transportation, and other expenses cost (on average) an additional $8,000 to $15,000 per year, depending on the area, whether you attend a public or private institution.

A car is often essential, as public transport is usually poor. Health insurance is compulsory, although students may be automatically enrolled in the university health insurance plan. All in all, paying for a child's college education is a major investment for parents, most of whom can expect to spend between $50,000 and $1,00,000 to put a child through college. Most families participate in savings and investment schemes to finance their children's college education, and an increasing number expect their offspring to take an active role in paying for their own education through loans and evening and summer jobs. Many students obtain part-time employment to finance their studies, during term-time and summer breaks (foreign students should check in advance whether their visa allows such employment), while others receive grants, scholarships and loans to help meet their living expenses.

Scholarships are awarded directly by universities as well as by fraternal, civic, labour and management organisations (around a third of students at Harvard receive a scholarship). Although public universities do not usually give financial aid to foreign students at the undergraduate level, it is possible for foreign students to obtain a scholarship or partial scholarship for their tuition fees from a private university. Full scholarships covering all tuition expenses are rare, so unless you are able to contribute at least 50 per cent from your own resources, it generally is not worth applying.

A foreign student can apply directly to an American university for aid, a scholarship or work-study option, and can also apply to educational programmes in his home country. American embassies can provide information about the range of scholarships and grants available. A request for financial aid from a college or university does not affect an entrance application in any way, as each is considered independently. Around half of all college students (some 5 million) receive some form of financial assistance, and having wealthy parents does not ban a student from receiving aid.

Qualifications for Overseas Students

Entry qualifications for American colleges and universities vary considerably; generally the better the university (or the better the reputation), the higher the entrance qualifications. Some specialist schools, such as law schools, have a standard entrance examination. Usually overseas qualifications which would qualify students to enter a university in their own country are taken into consideration.

It is important for mature students returning to full or part-time college education to provide any diplomas or certificates showing the education level they have attained (otherwise they must take basic tests). All foreign students require a thorough knowledge of English and those whose mother tongue is not English must take a TOEFL test. Some colleges and universities also require all foreign students to take the SAT. One needs to contact individual universities for details of their entrance requirements.

Applications

Applications must be made to the Director of Undergraduate Admissions at colleges and universities. For highly popular colleges and universities, such as those in California, one must apply in the summer or autumn (fall) for admission in the following fall term (August/September), i.e. one should start the process 18 months in advance. State universities in California are closed to foreign students by December for admission the following autumn. For less popular universities, the latest a foreign student can apply for September admission is March of the same year, as overseas applications usually take at least six months to process.

Accommodation

Following acceptance by a college or university, students are advised to apply for a place in a university dormitory (dorm) or in other college accommodation. Campus accommodation is limited, although many universities give priority to foreign students. The cost of college accommodation and board (meals) ranges from around $2,000 to $8,000 per year. Many students rent rooms in shared apartments or houses. However, in many areas this kind of accommodation is difficult to find and expensive.

Clubs and Facilities

All colleges and universities have a wide variety of societies and clubs, many organised by the students' union or council, which is the centre of campus social activities. Some universities ban alcohol on campus and there are no students' bars. Students found drinking alcohol on campus may face suspension or even expulsion.

American colleges and universities usually have excellent sports facilities and go to great lengths to recruit the best high school athletes. Most colleges provide full academic scholarships to athletes, often risking their academic reputation in the process. There is an unwritten agreement between college Directors of Admission and potential sports stars that they enrol in college purely to play sports (with luck they will use intercollegiate competition as a springboard to a professional career). Sports teams generate huge incomes for colleges and are a commercial necessity (inter-college competitions are big business), although the situation often embarrasses college administrators and angers other students, who resent the preferential treatment given to athletes. Faced with criticism, some universities have initiated support programmes to improve the academic performance and graduation rates of athletes.

All colleges and universities devote a lot of time to wooing their former students ('alumni/alumnae'), who are persuaded to keep in touch with their old college (alma mater), and most importantly, send lots of money. Many colleges have annual events called 'homecomings' (also held by high schools), when alumni are encouraged to return to college and take part in various activities. Colleges also hold other strange events such as a 'fathers' day' or 'siblings' weekend', which are often linked with sports events.

Information

American college catalogues are available in high school guidance offices, libraries and book shops. There are also numerous guides to choosing a college, including *Barron's Profiles of American Colleges*, US News and World Report magazine's *Ultimate College Guide* and Money Guide magazine's *Best College Buys*. Many State Departments of Higher Education have a toll-free 'education hotline' where you can obtain information about all aspects of higher and further (adult) education. One can also view course offerings from schools online such s www.gmc.edu.

References and Web Sites

Overviews of the U.S. Education System http://www.ed.gov/NLE/USNEI/toc.html http://www.edupass.org

Distance Education Information http://educationusa.state.gov

Information on Non-Degree Study in the United States http://educationusa.state.gov

http://www.educationusa.info/pdf/study/english1.pdf

https://www.justlanded.co.in/english/United-States/USA-Guide/Education/Higher-Education

https://www.epnuffic.nl/en/publications/find-a-publication/education-system-united-states.pdf

http://www.acenet.edu/news-room/Documents/Overview-of-Higher-Education-in-the-United-States-Diversity-Access-and-the-Role-of-the-Marketplace-2004.pdf

http://www.internationalstudentguidetotheusa.com/articles/american_education_system.html

7

System of Education in Brazil, UK and USA

Ismail Thamarasseri

The System of Education in Brazil

Brazil which is the largest country in the whole of South America was formally a federation of states but later divided into many municipalities as well as local districts. It should be noted that more than 80 per cent of the Brazilian population are Catholics and this to some extent prevents the blacks from being discriminated against. Like most democratic states, primary education in Brazil is not only free but also compulsory. This factor, among others, makes it possible for over 70 per cent of the Brazilian population to be literate. The government also pays attention to other forms of education such as adult as well as Non-formal education with the aid of radio and television.

Pre-Primary Education

This level of education is for children ages 2 to 6 years. Pre-Primary schools are being handled by the private individuals. At this level of education, children have to pay school fees. Primary education in Brazil is for children aged 7 to 14 years. As stated earlier, this level of education is not only free but also compulsory in Brazil. With the 1971 Basic Education Law in the country, pupils in primary schools are to spend 8 years. This level of education is divided into two stages and each stage lasts for four years. During the first stage, the pupils will be exposed to general studies while in the last stage (5-8 years) pupils will be exposed to vocational studies.

Secondary Education

This level of education in Brazil is designed for Brazilians aged 15 years. This level of education is purely academic. On the other hand, students who are interested in vocational education will be admitted into vocational schools where such subjects are being offered. Secondary school students in Brazil can run their secondary education on either full time or part-time basis. Students may spend three years on the programme and part-time students on the other hand may also spend four years. Since majority of Brazilians are Catholics, as it may be expected majority of the private secondary schools belong to the Catholics.

Higher Education

Higher education in Brazil was in the past a way through which the educated and rich Brazilians used to integrate their children into their parents highly stratified society. In Brazil, political activities have been a permanent feature of university life. In Brazil, there are both private and public universities. In most cases, best Brazilians in academics and perhaps in character have access to public universities while on the other hand, poor academically students, if not admitted by the public universities, may go to the private universities. In the Brazilian universities, both academic as well as professional subjects are being offered. The 1931 University Legislation empowered the Brazilians approved universities to teach and also to award degree to qualified students. However, there was legislation in 1968. The number of university graduates produced rose from almost zero in 1960s to about 40,000 in 1986. In the same vein, the percentage of university teachers with doctoral degree rose from 6.6 per cent in 1974 to 12.7 per cent in 1987 while teachers with master's degree rose from 9.7 per cent to 21.2 per cent within the same period.

Teacher Education

Primary school teachers in Brazil are expected to be professionally trained before they could be allowed to teach. It should be noted that in a few cases, untrained teachers might be allowed to teach particularly where there are inadequate qualified primary school teachers. Secondary school teachers must not only be trained but also, they are expected to receive their professional training in the university. However, like in some other places, secondary school teachers could also receive their professional training in the Teachers' Colleges. University teachers in addition to having a second university degree in most cases should also develop interest in research work. They are encouraged to develop themselves while still on the job.

Educational Administration

In 1988, a new Constitution was put in place by the Brazilian Government. With this Constitution, all public schools are to be tuition free. Generally, many educational decrees or educational laws were put in place by the Government in order to enhance the educational administration in Brazil. The formulation of the country's educational policy is the responsibility of the Federal Council of Education in collaboration with Ministry of Education. The Ministry of Education is also expected to supervise schools, to provide necessary assistance to federal universities.

Finance of Education

The Government funds the public schools at all levels while the private schools at all levels are also funded by their owners. Basically, bulk of the money spent on education in the country comes from various taxes including the compulsory private contributions. Higher institutions in Brazil at times receive aids from foreign individuals and organizations. Higher institutions are also encouraged by the Government to generate fund internally to complement the money they receive from the Government.

Education in England

Education in England at the initial stage was provided by voluntary agencies including the churches. However, such schools founded by the voluntary agencies were financially aided by the government. With the rapid growth in population as well as the expansion in the Industrial Sector and the enactment of Education Act of 1870, schools' boards were established to assist the Voluntary Schools, later, the Parliamentary Acts made Elementary Education compulsory and free. The beginning of a national education system in Britain can be traced to the Hadow Report of 1926. It was this report that brought about the reorganization of the Elementary Education. In the same vein, the SPENS Report of 1938 also assisted the reorganization of the Elementary Education and the recommendation of Technical Secondary Education. In the development of education in Great Britain, the Catholic played significant roles as quite a number of the Voluntary Schools were founded by them. However, the Education Act of 1902 gave the following three levels of education.

The Elementary School

This school is designed for the children aged 5-14 years, in order to ensure that majority of the children attend elementary school, Elementary education in England was not only tuition free but it is also compulsory for all the children who are within the age of 5 to 14 years.

Secondary School

This school was designed for children who have already completed the elementary education. It is designed for children whose parents are rich enough to pay the school fees. Unlike elementary education, it is not compulsory at all. Secondary Education after graduation offers the products clerical jobs among others.

Preparatory and Public Schools

These schools were very expensive and were meant for children of the upper class (the Aristocrats). These preparatory and public schools gave birth to the establishment of both the University of Oxford and the Cambridge University.

Types of Schools in England

The following types of schools are in existence in England:

Nursery Education

A nursery school is school designed for children aged 3-5 years. Nursery school also serves as a temporary home for the children whose parents are working. Nursery education can be dated back to 1850, through the efforts of Friedrich Frobel as well as Maria Montessori. It should be noted that day-nurseries where the children of working parents are kept are not the same thing as nursery school. The reason is that, real nursery education is for the children aged 3-5 years and it is also part of the school system. It is tuition free. The Hadow Report of 1933 and Plowden Report of 1967 greatly enhanced the development and improvement of nursery education in England.

Primary Education

The Balfour-Morant Act of 1904 gave the following as the objectives of Primary Education in England:

(a) Recognising the child from 7-11 is a total being whose character, intelligence as well as physical abilities are moulded and trained;
(b) Arousing in the pupils a lively interest in man's ideals, achievements, literature, history as well as language;
(c) Developing an awareness in the pupils limitation; and
(d) Demonstrating to the pupils how to acquire knowledge as well as learning for themselves. Primary School in England could be divided into:
    - Elementary, and
    - Higher elementary schools.

According to statistics, about 93 per cent of the children within the age of twelve years were in the elementary schools.

The Fisher Education Act of 1918 made Primary Education compulsory for children up to the age of fourteen years and it also recommended the re-organization of primary education. Simply, primary education in England can be described as the education of young children below the age of eleven years. For the purpose of administration, all the public primary schools were being administered by the Local Education Authorities. It was also the responsibility of the Local Education Authorities to control all forms of secular education in the privately owned (Voluntary) primary schools. Also, in England, there are some primary schools called Direct Grant School. Parents pay school fees in these schools. Primary school head is always given contract appointment. Inspectors only visit schools on request. Primary school subjects include: History, Geography, Nature study, Crafts, Arts and Physical Education, French, Religious Education. Also, the extra school activities include: Gymnastic, Swimming, Music among others. The 1944 Act increased the compulsory education in England to 15 years. It also recommended that the number of pupils in each class should be reduced to make it more manageable. The Plowing Report of 1967 had recommended a change in the age at which school pupils may transfer from eleven to twelve years. It was also recommended that the junior schools were recommended for pupils aged 8-12 years or 9-13 years to enable the Local Authorities have a better reorganization of the secondary schools.

Secondary Education

Secondary school in England may be day or boarding school which offers to each of its scholars, up to and beyond the age of 16, a general education, physical, mental and moral, given through a complete graded course of instruction of wider scope and more advanced degree than that in elementary schools. About four types of Secondary Education can be identified in England. They are:

- Secondary Modern Schools,
- Secondary Grammar Schools,
- Technical High School, and
- Comprehensive School.

Secondary Modern Schools: These are designed for students who are not academically inclined after their Primary Education. Secondary Modern Schools cater for secondary education for academically weak students up to the age of fifteen (15) years.

Secondary Grammar Schools: They are designed for the students who are academically inclined after their primary education. These schools in addition to giving sound formal education to the students also serve as the Custodian of English Tradition.

Technical High Schools: These schools, are provided for students who have an intension of working in the industry later in life. In other words, these schools are established to cater for the needs of commerce and industry. The products of this school are admitted into the faculties of engineering for engineering courses in the British Universities.

Comprehensive Schools: These schools are established to cater for children aged 11-18 years. The students in these schools offer the same subjects up to their second year. At the end of their third year, the students will be expected to choose three subjects apart from English language and Mathematics which they will like to study in their last two years. In the school, the students will have opportunity of learning one vocation or the other. As from the third year, the students will be exposed to one vocation or the other which he may want to do later in life. To assist the students, career officers are always provided by the school for the purpose of counselling the students on their future vocation.

Technical or Further Education in England

These are the institutions provided for young person's for the purpose of assisting them to develop their various aptitudes and also to train them to become responsible adults in life. Such schools among others include physical, practical as well as vocational training. An increased interest in the development of British Industry after the Second World War for the training of skilled manpower in the area of technology greatly contributed to the development of further or technical education in England. At the end of the course, the students could be presented for the examination of the city and guilds of London Institute or any other related professional examinations. For children under the age of sixteen years, tuition is free while those who are above the age of 16 years and are working have to pay fees. Technical colleges or further education are run on both part-time and full time basis.

Teacher Education in England

Teacher education is the professional training designed for teachers of all categories starting from the nursery school to the university. The first Teachers' College for the training of secondary school teachers was the College of Preceptors which was founded in the year 1846. With effect from 1904, the local education authorities were allowed to establish their Teachers Colleges. As from 1921, the British Universities include Teacher Education programme in their curricula. For the degree in education, students would spend three years and the fourth year would be for their teaching practice after which a university diploma or certificate in education would be awarded. In 1943, the Board of Education recommended that more Teachers' colleges should be founded so as to be able to solve the problem of inadequate qualified teachers. The Me Nair Report of 1944 among others, recommended that universities as well as Teacher Training Colleges should work hand in hand for the general improvement of teacher education. However, before the Education Act of 1944, the primary school teachers were of four categories:

- Certificated,

- Uncertificated,
- Supplementary, and
- Specialist teachers.

In case of secondary schools, the teachers are expected to specialize in a particular subject. While the teachers for the old elementary schools were trained in the two-year colleges after their secondary education, the secondary school teachers were trained in a one-year teachers' diploma course at the university departments after graduating either from the Faculty of Arts or Science. On the other hand, the teachers of independent public schools were degree holders.

Adult Education in England

Adult education in England can be described as education designed for people who have left school, adequate facilities for leisure-time occupation in organized cultural training and creative activities for persons who are above compulsory school age and can benefit from such educational programmes. The beginning of Adult education in both England and Wales could be traced to the activities of British Philanthropists who initiated the idea by first of all establishing Sunday schools for the Literacy Education of both the children as well as the adults. Many children and adults profited from this kind of education. The success recorded from this kind of education led to the establishment of London Mechanics Institution for the training of Mechanics in 1823. Within a very short time, similar institutions were cited in both England and Wales. The formation of the Workers' Educational Association which was affiliated to the Oxford University also contributed to the development of Adult Education in England. The association used to organize tutorial classes for its members in England. With effect from 1907, the Board of Education in England started to assist the university tutorial classes for general enhancement of Adult Education. Also, for the promotion of Adult Education, an Adult Education Committee was set up in 1921. Primarily, the Committee was to assist in the coordination of all the Adult education voluntary 60 agencies. To crown it all, an open university was founded between 1960 and 1970 to provide better education for both the Adults as well as the workers. With the open university education, workers in particular, were able to improve their working condition even though such Open University education was not tuition free.

University Education in England

Higher institutions in both England and Wales include: the universities, colleges of education as well as the polytechnics. The most popular universities are: the Oxford University founded in 1185 and Cambridge University in 1230. The two oldest universities were founded by the Church of England. In order to break the monopoly of both the Oxford University and the University of Cambridge, London University was established in 1828. School fees are being charged by the universities with which the universities are being financed in addition to financial aid from the public. Each university is autonomous in respect of admission, examination and award of degrees among others.

Administration of Education in England

The Education Minister is always appointed by the Prime Minister. The Minister has Permanent Secretaries to help him in carrying out his official duties. The Minister is the Controller as well as the Director of Education Board. He has the power to organize the schools at any time. The Local Education Authorities are elected bodies for the purpose of controlling schools under them. They also have voluntary schools under them. They employed teachers and pay their salaries as well. Each school has the power to select the textbooks for the use of its pupils. However, unlike primary and secondary schools, higher institutions are not under control of the Ministry of Education.

Financing of Education

Money is always voted for the Ministry of Education from the national revenue by the parliament. The Minister of Education will also disburse part of the money in form of grants to local Education Authorities.

Education in the United States of America

Each State in USA has the power to establish its own system of education. The local districts under the States also have the power to establish school boards and to found schools as well. The power of the States to set up schools does not in any way prevent the church from establishing schools in any of the states. The education levels in USA include:

- Nursery Education,
- Elementary or Primary Education,
- Secondary Education,
- Teacher Education, and
- University and Adult Education.

Nursery Education

At the beginning, nursery education was part of primary school between 1868 and 1873. By 1888, nursery education had spread to many places in America. The Lanham Education Act of 1940 also enhanced the development of nursery education in America by giving subventions from the Federal Government to nursery education. Later, individuals who had interest in the education of children started to part-take in the running of nursery schools. Also, the churches were participating in the running of nursery school.

Primary Education

Primary Education in America is the education given to the children which has the duration of six years. The purpose of American Primary Education includes:

- Turning out well-adjusted citizens.
- Helping the children to be active participants in the building of their own lives and also to assist them in understanding the roles expected of them in establishing a better American society.
- The Primary school subjects include: Mathematics, Science, Geography, History, Social Studies, English language, English literature, French, German and Spanish. However, religious subjects are not included in the school curriculum as Americans have freedom of worship.
- In the primary schools, the promotion of the pupils is always based on continuous assessment and not on any promotion examination. It is the duty of the Local Schools Board to provide some of the school materials.

A public primary school is headed by the principal who is the administrative head of the school. While the primary school teachers are expected to have a university degree, the principals are in addition expected to have master's degree of educational administration and supervision. The failure of the Federal Government to include Religious Instructions in the school curriculum was one of the reasons that forced the Catholic to establish their own schools where religious instruction was included in the school curriculum. By implication, there are both private and public primary schools in America.

Secondary Schools in America

Secondary Education in America is the type of education given to the adolescents on the basis of three years in the Junior Secondary School and three years in the Senior Secondary School. This can be referred to as 3-3 secondary education system. The aims and objectives of American Secondary Education include:

- Creating a strong egalitarian society where everybody will have equal opportunity.
- Preparing students for survival in the future.
- Preparing the students for their colleges and universities. Some States in America provide free secondary education and free textbooks for their citizens particularly up to the age of sixteen years. The products of primary schools are always admitted into the secondary schools.

There are both public as well as private secondary schools in America. The Ordinance Act, 1785 which made it mandatory for each township to set its sixteenth section for the use of education as well as the North West Ordinance of 1887 greatly enhanced the development of education in America. However, the problem of sub-standardized secondary schools and willingness to provide secondary education for many American children led to the introduction of Junior High School. In the Junior High School, the students are expected to spend three years after their primary education that is between the age of 12-15 years. After successfully completing the Junior Secondary Education, the students will start their Senior High School Education which is meant for the students, who are academically inclined. The public senior high schools are tuition free. Provision of learning materials for schools and the general financing of schools are responsibilities of the local schools district. In America, private high schools or secondary schools are also allowed by the Constitution. However, unlike the public high schools, tuition is not free and the teaching of religious education is allowed. It is on record that America has started operating 6+3+3+4 education system, yet, the old system of 8+4 years is still in operation (eight years of primary education and four years of secondary education).

Teacher Education in the USA

Teacher education in America like in other places refers to the professional training being given to the would-be teachers. The aims and objectives of American Teacher Education include:

- Preparing teachers for the needs and aspirations of America as a democratic nation.
- Preparing teachers who will later assist in the training of American children for the purpose of promoting their culture. The establishment of Jefferson College in Washington among others in the 1800s marks the beginning of teacher education in America.

The preparation of primary school teachers is always done by the *Normal Schools*. These normal schools are recognized by the State Boards of Education for the training of primary school teachers. The subjects being offered in the training institutions include: Administration, Psychology, Philosophy, History of Education. On the other hand, the secondary school teachers are expected to be university degree holders after a period of four years either in a college or in the university. In most cases, teachers' appointment is always on contract basis and it is renewable yearly, provided the concerned teacher is still interested in working in his school. At the same time, the School District Board of Education has the Constitutional power to terminate the contract appointment of any of its teachers.

The American University Education

In America, higher education is provided in the colleges of education, higher technical institutes and universities. In 1862, the American Government passed the Morrill Act which made it compulsory for the Americans to make land available to the American Federal Government for the development of Universities and higher institutions of learning. There are two major categories of higher education in America, they are:

- The state universities and colleges which are maintained by the state; and
- Independent universities and colleges which are run by various churches and private individuals. In these private colleges and universities, high school fees are charged. A degree programme lasts for four years.

Adult Education in America

The beginning of Adult education can be traced to the establishment of Lyceum in Massachusetts in 1826. Also, the Smith Lever Act of 1914 as well as the Adult Education Association of the United States in 1951 greatly contributed to the development of Adult Education in America. Adult Education in American is run by private individuals such as lawyers, physicians, architects, teachers and musicians for the purpose of self-culture, community instruction as well as the mutual discussion of common public interest. In 1906, the university extension was started and this has been extended to most of the universities in America.

Technical Education

There have been some technical institutions as early as the middle of 19th century. But there was no serious attempt to promote technical education until when the Mosco technical school was able to perform creditably well at the international exhibitions in the 1970s. Thereafter, more technical institutions began to spring up in America. Also, the Morill Act of 1862 assisted in the development of technical education, private individuals started founding both commercial as well as business colleges. The Smith-Hughes Act among other things recommended that a Federal Board of vocational education should be set up. It was on the basis of this that the Federal Board of vocational education was established in which a substantial amount of money was set aside by the Federal Government for the general promotion of vocational and technical education throughout America.

Administration of Education in America

Education in America is decentralized. Therefore, it is the responsibility of each estate as well as the private individuals to take care of their schools. In 1867, the National Officer of Education was set up and it is being headed by the Education Commissioner who is an appointee of the President of America. The Federal Government always assists the state governments in the funding of technical and vocational education. The state universities are financially aided by the Federal Government. At the State level, there is a state department of education under the headship of Education Director who is elected by the people within the state for a period of two to four years. Locally, each local government has a local board of education, usually headed by a Superintendent of Schools in the district. His duties include: appointing teachers and other personnel who will be working with him. He also works on the finance of schools funded by the local government.

Finance of Education in America

In the whole of America, less than 60 per cent of the total cost of both public primary and secondary schools comes from the taxes levied by the local school boards. Also, the state government always sets aside about 40 per cent of its annual budget for the running of the public schools. The bulk of this money is generated from the state taxes as well as the taxes paid by the state workers. In the private schools, starting from the primary school up to the university, the students pay school fees in addition to the taxes being paid by the parents. Also, some well-to-do individuals in America always assist the private schools financially.

References

Lawal, B.O. (2004). *Comparative Education.* Osogbo: Swift Publishers Nig. Ltd.

Lawal, B.O. *Comparative Education*, retrieved from http://www.nou.edu.ng/noun/NOUN_OCL/pdf/EDUs/EDU%20314%20-%20COMPARATIVE%20EDUCATION.pdf

Lawal, B.O., Salami, W.O. and Farayola, J.A. (2001). *Comparative Education.* Ibadan: Olu-Akin Publishers.

Thamarasseri, I. and Bhat, M.S. (2014). *Comparative Education.* New Delhi: Kanishka Publishers.

8
Understanding the Australian Higher Education System

Sadia Mahmood

Almost as challenging as obtaining an actual university degree is understanding the different higher education systems in operation across the world. So, let us make things simpler by breaking down Australia's higher education system into simple, straightforward terms.

Tertiary Education in Australia

The Higher Education in Australia is known as the Tertiary Education. Tertiary Education in Australia is primarily study at university or a technical college studying Diploma or above in order to receive a qualification or further skills and training. A higher education provider is a body that is established or recognized by or under the law of the Australian Government, a State, the Australian Capital Territory or the Northern Territory. VET providers, both public and private are registered by State and Territory governments.

There are several prominent universities located in Adelaide, Brisbane, Canberra, Melbourne, Perth and Sydney. There are 43 universities in Australia: 40 public universities, two international universities, one private university. The largest university in Australia is Monash University in Melbourne: it has five campuses and 75,000 students.

There are non-self-accrediting higher education providers accredited by State and Territory authorities, numbering more than 150 as listed on State and Territory registers. These include several that are registered in more than one State and Territory.

Australia's Tertiary institution system can be divided into two sections: universities and vocational schools.

Universities

The Australian university system is made up of 41 universities; of those, 37 are public and are, therefore, funded by the Commonwealth Government. Consideration for admission to Australia's public universities is a centralised process in each of Australia's states and territories, but international students are often selected by the universities themselves, instead of the wider selection body. Although domestic students frequently receive scholarships and financial aid from the Commonwealth, international students are not eligible for these awards. Most students who study abroad in Australia pay full tuition fees, unless they receive support from their home university or a third-party sponsor. A 2013 HSBC report announced Australia as the world's most expensive place to study abroad, with average tuition fees and living expenses totalling nearly $38,000 USD a year (the US ranked second most expensive, and the UK third). Regardless of this, it is also the world's most popular country for international students, suggesting that high costs have not deterred overseas students from investing in an Australian education.

Vocational Schools

The Australian public vocational system is known as TAFE (Technical and Further Education). These institutes are usually funded by the governments of the State or Territory in which they are located. TAFE institutes reward qualifications—Certificates I, II, III, and IV, as well as Diplomas and Advanced Diplomas—in line with Australia's Vocational Education and Training (VET) sector. In certain niche areas of study, some TAFE schools also award bachelor's degrees. Select number of TAFE institutes focus on just one area of specialized study, but generally the TAFE system offers courses and degrees in many fields of interest, ranging from business and hospitality to the visual arts and information technology. Very often, vocational schools have official agreements with universities, allowing students to transfer the credits they have accumulated at a TAFE institute towards an advanced Bachelor's degree. Universities also may offer guaranteed acceptance if a student achieves the minimum grade requirement from their TAFE coursework. Vocational degrees can also be obtained at private vocational institutes known as

Registered Training Organisations (RTO), of which there are over a thousand scattered across Australia. In addition to TAFE institutes there are many registered training organisations (RTOs) which are privately operated. In Victoria alone there are approximately 1100. They include:

- commercial training providers;
- the training department of manufacturing or service enterprises;
- the training function of employer or employee organizations in a particular industry;
- Group training companies;
- community learning centres and neighbourhood houses; and
- secondary colleges providing VET programmes.

In size these RTOs vary from single-person operations delivering training and assessment in a narrow specialization, to large organizations offering a wide range of programmes. Many of them receive government funding to deliver programmes to apprentices or trainees, to disadvantaged groups, or in fields which governments see as priority areas.

VET programmes delivered by TAFE institutes and private RTOs are based on nationally registered qualifications, derived from either endorsed sets of competency standards known as training packages, or from courses accredited by state/territory government authorities. These qualifications are regularly reviewed and updated. In specialised areas where no publicly owned qualifications exist, an RTO may develop its own course and have it accredited as a privately owned programme, subject to the same rules as those that are publicly owned.

All trainers and assessors delivering VET programmes are required to hold a qualification known as the Certificate IV in Training and Assessment (TAA40104) or the more current TAE40110, or demonstrate equivalent competency. They are also required to have relevant vocational competencies, at least to the level being delivered or assessed. All TAFE institutes and private RTOs are required to maintain compliance with a set of national standards called the Australian Quality Training Framework (AQTF), and this compliance is monitored by regular internal and external audits.

Educational Curriculum in Australia

The Australian Curriculum, Assessment and Reporting Authority (ACARA) is the independent authority responsible for the development of a national curriculum, a national assessment programme and a national data collection and reporting programme that supports 21st century learning for all Australian students.

ACARA's work is carried out in collaboration with a wide range of stakeholders, including teachers, principals, governments, State and Territory education authorities, professional education associations, community groups and the general public. It was established in 2008 by an Act of the Australian Federal Parliament. The authority is also responsible for the My School website and NAPLAN testing. The Australian Curriculum has been divided by ACARA into the following learning areas for the purposes of development of the curriculum, its assessment, and reporting (F being Foundation Year): Arts F-10, English F-10, English 11-12, Health and Physical Education F-10, Civics and Citizenship 3-10, Economics and Business 5-10, Geography F-1, History F-10, History 11-12, Languages F-10, Mathematics F-10, Mathematics 11-12, Science F-10, Science 11-12, Technologies F-10, National Trade Cadetships F-10, National Trade Cadetships 11-12. Progress of the development of each learning area is published and updated regularly.

Course Lengths

The majority of bachelor's degrees in Australia require three years of study. Students can opt to do a fourth year, referred to as "honours," in which a thesis is required. This honours qualification would then be listed as part of the degree; for example, 'Economics with Honours'. To obtain the bachelor's degree, students must pick a major, or focus on a particular subject area. Universities set specific general and major requirements that the student must fulfil in order to earn the degree.

In addition to a major, students have the option to minor in a particular field. Aminor requires fewer courses than a major, but is still a specialization in a certain academic area. Tacking on a minor does not usually increase the time needed to graduate. Some universities allow students to do double degrees, in which they major in two fields of study. This often delays the time required graduate and extends beyond three year period. Masters programmes across Australia are one to two years long, depending on the programme or the subject.

Academic Expectations

In the case of tertiary education in many parts of the world, students in

Australia are encouraged, but not required, to attend lecture. Final marks are usually dependent on one or two examinations per term. Of course, certain courses like laboratory work or language classes may place more emphasis on attendance, homework assignments and participation. The academic culture in Australia is very much based on student involvement. Students are encouraged to speak up in lecture, ask questions and offer opinions. Such active engagement is valued much more than simples copying or regurgitating notes. Similarly, it is expected that students demonstrate critical thinking in examinations rather than mere memorisation of lecture notes, and marks are rewarded accordingly.

Admission in the Courses

As Australia uses a Federal system of government, responsibility for education, and admission to Technical and Further Education colleges and undergraduate degrees at universities for domestic students, are in the domain of state and territory government. All states except Tasmania have centralized processing units for admission to undergraduate degrees for citizens of Australia and New Zealand, and for Australian permanent residents; however, applications for international and post-graduate students are usually accepted by individual universities. The Australian government operates the Higher Education Contribution Scheme (This has been replaced by the very similar HECS-HELP—Higher Education Loan Program) for undergraduate students, so admission is rarely limited by prospective students' ability to pay up-front. All states use a system that awards the recipient with an ATAR, and the award of an International Baccalaureate meets the minimum requirements for admission in every state. ATARs are awarded based on the level of attainment in each State's individual secondary schooling examinations (such as the NSW HSC). For individuals without an ATAR, or recent secondary schooling certificate, the Special Tertiary Admissions Test is used as the standard test to provide an ATAR. The maximum possible ATAR is 99.95, indicating that the student has achieved better than 99.95 per cent of their peers.

Funding of the Universities

Decision-making, regulation and governance for higher education are shared among the Australian government, the state and territory governments and the institutions themselves. Some aspects of higher education are the responsibility of states and territories. In particular, most universities are established or recognised under state and territory legislation. States and territories are also responsible for accrediting non-self-accrediting higher education providers. The Australian government has the primary responsibility for public funding of higher education. The Higher Education Support Act, 2003 sets out the details of Australian government funding and its associated legislative requirements. Australian government funding support for higher education is provided largely through:

- the Commonwealth Grant Scheme which provides for a specified number of Commonwealth supported places each year;
- the Higher Education Loan Programme (HELP) arrangements providing financial assistance to students;
- the Commonwealth Scholarships; and
- a range of grants for specific purposes including quality, learning and teaching, research and research training programmes.

The Department of Education has responsibility for administering this funding, and for developing and administering higher education policy and programmes.

Fee Structure

Students enrolled in courses at Australian tertiary education institutions are charged higher education fees. However, government loans and subsidies are in place to relieve the costs of tertiary education in Australia.

Some students are supported by the National government, known as the Commonwealth government. These students are only required to pay a part of the cost of tuition, called the "student contribution", while the Commonwealth pays the balance; and some Commonwealth supported students are also able to defer payment of their contribution as a HECS-HELP loan. Other domestic students are full fee-paying (non-Commonwealth supported) and receive no other direct government contribution to the cost of their education. Some domestic students in full fee courses can obtain a FEE-HELP loan from the National government up to a lifetime limit of $112,134 for medicine, dentistry and veterinary science programmes and $89,706 for all other programmes.

Australian citizens (and in some cases overseas professionals completing bridging studies in order to be accredited permanent residents) are able to obtain interest free loans from the government under the Higher Education Loan Programme (HELP) which replaced the Higher Education Contribution Scheme (HECS).

HELP is jointly administered by the Australian Department of Education and Training and the Australian Taxation Office (ATO). In addition, qualified students may be entitled to Youth Allowance or Austudy Payment to assist them financially while they are studying. These support payments are means and assets tested. Further assistance is available in the form of scholarships. Overseas students are charged fees for the full cost of their education and are ineligible for any loans from the Commonwealth, but may apply for international scholarships.

Quality Assurance of Education in Australia

The Tertiary Education Quality and Standards Agency (TEQSA) is a government body in Australia which monitors and accredits higher education providers for quality and compliance to the standards of the Australian Qualifications Framework. It operates under the Department of Education and Training of the Government of Australia. TEQSA was established on 30th July, 2011 by the Tertiary Education Quality and Standards Agency Act, 2011 as part of the Government of Australia's Transforming Australia's Higher Education System initiative, taking over the activities of the Australian Universities Quality Agency and integrating activities by similar state government regulatory bodies.

This makes Australia one of the leading countries imparting quality education and it can be very well fetched out that Australia offers one of the finest education system in world and helps many national and international students by brightening their future prospects.

References

"Academic Ranking of World Universities 2016". Shanghai Ranking Consultancy. Retrieved 17 December, 2016.

Breen, Jim (December 2002). "Higher Education in Australia: Structure, Policy and Debate". Monash University.

Cain, John; Hewitt, John (2004), Off course: From public place to marketplace at Melbourne University, Scribe.

Dodd, Tim (16 August, 2014). "Sydney Uni drops out of top 100; Melbourne Uni rises". *Financial Review*. Fairfax Media. Retrieved 17 August, 2014.

Foster, Gigi (20 April 2015). "The slide of academic standards in Australia: A cautionary tale". *The Conversation*. Retrieved 24 September, 2015.

"Higher education in Australia". Department of Education, Employment and Workplace Relations. Archived from the original on 28 December, 2010. Retrieved 13 July, 2010.

Knott, Matthew (30 December, 2014). "Work and pay prospects for graduates deteriorated in 2014, A survey shows". *Sydney Morning Herald*. Fairfax Media. Retrieved 1 January, 2015.

Marginson, S., National system reform in global context: The case of Australia. Reforms and consequences in higher education system: An international symposium, National Centre of Sciences, Hitotubashi Chiyoda-ku, Tokyo, 2009.

Marginson, S., (2000). Rethinking academic work in the global era. *Journal of Higher Education Policy and Management*, 22(1): 1-12.

"Monash returns to its inclusive roots". *The Age*. 16 March, 2015.

"Overview". Department of Education, Employment and Workplace Relations. Archived from the original on 6 September, 2010. Retrieved 13 July, 2010.

"Overview". Department of Education, Employment and Workplace Relations. Retrieved 13 July, 2010.

Papadopoulos, Toli (11 July 2014). "Overqualified and underemployed: Meet Australia's graduates". *Business Spectator*. Retrieved 13 September, 2014.

"QS World University Rankings". QS Quacquarelli Symonds Limited. Retrieved 17 December, 2016.

Schmidt, Lucinda (30 May, 2013). "A Matter of Degrees". *Sydney Morning Herald*. Fairfax Media. Retrieved 27 November, 2013.

"The White Hat Guide to Australian Nobel Prize Winners". *White Hat*. 1 January, 2014. Retrieved 5 July, 2014.

"Top Universities in Australia 2017". *Times Higher Education*. Retrieved 17 December, 2016.

"Universities and Higher Education—Study in Australia". Australian Government.

Williams, R., Van Dyke, N. (2007). "Measuring the international standing of universities with an application to Australian universities". *Higher Education*. 53 (6): 819-841.

9

United States Higher Education

An Overview

Mujibul Hasan Siddiqui and *Zaffar Ahmad Nadaf*

United States Higher Education borrows its Educational structure from both the British undergraduate college and German Research University, but its character is extremely influenced by three major philosophical beliefs that shape American public life.[1]

The Jeffersonian ideals of limited government and freedom of expression, states, religious communities, and individuals established and maintain a range of higher education institutions and continue to protect these institutions from the levels of government control seen in other countries.

The second set of influences is capitalism and the belief in the rationality of markets. American colleges and universities vie for students, faculty, and funding under the assumption that diversity and high quality are best achieved through competition rather than centralized planning. The final major philosophical influence on American higher education is a widespread commitment to equal opportunity and social mobility.

Higher Education was an elite activity for much of its history, excluding individuals based on gender, religion, race/ethnicity, and social class. However, during the 20th century, economic and social changes transformed higher education into a primary gateway to the middle-class, and women and minorities made inroads against longstanding exclusion from mainstream higher education. Americans came to view broad access to higher education as a necessary component of the Nation's ideal as a "land of opportunity".

Higher education responded by broadening access. Indeed, the one uniquely America type of institution—the community college—was founded in the 20th century to ensure open access to higher education for individuals of all ages, preparation levels, and incomes. Guided by these beliefs, US higher education reflects essential elements of the American character: independence, suspicion of government, ambition, inclusiveness, and competitiveness. This manuscript describes the major characteristics of American higher education and important issues that challenge it, linking back as appropriate to these essential philosophical underpinnings.

The Distinctive Characteristics of US Higher Education

American higher education is so diverse and complex, any description of "standard practice" inevitably misstates much about individual colleges and universities. Indeed, important exceptions to most of the characteristics described in this chapter exist. Nonetheless, this section provides an overview of how most colleges and universities are governed and financed, their students and faculty, and the nature of the curriculum and student life.

Size and Composition of US Higher Education

Other than diversity, autonomy, competition, and accessibility, size is a distinguishing feature of US higher education. The US Department of Education counts 6,500 post-secondary institutions that participate in its student financial aid programmes, including 4,200 colleges and universities that award degrees and 2,300 institutions that award vocational certificates. These 6,500 institutions enrolled approximately 16 million full- and part-time students, including 14 million undergraduates and two million graduate and professional students, in fall 2001. The 4,200 colleges and universities awarded more than 2.4 million degrees in academic year 2000–01. In addition, an untold number of other institutions offer post-secondary instruction of some type but do not choose to participate in the federal student aid programmes and therefore are not counted by the Federal Government (US Department of Education, 2003).

Degree-granting institutions are typically divided into four major groups, and a considerable amount of diversity exists within each group:

- America's 1,100 public two-year institutions, or community colleges, enrol the largest share of undergraduates (6 million students in 2001). These institutions award associate degrees in vocational fields, prepare students for transfer to four-year institutions, and serve their communities by providing a wide array of educational services. These services range from specialized training for large employers, to English language instruction for recent immigrants, to recreational courses. Almost 4 million students attended community colleges part-time in 2001. The US government does not track enrolment figures for non-credit adult education or recreational courses, but the American Association of Community Colleges estimates that an additional 5 million students enrol in these types of courses at community colleges every year.

- There are only 630 public four-year colleges and universities in the United States. But these institutions—which include regional comprehensive universities that concentrate on undergraduate teaching and graduate preparation in professional fields such as teaching and business, as well as research universities that offer a comprehensive set of undergraduate, graduate, and professional degree programmes—enrolled 6.2 million students in 2001. This figure includes 5 million undergraduates and slightly more than 1 million graduate students.
- Private not-for-profit institutions are extremely diverse, including research universities, four-year liberal arts colleges that focus on undergraduate teaching, a small number of two-year institutions, faith-based institutions that maintain strong links with religious denominations, women's colleges, historically black colleges and universities, and specialized institutions that focus on a single field, such as nursing or fine arts. Private not-for-profit institutions enrolled 3.2 million students in 2001, including 2.3 million undergraduates and more than 700,000 graduate students.
- For-profit institutions primarily offer vocational programmes that result in certificates rather than degrees. Of the more than 2,400 for-profit institutions counted by the US Department of Education, 500 offer two-year associate degrees and 320 offer bachelor's and/or graduate degrees. In total, for-profit institutions enrolled more than 7,50,000 students in 2001, all but 50,000 of whom were at the undergraduate level.

Table 9.1 provides an overview of enrolment in each of these four sectors. This large number and wide range of institutions offer both access and choice—two hallmarks of American higher education that respond to the previously described value placed on opportunity and faith in the market.

Table 9.1: US Post-secondary Institutions and Enrolments: Fall 2001

	Public	*Private Not-for-Profit*	*Private for-Profit*	*Total*
Institutions	**2,099**	**1,941**	**2,418**	**6,458**
Four-Year	629	1,567	324	2,520
Two-Year	1,165	269	779	2,213
Less than Two-Year	305	105	1,315	1,725
Enrolment	**12,370,079**	**3,198,354**	**765,701**	**16,334,134**
Four-Year	6,236,486	3,120,472	321,468	9,678,426
Two-Year	6,047,445	63,207	241,617	6,352,269
Less than Two-Year	86,148	14,675	202,616	303,439

Source: U.S. Dept. of Education National Centre for Education Statistics (2003).

Governance

Another of the philosophical underpinnings of US higher education is the Jeffersonian notion of limited and, whenever possible, locally controlled government. Based on this model, the US Constitution reserves for the states all government functions not specifically described as federal. Among those functions is education. As a result, each of the 50 States is responsible for governing public colleges and universities (which enrol 75% of students), rather than the Federal Government. The degree of control by the states varies tremendously. Some institutions, such as the University of California and the University of Michigan, enjoy constitutional autonomy as separate branches of state government. At the other extreme, locally elected boards of trustees govern some community colleges. In some states, a governing board appointed by the governor and/or legislature oversees all institutions, setting funding levels, establishing accountability measures, setting policies, and approving new academic programmes. In others, the state board plays only an advisory function and has little direct authority over institutions. In many others, a state agency is poised between the institutions and state government, implementing state-wide policy but also attempting to insulate institutions from ill-advised or overly intrusive state policies.

Some public universities are part of state-wide multi-campus systems in which an additional layer of oversight exists between the campus and state government. System administrators may oversee campus budgets, set policies such as admissions standards, coordinate degree programmes, and facilitate credit transfer and articulation between the state's public colleges and universities. Additionally, and importantly, they advocate to the legislature on behalf of public colleges and universities. In some states, more than one multi-campus system exists, such as California's distinct systems of community colleges, comprehensive state colleges and universities, and research universities.

Because the Constitution does not mention education as a federal responsibility, the Federal Government plays a limited role and the United States has never had an education ministry, such as those found in most other countries. With the important exception of the Morrill Land Grant Act of 1862, which donated federal territory to the states for the establishment of public universities, the Federal Government played almost no role in higher education until the middle of the 20th century, when Second World War necessitated the establishment of federal funding for scientific research at colleges and universities to build US military capacity. In 1944, President Franklin Roosevelt signed the GI Bill of Rights, which granted returning veterans funding to attend college as a way to integrate servicemen back into the US workforce. As the civil rights movement took hold in the 1960s, the federal role in supporting students expanded to include grant and loan programmes for low- and moderate-income students. Since that time, federal support has expanded so that it is now the primary financier of both scientific research and student financial aid.

While the Federal Government generally does not provide direct operational support to colleges and universities, this special purpose funding is an extremely important revenue source and, in turn, has increased the ability of the Federal Government to influence colleges and universities in areas outside research and financial aid. For example, in order for institutions to participate in the financial aid programmes, they must comply with a wide range of federal reporting requirements on topics ranging from teacher preparation to gender equity in intercollegiate athletics. However, despite the growing influence of the Federal Government, its role is still limited and has not yet intruded into core academic decisions, which are generally left to the institutions and, in the case of some public institutions, the states.

Two sets of voluntary organizations act as bulwarks against excessive government control of higher education: accrediting organizations that monitor quality assurance, and membership associations that represent institutions to the Federal and State Governments. Accrediting organisations are membership organisations of colleges and universities and rely on volunteers who work at colleges and universities and who agree to assist other institutions by providing evaluation through peer review. There are three types of accrediting organizations: regional organizations, which review the quality of entire institutions and focus almost exclusively on public and private not for profit degree-granting institutions; national organizations, which monitor the quality of most for profit and non-degree granting institutions; and specialized accrediting organizations, which evaluate academic programmes within a specific field such as medicine, law, or teacher education.

American accreditation differs from the type of quality assurance conducted by governments in most other countries. Federal and State Governments can and do impose their own accountability requirements on institutions, but they generally have left the assessment of academic quality to institutions themselves through the self-study and peer review processes of accreditation. The Federal Government, in particular, relies on recognized regional and national accreditation organizations to determine whether institutions are of sufficient academic quality and managerial soundness to merit inclusion in the federal student financial aid programmes. When the US Department of Education officially recognizes an accrediting organization, it certifies that the organization adequately monitors quality in areas mandated by the Federal Government, such as fiscal soundness and managerial competence, fair admissions and recruiting practices, and evidence of student success.

Accrediting organizations establish minimum standards that institutions must meet in a range of areas such as the curricula, faculty qualifications, student learning outcomes, co-curricular student services, and financial health. Accrediting organizations do not, however, mandate how institutions go about meeting those standards. Further, because accreditation measures institutions against a set of standards, it generally does not provide a gauge of how well an institution is performing relative to other institutions. Accreditation is accomplished through institutional self-study and a peer review process to determine whether the institution has met the organization's standards. Accreditors typically review institutions on a three to five-year basis (Eaton, 2000).

Membership associations, which can have either institutions or individuals (such as business officers) as members, represent the interests of colleges and universities to the Federal Government and, in some cases State Governments. Many colleges and universities also employ their own staff to advocate for them, but in most cases, those staff work only on issues of concern to the individual institution, such as state appropriations or federal research contracts for the institution. Membership associations champion those public policies that are in the collective best interest of either all or some major segment of higher education. In Washington, DC, colleges and universities are represented by hundreds of organizations, which also provide networking and professional development opportunities for their members.

Finance

Colleges and universities are financed in ways consistent with both the Jeffersonian ideal of limited government and the belief that market competition tends to improve quality and efficiency. While government plays a very important role in financing, American colleges and universities are supported further by diverse revenue sources that reflect the market choices of students and parents as well as other consumers of the goods and services that institutions provide. The major sources of revenue include tuition and fee payments from students and families (including the government-backed financial aid that students use to pay tuition); appropriations, grants, and contracts from federal, state, and local governments; private gifts; endowment and other investment earnings; and sales from auxiliary enterprises and services.

Some of these sources are more important to some types of institutions than to others. For example, local governments account for 18 per cent of revenue at community colleges but 1 per cent of revenue at private not-for-profit institutions. Similarly, private gifts contribute 14 per cent of revenue to private not-for-profit institutions, but only 1 per cent of revenue to community colleges (US Department of Education, 2003). While the revenue sources of American institutions are diverse, two sources are of particular importance to most institutions: state appropriations, particularly for public institutions; and tuition fees. These two sources (along with local appropriations at community colleges and federal research grants and contracts at research universities) provide the bulk of funds for general operating expenses. One of the perennial questions in American higher education finance is how much of the cost of education should be borne by government, and how much by students and families.

One of the perennial questions in American higher education finance is how much of the cost of education should be borne by government, and how much by students and families.

Traditionally, state appropriations have made up the bulk of institutional revenue at public institutions, but they are diminishing both as a share of state expenditures and as a percentage of institutional revenue. In response, state governments and public institutions have raised tuition, shifting the responsibility from taxpayers to students. In most states, higher education is the third largest item in the budget, after health care and elementary/secondary education. Because health care costs are escalating rapidly and voters demand that spending on elementary/secondary schools be protected, higher education falls logically into legislators' sights when they are forced to make budget cuts. Not only does higher education represent a significant portion of state budgets, but (unlike other programmes such as prisons) it has a natural alternative source of revenue—tuition payments from parents and students. Typically, in good economic times, states will raise appropriations to colleges and universities and demand that, in return, institutions keep tuition increases low. When the economy is in trouble and state tax revenue falls, states cut spending on higher education and expect institutions to make up the difference through tuition increases.

Private donations from individuals and corporations provide another source of revenue for American colleges and universities that is typically not found outside the United States. Total voluntary support for higher education, encouraged by the US tax structure, surpassed $23 billion in fiscal year 2003, of which $11 billion was donated by individuals (Council for Aid to Education, 2004). To this end, many colleges and universities construct sophisticated approaches to fund raising, and college and university presidents dedicate much of their time to raising private gifts.

A significant and growing set of expenditures at many private not-for-profit institutions is institutional financial aid, sometimes called "tuition discounting". Private colleges have a long tradition of providing financial assistance to low income students. In addition, most of these institutions (and, increasingly, many public institutions as well) have turned to institutional financial aid to attract students who may be able to pay the full price but who are unwilling to attend without a discount. For some institutions, tuition discounting is a way to compete with other institutions for the "best and brightest". For others, it is a necessary practice that fills enrolment places that otherwise would remain vacant. In either case, these discounts contribute to increases in the posted or "sticker price". All institutions face real increases in the cost of providing education. Technology and equipment costs are rising, as are the prices of journals and books, health care for employees, and building maintenance. Institutions are working to update and expand facilities and services to meet student demand for state-of-the-art technology, small class sizes, and world-class academic and recreational facilities.

In the face of these increased costs and reduced revenue from states and other sources, universities and colleges have three options. They can cut back, improve efficiencies, and/or generate new revenue. For the most part, institutions are engaged in some combination of all three. They cut back by reducing travel and equipment purchases, postponing salary increases, leaving vacant faculty and administrative positions, reducing administrative and support staff, and postponing building and renovation. Rarely do institutions cut academic programmes.

Institutions also strive to become more efficient. Much of this effort focuses on administrative and student service functions, such as lowering electrical usage, streamlining purchasing and procurement processes, and altering financial systems. Some institutions are pursuing efficiencies in academic areas, such as using technology to reach more students, increasing class size, and hiring adjunct instructors. However, most efficiencies are being sought outside the classroom.

Finally, American colleges and universities are pursuing many efforts to diversify and expand their revenue streams, such as developing online education and niche oriented degree and non-degree academic programmes, expanding research capacities, engaging in licensing and sponsorship agreements, and pursuing auxiliary enterprises, such as managing real estate and running conference centres. Because a primary source of additional revenue is student tuition and fees, they have risen at twice the rate of inflation over the past 20 years, outstripping increases in both family income and financial aid resources.

The implications of increasing prices for students and families are a matter of constant policy debate. Despite tuition increases, demand for higher education continues to increase. Further, a wide array of government and private financial aid programmes provides assistance to students, based on both financial need and academic merit. Financial aid to students totaled more than $105 billion in 2002-03, including $71 billion in federal grants, loans, and tax credits; $6 billion in state grants; and $20 billion in grants provided by colleges and universities, as well as private organizations (College Board, 2003). Despite these resources, access and success in higher education continue to be stratified according to income, with students at the upper end of the income spectrum far more likely to attend college and earn a degree than those from disadvantaged backgrounds. Of course, many factors play into college access and success, not the least of which is students' level of prior academic preparation.

Because the quality of US elementary and secondary schools varies widely depending on the wealth of communities, tuition prices alone cannot be blamed for disparities in education opportunity. However, even if low-income students are able to overcome the academic and financial barriers to enrolling in college, their ability to succeed once enrolled can be impeded because they must work and attend part-time in order to pay their tuition, suggesting that financial matters play a crucial role.

Students

Despite increases in the price of attending college, the American student population continues to grow rapidly in both size and diversity. As noted previously, there are more than 16 million individuals seeking degrees at US post-secondary institutions and an estimated 5 million additional students enrolled in non-credit courses.

American college students are diverse in age, race/ethnicity, gender, socio-economic status, and academic interests. The majority of undergraduate students are women and despite increases in the price of attending college, the American student population continues to grow rapidly in both size and diversity. One-third are racial or ethnic minorities.

More than 40 per cent are of age 25 or older (US Department of Education, 2002b). About 20 per cent come from families with incomes at or below the federal poverty level (King, 2004). Three out of four American college students are considered non-traditional—that is, they possess one or more of the following characteristics:

They are of age 25 or older, have delayed entry into higher education after completing high school, did not earn a traditional high school diploma, are married, attend part-time, work full time, or have children (US Department of Education, 2002a). Eighty per cent of students work during the academic year. Half attend part-time (US Department of Education, 2002b). In part because most non-traditional students juggle college attendance with work and family responsibilities, it is becoming increasingly unusual for students to enroll at one institution and remain there for their entire undergraduate career. Sixty per cent of bachelor's degree recipients attend more than one institution. In about half of these cases, the student formally transfers from one institution to another. The most common form of transfer is from a community college to a four-year institution. In the remaining half of these cases, students may maintain their primary enrolment at one institution but also take classes at other institutions, sometimes attending two different institutions simultaneously.

Students also may move among multiple institutions, often suspending enrolment (or "stopping out") for some period before enrolling at a new institution. This student mobility is possible because the American system of higher education uses a common "currency" to measure academic progress—the credit. Students earn credits towards their degrees by completing courses. These credits can then typically be transferred to another institution if the receiving institution agrees that the academic rigour and material in the courses is roughly equivalent to its own similar courses. Many institutions develop transfer or articulation agreements to help facilitate student mobility, determining in advance which courses are of equivalent value. Institutions struggle to balance the goal of expanding access by allowing students to take classes where and when they want with the need to maintain the academic integrity of their degree programmes and capture much-needed tuition revenue.

Although American college students enjoy a level of mobility unknown to most of their peers around the world, they still must compete for admission to the more selective colleges and universities. American higher education includes institutions with a wide range of admissions selectivity, from open-access two-year and four-year institutions that admit all students, to highly selective research universities and liberal arts colleges that admit only a small fraction of those who apply. Many students apply to more than one college or university and enrol in one from among those that offer them admission.

Admissions decisions at selective institutions are based on a fixed set of academic criteria, including high school coursework, grade point average and class rank, and admissions test score, as well as a more flexible set of non-academic characteristics, such as demonstrated leadership ability, creativity, and community service. Because the United States has no national secondary school curriculum or high school exit examination, colleges rely on two privately developed admissions examinations—the SAT and ACT. These tests, while important, are only one criterion among many that institutions consider. Indeed, the admissions decisions at highly selective institutions are so complex and consider so many factors that wealthy families often hire private admissions counselors to help them anticipate which factors a given institution is likely to weigh most heavily and to help their child craft an application that best meets those criteria.

Consistent with American faith in the market, institutions compete heavily to attract the most talented students. While this competition spurs improvements in quality and keeps institutions focused on meeting student needs, it also can have negative effects, sometimes prompting institutions to make academic and financial choices that may improve student recruitment but that are inconsistent with the institution's mission, the best interests of the public, or the long-term financial health of the enterprise.

The Curriculum and Degrees

Five types of degrees exist in the United States. Two-year colleges (community colleges) and a small number of four-year institutions grant associate degrees, typically awarded after the completion of 60 credits.

Associate degrees may represent a terminal degree in a vocational field or may prepare students to complete a bachelor's degree at a four-year institution. The bachelor's degree is by far the most common type of degree awarded, preparing students for most jobs that require a college degree and for further graduate study. Three degrees exist at the graduate level:

1. The master's degree is the most common type of graduate degree. About 75 per cent of graduate students are enrolled in master's degree programmes, divided roughly evenly among students in education, business administration, and all other fields (US Department of Education, 2002c). A master's degree may have either a professional or theoretical focus and usually requires a comprehensive examination and/or thesis or other original piece of work. The master's degree either prepares graduates for future advanced study at the doctoral level or is itself a terminal degree.
2. A professional degree provides access to advanced professions in fields such as law and medicine.
3. The doctoral degree is the highest academic award and recognizes the graduate's ability to conduct independent research. The most common degree of this type is the doctor of philosophy (Ph.D.), but it also includes the doctor of education (Ed.D.).

No national laws govern the titles of degrees, although each state typically regulates the level of degree that institutions located within its borders can award. Each institution has the autonomy to determine its own programme requirements, typically following broad degree guidelines set by the states or by specialized accrediting agencies.

> The bachelor's degree is by far the most common type of degree awarded, preparing students for most jobs that require a college degree and for further graduate study.

The undergraduate curriculum typically consists of two components—general education and the major field of study (the major). The purpose of general education is to provide students with broad knowledge and prepare them to be engaged and informed citizens. General education is delivered predominantly through either a core curriculum, in which all undergraduate students take the same courses, or an elective or distributive format, in which students choose courses from a pre-specified list representing a range of topics (such as science, art and aesthetic appreciation, mathematics, humanities etc.). General education requirements typically constitute between one-quarter and one-half of a student's courses, depending upon the institution and the student's major. The other courses include those related to the major. Students choose their major either upon enrolling or after completing their second year of studies, depending upon institutional policy. Students may change their majors if their interests change and keep most of their credits earned towards their degree. Although most institutions continue to rely on a traditional nine-month (two semesters) academic calendar, many colleges and universities are innovating with their academic calendars, and additionally offer short month-long courses, overlapping semesters, and courses in a condensed weekend format, as they try to create programmes that meet student needs and schedules.

Faculty and Their Appointments

More than 1 million academic staff (faculty) work at American colleges and universities. Faculty appointments may be full time or part-time and may be tenured/tenure-track or no tenure-track. Tenure is an academic employment arrangement, granted after a probationary period, which ensures holders a series of rights, including academic freedom and participation in institutional governance. It often implies continuous employment, barring dismissals for cause or financial exigency. Not all academic positions carry tenure. *See* Table 9.2 for a list of faculty titles in the tenure and no tenure tracks.

Faculty responsibilities typically fall into three basic categories: teaching, research, and service to the campus and/or community. However, faculty jobs are by no means uniform, and the time and attention that faculty devote to these three roles depend upon the mission of the institution at which they work, their academic discipline, and their rank and career stage. For example, faculty at community colleges more often tend to teach and be engaged in service activities, while many senior faculty at research universities spend more time engaged in research than in the other two areas.

Thirty-eight per cent of all full-time faculty are women, but women hold only 21 per cent of full professorships. At the assistant professor rank, 46 per cent of full-time faculty are women. However, women's larger presence at the junior ranks does not guarantee future proportionality at senior ranks. The number of full-time faculty from racial/ethnic minority groups almost doubled over the last 20 years, yet only 14 per cent of all full-time faculty are racial/ethnic minorities. The largest minority group is Asian American/Pacific Islander, comprising 6 per cent of the total full-time faculty population, with African Americans at 5 per cent, Hispanics at 3 per cent, and Native Americans at less than half of 1 per cent (Harvey, 2003).

Table 9.2: Faculty Rank and Titles, by Tenure/Non-tenure Track

	Tenured/Tenure Track	*Nontenure Track*
Full Time	Professor Associate Professor Assistant Professor Research Professor	Lecturer Instructor Professor of Practice Research Professor
Part Time	Professor Emeritus	Adjunct Professor Lecturer Instructor

Source: American Council of Education 2001).

In 1999, according to an American Council on Education study (Anderson, 2002), approximately half of all faculties were employed part-time and/or in no tenure-track positions. These faculties include those who are qualified for and seek full-time, tenure-track appointments yet do not obtain them, as well as individuals who do not have doctorates and/or teach in addition to other professional responsibilities. Debate and discussion continue to focus on the increasing use of part-time and no tenure-track faculty. Much of this growth accommodates increasing student enrolments. Another important reason for hiring part-time and no tenure-track faculty is to reduce personnel costs and increase institutional flexibility in course offerings, as these faculty can be hired and fired as interest in their academic fields ebbs and flows. However, critics charge that reliance on part-time and no tenure-track faculty has hidden institutional and educational costs, lowering quality as these individuals do little student advising and research and do not participate in non-instructional activities such as faculty governance.

University Administration

Although the internal organization and structure of US institutions vary based upon size and mission, some common elements exist. Lay boards of trustees who tend not to be academics govern most college and universities. These boards are the legal agents for the institution and are responsible for ensuring and monitoring its financial health, setting strategy to fulfil its mission, and evaluating both institutional and presidential performance. The size, structure, and appointment of boards vary. For example, some boards of private non-profit institutions exceed 50 members. Public institution boards tend to be much smaller. According to the Association of Governing Boards of Universities and Colleges (AGB), the mean size of public boards is approximately 10 people and the mean size among independent institutions is 30. For most public institutions, the state government typically appoints board members, often after nomination by the governor and approval by the legislature. However, in some states and at many community colleges, board members are chosen through general elections. For private institutions, boards select their own members (called self-perpetuating boards). The length of board members' terms varies from four years to as long as 12 years. In some cases, board members can be reappointed to additional terms.

Boards hire and delegate much of the administrative responsibility for managing the institution to the president (sometimes called a chancellor). The president is responsible for providing overall leadership to the institution, managing its finances and budget, developing and executing the institution's strategic plan, and establishing systems of accountability and performance. However, much of the president's work lies outside the institution. The president advocates for the institution's needs and seeks support from legislative and other external audiences, meets with alumni and prospective students, develops relationships with corporations and community groups, and provides the public persona of the institution. The president serves either at the pleasure of the board or on a fixed-term contract, eligible for renewal.

Beyond the president, other senior administrators provide the leadership for the institution's various divisions. The typical structure includes academic affairs, responsible for academic programmes and research; student affairs, overseeing student services and student life; business and administration, accountable for the financial operations, auxiliary services, and campus facilities; and development, focusing on fund raising and alumni relations. Within each division, a variety of deans, directors, and department chairs complete the administrative structure. Figure 9.1 provides an overview of a typical college or university administrative structure (American Council on Education, 2001).

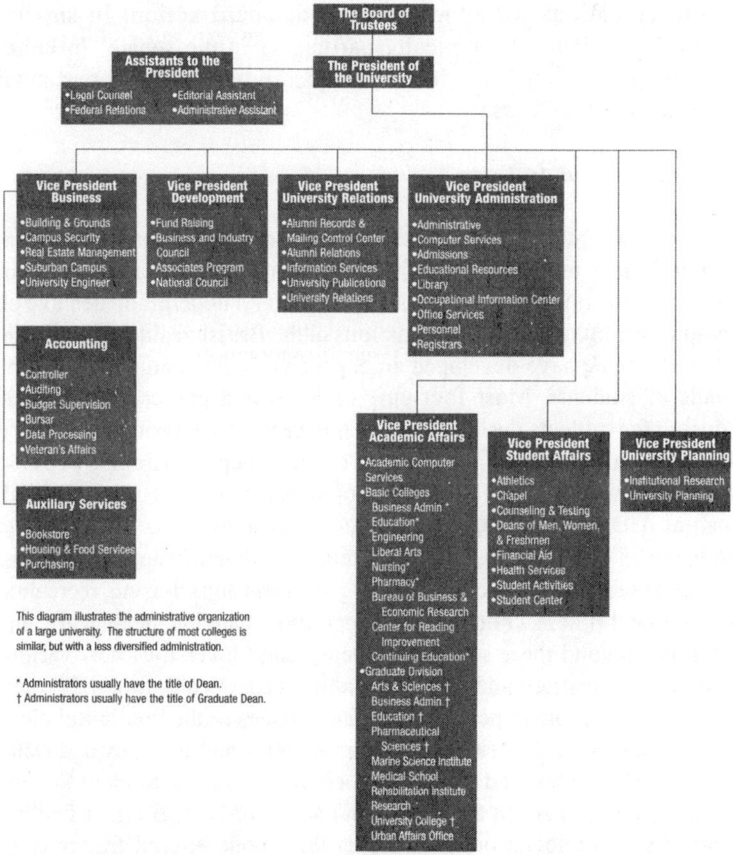

Fig. 9.1: The University: Administrative Organization

Source: Eckel & King (2004), An Overview of Higher Education in the United State.

Although presidents have primary responsibility for the institution, most rely upon a system of shared governance between faculty and administrators for key institutional decisions. The primary organizational structure for shared governance is the faculty senate. The senate is responsible for recommending academic decisions and policies, such as those affecting new curricula and courses, degree requirements, and academic hiring and workloads. Its members typically include full-time faculty, although students, administrators, staff, and part-time faculty sometimes participate as well. At some institutions, the senate has the ability to make final decisions; at others, the senate makes recommendations for administrative or board action. In smaller institutions, all faculty typically participate in the senate. In larger institutions, senators are elected, frequently representing particular departments or colleges.

Student Life and Athletics

The US collegiate experience is strongly shaped by a residential tradition, although today more than half of undergraduate students are older and/or enrolled part-time and less than 20 per cent of all undergraduates live on campus. Building upon the foundations of the British residential college, US institutions have developed an expansive infrastructure to meet the needs of students. Most four-year colleges and universities provide housing for students during the academic year. These residence halls, in addition to providing food service and sleeping rooms, provide programming to students on a variety of topics, both academic and social, such as AIDS awareness, alcohol abuse, and study skills. Colleges and universities additionally provide a range of student support services, including personal counselling, career placement and advising, recreation and physical fitness, child care, transportation, banking, health care, and tutoring. Beyond these services, colleges and universities host various student organizations and clubs, including academically focused groups (such as the National Society of Black Engineers or the Public Relations Student Society of America), as well as athletic (such as rugby and water polo clubs), cultural and religious (such as the Muslim Student Society or Association of Asian Students), and social organizations. A familiar type of student social organization is the Greek-lettered fraternity or sorority. Another important student organization is student government, which is the formal, recognized student advocacy body on campus. However, for the most part, its influence is limited and its agenda constrained, particularly when compared with similar student governments or student unions in Latin America and Europe.

Finally, any discussion of student life at American colleges and universities must include athletics, which plays a major role on many—but not all—campuses. The influence of athletics on campuses tends to be disproportional to the small number of student athletes. At institutions with "big-time" sports programmes, the athletics budget can reach millions of dollars, dwarfing those of academic departments, and coaches of men's basketball and football teams are frequently the university's highest-paid employees. At these institutions, athletic teams are divided into revenue sports (football, men's and increasingly women's basketball, and in some cases, ice hockey) and non-revenue sports (for example, track and field, swimming, wrestling, golf, tennis, field hockey, and soccer).

The majority of student-athletes participate in the non-revenue sports. The revenue sports tend to be highly commercialized, garnering national television coverage and athletic apparel endorsement deals. Athletics on US campuses is a double-edged sword. In some situations, it can provide a unifying catalyst for the institution and its community and teach its participants valuable lessons. In other situations, it has been described as an unstoppable "arms race," exemplifying a winner-take-all attitude, spurring scandal, academic dishonesty, excessive commercialization, abuse of student-athletes, and distraction from the institution's academic priorities.

Current Challenges Confronting US Higher Education

The introduction described the fundamental belief systems that shape the character of American higher education and distinguish it from higher education in other countries. This section expands on that discussion, describing how the inherent tensions among these central beliefs have created serious challenges for US higher education. The section concludes with a short overview of additional issues on the national higher education agenda.

The Marketplace (Not Government) as Key External Driver

Many believe that the marketplace has overtaken state government as the dominant external force shaping (and reshaping) American higher education, even for public colleges and universities. As noted earlier, government support is not keeping pace with educational expenditures.

Thus in many ways, the market is having more bearing on higher education than government. To create more flexibility, many public colleges and universities are asking for less government regulation and oversight. In some instances, they are even asking for less state money in return for more autonomy. Their argument is that the current structures and accountability requirements impede their capacity to be effective and efficient. The ability to set tuition, seek block-grant funding, and secure freedom from state policies and regulations in areas such as purchasing Current Challenges Confronting US Higher Education and building represent just some of the additional autonomy that public institutions are seeking. Many are pressing for new legislation to provide this freedom through a range of innovations, including public corporations, charter colleges, state enterprise status, and performance contracts. The result is that activities and research in certain fields and disciplines (such as engineering, applied natural science, and agricultural science) become higher institutional priorities because they have stronger market value than do other programmes (such as humanities).

> Many believe that the marketplace has overtaken government as the dominant external force shaping (and reshaping) American higher education.

Institutions create new programmes, alter academic calendars, and pursue different financial aid policies to capture more and better students—particularly those who can afford to pay high tuition prices. For instance, executive MBA programmes are increasingly popular. Institutions seek contracts and partnership agreements, and enhance research programmes with practical applications that have large financial pay-outs. They are changing their institutional structures—for example, by adding new units that focus on generating external grants and bringing new technology to market, by building conference centres, and by creating for-profit subsidiaries. The implications of the growing privatization are that academic research is increasingly focused on marketable knowledge, entrepreneurial priorities are taking precedence, services are being outsourced, and students are carrying an increasing burden to pay higher tuition and fees for their education.

Administrators see little option except to respond to the marketplace, for if their institution does not react effectively, it will not have the necessary resources to offer high-quality and diverse academic programmes. Institutions unable to compete may face trying circumstances as public support continues to fall, students become better-informed consumers, and advances in technology and new entrants into higher education widen the number and reach of competitors. In turn, the ability to compete—for students, resources, faculty, and prestige—becomes a driving strategic force. At its extreme, competition can overtake more traditional academic values such as unfettered inquiry, access and choice for a diverse student population, and critical social commentary. The downside of pursing market goals without appropriately balancing them against the public good is that institutions will no longer be able to uphold their part of the social compact to produce a well-educated citizenry and face the threat of losing their privileged place in American society as they resemble more closely other market-driven organizations.

Higher Education as an Engine of Mobility

Since Second World War, US higher education has been engaged in a process of "massification", that is, expanding to serve students from all walks of life. Motivating this effort is a widespread belief in the power of education to create social and economic mobility and in the morality and social value of making higher education accessible to everyone. Longitudinal data bear out public perceptions: Young people from low-income backgrounds who complete a bachelor's degree have income and employment characteristics after graduation equivalent to their peers from more affluent backgrounds (Choy, 2002). Education truly can be "the great equalizer".

Despite widespread public faith in the value of higher education, the process of massification has not been without its detractors, and progress has been slow and uneven. Higher education did not admit significant numbers of racial and ethnic minorities until after the civil rights movement of the 1960s forced change. Further, despite significant expenditures on financial aid, minority and low-income individuals are still less likely to attend college than whites or students from middle and upper income families—although these gaps have narrowed somewhat. Despite progress in narrowing the access discrepancies, large gaps remain between completion rates. Low-income students come to college less prepared, and must balance academic demands with work and family responsibilities.

Finding ways to increase the enrolment rates of low-income students and encourage their success once enrolled are two of the most important problems facing American higher education. One of the challenges to meeting these goals is that they can conflict with the other central tenets of American higher education: market competition and resistance to government control. For example, institutional competition for the most academically talented students is likely to foster increased use of tuition discounting for students without financial need, which could divert resources away from need based financial aid for low-income students. Similarly, institutions may seek to distinguish themselves in the academic marketplace by becoming more selective in admissions decisions, thereby reducing the number of low income students admitted. A primary role of government in the United States is to mediate the potentially negative effects of competition by insisting that institutions adhere to their missions, providing need-based financial assistance to students, and holding institutions accountable for their performance. Institutional resistance to government control provides a useful check on the ambitions of government, pushing policy makers to focus on ends rather than means and to leave core academic decisions largely in the hands of institutions. Nonetheless, a constant preoccupation of American higher education is this tension between the competitive, ambitious nature of institutions and the interests of government in promoting important public goals, primary among them broad access and widespread success for all students.

Other Current Issues

This section explores some of the other challenges currently facing American higher education. This list is not inclusive, but rather reflects some of the key issues creating sleepless nights for academic leaders.

> Public colleges and universities are in many ways becoming private, as the percentage of state funds in their budgets is dropping—in some cases, to less than 20 per cent.

The Blurring of Institutional Types

American higher education is known for its institutional diversity. However, the characteristics that make many types of institutions distinct are fading. For instance, in some states, community colleges are seeking to offer four-year degrees to meet growing demand for higher education. Public colleges and universities are in many ways becoming private, as the percentage of state funds in their budgets is dropping—in some cases, to less than 20 per cent. They are soliciting gifts and working to build endowments in ways similar to their private counterparts, and are seeking more procedural autonomy from state oversight. At the same time, for-profit institutions are vying for public funds previously reserved only for non-profit institutions.

Documenting Student Learning

American colleges and universities are facing increased external scrutiny of the effectiveness of undergraduate education. As budgets become tighter and tuition continues to rise, taxpayers and policy makers—as well as students and their families—are asking the extent to which their investment is producing real educational results. Simply put, they want to know what and how much students are learning. Outside pressure is mounting on institutions to document student learning, in much the same way that the elementary and secondary education sectors document learning through assessments linked to standards of what students should know and be able to do. Of course, the challenge of demonstrating student learning is much more difficult in higher education because of the diversity of the curricula. Nonetheless, higher education leaders are being challenged to find some way to show that real learning takes place at their institutions.

Internationalizing the Undergraduate Experience

Many US colleges and universities are making a concerted effort to make their institutions and curricula more international and to provide experiences for students that broaden and deepen their understanding of other cultures. At the same time, US institutions continue their efforts to train and educate foreign students, both by bringing them to campus but also through distance education and satellite programmes abroad (although we do not know the extent of US involvement in such cross-border education). However, recent US visa and homeland security policy changes, coupled with an increased desire by foreign universities to recruit abroad, mean that the US share of the international student market is shrinking. Institutions from England, Australia, Canada, and New Zealand, for instance, are establishing a presence abroad and benefiting favourably from their governments' policies. The effect is slowed growth in the number of international students enrolling in American colleges and universities.

Increasing Productivity and Efficiency

Because of increasing pressure to reduce costs, keep tuition increases small, and serve more students, institutions are seeking ways to improve their productivity and efficiency. They are creating administrative efficiencies, such as by streamlining business processes. They are innovating with technology-based teaching to reach more students both on campus and in the broader community through distance education. Many institutions are also beginning to view collaboration as an important strategy. Partnerships include (among other things) joint research, collaborative purchasing arrangements, shared financial services, and inter- institutional academic programmes. These alliances allow partners to extend capabilities; develop research, courses, and services more quickly; generate greater economies of scale; share costly investments; gain access to knowledge and skills; and reduce expenses.

Conclusion

In many ways, the American system of higher education is unique in the world. In its size, diversity of institutions and students, freedom from government controls, and reliance on market forces, it is without peer. However, higher education systems around the globe are struggling with many of the same issues as the United States and are exploring similar strategies, such as imposing tuition to create greater access while instituting student aid programmes, creating a credit system to facilitate student mobility, and standardizing degree programmes. Other nations wrestling with these challenges may benefit by understanding the philosophical beliefs that shape US higher education—distrust of government, faith in markets, and reliance on education as a gateway to social mobility—and the ways in which the United States continually struggles to balance market forces, government intervention, and access to high-quality education.

Note

1. In the United States, several important terms differ in meaning from most of the rest of the world. The term college refers to an institution that typically awards only undergraduate degrees. The term faculty can refer either to an individual professor or to all instructors (e.g., "The Harvard faculty approved a new degree programme.")

References

American Council on Education (2001). *A Brief Guide to US Higher Education*. Washington, DC: American Council on Education.

Anderson, E. (2002). *The New Professoriate: Characteristics, Contributions, and Compensation*. Washington, DC: American Council on Education.

Choy, S. (2002). *Access and Persistence: Findings from 10 Years of Longitudinal Studies of Students*. Washington, DC: American Council on Education.

College Board. (2003). *Trends in Student Aid: 2003*. New York: College Board.

Council for Aid to Education. (2004). *Charitable Giving to Higher Education Stabilizes in 2003; Gifts from Alumni Rebound After a Sharp One-year Decline*.

Eaton, J. (2000). *An Overview of US Accreditation*. Washington, DC: Council for Higher Education Accreditation.

Harvey, W.B. (2003). *Minorities in Higher Education: Annual Status Report*. Washington, DC: American Council on Education.

King, J.E. (2004). *Choice of Institution: Changing Student Attendance Patterns in the 1990s*. ACE Issue Brief. Washington, DC: American Council on Education.

Santa Monica, CA: RAND Corporation, Council for Aid to Education. *See* http://www.cae.org/content/pdf/2004FullPressReleaseVSE2003.pdf.

US Department of Education, National Centre for Education Statistics (2002a). *Findings from the Condition of Education 2002: Non-Traditional Undergraduates*. Washington, DC: Government Printing Office.

US Department of Education, National Centre for Education Statistics (2002b). *Profile of Undergraduates at US Post-Secondary Institutions: 1999-2000*. Washington, DC: Government Printing Office.

US Department of Education, National Centre for Education Statistics (2002c). *Student Financing of Graduate and First-Professional Education, 1999-2000*. Washington, DC: Government Printing Office.

US Department of Education, National Centre for Education Statistics (2003). *Digest of Education Statistics: 2002*. Washington, DC: Government Printing Office.

10
Higher Education in the United States of America

Bilal Ahmad Bhat and *Mujibul Hasan Siddiqui*

Higher education in the United States like other countries of the world is the final stage of formal learning followed by secondary education. This stage of learning, also named by post-secondary education, third stage, or tertiary education occurs most commonly either in colleges or universities in the country. These may be universities, private, liberal arts colleges, or community colleges. Strong research and funding have helped in making American higher education system among the world's most prestigious, making them particularly attractive to students from other countries, professors and researchers in the pursuit of academic excellence. Unlike Tertiary Education System of UK (and in addition Australia), American education is unique in the world by placing a strong emphasis on Liberal Arts Education in its higher education curriculum. US Higher Education is decentralized, complex, diverse, and inclusive. At the national level, there is the Department of Education, but its authority and focus are limited; rather, every 50 states have primary responsibility for supervising Higher Education within their borders. The United States has no equivalent to the centralized national ministry of education found in many countries like India. In the United States, State Governments grant licences/recognitions to higher education institutions, but accreditation, which recognizes academic legitimacy, is a non-governmental, voluntary process carried out by non-profit organizations.

In the modern times, the colleges and universities have assumed an importance far beyond their character and role in earlier times. They are now the world's chief supplier of three ingredients essential to national progress––new inventions, discoveries in science, technology, and other fields of inquiry; expert knowledge of the kind essential to the work of most essential and important institutions; and well-trained adults with the skills required to practice the professions, manage a wide variety of organizations, and perform an increasing proportion of the more demanding jobs in an advanced, technologically sophisticated economy. In addition, they help a nation in strengthening their democracy by educating its future leaders, preparing students to be active role players, knowledgeable citizens, and offering informed, valued, and positive critiques of government programmes and policies. Not least, they supply the knowledge and ideas that create new industries, new organizations, protect us from disease, preserve and enrich our culture, tradition and inform us about our history, our environment, our shared goals, our society, and ourselves. Because of the essential role that higher education play, almost everyone has a right of sharing things in having them perform well. By several measures, American Higher Education System has succeeded handsomely. In a recent ranking compiled by times higher education, six out of the ten highest-rated universities in the world were located in the United States. More than half of all Nobel Laureates in science and economics since Second World War did their most important work while serving on faculties in this country. The colleges and graduate schools of America have long been the destination of choice for students around the world who have the chance to study outside their own country. Because of these achievements, more and more nations around the world are adapting their systems of higher education to conform more closely to the American model.

Great Strengths of US Higher Education

The higher system of education in the US is unlike those in Europe or Asia or South America in one simple way: the United States has no central Ministry of Education for maintenance and other things. This is the characteristic feature of American higher education. This is why America has the best universities in the world (by pretty much on any measure), they do have a Department of Education, but it has little role. It does not run schools or universities. It does not issue diplomas, certificates. It does not write or choose or frame curricula. So, each college or university decides for itself how best to teach its students in their own ways. This is the first great strength of US Higher Education. It has diversity in higher education. With over 4,000 accredited colleges and universities, the US system provides so many learning options that virtually all students can study what they want in a way that works for them as per their choice and need. For example, though most colleges teach mathematics and science traditionally, others go deeper into the historical roots of these subjects. St. John's College (with campuses in New Mexico and Maryland) teaches every subject through its great books. So, physics students read Sir Isaac Newton's Principia Mathematica and geometry students read Euclid's Elements.

The decentralized nature of US Higher Education gives colleges and universities the flexibility to change with new generations of students and with our evolving world around us. In fact, flexibility—the second great strength of the US system—continues to put US universities at the top of almost every international university ranking published. The reason is simple: US universities can do what other universities can't do by putting themselves under some central boards. For instance, consider interdisciplinary research. Some of the most exciting and relevant research requires input from several different disciplines, and since US professors are not bound by Ministry- approved curricula, they can reach out across disciplines and specializations to create cutting edge institutes or departments in completely new fields of study, like Psycholinguistics (MIT, 1956) or Bioethics (Georgetown, 1971).The feature not only attracts attention to US university research, it also gives students at all levels the opportunity to study topics not offered elsewhere in the world. The flexibility is of the nature that most degree programmes require a certain number of classes in the discipline and students can choose the rest of their schedule. This means that if two students are studying a subject (international relations) at the same university at the same time, one can focus on the developing economies in Sub-Saharan Africa, while the other can focus on twentieth century totalitarianism in East Asia.

In short, the decentralized nature of the US educational system allows each university and college to decide, how it will teach its students. It also allows students and professors within each university a lot more freedom. Because, no one is restricted or bounded by Ministry regulations, students and teachers can work across disciplines and even create new fields of study as long as they are fulfilling university requirements.

The third strength US universities have its international students. International students bring new opinions, ideas to the classroom, new experiences to campus, and new ideas to the research conducted in laboratories and libraries nationwide. And US universities love it to have great international students just like international students want to find great universities. Because, we know that helping the best students find their way to our universities benefits us as much as it helps students.

Authority and Responsibility for US Higher Education

The Role of the Federal Government and the US Department of Education

The Federal Government does not control or serve as the primary foundered US Higher Education, as the governments of most other countries do through their ministries of education. (The exceptions in the United States are several federal institutions, including Howard University, the military academies, and 28 tribal colleges.) Instead, each state is responsible for most aspects of education within its territories. State authority on private colleges and universities generally is very limited. The American Department of Education is involved in the regulation of education in a limited way. Its primary areas of concern are: (1) the use of federal funds granted to higher education institutions through grants and to students attending those institutions; (2) the implementation of legislation, such as the Civil Rights Act, which involves higher education; (3) programmes designed to encourage particular types of curriculum development, such as foreign language training and area studies programmes; (4) special programmes designed to help make higher education opportunities available to people with various type of challenges like visual challenge, hearing challenge etc.; and (5) federal funds for research in a wide range of areas, including health, science, international studies, space, and the environment.

The Role of the States

As it has been mentioned that there are two types of higher education institutions in the US which are mostly established by the state (public colleges and universities) or receive their charters from them (most private institutions). State governments of 50 states of US possess legal authority to regulate and approve their continued operations, even though independent non-governmental bodies carry out the accreditation. The state departments of education, state boards of higher education, and in some cases, state universities or special state commissions share responsibility for the institutes of higher education. Private higher education institutes like colleges and universities have their own governing boards but are subject to state laws governing non-profit and for-profit organizations. It is important to emphasize that state licensing does not imply accreditation of these institutes. In fact, some state-licensed "colleges" or "universities" are not legitimate education institutions at all, but rather "diploma mills"—business operations that issue bogus degrees with the purpose of business in mind.

Governance of Higher Education in the United States

The issues of power, authority, and responsibility in higher education remain debatable. Conflicts between governing boards and presidents are recurrent. Issues pertaining to the authority regarding faculty senate are commonplace, especially insofar as academic matters are concerned. Governing boards have the ultimate executor responsibility for their institutions, but their recurrent tendency to become directly involved in the day-to-day functions of the institution is a repeated cause of tension among boards, presidents, and faculty. Similarly, some presidents believe that the faculty (and often the senate) has too much power in their hands. Many faculty members are of the opinion that the academic aspects of the institution are (or should be) run by the faculty, with the board and the president providing an effective teaching and working environment conducive for best results. In public institutions, conflict of governance may be solved with the help of political intervention by the governing board, the members of which often are appointed by the governor or by legislative action. Private institutions appoint their own boards and are protected from direct political interference. The role of students in the governance structure also remains a debatable issue at some institutions.

Administrative Structure in Higher Education Institutions

The organizational structure of the higher education institutes in the US reflects the institution's size, philosophy, and objectives and usually is influenced by the interrelated priorities placed on teaching, research, and extension. These institutes (colleges and universities) have multiple levels of administration, each with specific functions. The structure of the higher is as under:

(i) The Board, (ii) The Chief Executive Officer, (iii) Academic Vice President, (iv) Graduate Dean, (v) Dean of Students, (vi) School Dean, (vii) Department Chair, and (viii) Other Administrators.

The Board

In the area of administrative activities, higher education institutions in the United States have many similarities. In all cases and in all states, the highest level of administration is the governing or policy-making body. This body may be called with different nomenclatures like aboard of regents, the board of trustees, or board of governors. Members of public boards may be appointed by the governor, elected by voters, or chosen in part by the groups they represent (such as alumni). Boards of Private Institutions often are "self-perpetuating": the board members themselves select new members as others' terms expire. In most cases, some constituencies (such as alumni) elect their own representatives. Governing boards are responsible for appointing the president (or chancellor) to the institution and creating general, fiscal, and academic policy to ensure their institutions' effective and efficient operation. While boards typically are an institution's highest authority, they share power and responsibility with the president, senate, and other bodies. For example, in academic areas, primary authority usually resides with the faculty, often represented by the senate and committees. Nevertheless, many academic issues require final approval by the board.

The Chief Executive Officer (President or Chancellor)

The chief executive officer oversees the day-to-day activities of the institution; ensures that the policies/rules of the governing board are implemented; and facilitates the academic programme of the institution by working with various stakeholders, such as students and faculty. An increasingly important expectation of the president is fund raising from different sources. The president also is the mediator between the board and the college or university community. He or she may also make policy recommendations to the governing board on behalf of the academic community. At most institutions, the president is selected by and reports directly to the board.

Academic Vice President or Dean

The academic vice president—sometimes called the dean of the college, the provost, or the dean of the faculty—is the chief academic officer of a college or university. He or she reviews or approves individual faculty appointments, appoints and supervises the academic administrative officers, reviews and approves administrative policies in all educational areas, and assists department chairs in evaluating and advising faculty members. The academic vice president works in close with the faculty on academic matters and is framer of curriculum development. Most institutions in the US have several other vice presidents for such areas as planning, finance, or student affairs, depending on their size and structure.

Graduate Dean

The chief graduate school has institution-wide responsibilities for graduate programmes and research carried out in conjunction with institutional activities. Included within these responsibilities are programme evaluation, programme initiation and termination, supervision of graduate faculty, and research administration. Depending on the size of the institution and the degree of centralization of administrative efforts, these responsibilities may be carried out by the vice president or dean or coordinated among a variety of semi-autonomous, discipline-based units. The chief graduate school research officer also is responsible for coordinating the university's research efforts involving federal, state, and private industry funding.

Dean of Students

In undergraduate life, experiences outside the usual classroom make an important contribution to student learning in their lives. These sometimes are referred to as the "co-curriculum," campus life programmes and events include clubs, speaker series, student newspapers, theatre etc. Deans of students or vice presidents of student affairs look after these activities, as well as hostels and student conduct issues.

School Dean

At universities with separate schools or faculties or departments, these units usually are headed and look after by a school dean.

Department Chair

The basic or fundamental unit of academic organization in most institutions is the department (e.g. physics, economics etc.). The department chair is bound with the administration of instruction; represents the department's academic, financial, and personal interests; and initiates searches for new faculty members like assistant professors, associate professors etc. The chair serves as a medium of interaction between the dean of a school or college (in a large unit) or the chief academic officer and the department members. Among the several responsibilities of the chair the most chief responsibilities, with other tenured members of the department, are faculty recruitment, evaluations for reappointment, and salary increases. The chair works and coordinates with the registrar to address the department's classroom needs, serves as a mediator with other units, develops relationships with students majoring in the department, and addresses and identifies teaching problems within the department. Chairs may be elected by the members of the academic department or named by the administration, or some combination of the two.

Other Administrators

Other appointments are made as per the need of higher education institutes for deans or directors, according to the institution's size. These chairs are responsible for such areas as graduate programmes, institutional budget, and business affairs, student admissions, financial aid, supervision of hostels, foreign student advising, and other academic and non-academic activities.

Registrar

The record keeping officer of the institution is named as the registrar. The office of the registrar organizes student course enrolment, frames academic requirements for degrees, certifies students for academic honours, requests grades from faculty members, keeps records of student grades, notifies the advising office of academic deficiencies, and notifies officers or committees of students who do not meet the institution's minimum standards. Its office prepares directories of registered students; schedules and enforces deadlines; determines class hours, classrooms, and final examination schedules; and considers requests from applicants for changes in any of these.

Chief Development Officer

This position is occasionally referred to as vice president for development (or community and external relations) or director of development. Functions of the office include fund raising, publicity, alumni relations, and records.

Government Relations Officer

A government relations officer—especially at a public institution—is responsible for serving as a medium with state and Federal Governments. The office frequently is chaired by a vice president for external affairs. Duties/functions include legislative affairs, public relations, and communicating with state and national agencies.

The Faculty and the Senate

The faculty is an important part of the shared structured US higher education system. The primary responsibility of the faculty members is the institutional curriculum and research and often involved in finance, student discipline, and strategic planning. Faculty exercises its control through an elected senate and committees. At most institutions, academic functions are handled separately from operations and financial management. The former are much more hierarchical, representing at least a division of labour (especially at research universities), if not a clear demarcation of authority. At some higher education institutions, both administrative and academic functions are operated according to a strict hierarchy in which the board and the president are at the top and faculty authority is having limited authority. In institutions at which the faculty is unionized, management functions are very much clearly differentiated from teaching, research, and service.

Types of US Higher Education Institutions

There are two types of higher education institutions in America, namely community colleges and four-year colleges and universities.

Community Colleges

The 2-year institutions or technical or junior colleges award associate degrees upon completion of a 2-year programme of study. There are nearly 1,200 two-year institutions in the United States, serving more than 11 million students. An associate degree enables students to Transfer to a 4-year college or university to obtain a bachelor's degree, usually after 2 additional years of study.

Four-Year Colleges and Universities

The other institutions are known as four-year colleges and universities which award bachelor's degrees in arts or science (BA or BS) and also may award graduate and professional degrees. The points or credits earned at community colleges are accepted for transfer into almost all 4-year college and university bachelor's degree programmes. Four-year higher education institutions provide a variety of degrees including bachelor's, master's, and doctorate, and professional degrees in fields such as business law, and medicine.

The Academic Year

The academic year of US higher education institutions is usually divided into two semesters of four months each, or three-quarters of three months each. A full-time enrolled student takes four or five courses in each semester or three or four courses in each quarter. The first academic year of higher education (called the freshman year) and the second year (called the sophomore year) are mainly focused on general studies. Students having completed their freshman and sophomore years at a community college obtain an associate degree .The third academic year called by the junior year and focuses on amore intensive study in the chosen major area. The fourth and final academic year towards obtaining a bachelor's degree is called the senior years. It is commonly referred to students by their academic year of study, viz. students are called by freshmen, sophomores, juniors, or seniors as per their academic years.

Freedom of Choice

There is a choice for students to choose their own courses and class schedules. Due to this freedom, there is great responsibility on students for making the right choice to achieve their educational goals. There are advisers, always ready to give advicethat will help students make the right decisions among the available choices.

Course Credits

There are certain credits for each course successfully completed. The number of credits is directly related to the number of hours assigned to the course by the college or university. For example, successful completion of a course that meets for 1 hour, four times a week equals a total of 4 credits. The same course for which lab is necessary, with an additional hour of laboratory work equals 4 credits.

Course Grades

Grades received by the student at the end of a course are used to indicate how well the student performed, how much, and whether the course was successfully completed. The range of grades is from A to F, with A as the best possible grade. An F indicates failure. All grades received by a student during a course of study are combined to determine the student's grade point average (GPA).

Accreditation, Quality, and Standards

The two core values of higher education institutions that shape the quality assurance process, that is, the importance of quality and high standards, and institutional autonomy. In that context, the accreditation process has developed on voluntarily, non-governmental, self-regulatory structures basis. The US Department of Education is not responsible for accreditation, quality control, or standards, as there are ministries in many other countries for such purpose. In US, there are two basic types of accreditation: institutional and specialized.

Institutional accreditation gives recognition for an institution as a whole, while specialized accreditation recognizes a programme or unit within an institution. Specialized accreditation is most common in professional courses such as medicine, law, social work, and journalism. The accreditation process ensures that colleges and universities maintain academic standards, are adequately managed and are eligible to have participation in certain federal programmes. There are accreditation associations, guided by a framed set of expectations about quality and integrity. These associations send teams of administrators and faculty members from other institutions for a site visit to the institutions which are to be accredited. Sometimes, professionals from the subject area are being involved in reviewing the accreditation process. The teams of creditors then make judgments and communicate the decisions to the institution. If a programme or institution falls below established standards, then the institution is being given a notice that it could lose accreditation if standards are not achieved within a reasonable set the team of experts. The accreditation process is coordinated, and to some extent overseen or overlooked by the Council for Higher Education Accreditation (CHEA).

Institutional Accreditation

The accreditation of Institution is granted by the regional and national accrediting associations, which collectively serve in most of the institutions chartered or licensed in the United States for Higher Education. The eight such regional associations accredit most of the non-profit two-year and four-year-degree-granting and some preparatory institutions in America. The national level associations accredit many for-profit universities and professional schools, both degree-granting and certificate programmes. Some bible colleges and seminaries also are being accredited by these national associations. Although accreditation is generally being granted for a specific term, usually 10 years of duration, accrediting bodies have the right to review member institutions or programmes at any time of academic year. Institutional accreditation, though voluntary, is necessary for the survival of colleges. It is a basic consideration of parents, prospective students, and counsellors in choosing an institution; loss of accreditation, or threat of loss, would always adversely affect student enrolment in the institution. It would destroy the institution's ability to recruit good faculty members. The Institutions must be accredited to receive federal funds from the government, and it is always a prerequisite for funding from other foundations as well. Graduation from an accredited institution generally is a minimum requirement for admission to graduate school. Employers in the market seldom recognize credentials obtained from a non-accredited institution.

Specialized Accreditation

Specialized accreditation of occupational and professional schools and programmes is granted by commissions set up by national professional organizations in fields such as business, medicine, art, dance, journalism, engineering, and law to provide assurances of educational preparation. Each of these groups has a distinctive and characteristic definition of eligibility, criteria for accreditation, and operating procedures. Many only consider requests for accreditation reviews for programmes affiliated with colleges that are holding institutional accreditation. However, some specialized agencies accredit professional programmes at independent institutions that only offer the particular discipline or course of study. Because this accreditation given is often been used by state licensing authorities, graduation from an accredited programme is essential for most students seeking licensure as, dentists, practicing architects, engineers, lawyers, physicians, and many other professions.

Council for Higher Education Accreditation (CHEA)

The Council for Higher Education Accreditation (CHEA) helps in preserving the independence and autonomy of the accreditation process. CHEA is a national level membership organization of colleges and universities in the USA. It focuses on the quality and process of accreditation. It constantly engages itself in re-evaluating and resetting expectations for recognition of accrediting organizations and recognizing those which meet its expectations. It coordinates research, analysis, and debate; collects and disseminates information about good practices in accreditation and quality assurance; and helps in solving disputes between higher education institutions and creditors.

Internationalization

Many American Higher Education Institutions are constantly intensifying their efforts to internationalize their curriculum, research, and service functions. In 1946 a Fulbright Programme for student, scholar and teacher exchanges was established to encourage international exchanges. Many interdisciplinary area studies programmes were developed at most major research universities between the 1950s and 1960s, (and some other institutions) to study Latin America, Africa, Russia, Europe, the Middle East, and Asia; attention was also focused on language study and a broad range of political, social, and cultural aspects of other parts of the world to internationalize the institutions in America. The Cold War between two blocks after Second World War added urgency to the efforts of internationalization, and the Federal Government provided substantial funding for training, scholarship, and travel through a variety of programmes, including foreign language and area studies grants. With the end of the Cold War, this funding was reduced somewhat. Because of the financial pressures in the 1980s, many faculty members in languages and international studies were not replaced. Federal support for international programmes also fell down; for example, funding for Fulbright-Hays and Title VI programmes get dropped by 43 per cent and 14 per cent, respectively, from their high points in the 1960s. On the other hand, the number of students studying foreign languages increased slightly from 1990 to 1998, languages, as a percentage of total enrolments, dropped from 8.2 per cent in 1990 to 7.9 per cent in 1998, only half of that what was there in 1960. A major concern is that whether the graduates of US colleges and universities will have the knowledge and language skills they need to be effective to act as global citizens in the new millennium. Will the America be able to compete effectively in an increasingly global scenario of the economic, intellectual, and political arena, taking consideration of its diminished pool of area specialists and graduates who are less well-prepared to understand and operate in an international environment than in other countries' graduates? As the problems of political, economic, social, health and environment become acuter with each passing day; there is a need for effective economic, political, and social relations that will depend on the ability of citizens of different nations to understand and communicate effectively with one another.

References

American Council on Education. (2001). *A Brief Guide to US Higher Education.* Washington, DC: American Council on Education.

American Council on Education. (2001). *American Universities and Colleges.* New York: Walter de Gruyter: James J. Murray III.

Eaton, J. (2000). *An Overview of US Accreditation.* Washington, DC: Council for Higher Education Accreditation.

Haidar, H. (2014, May 28). *What is Liberal Arts Education*? Retrieved from http://www.topuniversities.com/blog/what-liberal-arts-education

Jeffrey, J. (2013, May 8). *With Gorgeous Dorms but Little Cash, Colleges Must Adapt.* Retrieved from http://www.npr.org/2013/05/08/181580716/with-gorgeous-dorms-but-little-cash-colleges-must-adapt

Peter D. Eckel and Jacqueline E. King, R. (2006). *An Overview of higher education in the United States: Diversity, Access, and the Role of the Marketplace.* In J. Forest and P. Altbach, (Eds.), Retrieved from http://www.acenet.edu/news-room/Documents/Overview-of-Higher-Education-in-the-United-States-Diversity-Access-and-the-Role-of-the-Marketplace-2004.pdf.

Phil Batty. (2010, September 16). *The World University Rankings: Measure by Measure: the US is the best of the best.* Retrieved from https://www.timeshighereducation.com/world-university-rankings/2010-11/world-ranking/analysis/usa-top-universities

USA Education. (2016, April 13). Retrieved from http://www.hitost.com/2016/04/usa-education.html

World University Rankings 2015-2016. (n.d.). Retrieved from https://www.timeshighereducation.com/world-university-rankings/2016/world-ranking#!/page/0/length/25/sort_by/rank_label/sort_order/asc/cols/rank_only

Section-II
Comparative Perspective

11

Higher Education in India and Abroad Comparatively

Shah Raziq Khalid

Enrolment of international students in institutions of higher education in the United States continues to rise, and US colleges and universities increasingly recognize the need to prepare domestic students to work in a global economy and to function effectively as global citizens and leaders. Although institutions of higher education in the US are academically among the top worldwide, they are nonetheless continually challenged by the need to simultaneously address the cognitive, social, and intrapersonal development of students—a linked, integrated activity now called learning (Keeling, 2004). Even still, programmes, services, and systems of support may remain fragmented and unintegrated despite the interwoven nature of learning. In the past, such fragmentation had been common among US institutions, but in recent years sophisticated student affairs, models and infrastructures have developed, which have dramatically improved the student experience (and therefore, student success) in US colleges and universities. The questions we address in this article are: Can these methodologies be effectively transported to higher education institutions in developing nations, like India? How should they be modified to coalesce with the current departmental and administrative structures within Indian institutions? Have Indian institutions begun to make similar realizations about the global economy and taken logical, subsequent steps? We focus our attention in this article on India — which has arguably the fastest growing higher education market in the world — but similar changes are rapidly occurring in many other developing nations.

Some Indian institutions have already initiated the process of change. Surprisingly, it has not been among traditional public Indian universities, but among privately funded campus-based institutions and distance learning programmes, which are both trying to fulfil a national demand and distinguish themselves among the elite world institutions. By incorporating student affairs programmes and services—and endeavouring to reach out to aid underprivileged students—these newly created, non-traditional institutions could promote a different kind of graduate in India; one who is socially, developmentally, and globally competent. Striving to be more than diploma mills, these institutions are aware of the skills needed to be successful in a global environment, and are beginning to respond in kind.

Higher Educational Reform in India

Despite political and economic constraints—due to which India may have to accept slower economic growth than that forecasted in its fiscal and political agenda—Indian Prime Minister Manmohan Singh has unveiled a rigorous plan to create forty new universities, mostly in information technology, management, science education and research (Neelakantan, 2007). Waylaid by Parliament, progress in improving current institutions and increasing the number of Central Universities has been scant—even with the establishment of political entities like the National Knowledge Commission, a high level advisory body to the Prime Minister with the objective of transforming India into a knowledge society (Sinha, 2006). The Knowledge Commission indicated through a recent report that it must increase the number of current universities, 350 to 1,500 by 2015 in order "to raise the proportion of 18 to 24 year old entering higher education to at least 15 per cent" (Neelakantan, 2008). Political roadblocks notwithstanding, such statistics indicate a strong demand for quality higher education programmes in India.

With a new generation of successful Indian professionals anxious to give back to their country, and the remarkably increased interest in private investment in Indian education, a new breed of Indian educational institutions has recently surfaced, unfettered by the constraints of governmental funding and bureaucracy. One must inquire whether contemporary private institutions are in a better position and/or better qualified than their traditional and esteemed publicly funded competitors for reaching the goal of delivering quality education to a broad sub-section of the Indian population. Given their private funding, do they promote labour skills over critical faculties, and threaten to suppress voices of imagination in the educational culture? Martha Nussbaum (2007) wrote in the *Chronicle of Higher Education* that in India, "such [imaginative] voices have now been silenced by the sheer demand for profitability in the global market." Explicit in Nussbaum's statement is the notion that learning has become second priority; in order to respond to the present economic boom and fuel these thriving businesses, creativity and innovation are being replaced by mechanization and standardization. Indeed, for many—not just in India—higher education has become an entrepreneurial enterprise. For profit institutions have often neglected student development and learning activities and focused instead on analysing profit margins and actively seeking investors. In this regard, some concern should linger about whether or not appropriate skills befitting a knowledge society are even being developed, and consider the indelible effects of a system that may be devoid of channels for academic innovation.

Nonetheless, it is important to bear in mind that in a developing nation such as India, where only 7 per cent of the college-age population currently receives any form of higher education at all (with similar fractions matriculating in other developing countries), it is essential for the near-term economic development of the nation to explore new channels for educational delivery. Moreover, current dogmas concerning the comparative quality of education at small, for profit institutions *versus* public schools must be carefully reassessed in the Indian context. Even the oldest, most highly ranked schools in India could benefit from some degree of academic overhaul. India currently has 350 universities and 15,600 colleges, most of them public, graduating 2.5 million students each year. Every year, 350,000 students graduate with degrees in engineering—twice the number of engineering graduates in the US, but still a tiny fraction of the total population of 18 to 24 year old. Despite its sheer number of university and college graduates, not one Indian public university ranks among the top 300 schools worldwide. Of course, there are several Indian public universities, such as the Indian Institute of Science (IISc), which ranks in the top 400, and the Indian Institutes of Technology (IITs)—that excel in both teaching and research. But by and large, India's public education system is lagging behind international standards. For example, China has 6 public universities in the top 300. The top 100 world universities are largely concentrated in the US, Canada and Europe (Liu & Cheng, 2005).

What is it that distinguishes these latter institutions from the rest? Certainly, faculty quality and educational resource budgets play a dominant role, but at an undergraduate level, middle-tier schools generally teach much the same academic curriculum as their top-tier counterparts. In the US and Europe, numerous studies have indicated that a dominant factor that contributes to the success of the most highly ranked schools is the attention afforded directly to the student and complementary support structures that exist for the primary goal of maximizing the productivity of the student experience (Schulz, Lee, Cantwell, McClellan, & Woodard, 2007). Historically, such attention has been lacking in India, and indeed in developing nations as a whole. However, some institutions—most of them private—are proving to be the exception; they understand the advantages in providing more comprehensive student services, how they can be integrated throughout the whole institution, and how they are essential for entrepreneurial success. For example, defining and implementing a student affairs model and structure can lead to a greater level of institutional uniqueness, which in turn, could make a university more competitive by providing a superior student experience. A drive towards globalization in higher education—especially in the form of educational partnerships and student exchange programmes across international boundaries—is providing further impetus for the implementation of compatible student affairs models in developing nations (Schulz *et al.*, 2007).

In what follows, we survey the role that such student support and institutional assessment strategies play in Indian public and private traditional universities, Indian distance learning institutions, and collabourative international initiatives between Indian and foreign institutions. We illustrate our observations with specific examples drawn from institutions visited first-hand in the state of West Bengal.

A New Breed of Indian University: Private Institutions with Student Support Structures

Broadly speaking, Indian universities—especially those supported by the Central Government—have not been held to any level of institutional accountability with respect to student support structures. Throughout the United States, variations exist around a strong commitment to address student needs and issues that affect student learning and engagement; for example, many US institutions have health services departments, including counselling services, disability services, health promotion, and mental health services. Provoked by recent public attention, parents, students, and prioritization by Secretary of Education Margaret Spellings, institutional accountability has increased across the board (Spellings Commission Final Report, 2006). For parents of upper middle class US students, a primary attractor of top-tier universities is their doting attention to individual student needs. For example, students at top US institutions are assigned individual tutors, receive access to clubs and state-of-the-art athletic facilities, and have readily available health services and mental health advising; such individualized services do not exist in India.

In India, institutions such as Presidency College, the IITs, and the University of Delhi are the analogue of top-tier Western universities. These universities are highly selective in their entrance requirements, and typically, most admitted students come from upper or middle class Indian families. However, similar student support services are lacking from almost every Indian traditional top-tier university. In India, the traditional lack of competition in providing high quality higher education has resulted in a lack of motivation for the development of such infrastructures even in the top schools.

For example, a visit to Presidency College in Kolkata, a premier college affiliated with the University of Kolkata in West Bengal, indicates a curious admixture of the best and brightest young minds and Indian faculty, but essentially absent horizontal communication channels between them. Many Presidency students, recognizing the difficulty of gaining acceptance to this leading Indian institution for undergraduate studies, find receiving lectures from distinguished professors sufficient in itself, and do not press for more progressive opportunities for interactive learning. Still, interviews with undergraduates at top public Indian universities reveal that many students find it increasingly difficult to cope with the competition inherent in an oversaturated market where only the top graduates will gain acceptance to a premier graduate programme or even find a well-paying job (personal communication with students from Presidency College, July 3, 2007). These interviews indicate that student depression may be pervasive, but there is no formal record of such reports or actions taken to counsel despondent students. Over the last decade, however, India has developed new and progressive institutions—some of which are beginning to emulate foreign models, and some of which are innovating themselves in order to provide a better comprehensive student experience. Heritage Institute of Technology (HIT) in Kolkata—a premier privately funded educational institution, created and financed by the Kalyan Bharti Trust (established by a consortium of successful

North Indian Entrepreneurs and Professionals), has only been in existence for six years. It has become a model for the new generation of private Indian institutions of higher education, even pulling faculty away from prestigious government funded universities because of the depth of financial resources from which to draw (Probir Roy, Vice Chancellor, HIT & Pradip Agarwal, CEO, Kalyan Bharti Trust, personal communication, October 28, 2007). HIT has been focusing on enhancing the overall student experience and creating structures and metrics that will accurately gauge student success. HIT is adjacent to the K-12 Heritage School, which provides and mandates diverse extracurricular activities such as yoga and swimming. HIT formed a functional Alumni Association, created a Student's Council consisting of committees like Cultural, Academic, Magazine, Games, and Sports, and approved of student chapters of Computer Society of India (CSI), Instrumentation, Systems, and Automation Society (ISA), Indian Institute of Chemical Engineers (IIChE) and Institute of Electrical and Electronics Engineers, who frequently organize seminars and workshops.

HIT is in pursuit of very progressive student support systems, which may inform and be informed by the most popular student support models currently employed in the US and Canada—inclusive among these models are the best practices for primary care and mental health services. HIT provides medical insurance for all students (virtually non-existent among Indian public universities) as well as free textbooks and laptops. A sophisticated IT infrastructure, engineered in collabouration with private industry, supports the dissemination of these services. Throughout these efforts, HIT maintains a strong relationship with students in advancing their standing in a global setting. One student received an academic award as the World Wide Topper, an achievement that has always been a priority of both the Indian and British educational systems. Others have won international engineering contests, due increasingly to efforts by the Heritage administration to promote participation.

These remarkable achievements are enabled in part through the consistent training of faculty in the latest communication technologies and teaching methodologies. Pradip Agarwal, Chief Executive Officer of the Kalyan Bharti Trust, highlighted the faculty enrichment programme at Heritage, which provides on-site training in both technical and administrative skills to faculty and community members at select corporate institutions (P. Roy and P. Agarwal, personal communication, July 3, 2007). HIT students are also encouraged to reach beyond the walls of the university to partake in integrative and service learning programmes, such as teaching computer software skills to underprivileged children in India. Such service programmes are especially important in developing nations, since they foster a sense of national awareness in students who might otherwise lose touch with their roots in an effort to modernize.

US and other foreign universities have begun to contact private Indian universities in search of collabourative student exchange programmes. For example, the London School of Economics (LSE) and New Jersey Institute of Technology (NJIT) have recently entered into negotiations with HIT. As discussed further below, the progressive approach of private institutions increases their willingness to send Indian students to take courses in the US for a semester, as HIT is doing in 2008 with NJIT. In turn, HIT seeks to offer international students an academic experience comparable to that they would receive at a top-tier Indian institution, while simultaneously offering a student experience on their own campus not unlike that at Western institutions. Established public universities may possess an advantage in terms of name recognition, but progressive Indian higher education institutions have a substantial advantage over public institutions in developing compatible student affairs structures, due to their flexibility and willingness to adopt infrastructures aligned with those of Western schools.

Despite these developments, a primary challenge facing both the Heritage Institute and Presidency College is the cultivation of a student affairs structure that supports innovation. In order to achieve this goal, it is necessary that students can regularly and freely interact with members of multiple departments, such that cross-departmental collabouration can be achieved. This might be implemented through the engineering of effective horizontal and vertical structures that bridge the existing gap among faculty, administrators and students (Keeling, Underhile & Wall, 2007). Western educational leaders have recently begun to implement such structures within US, Canadian, and European schools; many of the same lessons are likely to be equally applicable within India.

HIT's efforts mirror in many ways developments at the Harrisburg University of Science and Technology (HUST) in Pennsylvania. Both institutions were founded in 2001 with a focus on science and technology, and both have taken a unique, accelerated path towards becoming a full-fledged university. HIT will undergo a review for university status by the National Board Accreditation next year. HUST seeks Middle States accreditation in 2009. Despite these similarities, the market demand and potential for growth of new private Indian institutions like HIT is substantially higher than that of comparable US institutions. Further efforts on the part of international educators to deploy their expertise on student support structures would have a tangible impact on the quality of the private sector of the Indian educational system.

Higher Education for the Masses: Innovations in Distance Learning

Whereas private institutions like Heritage have a substantial charitable endowment from which to draw in their efforts to design sophisticated student support structures, distance learning institutions—largely publicly funded at present and in the eyes of many the most essential component for transforming a developing nation into a knowledge community—must find innovative ways to deliver quality higher education to the underprivileged masses of the country under tight resource constraints.

Due to their more affordable tuition fees, distance learning schools do not typically provide traditional student support services. Experiments with distance learning in the United States indicate that it is nonetheless possible to effectively monitor learning outcomes through a dialogue with students. For example, the University of Phoenix, the largest US virtual university, does not offer traditional services, having no sports, fitness centres, student unions, fraternities, museums, research labouratories, or alumni events (Bachorz & Cronin, 2006). In fact, the majority of students at such institutions are too busy with employment and family affairs to be able to spend time on such services, even if they were to be offered. Still, Phoenix cares about students, especially student retention and persistence, ensuring that students who start a degree ordinarily complete a programme. For example, Phoenix staff instructs online students they are expected to log on four times a week; if they do not, a representative phones them to see what is wrong and what help they need. By contrast, most traditional colleges do not check in until mid-semester warning time, which is often too late. Another Phoenix trademark is a tailor-made curriculum for distance learning students that differs fundamentally from the semester system at traditional schools. Courses are designed by a committee of subject-matter experts and standardized across the system in short semester blocks of five to six weeks.

Granted, distance learning institutions in the US are vastly different from those located in India. In the US, although more than 2,700 campus locations span the 50 states, the geographic size of the sector is matched by low enrolment numbers (Kinser, 2006). The opposite holds true in India, where some institutions now exceed enrolment of 100,000 students. In fact, the five largest distance learning programmes in the world are all based in developing countries. They claimed an aggregate enrolment of roughly 2 million students even in 1997, and account for 10 per cent of enrolment growth in developing countries during the past two decades. Quality control and institutional assessment take on entirely new meanings in such a context. Moreover, a distinguishing feature of distance learning initiatives in India (as well as those in Europe) is that several of the largest such initiatives are government-funded. Is attention to student learning outcomes the norm in Indian distance learning initiatives? Is it reasonable to expect such attention to detail with a much larger student body and a greater dearth of qualified faculty?

Surprisingly, the answer is a resounding yes. Netaji Subhash Open University (NSOU), located in Kolkata, is currently a leader in the field of Indian distance learning, experiencing phenomenal growth since its founding in 1997 with the mission of "providing wider access to higher education especially to the backward and weaker sections of society." (Surabhi Banerjee, Vice Chancellor, NSOU, personal communication, July 4, 2007). This includes a 2646 per cent increase in enrolment, 346 per cent increase in study centres, and 367 per cent increase in the number of courses offered since 2002. In addition to undergraduate and masters programmes in all the central natural sciences and IT disciplines, since 2004 NSOU has been offering a Ph.D. programme in 8 different subjects (NSOU, 2007). These growth metrics dwarf those of US institutions like the University of Phoenix and provide an indicator of the tremendous opportunities surfacing in the Indian distance learning arena. This growth has been accompanied by an attention to student learning outcomes that is uncommon among traditional mega universities. NSOU was recently recognized and awarded for its attention to student success through the Commonwealth of Learning Excellence in Distance Education Award at the Pan Commonwealth Forum Conference on distance learning held in Jamaica in 2006 (NSOU, 2006).

NSOU has embraced developments in affordable information technology in its drive to establish a vital two-way learning interface to students that would be impossible to achieve under traditional models. Indeed, administrators like Vice Chancellor Surabi Banerjee have attributed much of NSOU's recent success to its ability to deploy high-speed communication links to the rural villages of West Bengal. Historically, a major bottleneck for advancing virtual education had been in the availability of sufficient IT resources in rural settings. The Indian government's strong new commitment to enhancing distance learning opportunities through cutting edge information technology is perhaps most clearly demonstrated *via* its launch of EduSat, a satellite intended solely for transmitting virtual distance learning programmes to all parts of India, in particular its remote rural sectors. EduSat will support 25 to 30 uplinks and about 5000 remote terminals per uplink. The Indian government, fully aware that the success or failure of the EduSat initiative is contingent on the quality of the content, has organized five regional and one national conference to discuss the capabilities and future use of the system, especially by distance learning institutions. NSOU currently has one on-campus EduSat receive terminal and has taken steps to establish an audio-visual studio that will be used to transmit teaching programmes to the remote sectors of West Bengal (Indian Space Research Organization, 2004).

Still, there is often a substantial gap between access to information technology and its efficient exploitation by users in rural settings. There are many outstanding challenges to be met in properly assessing learning outcomes associated with curricula transmitted through EduSat. In the meantime, established US distance learning institutions including the University of Phoenix and Thomas Edison State College are eyeing India and China as their next frontier for growth. As such, the pressure will continue to mount for Indian distance learning institutions to instate additional assessment metrics.

Partnerships with Foreign Institutions

Although the drive to develop student support structures has been concentrated in Indian private and distance learning institutions, many traditional Indian centres of higher learning are also endeavouring to modernize in a less costly manner, through the development of partnerships with foreign schools. Within the last few years, the Central Government of India has become more flexible and progressive in its education laws as they relate to foreign institutions. Much excitement has been generated around foreign investment in Indian institutions of higher learning as well as foreign institutions looking to open branches of their schools within India. According to one recent report, there are currently over 130 foreign universities that have tied-up with various Indian academic institutions (Sengupta, 2007); this list includes a wide range of Indian private, traditional public, and distance learning schools.

The drive to fashion such partnerships with Western institutions is fuelled by two primary factors. First and foremost, Indian institutions are seeking to establish within their students a global competence and social maturity that is essential for success in today's job market, but is often lacking from the education received at a traditional public institution. Second, Indian schools are pushing to establish the mark of quality that may render them competitive with their public counterparts. From the perspective of Western institutions, the opportunity to tap into a huge new student base in India for immediate tuition income and endowments is the primary motive, but in addition, these schools are hoping to establish strong ties during the nascent stages of India's economic development, so as enjoy a privileged relationship that will enhance their international presence in the future. In March 2007, Karen Hughes, US Under Secretary of Public Diplomacy and Public Affairs, travelled to India with a delegation of American higher education administrators for the purpose of articulating these goals. In the words of Ms. Hughes, "The past few years have seen an explosion of business ties in which Indian and American businesses have found new productive ways to work together...Much like their business counterparts, American universities are exploring new strategies for collabouration" (Hughes, 2007).

Foreign partnerships with private Indian institutions have already been highlighted above. Recent examples of alliances between top US institutions and top Indian public institutions, as well as distance learning initiatives, also abound. The following is a short list.

Cornell University's President signed a three-year agreement with Indian Prime Minister Manmohan Singh to send visiting faculty—especially those from science, engineering, and computing departments—to Indian campus-based institutions. Moreover, Cornell has made a commitment to make its lectures available to Indian institutions through the EduSat service. Carnegie Mellon University, the University of Buffalo, UC Berkeley and UC San Diego are partners in the EduSat effort.

The Canadian government, through its Department of Foreign Affairs, recently set up a committee to work on educational collabourations with Indian institutions including the IITs.

Rutgers University currently has an exchange programme underway with the prestigious St. Stephens College of the University of Delhi, generating demand at a level that is currently twice that of capacity.

Brown University has developed similar programmes at the University of Delhi, and Dartmouth College and Antioch College have established student exchange programmes with universities in Pune and northern India, respectively.

The Indian School of Business (ISB) has exchange programmes with 32 leading business schools in the US, Europe, Israel, Africa, China, and the UK.

In the United States, interest in Indian study abroad programmes is not limited to Indian-American students; applications have been received almost equally from Indians and non-Indians. US students have become increasingly aware of the growth in the Indian market, and many see the opportunity to spend a semester studying in India as a step towards landing a prestigious international appointment, especially in the consulting or financial services industries. As an indicator of interest, consider Harvard's new ambitious new South Asia Plan—spearheaded by new President Drew Faust—which Vice Provost for International Affairs Jorge Dominguez said "is [Harvard's] most fully developed plan related to any geographic region outside the US...South Asia is very much a model for us" (Haniffa, 2007).

The market for India-US student exchange programmes is underscored by the prolific numbers of Indian students enrolling each year as full-time students in US schools. According to Open Doors 2006, an annual report released by the Institute of International Education (IIE), India remains the leading country of origin for international students studying at US universities. Although the report shows a decline of 4.9 per cent in the 2005-06 academic year compared to the previous year in the total number of students from India studying the US, other recent reports have indicated totals may increase in the coming years. Since the 2000-01 academic year, the number of Indian students has risen from approximately 55,000 to more than 80,000 in 2004-05. 73.7 per cent are enrolled at the graduate level, while 16.6 per cent are undergraduate students and 9.6 per cent are enrolled in other programmes. India also has the third largest number of international scholars—teachers and researchers who are not enrolled as students—at US universities. By comparison, the number of Chinese students granted US visas was 20,200 in 2005.

The push within Indian higher education for Western partnerships is by no means limited to the US. Within the last year, the governments of Britain and India launched the $50 million UK-India Education and Research Initiative, with top-tier UK schools vying to tie up with relatively young Indian institutions. This programme will fund 40 courses for approximately 2,000 students over the next several years. For example, the University of Greenwich has won funding to offer masters courses in business and IT subjects in partnership with privately funded ITM Universe in Gwalior. Commenting on the arrangement, Lady Blackstone (2008), Vice Chancellor of the University of Greenwich, highlighted the complementary motives of the two universities in establishing a link:

"The UK has an international reputation for excellence in higher education, with long experience of developing policy and practice in teaching and research, backed by a national system of quality assurance… on the research side, there will more Indian students completing research degrees in the UK, and more UK researchers undertaking work in India, along with joint research projects."

Such faculty exchange and information exchange between Western and Indian institutions are increasing hand-in-hand with student exchange. For example:

Rutgers University South Asian Studies programme is currently negotiating plans to bring experts in Indian literature and poetry from Visva Bharati University in West Bengal to their campus to teach undergraduate students (Professors Sumit Guha and Dipak Sarkar, Rutgers University, personal communication, November 16, 2007).

IIT Kharagpur, one of India's most highly rated universities, has acknowledged faculty shortage in engineering disciplines, pushing for joint international programmes to train faculty members.

Conclusion

As competition in the Indian higher education market grows, it will become increasingly difficult for top domestic Indian institutions to retain the pre-eminence of their degree programmes without student support services and methods for gauging student learning outcomes. Since private institutions are unfettered by the need to pass decisions through bureaucratic committees, they have an advantage in developing such programmes. Although in the West the value of a degree from a top traditional university holds a value with which for profit institutions are unable to compete, institutions of higher education in India operate on an increasingly level playing field where integrative programmes can make even the newest university an attractive candidate for international partnerships, exchange programmes, and domestic demand.

Once assessment metrics are in place, institutions will be able to illustrate the impact of such programmes and services. Assuming that students value these additional services, future Indian universities will need to take into consideration such models. Even government-funded institutions will have to take notice, since they have a vested interest in providing competitive job opportunities to their students, opportunities that may only be available to globally aware and socially competent graduates.

Still, it is clear that the future economic development of developing nations like India rests largely on the shoulders of the success of their distance learning programmes. The ultimate balance in distance and online education in India *via* Government-funded and private channels has yet to be determined. The Indian Government has already put substantial resources into distance learning initiatives, but with such support comes the added responsibility of developing and instating appropriate metrics for student success in such non-conventional learning environments. The ability, or lack thereof, of Government funded distance learning programmes to adhere to a high quality standard—through interaction with international accreditation agencies and advisory boards—will likely play a decisive role in determining the preparedness of the majority of the Indian population to compete in the modern economy. Premier Indian public universities undoubtedly possess the greatest name recognition today.

However, progressive institutions of higher education in India are well on their way towards obtaining seals of approval from Western institutions and international experts. Who will be the next Harvard or Stanford equivalent? Or, rather, will India develop a new model for egalitarian education ideally suited to meet the challenges inherent in its socio-economic development? With minimal international standards for assessment and student support services, such progressive institutions could witness a growth far exceeding that of similar institutions in the West, where the target audience is much smaller and more limited in scope.

References

Arjun has the last laugh, shelves proposal. (2008). Retrieved February 29, 2008 from http://academicsindia.com.

Bachorz, P. and Cronin, J. (2006). The Rising of Phoenix, and What It Means for Higher Education *Journal of Education*.

Basu, K. (2006, August 18). India's faltering education system. *BBC News*. Retrieved January 28, 2008 from http://news.bbc.co.uk/2/hi/south_asia.

Blackstone, L. (2008). Playing our ace. *Education Guardian*, United Kingdom.

David, R. (2007, October 25). *Indian crackdown likely to hurt hedge funds*. Retrieved January 28, 2008 from http://forbes.com

Das, G. (2008, February 10). End this killer Raj. *Times of India*.

Haniffa, A. (2007). *Harvard unveils South Asia plan*. Rediff India Abroad.

Hughes, K. (2007, March 24). Higher education: A keystone in US-India relations. *The Times of India*.

Indian Space Research Organization (2004, July). *Press release.*

Joshua, A. (2007, May 31). Foreign varieties can't repatriate earnings. *The Hindu.*

Keeling, R.P., Underhile, R., and Wall, A.F. (2007). Horizontal and vertical structures: The dynamics of organization in higher education. *Liberal Education.* Washington, DC: Association of American Colleges and Universities.

Keeling, R.P., ed. (2004). *Learning Reconsidered: A Campus-wide Focus on the Student Experience.* Washington, DC: National Association of Student Personnel Administrators and American College Personnel Association.

Kinser, K. (July/August 2006). What Phoenix doesn't teach us about for-profit higher education. *Change*, 38(4): 24-29.

Liu, N.C and Cheng, Y. (2005). The Academic Ranking of World Universities—Methodologies and Problems. *Higher Education in Europe*, 30(2): 127-136.

Neelakantan, S. (2007, August 17). Indian Prime Minister describes plan to create 40 new Universities. *The Chronicle of Higher Education.* New Delhi.

Neelakantan, S. (2008, January 24). Overregulation Hampers Higher Education in India, an Advisory Group Reports. *The Chronicle of Higher Education.*

Netaji Subhash Open University. (2007). Ascent: A Publication of the Netaji Subhash Open University, 6(1).

Netaji Subhash Open University. (2006, December). Ascent: A publication of the Netaji Subhash Open University, 5(2).

Nussbaum, M.C. (2007, May 18). Fears for Democracy in India. The Chronicle of Higher Education.

Rajagopalan, T. (2001, October 30). Ensuring quality in education. Book Review on Assessment and Accreditation in Higher Education. *The Hindu.*

Rena, R. (2007, Jan. 3). *Indian higher education and foreign universities.* Retrieved January 28, 2008 from http://Worldpress.org.

Roy, R. (2007). *Allow foreign varsities on Chinese model.* Retrieved January 28, 2008 from http://Educationalpartnershipsindia.com

Schulz, S.A., Lee, J.J., Cantwell, B.J., McClellan, G. and Woodard, D. (2007). Moving Toward a Global Community: An Analysis of the Internationalization of Student Affairs Graduate Preparation Programmes. *NASPA Journal.*

Sengupta, S. (2007, March 26). India attracts universities from the US. *New York Times.*

Sinha, P.M. (2006, November 29). *National Knowledge Commission Note on Higher Education.* http://knowledgecommission.gov.in

Spellings Commission Final Report. (2006). A Test of Leadership: Charting the Future of U.S. Higher Education. Retrieved January 28, 2008 from http://www.ed.gov/about/bdscomm/list/hiedfuture/reports.html

12

Status of Higher Education of the World and India

Vibha Singh Kushwaha

Overview

The University of Oxford has become the first UK University to top the Times Higher Education World University Rankings in the 12-year history of the table. It knocks the five-time leader, the California Institute of Technology, into second place in the world University Ranking 2016-17.

Oxford's success can be attributed to improved performances across the four main indicators underlying the methodology of the ranking—teaching, research, citations and international outlook. More specifically the institution's total income and research income is rising faster than its staff numbers, its research is more influential, and it has been more successful at drawing in international talent.

But when looking at country level, nations in Asia stand out. Two new Asian universities make the top 100 [Chinese University of Hong Kong and Korea Advanced Institute of Science and Technology (KAIST)]. While another four join the top 200: City University of Hong Kong, University of Science and Technology of China, University of Hong Kong, University of Science and Technology of China, Fudan University and Hong Kong Polytechnic University.

Furthermore, China's two flagship universities have both made gains—Peking University joins the top 30 at 29th (up from 42nd last year), while Tsinghua University joins the top 40 at 35th (up from joint 47th). Asia's leading institution, the National University of Singapore, is at 24th—its highest ever rank.

Meanwhile, India leading university—the Indian Institute of

Science—is edging closer to the top 200, claiming a spot in the 201-250 band, its highest ever position.

Overall, 289 Asian universities from 24 countries make the overall list of 980 institutions and an elite group of 19 are in the top 200, up from 15 last year.

When analysing which countries achieve the highest average scores, Singapore comes top on all five of the pillars underlying the ranking—teaching, research, citations, industry income and international outlook. Hong Kong is second for teaching, third for research and fourth for citations.

Rajika Bhandari, deputy vice-president of research and evaluation at the Institute of International Education and co-editor of the book Asia: The Nest Higher Education Superpower?, said that the "sharp rise" of Asia's universities is due to three main factors; rapidly growing population and demand for higher education in the region; governments making "significant investments" in universities; and improvements by individual institutions.

On advances at university level, that said that many Asian scholars who studied at Western universities are now academics in their home countries and have "really begun to transform their own higher education sectors".

They have "brought back to (their) home campuses some of the leaching values of critical thinking and liberal education, as well as the idea of promotion based on merit and research outputs", she said.

World University Rankings 2016-17: The nine big challenges global higher education must confront over the next five years.

To remain relevant in a rapidly changing world, the global university sector must work harder to convey its value to policy-makers and the wider public, says Hamish Coates, professor of higher education, university of Melbourne current global crises imperil exactly the kinds of progress higher education has helped to create. Higher education must contribute now like never before. But the sector must get its own house in order and do a better job of conveying its transformative potential.

Big Challenges must Higher Education Confront Over the Next Five Years

Research Grows Geopolitical

First, let us consider research, which I believe will further crystallize around geopolitical lines it step with wider global shifts. Serious research kit blows the budget of many countries. Large questions need big teams sharing diverse perspectives and advanced expertise. Nations will tighten investments around strategic interests, strengthening transnational networks that garner required capability. This puts new heat on every researcher to demonstrate not just the activity or quality of their work but its broader public impact. It demands fresh courage from universities to invest in basic fields that yield long-run returns. We need reports that celebrate the value of such "show leadership". The Organisation for Economic Cooperation and Development's new system benchmarking initiative could play a role.

National Competition for Students

At the same time, competition between nations over education will intensify. As economies mature, both higher education and the professional workforce that it forms will become more significant. Countries will compete not just to recruit the most promising students but also to retain the most successful graduates. They will entice the most talented people through targeted incentives, creating new student flows and diasporas. Countries are searching for differentiating means for demonstrating the value returned from studying and working with them. This is signaled by work on learning gains and teaching excellence in the United Kingdom, by ROI (return on investment) calculators in the US, and by outcomes assessments unfolding across Europe, Asia and South America.

Clarifying Value: The public will ask more about the value of higher education. Is higher education worth the cost, time and effort? More deeply, does it improve people, make them better citizens, create a more open and scientific society? Dose academic research serve as a catalyst of innovative change? Tonnes of research make clear that higher education creates enormous value. Articulating this contribution to people who do not know or perhaps do not care about higher education has been difficult. New conversations are required that help people to see how higher education can help them succeed. The stories that higher education tells a more interested public are essential. Rather than talk about their own immaculate histories, the sector must engage people and communities in imagining their own future options.

Implication: Transparency on Education

A big part of demonstrating value higher on better information about education. Information on research reputation muddles thinking about education activity, quality and impact. Market get distorted, individual futures are compromised, quality itself degrades. Globally, less than 5 per cent of institutions are serious research players. Reports clarifying what students know and can do are sorely needed. Although politically vexed, the OECD's Assessment of Higher Education Learning Outcomes proved what it is feasible to achieve, paving the way for myriad ambitious initiatives unfolding today. Changes in markets, institutions and technologies are spurring changes in assessment of the sort that have already revolutionized curriculum and teaching. Information on education outcome will become more widely available, revolutionizing discourse about what higher education contributes.

Commercialising Core Business: Core education and research business is changing, in turn changing institutions. Many traditional academic approaches were never designed for the kinds of provision apparent today. Scaling them can be expensive and risky. Instead, savvy designers are creating novel architectures that offer viable quality at scale. Universities are partnering with commercial firms to co-source and outsource core teaching work. Research is shifting into specialized units. New business models are given life in these changes, as are the new institutions that create and sustain them. While typically tinged with commercial intent, institutions must be clear about the corporate changes underway.

Twenty-first Century Academic Work: Such reforms impel changes in academic work, roles and workforces. New forms of education, research and engagement are seeding new and more specialised forms of work. Changing academic work is creating new kinds of roles. Academics build expertise in niche areas rather than strive to be "superdemics" doing everything for everyone. Over time, wide-scale role changes reshape the workforce itself. Incumbents, however, will temper the pace of such change, not least as the baby boomers are retiring slowly. Even so, large-scale workforce renewal is under way in many countries. But hiring teachers on one-hour contracts is far from a sustainable solution. Much more must be done to make the sector an employer of choice that attracts the best talent.

Broadening Leadership Capability: New forms of leadership are required to embrace future challenges. Working up through academic and managerial ranks does not necessarily grow the capabilities needed to respond to mounting expectations of governments, fluctuating requirements of industries or diverse needs of communities. New formal and no-the-job training is required, as are new kinds of track record and recruitment. Leaders will benefit from the kind of commercial acumen gained through industry experience. Rather than spend a sabbatical at a similar university, more return may be procured from a secondment at in industry partner or government agency.

Co-creating New Contributions: This brief survey is only the start of it. New system architectures and forms of governance are taking shape. Funding reform is a huge issue to address, which leads quickly to questions about the cost of teaching and research, and sensitive matters around cross-subsidizations and executive incentives. Much must be done to create more sustainable and equitable societies, looking at disadvantaged groups and also across generations. Higher education will keep swinging East as Asian institution mature, revealing new academic cultures, alignments and disparities. Accreditation agencies must ensure compliance with clear standards to sustain sector legitimacy. At the same time, ministries are seeing new limits to their power, and instead the need to co-create policies with the communities they represent.

Transparency a Linchpin to Success: Like never before, the world needs higher education to help work through meltdowns and create better futures. To engage best, institutions also need to address their own challenges and take leadership over communicating the value they create. As higher education transforms, effective leadership in terms of transparency will play an important role in making good with the future.

Table 12.1: Data on Indian Higher Education

(in crore)

	2001	*2016*
Total	102.80	121.02
Male	53.20	62.37
Female	49.65	58.65

Data Score: O/O RGI, Census 2001 and 2011.

Global Challenges and Issues: Indian Higher Education

Introduction

The world has made some remarkable progress in education since 2000, when the six Educations for All (EFA) goals and the Millennium Development Goals (MDGs) were established. Those goals were not,

Table 12.2: Estimated Population by Age Group 2012-13

(Figure in '000)

Age group	*Estimated Population 2012*			*Estimated Population 2013*			*Corresponding Level of Education*
	Total	*SC*	*ST*	*Total*	*SC*	*ST*	
6-10 year	131144	23362	13068	130896	23324	13020	Primary (I-V)
11-13 year	76044	13394	7312	75223	13259	7194	Upper Primary (I-V)
6-13 year	217177	36756	20380	206119	36583	20214	Elementary (I-VIII)
14-15 year	50691	8882	4662	50244	8803	4610	Secondary (IX-X)
6-15 year	257879	45638	25042	256363	45386	24824	I-X
16-17 year	45438	7819	3990	45085	7749	3963	Sr. Secondary (XI- XII)
6-17 year	03317	53457	29032	301448	53135	28787	I-XII
18-23 year	140559	24049	11904	140802	24077	11926	Higher Education

Data Source: Population projection of MHRD.

however, reached by the 2015 deadline and continued action is needed to complete the unfinished agenda. With Goal 4 of Transforming our world: the 2030 Agenda for Sustainable Development. "Ensure inclusive and equitable quality education and promote lifelong learning opportunities for all" (hereafter referred to as SDG4-Education 2030)—and its associated targets, the world has set a more ambitious universal education agenda for the period from 2015 to 2030.

The new figures are staggering. In world 263 million children and youth are out of school, (out-of-school children of primary age in India 2.9 million) according to UIS data. This number includes 61 million children of primary school age (about 6 to 11 years), 60 million young adolescents of lower secondary school age (about 12 to 14 ears) and 142 million youth of upper secondary school age (about 15 to 17 years) for the school year ending I 2014. 11.1 million Secondary school age out-of-school population in India and also 47 million youth of upper secondary age are not in school, representing nearly half of the population for the age group.

The Indian Higher Education system, which includes Technical Education, is one of the largest of the world, just after the United States and China. Higher Education is the most powerful tool to build a knowledge-based society for the future. Higher Education is the most powerful tool to build a knowledge-based society for the future. Higher Education provides people with an opportunity to reflect on the critical social, economic, cultural, moral and spiritual issues facing humanity. It contributes to national development through dissemination of specialized knowledge and skills. Being at the apex of the educational pyramid, it plays a key role in producing quality teachers for the country's education.

Higher Education system has witnessed significant expansion in last few years, both in terms of the number of institutions and colleges as well as the student enrolment in various courses. India has more than 600 universities and over 30,000 colleges with 285.63 million students till end of 2013. Some Indian institutes, such as Indian institutes of Technology (IITs) and Indian Institute of Management (IIMs), have been globally recognized for their education standards. According to the *London Times,* Higher Education (2009)—Quacquarelli Symonds (QS) World University Rankings—There was no Indian university in Top 100 universities but many other Asian Universities were included. Hong Kong and Singapore have two ranked at 30 and 73, South Korea also has two ranked at 47 and 69 and Taiwan one in the 95th position. China also managed to get two universities ranked at 49 and 52. There is no Indian

Institute till 200. Only the IIT, Kanpur, Madras and Delhi University got rank 237, 284 and 291 respectively. Shanghai University conducted a research on universities and institute all over the world. Its research shows that there is no single Indian university in top 300 universities while China has six universities. The first institute to make its appearance in top 400 is the Indian Institute of Science, Bangalore. The IIT, Khargpur is also counted in top 500.

At the end of XI Plan (31.3.2012), there were 573 University (43 Central, 129 Deemed and 397 State Universities (State Public 286 and 111 Private) and 4 Institutions established under Special State Legislature Acts and 35.539 Colleges in the Country. During the year 2014-15 there were 711 University and university level institutions (Listed by UGC) (46 Central, 128 Deemed 329 State Public, 205 State Private and 3 Institutions under Special State Legislature Act) and 40760 Colleges. Maharashtra (716), thus registering an increase of 24 per cent in the number of Universities and 14.69 per cent increase in colleges during the 3rd year of XII Plan in comparison to the figures at the end of XI Plan. During the reporting year 2014-15, 1 Central University, 30 State Private Universities and 18 State Universities were included in the UGC list of universities and 6 universities were declared fit to receive central assistance under section 12B of the UGC Act, 1956. Detailed information on State Universities, State Private Universities, Deemed Universities and Institutions established under State legislature and is also available on UGC website.

Objectives of Study

- To analyse the current scenario of higher education system in India.
- To identify on the Emerging Challenges and issue of higher education in India.
- Suggestions for improving quality of higher education and conclusion.

The present paper is a macro level and descriptive study in nature, based on secondary data collected from the published and unpublished records, reports and contributions of several institutions, organizations and individuals in India. Specifically, the secondary sources include Annual Reports of UGC, Education Department of Ministry of Human Resource Development, Economic Survey and other journals, and websites.

Emerging Issues in Higher Education in India

The role of Higher Education in the emerging scenario of knowledge economy is very crucial and multifaceted for any country in general and India in particular. There are many basic problems faced by higher education system in India. These include lower level of teaching quality, Financing of Higher Education, more concentrated on theories and rather than practical knowledge Corruption in Education, privatization, Inadequate facilities and infrastructure Quota system.

- **Lower Level of Teaching Quality:** Our education system is torture by issues of quality in many of its institutions and universities. Many of the issues like lack of faculty, poor quality teaching, Traditional teaching methods, outdated and rigid curricula and pedagogy, lack of accountability and quality assurance and separation of research and teaching are raise questions on Indian education system.
- **Financing of Higher Education:** One of the most important things that have to be noticed is the issue of financial constraints regarding higher education before the government. Expenditure on education in common and on higher education in particular by the government, is one of the parameters to judge the quality in education for at all nation. The State Government have already been spending 20-30 per cent of its revenue budget on education. It cannot afford to spend more. In India, higher education has received less attention in terms of public spending than other levels. It is not feasible for India to make.
- **Corruption in Education:** Corruption in Indian education system has been eroding the quality of education and has been creating long-term negative consequences for the society. Educational corruption in India is considered as one of he major contributors to domestic black money.
- **Facilities:** A study of 188 government-run primary schools found that 59 per cent of the schools had no drinking water and 89 per cent had no toilets. 2003-04 data by National Institute of Education Planning and Administration revealed that only 3.5 per cent of primary schools in Bihar and Chhattisgarh had toilets for girls. In Madhya Pradesh, Maharashtra, Andhra Pradesh, Gujarat, Rajasthan and Himachal Pradesh, rates were 17-26 per cent in 2014. In fact,

the number of secondary schools is almost half the number of upper primary schools available in the country.

Emerging Challenges in Higher Education India: The system of Indian Higher Education in the second largest in the world which fulfils the education different sections of the society since it is the student community that can help to generate health academic atmosphere in institutions of higher learning. No doubt that India faces today a number of problems pertaining to poverty unemployment disappearance of moral and spiritual values. But in the last few decades a country wide problems challenges have emerged in Higher Education system in India they are discussed as under.

Our Heterogeneous Education System: Our heterogeneous education system based on geographical, rural-urban, rich-poor set up has posed in great challenge for the educational institutions. Varieties of colleges, universities, technical institutions have produced and different types and quality of Education. Some of them are really imparting qualitative education which a few others are doing the dirtiest job. Thanks to UGC, for publishing the list of such a fake Universities and Institutions indulging in educational malpractices.

Economic Difficulties: Is one of the most troublesome changes that the present higher education system has imposed on the communities? The number of students are coming from the ordinary classes; many of them are unable to provide the minimum necessities of life for themselves. Economic miseries have grown due to the rising prizes, habits of wasting money on luxuries, increasing population, shortage of food supply, selfish etc. students hold part-time jobs in order to pay for the their educational expenses and must divide their attention between a job and college/ university education. Near about seventy five per cent of the total students community today have been facing the financial problems. Earn while learn scheme cannot adequately support student to face economic challenges.

Lack of Resources: Lack of Resources has been a major issue. Within a system that is overloaded, the growth of private higher education in India has been rapid, but is taking place in a policy vacuum, as a major private education bill has languished in the Indian parliament for over two decades. At the same time, the regulatory framework, accreditation mechanisms and the processes of quality assurance remain confused. The techno savvy generation of students has increased their potential and aspiration for techno based learning cannot be ignored and therefore, keeping pace with this new generation learners is emerging as one of the most important issues in Higher Education. Although individual researchers and some institutions perform creditably, serious problems afflict research performance in India. In various global ranking systems, such as Shanghai's Jia Tong, Indian universities perform poorly, with only the Indian Institutes of Technology and Management ranked on the top three hundred.

The Supply-demand Gap: India has a low rate of enrolment in higher education, at only 18 per cent compared with 26 per cent in China and 36 per cent in Brazil. There is enormous unmet demand for higher education. By 2020 the Indian government aims to achieve 30 per cent gross enrolment, which will mean providing 40 million university places, an increase of 14 million in six years.

The Low Quality of Teaching and Learning: The system is beset by issues of quality in many of its institutions: a chronic shortage of faculty, poor quality teaching, outdated and rigid curricula and pedagogy, lack of accountability and quality assurance and separation of research and teaching.

Indian Higher Education Global Challenges and Issues Overview

Introduction

India, with more than 1.4 million schools and more than 230 million enrolments, is home to one of the largest and complex schools education systems in the world along with China. The structures of the educational system in the independent India were inadequate to build potential human resources required for the self-reliant socio-economic development. In an attempt to remove the infirmities of these inherited structures Radhakrishnan Commission (1948-49) and Kothari Commission (1964-66) were appointed and their reports formed the base for New Education Policy (1986) and Programmers of Action (1992) adorned with broad goals such as enhancement of the student enrolment, provision for equal access to all, quality education and promotion of relevant education.

Emerging Issues

The role of higher education in the emerging scenario of knowledge economy is very crucial and multifaceted for any country in general and India in particular. There are many basic problems faced by higher education system in India. These include Lower level of teaching quality, Financing of higher education, More concentrated on theories and rather than practical knowledge, Traditional methods of teaching, Privatization, inadequate facilities and infrastructure Quota system.

Lower Level of Teaching Quality: Our education system is torture by issues of quality in many of its institutions and university. Many of the issues like lack of faculty, poor quality teaching, traditional teaching methods, outdated and rigid curricula and pedagogy, lack of accountability and quality assurance and separation of research and teaching are raise questions on Indian education system.

Financing of Higher Education: One of the most important things that have to be noticed is the issue of financial constraints regarding higher education before the government. Expenditure on education in common and on higher education in particular by the government, in one of the parameters to judge the quality in education for at all nation. The State Government has already been spending 210-30 per cent of its revenue budget on education. It cannot afford to spend more. In India, higher education has received less attention in terms of public spending than other levels. It is not feasible for India to make massive state investments in research and development that produced research led universities in the West such as same of the University vocational oriented knowledge. More concentrated on theories and rather than practical knowledge: Indian education system is more focused on theoretical knowledge rather than practical knowledge. In many jobs there is also a minimum requirement of percentage which is high.

Traditional Methods of Teaching: Professors still stick to those older methods of teaching like board, marker. They do not like to make use of audio visual aids in teaching. Also they are not up-to-date with the information available and what global industry demands.

Privatization: In the present scenario, privatization of higher education is apparently a fledging but welcome trend and is essential to maintain creativity adaptability and quality. The economic trail of liberalization and globalization demands it. In India both public and private institutions operate simultaneously. Approximately 50 per cent of the higher education in India is imparted through private institutions, mainly unaided involving high cost. However, the situation is not so simple. Private providers, in the interest of maximizing profit, every incentive to 'minimize costs' by compromising on the quality of education provided in their institutions. Last but not least, quality of teaching staff is one of the considerable issues for higher education sector to one of the considerable issues for higher education sector to sustain in the future. Earlier, they were committed to their students to their subjects and to their profession. Today high salaries are available but the commitment is less. Thus, it is the need of the hour to free the higher education system from unnecessary constraints and political interference.

Inadequate Facilities and Infrastructure: In India, many of the universities do not have adequate infrastructure or facilities to teach students. Even many private universities are running courses without classrooms, Internet and Wi-Fi facility is still out of reach of many students.

Quota System: Bringing the reservation and quota system for different categories in education lost its quality. Even deserving candidates of general categories are ignored and on quota we have to select other persons from reserved category even though he is not suitable.

Emerging Challenges

The system of Indian Higher Education is the second largest in the world which fulfils the education requirements of millions of students who come form different section of the society since it is the student community that can help to generate health academic atmosphere in institutions of higher learning. No doubt that India faces today a number of problems pertaining to poverty unemployment disappearance of moral and spiritual values. But in the last few decades a country-wide changes have emerged in Higher Education System in India they are discussed as under.

Our heterogeneous education system, based on geographical, rural-urban, rich-poor set up has posed in great challenge for the education institutions. Varieties of colleges, universities, technical institutions have produced and different types and quality of Education. Some of them are really imparting qualitative education although a few others are doing the dirtiest job. Thanks to UGC, for publishing the list of such a fake Universities and Institutions indulging in educational malpractices.

Interference of Political Factors: Most of the institutions imparting education (Aided-non-aided) are owned by the dominant political leaders, now playing key role in governing bodies of the University. They have established their own youth cells and encourage students organization on political basis. They exploit the students' energy for their political purposes. The students forget their own objectives and begin to develop their career in politics.

Economic Difficulties: Is one of the most troublesome changes that the present higher education system has imposed on the communities? The number of students are corning from the ordinary classes; many of them are unable to provide the minimum necessities of life for themselves. Economic miseries have grown due to the increasing prizes, habits of wasting money on luxuries, increasing population, scarcity of food supply, corruption, selfish etc. students hold part-time jobs in order to pay for the their educational expenses and should divide their attention between a job and college university education. Near about seventy five per cent of the total students community today, have been facing the financial problems. Earn while learn scheme cannot adequately support student to face economic challenges.

Lack of Moral Values: Rapid growth of science and technology and subsequent industrialization has caused a great and danger to our old moral and value. The younger generation's dissatisfaction and revolt is the outcome of a decaying system of values.

Suggestions for Improving Quality of Higher Education

There are some suggestions and expectations from government, industry, educational institutions, parents and students for improving quality of higher education.

Student-Centered Education and Dynamic Methods: Methods of higher education also have to be appropriate to the needs of learning to learn, learning to do, learning to be and learning to become, student-centred education and employment of dynamic methods of education will require from teachers new attitudes and new skills. Methods of teaching through lectures will have to subordinate to the methods that will lay stress on self-study, personal consultation between teachers and pupils, and dynamic sessions of seminars and workshops. Methods of distance education will have to be employed on a vast scale.

Examination Reforms: Examination reforms, gradually shifting from the terminal annual and semester examination to regular and continuous assessment of student's performance in learning must be implemented.

International Cooperation: University in India have been a primary conduit for the advancement and transmission of knowledge through traditional functions such as research, innovation, teachings, human resource development, and continuing education. International cooperation is gaining importance as yet another function. With the increased development of transport and communication, the global village is witnessing a growing emphasis on International Cooperation and Action to find satisfactory solutions to problems that have global dimensions and higher education is one of them.

To Increase Quantity of University: We need more universities because we are more in number and present number of universities is too less. On 13th June, 2005, Government of India constituted a high level Commission (NKC) to advise the PM about the state of education in India and measures needed to reform this sector. It was headed by Sam Pitroda and submitted its report in November 2007. NKC has recommended setting up of 1500 universities by 2015 so that gross enrolment ratio increases to 15 per cent. It has also called for Higher Education (IRAHE) to monitor the quality of overall higher education in India.

Cross Culture Programmers: After education tour to every place in India and world as far as possible with the cooperation of government is necessary so that one can understand about people, culture, arts, literature, religions, technological development and progress of human society in the world. Action plan for improving Quality- Academic and administrative audit must be conducted once in three years in college by academic experts for ensuring quality on all aspects of academic activities. The self-finance-colleges must come forward for accreditation and fulfil the requirements of accreditation. Universities and colleges should realize the need for quality education and come forward with action plan for improving quality in higher educational institutions.

World Class Education: Indian Government is not giving priority to the development of Standard in Education. India must aspire for the international standard in education. Many national universities like to the USA, UK, Australia etc. allow studies in higher education for foreign students in their countries and through correspondence courses as well. In the same way, Indian Universities of world class education can also offer courses of studies to foreign students taking advantage of the globalization process. To achieve that goal it must adopt uniform international syllabus in its educational institutions.

Higher-tech Libraries: Our university libraries have a very good collection of books, but they are all in mess. A library must be online and conducive for serious study. Indian universities should concentrate more on providing quality education which is comparable to that of international standards.

Vocational Education—Affordable in New Skill: The one issue that needs attention at policy level is the reform of vocational education in the state for making the education relevant and inclusive of the poor. The new entrants in the higher education system will necessary come from rural area and economically and social disadvantaged background. Bulk of them will be first generation learners. The proportion of drop-outs at higher secondary level is higher among the lower income group. It is also low for ST, OBC and Muslim. It is for these groups that the government should reform the policy of vocational education, with a provision for upward mobility. The vocational education will have to be affordable and relevant which will enhance their employability. The vocational should necessarily be in the skills which are in demand in current and medium term period and also suits the needs of farm and non-farm wage labour in rural area and small and marginal Farmer's households in general and particularly form ST, OBC, economically weak OBC and Muslim and Buddhist.

Multi-cultural Education to Enhance Knowledge and Skill to deal with Diversity and Prejudices for Harmonious Students Community and Campus Life

There also need to enhance understanding and skills of students who come from diverse social/cultural/religious background to deal with diversity and for reducing cultural barriers. Recently the issue of social distance and discrimination of students from certain caste, ethnic, religious and regional background has surfaced in major way and some efforts are underway to develop policies, legal and positive to deal with discrimination and social distancing in the universities and educational Institutions. The countries like USA, South Africa, UK and others have developed multicultural education, including courses at undergraduate and post-graduate level enhance the understanding of various cultures, so that students recognize and respect diversity of culture and develop participatory community life on university and campus which is socially inclusive, mixed and harmonious. The state of Maharashtra can take lead in this matter and develop a policy for multi-cultural education to create attitudes among the students which is secular, mixed and harmonious, so that all can learn from each other and from their diversity of experiences.

Various Issues of Teacher Education in Higher Education in India

Introduction

There are many problems and issues planning the system of teacher education. The teachers preparation has been a subject of discussion at all levels from the government ministers, regulatory bodies and schools and teachers themselves. A lot of planning and resources has been used for improving the quality of teacher education. New technologies education could not grow up to the expected level. It is lacking behind somewhere in realizing its purpose. Its scope has broadened and its objectives have becomes focused during the last thirty five years, but teachers could not realize its objectives fully no doubt education plays a significant role in nations development but the quality of education is greatly depend on the quality of teachers, therefore, great were made of teachers education.

Defective Admission Process

The admission process in India procedure many vary from state to state. In many states students needs to past CET examination for admission but in many states there is no need to pass examination, students get admitted on merits basis. The selection procedure of the students teachers is not proper. Improper selection procedure leads to wakening of the quality of teachers. Better selection method would not only improve the quality of training but also save the personal and social wastage.

Inadequate Teaching Training Programmes

The period of secondary teachers training programmes is one of the year after the graduation one year duration of teacher education programme has been on issue of much long debate, but because of late admission procedure, the effective session of training is behind of eight and nine months. The main purpose of teacher education programme is to develop healthy attitude board interest in values in students teachers, but it is not possible during the short duration of eight to nine months. The teacher education curriculum which includes theory and practical and internship in actual schools require much more to enlarge the time period of present teacher education programmme. Now-a-days, the NCTE had announced that to implement B.Ed. and M.Ed. programme of two years from 2015-16.

Incompetency Between Student and Teachers

The exising teacher training programme does not provide enough opportunities to the student teachers training programme are not sensitive about the existing problem of schools. Therefore there should be close corresponding between the work for teachers preparation in training colleges. A student teacher should know the meaning of education, its objectives, the socio-cultured and politico economics background the principles the guide construction of curriculum etc. but a proper preparation towards a good orientation is impossible due to short duration of teacher training.

Problems of Practice Teaching

The teaching practice plays a significant role in teachers training programme. But the ratio of marks between theory and practice generally remains at 5.2. In spite of all kinds of elabourate preparations regarding practice teaching student teachers are not serious about the task of teaching, poor in sense of duty irresponsible, aimless indifferent to children lacking innovative measure in teaching which is great barriers in the development of pedagogical skills.

The supervision of practice teaching aims to bring improvement in the student teachers by using various techniques and practical skills in teaching. Also it helps them to develop confidence in facing the classroom situations. But in most of the teacher training colleges it is done by teachers who are not method specialist generally. The percentage of lessons supervised by the defective time table etc.

Lack of Subject Knowledge

Now-a-days, because of unaided colleges, the students admitted in the colleges were very poor in their basic subjects, because the B.Ed. programme give emphasis to the knowledge of the basic subject. The whole teaching practice remains indifferent with regard to subject knowledge. Due to the lack of subject of knowledge they could not explain the difficult concepts at the time of practice.

Traditional Curriculum and Time of Practice

Curriculum of Teacher Education Programme in India has been criticized much more, some educationists feel that it does not fully concentrate on the need of existing Indian schools and society. And also, it does not include relevant contents for teachers who are to communicate quality education in schools.

In India teacher education is unenthusiastic to innovation and experimentation in the methods of teaching. Because, most of the teacher education is not acquaint with modern class room communication devices. They are not introduced with new teaching-learning methods for teaching.

No Coordination Between Schools and Training Institutions

It has been observed by Education Commission, the teacher education has become isolated from schools and education. The school considers that teacher education department is an unfamiliar institution and not a nursery for the professionals observed the formality of finishing the approved number involved in the procedure. In last decade, NCTE had permitted number of colleges on unaided basis. So the number of seats for admission increased but the quality of the students decreased. Most of the candidates do not have the necessary motivation and an academic background for a well deserved entry in teaching professions.

Lack of Proper Resources and Amenities

The quality of teacher education institution is mainly depending on the physical resources, human resources and the work done by the colleges. But in India, the teacher education programme is being not given a good treatment. About 20 per cent of the teacher education institutions are being run in rented buildings without any facility. Number of unaided colleges has not sufficient physical and human resources such as science labouratory, guidance rooms and other equipments necessary for a good teacher education department. Also there are no separate hostel facilities for student teachers.

Some suggestions to remedy of problems of teachers education—

- Curriculum of teacher education programme should be revised from time to tie according to changing need of society. The course of studies both in theory and practices should be recognized.
- The method of teaching in the teacher education departments should be such tat it inspires a sense of appreciation among other departments of universities and colleges.
- The admission process of B.Ed. should be completely systematized and steps should be taken to make it full proof against tempering and meddling as far as possible.

- Teacher language must be well qualified and experienced with language proficiency.
- Privatization of teacher education should be regulated.

Role of UGC in Higher Education in India

Introduction

India's Higher Education System is the third largest in the world after China and the United States. In future, India will be one of the largest education hub. The University Grants Commission (UGC) came into existence on 28th December, 1953 and became a statutory body of Government of India by an Act of Parliament in 1956 for the coordination, determination and maintenance of standards of University Education for the purpose of performing its functions. The Commission may allocate and disburse, out of the fund of the commission, grants to universities and colleges for the maintenance and development; Advise Central Government, State Governments and Institution of Higher Learning on the measures necessary for the promotion of university education; Make Rules and Regulations consistent with Act etc. As per section 18 of the UGC Act, the Commission shall prepare once every year an Annual Report, giving a true and full account of its activities during the previous year and copies there of shall be forwarded to the Central Government and the Government shall cause the same to be laid before both Houses of Parliament need and importance of the study.

Objectives

- To study the of UGC in the establishment of NAAC and IQAC.
- To study how the college promote social responsibilities and citizenship roles among the students.
- To find out how the extension activities enlarge after the establishment IQAC in the college.

Objective of Twelfth Year Plan

The plan lays out the following as the objectives that must guide central, state and private institutions in the country:

- Higher education in India to be brought in line with and at the frontiers of;

- Global Trends in higher education and knowledge development;
- Improvement in overall quality of teaching learning in an average higher education institution in the country;
- Arresting and reversing the trend of group inequalities in access to quality higher education;
- Creation of an additional capacity for 2 million more students from eligible age cohort to have access to higher education in a demand driven manner; and
- Undertaking government and regulatory reforms that focus on institutional autonomy within framework of accountability and build adaptive capacity of the system.

The major objective of the Twelfth Five Year Plan in the sphere of equity should be to eliminate gender disparities and to significantly reduce urban-rural interregional and inter-social group disparities.

Role of UGC in Higher Education in India

The Higher Education System in India has grown in a remarkable way, particularly in the post-Independence period to become one of the largest system of its kind in the world. The UGC serves as a vital link between the Union and State Governments and the Institutions of higher learning, in addition to its role of giving grants to universities and colleges the University Grant Commission also devices Central and State Governments on the measures necessary for the improvement of University education. It also frames regulations of teachers on the advice of subject specialists and academicians with whom it frequently interacts and connections with the formulation, evaluation and monitoring of programmers. In the next few decades India will probably have the world's largest set if young people. Even as other countries begin to age, India will remain a country of young people. If the proportion of working population to total population increase that should be reflected in a sharp increase in the country's saving rate. If India can find productive job opportunities for working population, that would give India big opportunity to leapfrog in the race for social and economic development and as a result growth rates would go up.

In an environment of global competitiveness it is important that Indian products of the higher education institutions are as competent as graduates of any other country, not only in their scholastic attainments, but also in term of the value system and richness of their personality. Unless the quality and standard of Indian higher education institutions is enhanced zealously and sustained at a higher level through innovation, creativity and regular monitoring, it seems to be difficult for the Indian academics/ professionals to complete in the world scheme.

In India there were only 20 universities and 500 colleges with 0.1 million students at the time India attained Independence. This has increased to 611 universities and university-level institutions and 31,324 colleges as on August 2011. The concern the merely increasing the number of higher education institutions and their enrolment capacity will not achieve the national developmental goals without concurrent attention to quality and its access to all those who desire it, is addressed in the Twelfth Five Year Plan. Also special efforts need to be made to ensure fair and impartial treatment to the disadvantaged sections of the society in making available to them benefits of higher education.

Recent Reforms in Higher Education

In the past, public investment and subsidies promote access to higher education, however, currently, the individual capacity to buy and private incentives to invest influence higher education provisions.

A growing social demand for higher education coupled with a decline in state funding, led to cutback budgetary constraints became a regular and permanent feature, universities had to discover long term sustainable solutions for their survival and growth. In other words universities started looking more for sources of regular income flow rather than one of contributions.

Some of the reform measures adopted by various universities include:

(1) Cost-saving measures such as a freezing both staff salaries and recruitment;
(2) Cost-sharing measures, such as enhancing student fees and introducing student loans;
(3) Resources-mobilizing measures, including short courses or training programme on a full cost-recovery basis, undertaking contract research and consultancies and variety of other income generating activities;
(4) Efficiency-enhancing measures such as changing resource allocation policies and emphasizing accountability and evaluation procedures for performance assessment; and
(5) Quality-assurance measures, such as establishing accreditation agencies.

Establishment of NAAC and IQAC

The University Grants Commission (UGC) established the National Assessment and Accreditation Council (NAAC) in 1994 at Bangalore. NAAC has given guidelines to all the accredited institutions to establish an Internal Quality Assurance Cell (IQAC) to ensure qualitative growth of the institution. Internal Quality Assurance Cell (IQAC) is established as a post-accreditation quality sustenance measure. Since quality enhancement is a continuous process, the IQAC has become a part of the institution's system and work towards realizing the goals of quality enhancement and sustenance Internal Quality Assurance Cell (IQAC) Part A of guideline of XI Plan of University Grants Commission directs all the Higher Quality Assurance Cell (IQAC). The motive behind setting up of IQAC is crucial to HEIs. IQAC is a mechanism to build and ensure a quality culture at the institutional level, and is meant for planning, guiding and monitoring Quality Assurance (QA) and Quality Enhancement (QE) activities of the HEIs Complying with the aim a UGC, IQAC has been constituted in the University to review the performance for the entire gamut of academic programmes encompassing the faculty, research scholars and students. IQAC was constituted strictly as per the guidelines of UGC, and Prof. K.V.S. Sharma was given the responsibility to act as the coordinator. The cell IQAC started to function immediately with clarity of vision and plan of action.

Conclusion

It is clear higher education institutions come in all shapes and sizes, and this means that solutions will need to be organic; a standard set of remedies will also not work when countries are so diverse. Despite this diversity, the main objective of the task force has been to determine strategies for higher education reform, as well as general guidelines and principles for assessing the operation of higher education systems and institutions. These benchmarks offer guidance for informed dialogue aimed at educational reform helping to cut through the often confusing thicket of institutions and practices.

There may be a danger that SDG 4 is treated as an 'education' goal, focusing on basic literacy for children and young people. We need to acknowledge an expansive definition of 'education' that reflects the many different spaces and ways in which people can learn, be taught, and 'educate' themselves and each other. Lifelong learning may be the key to this, but it cannot be seen as falling outside the responsibility of government. It is important to build on what people already know, in ways that are respectful of local cultures and local knowledge. Harnessing the potential of ICT and new technologies in inclusive ways, and expanding the focus of 'literacy' more fully across spaces, not only in schools but in technical and vocational centres, universities and workplaces, will also be critical. A holistic approach to the SDGs can thus take forward much of the good thinking and action around adult literacy. Historical efforts to improve adult literacy may have not been 'effective' according to the narrow framing of basic literacy skills, but they could be seen as extremely valuable once it is commonplace to employ an expanded notion of literacy and sustainable development that goes beyond function and binary understandings. Neither 'literacy' nor 'women' should be seen as a homogenous category; both gendered identities and literacy practices develop and shift over the lifecycle and according to contexts. 44 Girls' and women's literacy with a lifelong learning perspective the final targets of SDG 17 suggest some ways to do this at the national and community levels: by enhancing capacity by sharing knowledge, expertise and technology as well as financial resources; and by enhancing capacity to increase the availability of high quality, timely and reliable data. Strengthening the evidence base across the SDGs to include non-instrumental understandings of literacy, going beyond women-as-mothers, and focusing on girls and women as active agents of change, will be crucial to achieve positive, sustained change for women's and girls' literacy and sustainable development.

After independence, there has been tremendous increase in higher education institutions of learning in all disciplines. But still India is way behind in providing world class education. Today, India is one of the fastest growing countries of the world with the annual growth rate going above 9 per cent. In order to sustain that rate of growth, there is need to increase the number of institutes with quality education. To achieve and reach the future requirements there is an urgent need to relook at the Financial Resources, Education Policies, and Higher Quality of Teaching in only English language no other language. Access and Equity, Quality Standards, Relevance and at the end the Responsiveness.

Suggestions for Improving the System of Higher Education:

- There is a need to implement innovative and transformational approach form primary to higher education level to make Indian educational system globally more relevant and competitive.

- Higher educational institutes need to improve quality, reputation and establish credibility through student exchanges, faculty exchange programmes and other collabourations with high quality national and international higher educational institutes.
- Government must promote collabouration between Indian higher education institutes and top International institutes and also generates linkage between national research labouratories and research centres of top institutions for better quality and collabourative research.
- Regulations and control on private higher educational institutions.

Teacher and his education are very significant aspects of any nations. The education gives a new shape to the individuals and the nation as well. It is well known saying that teacher is nation builder. So the quality of teacher education programme needs to be graded. The teacher education programme needs a comprehensive reform and reconstruction of curriculum and needs to revise according to changing needs of society. Since the teacher has the vital role in the entire educational system and it is the main agent for introducing essential and advantage changes in the teaching learning process, efforts need to be made for motivating teachers to become innovative and creative.

In this way India partakes the challenge of higher education all over the globe. An unprecedented rise in the number of university students, their changing social profile, rise of interconnected network of knowledge facilitated by new technologies, greater integration of world economy. Increasing recognition of cultural plurality and the emergence of new problem that defy existing solution define the context of higher education all over the globe in the coming decades. India can play a major role in balancing the fast growing globe demographic skew due to increasing preponderance of an aging population and can emerge not gust as a knowledge creating country but also as knowledge provider. This context is pressing for a fresh thinking on future university as a place of the generation and transmission of knowledge and values.

References

All-India Survey in Higher Education, Ministry of Human Resource Development, 2010-11 (Provisional).

Avhad, S., (2013), "Emerging Issues and Challenges in Higher Education", *IMJRMT*, volume 2, January, 2013.

Basu, Kausik, (2004), "Combating indies truant teacher", *BBC*. Retrieved 20/09/2016.

Chahal, M., "Higher Education in India: Emerging Issues", *International Journal of Business, Quantitative Economics and Applied Management Research,* Vol. I, Issue II, April 2015.

FICCI, (2015), "A study on widening of tax base and teaching Black money", February 2015. Retrieved 20/09/2016.

GOI, *Annual Report* (2014-15), "Department of Higher School Education and Literacy Department, Ministry of Human Resources, Government of India", New Delhi.

Iman, A. (2011), Quality and excellence of teacher education: issues and challenges in India, *International Journal of Multidisciplinary Research,* Vol. II, Issue 7.

Jamwal, B.A. (2012), Teacher Education, Issues and Their Remedies, *International Referred Research Journal,* Vol. 2, Issue 19.

NAAC. (2015), Guidelines for the creation of the Internal Quality Assurance Cell (IQAC) in Accredited institutions.

National Knowledge Commission Report 2006-09.

Naveen Chahal, Hafizullah Dar, (2015), "Higher Education Sector in India: Challenges of sustainability", *Journal of Management Research and Review,* Volume 5, Issue 3, March 2015.

Patil, D., (2015), "Indian Higher Education: Issues and challenges", *ASM's International E-Journal on ongoing Research in Management and IT.*

Power, K.B. (2002), *India Higher Education,* Concept Publishing Co., New Delhi.

Report of Twelfth Five Year Plan, Planning Commission of India, New Delhi, 2002.

Singh, Shivani, (2005), Education chess: Are Government School any better now. *The Times of India,* Retrieved 20/09/2016.

UGC, *Annual Report 2014-15*, UNESCO, (2015) Education 2030 Incheon Declaration and Framework for Action for the Implication of Sustainable Development Goal", December 2015, Paris.

UNESCO, (2016), "Global education monitoring Report" de Fontenog 75352, Paris 07 sp France Retrieved.

www.academia.edu/..../HigherEducation in the world 5._knowledge-engagement.

www.google.co.in major issues and problems of teachers education in India.

www.palgrave.com/us/book/978023053365pure.pascalobservatory.org/sites/default/files/guni_report_press_release_1.pdfwww.guninetwork.org GUNiTopics Engagementhttps:/www.bookdepository.com/Hiogher-Education-World-5..../9780230535565

www.ugc.ac.in

www.UGCac in page NAAC asp.
www.unesdoc.unesco.org
www.tfhe.net/report/conclusions.html
www.universitywotrldnews.com/article. php?story=20101008113124222https:/ /en.wikipedia.org/wiki/Higher_education_in_India
www.unesco.org/education/uedocs/cms_ data/does/pressdata/en/educ/ 139717.pdfhttps:/books.google.co.in/books?isbn=9811010560www. highereducattion.org/reports/cal_highered/conclusion.shtml.
https://education-2025.wikispaces.com.Conclusion
https://www.ncert.nic.in/htm//pdf/final NCERT profile Brochures pdf.
https://www.tfhe.net/report/conclustions.html
https://www.taimeshighereduction.com/world-university rankings2016 worlds-ranking.
https://www.timeshighereducation.com/features/conclusion/192440.aricle
https://www.timeshighereducation.com/features/conclusion/192440.article
https:/education-2025.wikispaces. com?Conclusionsitersorces.worldbank.org. EDUCATION/Resources/278200…./peril_promise_en.pdf
https://www.universityworldnews.com/article.php?stor=20101008113124222
https:/www.timeshighereducation.com/world-university-rankings/….world-ranking.

Section-III
Development Perspective

13
Higher Education and Industrial Development

A Comparison Between India and Other Countries

Vivek N.

Introduction

India holds an important place in the global education industry. The country has more than 1.4 million schools with over 227 million students enrolled and more than 36,000 higher education institutes. India has one of the largest higher education systems in the world. However, there is still a lot of potential for further development in the education system.

India has become the second largest market for e-learning after the US. The sector is currently pegged at US$ 2-3 billion, and is expected to touch US$ 40 billion by 2017. The distance education market in India is expected to grow at a Compound Annual Growth Rate (CAGR) of around 34 per cent during 2013-14 to 2017-18. Moreover, the aim of the government to raise its current gross enrolment ratio to 30 per cent by 2020 will also boost the growth of the distance education in India.

Education Sector in India

Market Size

The education sector in India is poised to witness major growth in the years to come as India will have world's largest tertiary-age population and second largest graduate talent pipeline globally by the end of 2020. In FY 2015-16, the education market was worth about US$ 100 billion and is expected to reach US$ 116.4 billion in FY 2016-17. Currently, higher education contributes 59.7 per cent of the market size, school education 38.1 per cent, pre-school segment 1.6 per cent, and technology and multi-media the remaining 0.6 per cent. Higher education system in India has undergone rapid expansion. Currently, India's higher education system is the largest in the world enrolling over 70 million students while in less than two decades, India has managed to create additional capacity for over 40 million students. At present, higher education sector witnesses spending of over Rs. 46,200 crore (US$ 6.78 billion), and it is expected to grow at an average annual rate of over 18 per cent to reach Rs. 2,32,500 crore (US$ 34.12 billion) in next 10 years.

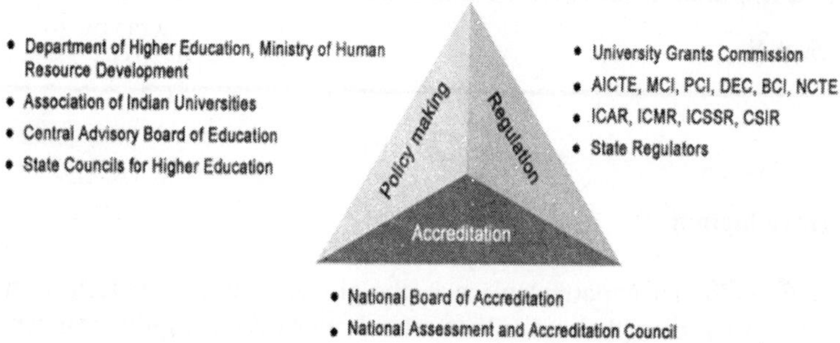

Fig. 13.1: Regulatory Framework of Higher Education in India

Source: Govt. of India

Investment

- The total amount of Foreign Direct Investments (FDI) inflow into the education sector in India stood at US$ 1,256 million from April 2000 to March 2016, according to data released by Department of Industrial Policy and Promotion (DIPP).
- The education and training sector in India has witnessed some major investments and developments in the recent past. Some of them are:
- The Government of India aims to increase digital literacy to at least 50 per cent of Indians from currently 15 per cent over a period of next three years.
- Training and skills development firm NIIT has partnered with US-based edX to offer online courses from leading international universities including MIT and Berkeley to about 5 lakh people over the next three years.
- Byju's, an education technology start-up, has raised US$ 50 million from the Chan Zuckerberg Initiative, founded by

Facebook founder Mark Zuckerberg, and existing investors Sequoia Capital, Sofina SA, Lightspeed Venture Partners and Times Internet Ltd.

- India and Germany have signed an agreement on vocational education and skill development with a budget of US$ 3.37 million, which will help create and improve cooperative workplace-based vocational training in India's industrial clusters.
- Cisco Systems plans to invest US$ 100 million in India over the next 2 years, will be used to fund early-stage and growth-stage companies in the country, open six new innovation labs, three centres of expertise and train around 250,000 students by 2020.
- Neev Knowledge Management Pvt. Ltd., which offers online and classroom-based certification courses under the brand name EduPristine, has raised US$ 10 million from Kaizen Management Advisors and DeVry Inc., which will be used to increase its course offerings, and increase its presence to 15 cities across the country.
- BRS Ventures and Holdings Ltd., owned by Abu Dhabi-based billionaire Mr. B.R. Shetty, plans to invest US$ 1.8 billion in Amaravati in the state of Andhra Pradesh across projects in healthcare, tourism, hospitality, infrastructure, and education sector.
- Byju's, an education technology start-up, has raised US$ 75 million from US-based venture capital firm Sequoia Capital and Belgium-based investment firm Sofina, which will be used to improve content delivery, expand product pipeline, launch in new markets and continue to build its talent pool.
- US based multinational technology major Intel Corporation has partnered with Extramarks Education, a digital learning solutions provider, to tap the US$ 40 billion private school sector in India and thereby provide optimised learning solutions and extend computing technologies to students and schools in the country.
- EdCast, a technology education start-up based in Silicon Valley, plans to invest up to US$ 50 million in education based technology and tie-up with around 500 educational institutions to build digital content and curriculum for educational institutions in India.
- Tata Trusts, part of the Tata Group, has entered into a strategic partnership with web-based free learning portal, Khan Academy, and seeks to use technology to provide free education to anyone, anywhere in India.

- Venture capital fund Acumen has invested in two Hyderabad-based education start-ups—Ignis Careers (US$ 250,000) and SEED (US$ 650,000)—working in the low-cost school education space.
- Anuna Education, a partner to National Skills Development Corporation (NSDC) has announced the eEntrepreneurship Programme in collabouration with eBay India. Anuna Education will train entrepreneur to sell their products on eBay globally in collabouration with eBay India along with a practical training on how to sell the products to global buyers.
- The Central Board of Secondary Education (CBSE) has mandated the appointment of a special educator for children with learning disabilities so that they could be assimilated with other students. This directive came as a part of "inclusive practices" philosophy of CBSE and strict guidelines of "Right to Education" Act.
- In an attempt to improve health care infrastructure in West Bengal, nine new medical colleges will be opened, out of which five will be government-run while the other four will be set up under the Public Private Partnership (PPP) model.

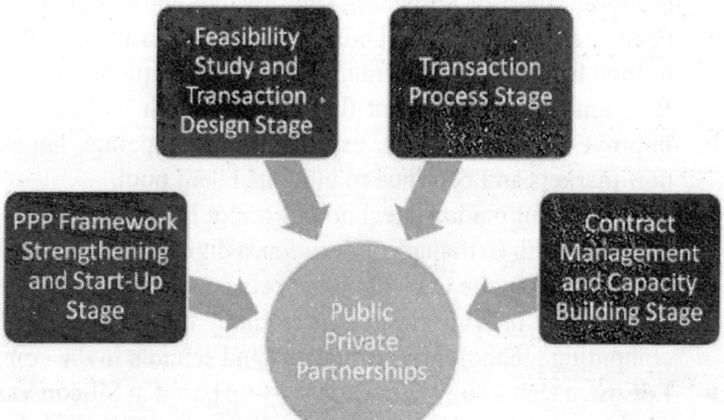

Fig. 13.2: Public-Private Partnerships

Government Initiatives

Some of the other major initiatives taken by the Government of India are:

- The Union Budget 2016-17 has made the following provisions for the education sector.
- 10 public and 10 private educational institutions to be made world-class.
- Scheme to get Rs. 500 crore (US$ 73.36 million) for promoting entrepreneurship among Schedule Caste/Scheduled Tribe (SC/ ST).
- Digital Repository for all school leaving certificates and diplomas.
- Rs. 1,000 crore (US$ 146.72 million) allocated for higher education financing.
- Rs. 1,700 crore (US$ 250 million) allocated for 1500 multi-skill development centres
- 62 new Jawahar Navodaya Vidyalayas (JNV) to provide quality education.
- Digital literacy scheme to be launched for covering six crore additional rural households.
- Objective to skill one crore youth in the next three years under the Pradhan Mantri Kaushal Vikas Yojana (PMKVY).
- The Government of India has announced plans to digitise academic records such as degrees, diplomas, mark sheets, migration certificate, skill certificate etc. from secondary to tertiary-level institutions into a National Academic Depository (NAD).
- The Government of India plans to set up an advanced research and training institute in chemical engineering, which will offer support services to businesses in technology, design and testing and will train engineers and scientists through its various centres in different parts of the country.
- The Government of India has signed a financing agreement with The World Bank, for International Development Association (IDA) credit of US$ 300 million, for the Madhya Pradesh Higher Education Quality Improvement Project, which aims to improve student outcomes, especially of disadvantaged groups in selected Higher Education Institutions (HEIs) and increase the effectiveness of the higher education system in Madhya Pradesh.
- The Human Resource Development (HRD) Ministry has entered into a partnership with private companies, including Tata Motors Ltd., Tata Consultancy Services Ltd. and real-estate firm Hubtown Ltd., to open three Indian Institutes of Information Technology (IIITs), through Public-Private Partnership (PPP), at Nagpur, Ranchi, and Pune.

- Prime Minister Mr. Narendra Modi launched the Skill India initiative—"Kaushal Bharat, Kushal Bharat". Under this initiative, the government has set itself a target of training 400 million citizens by 2022 that would enable them to find jobs. The initiatives launched include various programmes like: Pradhan Mantri Kaushal Vikas Yojana (PMKVY), National Policy for Skill Development and Entrepreneurship 2015, Skill Loan scheme, and the National Skill Development Mission.
- PMKVY is the flagship programme under the Skill India Initiative and it includes incentivising skill training by providing financial rewards on completion of training to the participants. Over the next year 2.4 million Indians are believed to be benefited from this scheme.
- National Policy for Skill Development and Entrepreneurship 2015 is India's first integrated programme to develop skill and promote entrepreneurship simultaneously. The vision of this programme is to skill the Indian youth rapidly with high standards and at the same time promote entrepreneurship thus creating wealth and gainful employment for the citizens.
- Skill Loan Scheme is designed to disburse loans of Rs. 5,000 (US$ 75.3) to Rs. 150,000 (US$ 2,260) to 3.4 million Indians planning to develop their skills in the next five years.
- The National Skill Development Mission is developed to expedite the implementation of skilling activities in India by providing robust institutional framework at the centre and the state.
- India and Australia have signed a Memorandum of Understanding (MoU) to boost partnerships between the two countries in the fields of higher education and research, including technical and professional education, schools, vocational education and training.
- The National Skill Development Corporation of India (NSDC) under a Public Private Partnership promoted by the Ministry of Finance, Government of India signed a Memorandum of Understanding with Centre for Research and Industrial Staff Performance (CRISP), India to explore national and international opportunities for strengthening skills development in India.

Road Ahead

Various government initiatives are being adopted to boost the growth of distance education market, besides focusing on new education techniques, such as E-learning and M-learning.

Education sector has seen a host of reforms and improved financial outlays in recent years that could possibly transform the country into a knowledge haven. With human resource increasingly gaining significance in the overall development of the country, development of education infrastructure is expected to remain the key focus in the current decade. In this scenario, infrastructure investment in the education sector is likely to see a considerable increase in the current decade.

Moreover, availability of English speaking tech-educated talent, democratic governance and a strong legal and intellectual property protection framework are enablers for world class product development, as per Mr. Amit Phadnis, President-Engineering and Site Leader for Cisco (India).

The Government of India has taken several steps including opening of IITs and IIMs in new locations as well as allocating educational grants for research scholars in most government institutions. Furthermore, with online modes of education being used by several educational organisations, the higher education sector in India is set for some major changes and developments in the years to come.

By 2030, India will be amongst the youngest nations in the world. With nearly 140 million people in the college-going age group, one in every four graduates in the world will be a product of the Indian higher education system.

Over the last two decades, India has remarkably transformed its higher education landscape. It has created widespread access to low-cost high-quality university education for students of all levels.

With well-planned expansion and a student-centric learning-driven model of education, India has not only bettered its enrolment numbers but has dramatically enhanced its learning outcomes.

A differentiated three-tiered university system—where each tier has a distinct strategic objective—has enabled universities to build on their strengths and cater across different categories of educational needs.

Further, with the effective use of technology, India has been able to resolve the longstanding tension between excellence and equity.

India has also undertaken large-scale reforms to better faculty-student ratios by making teaching an attractive career path, expanding capacity for doctoral students at research universities and delinking educational qualifications from teaching eligibility.

The Road to Progress: 2013 to 2030

In recent years, India has undertaken massive structural and systemic changes that have started to yield encouraging results. The country has been touted to have the best-in-class post-secondary education system at present. Some of the significant factors that have contributed to this growth and can help envision the 2030 dream includes:

- Expansion of a differentiated university system with a three-tiered formalized structure.
- Transition to a learner-centred paradigm of education.
- Intensive use of technology.
- Reforms in governance.

Need for Greater Role of Industry in Higher Education in India

For India to become economically, politically, and socially developed, education is critical. As a result the government must assume the responsibility for providing and financing education, especially basic education. Today, India already produces some of the most talented and intelligent students and workers, but questions related to quality, access, and equity still challenge educational planners. In corroboration, a recent study titled Effective Education for Employment (EEE) by Edexcel stated that there is a huge mismatch between what is being taught in schools, colleges and universities and the knowledge, skills and behaviour businesses and organisations are looking for, in new recruits. Even students felt that their education lacked relevance to the jobs they were hoping to apply for in the future which reinforces the missing element "linking education to careers".

The former HRD Minister, Mr. Kapil Sibal called for significant reforms in the Indian education system in order to address these deep-rooted issues that are hampering the modernization of the sector. However, taking on such a responsibility is immensely compound, making it important for the government to explore diverse ways of financing and providing educational services. The Indian education system has a multitude of governing bodies—employer associations, chambers of commerce and other business organizations all of which work somewhat in silos. In fact in most developed and developing countries it is the Chamber of Commerce that leads from the front and represents employers and businesses.

The complexity of this challenge calls for a bold and timely response—a solution that can allow us to leapfrog costly stages in the development and expansion of our education systems, while still enabling institutions to incorporate 21st century skills into a demanding curricula. At this stage we would do well to encourage public-private partnerships, attract foreign direct investment (FDI), provide independent accreditation rating systems and grant autonomy in governance, amongst many other initiatives. Moreover, if such a system could be guided by a comprehensive roadmap of curricular and assessment reform, new teacher recruitment and training strategies, leadership development, and the integration of collabourative technologies, we will be able to address some of the challenges we face.

The end goal here is the systemic improvement of the quality, inequity and accessibility of education to everyone. Following such an approach enables us to address the existing skills gap that is been echoed from various quarters, particularly from the industry which has long been reeling under a talent crunch. And from past experiences in India and in other countries, the way to go forward is clearly to build strong public private partnerships.

The main rationale for developing public private partnerships (PPPs) in education is to maximize the potential for expanding equitable access to schooling and to improving education outcomes, especially for marginalized groups. Following a PPP model especially when it comes to higher education can bring multiple benefits. To begin with, the challenges that institutes face have a direct impact on corporations and the future of their business. Sustainability for the private sector depends on the innovation and expertise of their employees. Hence their priority will always be the recruitment and retention of top talent.

Finally, we know that although today's global, Internet-based economy provides numerous opportunities not available before, there is still a critical need for universal access to quality education and visionary leadership. And PPPs, when implemented correctly, can increase efficiency and choice as well as expand access to education services, particularly for households that tend to be poorly served by traditional delivery methods. PPPs also allow governments to take advantage of the specialized skills offered by certain private organizations and to overcome operating restrictions such as inflexible salary scales and work rules that may prevail in the public sector. Unfortunately quality in India is viewed when private institutions are able to surpass the standards set by Government institutions and are able to garner students based on this fact. But, while many corporations invest heavily in ongoing education and skills training of employees, they still depend on the solid foundation taught during primary, secondary, and tertiary education.

IT majors such as Infosys, Wipro, Cisco, Autodesk have been leading the way in building sustained programmes to impart the desired skills at a college level. For example, Dr. Reddy's Foundation's Livelihood Advancement Business School (LABS) works towards assimilating its students into the competitive job market, it also helps them acquire the required livelihood and social skills in an environment of learning and mentoring that is responsive to the student's emotional and developmental needs.

Such success stories now need to be scaled-up in association with other corporates to make a sizeable impact on the system. For a country betting on its demographic dividend, these kinds of partnerships help build scale. On the other hand, government also plays a role in defining and monitoring the role corporates play in the education system. The proposed new National Council for Higher Education (NCHE) which would take over the academic, accreditation and financial functions of the regulators is one such example. In essence, because corporations are consumers of the talent developed by the education system, engaging in strategic initiatives for education reform in partnership with the public sector becomes mutually beneficial.

Education has been the passport to opportunity and prosperity—It has enabled individuals, whether in developing or developed countries, to become academics, entrepreneurs, and business and government leaders. And by working together, both private and public sectors can help achieve this goal.

Focus towards Qualitative and Quantitative Development

The National Policy on Education (NPE) 1986 defines, *inter alia*, the Government policy in the area of technical and management education. The NPE 1986 underlined the need for re-organising the technical and management education system to effectively deal with the changes in the economy, social environment, production and management processes, rapid expansion of knowledge and advances in science and technology. The NPE 1986 laid specific guidelines for the qualitative and quantitative development of the technical and management education sectors, establishment of linkages amongst the concerned agencies, manpower assessment and technical education forecasting, increasing effectiveness of technical education management system, proper delivery systems, measures to achieve greater cost effectiveness and generation of resources through suitable means. The National Policy on Education has also laid emphasis on modernisation and removal of obsolescence of labouratories and workshops of engineering colleges and polytechnics in order to enhance functional efficiency.

As a consequence of continuous efforts, phenomenal growth has occurred in the facilities of Technical Education in the country since 1947. This has been possible through planning and setting the objectives, implementation and conducting reviews and corrections whenever and wherever needed.

The formal educational opportunities have increased tremendously and this can be gauged from the fact that there has been a ten-fold increase in the number of engineering colleges and almost a twenty-fold increase in the diploma polytechnic institutions since independence. In 1947, there were 43 diploma polytechnic institutions with a student intake of 3,670 which increased to 1,102 with an intake of 1,84,648 in 1997. Likewise, in 1947, there were 44 degree-level institutions with a student intake of 2,500, which increased to 547 institutions with a student intake of 1,30,947 in 1997.

The Indian technical education system during the post-Independence period is, therefore, characterised by a massive growth in the number of institutions and student enrolment, vast coverage of subject areas and specialisation, establishment of institutions of national importance, establishment of regional-level institutions of excellence, emergence of unaided private institutions and the emergence of non-formal sector in technical education besides establishment of national and State-level distance learning programmes.

The expansion in technical education has been possible on account of reasonable investments made in all the Five Year Plans. The role of the private initiatives in the massive expansion of technical education facilities is also prominent. The Government has played a proactive role through granting income tax exemption for the donations received by the educational institution from private sources. In addition, based on a Supreme Court judgement, the rationalisation in tuition fees has been responsible for an enthusiastic response from the private sector for its participation.

What Role will Higher Education Play in the Fourth Industrial Revolution?

The Fourth Industrial Revolution urges us to think creatively about the manufacturing process, value chain, distribution and customer service processes. In the meanwhile, the future of education emphasizes the immense need to look beyond these areas and strategically utilize the "Internet of Things" to prepare the coming workforce for the challenges ahead.

Universities emphasize their role in shaping future technology by being the test beds for innovation and educating future generations. Traditional education has contributed greatly to the current levels of industrial evolution and technological advancement. However, in order for higher education to deliver future generations with the right set of skills and knowledge; an imperative question has to be asked regarding how higher education institutes would be affected by the Fourth Industrial Revolution and how the delivery of education will be transformed.

There are different opportunities available that will shape the role which can be undertaken by higher education in the Fourth Industrial Revolution. Combining the strength of the traditional higher education with the increasing trend of MOOCs represents necessary steps to scale quality education. On the other hand, "Global Identity" and "Education for You" embody aspects, if globally embraced, that would transform global higher education. Let's explore these in more detail.

A Mix Between Traditional Education and MOOCs

At times where the boundaries between the internet, physical world and people are becoming more blurred by each passing day, the need for education in general and higher education in particular to be "Place-based" is diminishing. Currently, education is being connected to mobile devices through applications in the cloud and is no longer limited to knowledge but extended to skills acquisition. With the expansion in networking services nationally and globally, physical boundaries are no longer barriers to education.

Massive Open Online Courses (MOOCs) are a potentially disruptive innovation. The number is increasing exponentially across the globe, making learning more accessible to people. According to MOOCS in 2015, the number of participants has doubled from 16-18 million students to 35 million students across all MOOC providers; even universities are digitizing some of their courses. However, one can not overlook the importance of direct and face-to-face interaction between the learners and teachers as an influential part of a quality education. Therefore, a mix between MOOCs, which are gaining more and more popularity, and traditional ways of delivering education is extremely vital for meeting the global job markets' needs.

One of the main issues facing MOOCs is related to accreditation and trust in the associated credential. On the other hand, higher education institutions are trusted and have had a long experience in accreditation. The future mix between MOOCs and traditional education can provide higher education institutes the opportunity to expand services to offer credentials using the experiences of the lecturers and teachers. One of the main services universities offer is the provision of certification for students upon the completion of their studies. Nonetheless, there are many students whose education is disrupted whether because of war, conflicts, or a lack of financial resources. The higher education community might address this great challenge by creating micro certificates recognizing the level of knowledge or skills acquired by the sum of a person's education until the moment of its interruption.

Global Identity

At a time when the world is witnessing the largest refugee crisis since the Second World War; education is being stressed more than ever for those millions of refugees around the globe. According to the report "Uncounted and Unacknowledged" about Syria's refugee university students and academics in Jordan, one of the main challenges facing the provision of higher education to refugees and their inclusion in their host countries' educational system is the lack of official documents verifying the educational levels acquired in their home countries. Having a digital identity that is trusted, portable and secure, which stores an individual information and can be used across countries especially in case of conflict eruption or natural disaster, would address this challenge.

As individuals gain education from different universities, work at diverse and global organizations and participate actively with different initiatives, his/her identity is no longer tied to one organization. Creating identities based on every institution one learns from or organization one works at could be very confusing and overwhelming; which raise the question of "What is our identity and where can we find it?" Douglas Van Houweling, the founding President of Internet and Professor in the

School of information at the University of Michigan, predicted the creation of "Global Identity" as key development in Higher Education in 20 years' time. The trust placed in Higher Education Institutions could be the driver for Higher Education to be leading the creation of a global identity that is portable across universities and organizations. Higher Education is not proprietary nor limited to one ideology; its openness and long history of tryst makes it eligible to act as a custodian for protecting this identity and continuously create environment for knowledge and skill attainment.

As a first step to the Global Identity, the need for federated identity is being recognized globally; where a local login access to global resources is facilitated. The Research and Education Federations REFEDs group, a place to exchange Identity Federation processes, practices and policies and holds discussion to facilitate inter-federation work, has participants from 61 countries; with 43 countries producing federated identity and 18 countries in the pilot stage. Nonetheless, privacy remains a main concern for every individual in the digital world; where individuals would like to maintain control over their identity. Unlike commercial companies that aim to maximize control over ones' data, Federated Identity and privacy management give users much more control over what to be shared with minimal disclosure of relevant data.

The shift for "Inter-federated Identity" is scaling the process of sharing entity metadata globally between different national federations with minimum barriers. The student or researcher's behaviour can indicate his/her identity and tracking such behaviour, which is becoming more possible than ever through the fourth industrial revolution, will ensure the verification of the identity; a vital step for accreditation. These efforts could lead to the vision of "Global identity" which can extend beyond the education sector to health sector and others and across countries.

Education for You

Data analysis and automation help companies not only to survive but also to thrive in the future. Similarly, Higher Education institutions are embracing data mining in order to gain better understanding of student performance and deliver "Education for you" that is tailored to meet the demand of the job markets while considering the students' needs. Alan Blinder, an economist at Princeton University, argued in "Education of the Third Industrial Revolution" that for students to adapt to the information age, a great focus should be of the type of education students receive rather than the quantity they receive. Education is increasingly becoming "just in time" rather than "just in case"; it is more about what you need to know for a certain time than compiling knowledge that may never be needed. Data regarding student performance, behaviour, development, and interaction inside classrooms and on the online platforms of MOOCs as well as data from smart campus would create diverse and fast-changing data. The ability of Higher Education institutions to integrate this information into smart data would result in intelligent decisions in regards to the delivery of customized education and personalized learning experience for students.

The Challenges Ahead

Altering higher education is more necessary than ever before. However, the challenges ahead have to be considered in order to ensure effective and immediate transformation. With the reduced public financial support for higher education; universities need to think strategically regarding methods to utilize their experience in credentials, trust and identity to offer new services. Furthermore, higher education leadership needs to be less risk averse especially in this world of disruptive change. It is no longer an option to keep doing things the old way; innovation and accepting change are now prerequisite for survival.

Inequality would still be a concern for digital higher education since more than 4 billion people are still offline without access to the internet according to a study by McKinsey & Company. Most of those people are marginalized families who live in developing countries with no access to an affordable education. Although digital higher education can be more affordable compared to other education options, higher education institutions need to consider the best ways to reaching underserved populations where education can serve as a strong empowerment and change tool.

Risk, privacy and security are other challenges facing higher education. Collabouration, integration and aligning security process are key words for scaling higher education efforts and bringing sustainability. During the World Engineering Education Forum 2015, Professor Sabina Jeschke from RWTH Aachen University said, "the complexity of the systems developed to meet the demands of the fourth industrial revolution necessitate interdisciplinary and collabouration as a precondition for innovation."

This is the time to ask whether the global higher education community will only react to how the business world is shaping the Fourth Industrial

Revolution or if it will be among the key players of shaping the Fourth Industrial Revolution! Furthermore, the annual meeting of the World Economic Forum happening in Davos, 2016 is the place to investigate and explore further the previously mentioned question and challenges.

The Role of Higher Education in High Tech Industry Development

There is much written on the role of American universities in high tech industries and more generally in their industrial development, including some that compare their roles against those in Europe or Japan. For other countries, there are studies which conclude that a significant role was or is being played by well trained engineers and scientists, and by implication higher education systems. However, few studies go beyond referring to higher education as one of multiple—albeit often critical—factors. The comparative higher education literature describes similarities and differences across national higher education systems, but there tends to be little emphasis on different roles they play in economic development.

Lester (2005) makes an important step in arguing that different types of industrial transformations require different roles to be played by universities based on a comparative study of several countries. There is also an emerging literature on university-industry relationships in developing countries (Chun and Kenny, 2007; Kroll and Leifner, 2008; Ma, 2007; Wu, 2007; Yusuf and Nabeshima, 2007), with some papers beginning to discuss the role of universities in economic development in a more specific way (Mazzoleni and Nelson, 2007; Leifner and Schiller, 2008). Mazzonleni and Nelson provide an in-depth analysis of the role of public research in economic catch up, and argues for the increasing importance of research for economic catch up particularly in application oriented sciences and engineering (2007). They also provide a helpful summary about the nature of American research universities and their economic roles. Leifner and Schiller contribute to the debate through introducing the notion of 'academic capabilities' to think about the roles universities play in technological capacity development (2008).

This chapter seeks to extend our understanding about the role of higher education in the development of high tech industry from a range of countries. Wherever possible, this has been complemented by country specific literature on higher education systems and their development. The main emphasis has been given to two 'recent' high tech industrial sectors: ICT (including hardware as well as software) and biotechnology.

The point of this chapter is not to provide a full contrast of the paths taken, nor to examine all the contributing factors to high tech industry development. That high tech industry took off for a variety of reasons is taken as a given, and the chapter focuses on what possible specific roles higher education has played within that context. The chapter examines differences in high tech industry capabilities among countries—but only to the extent that they are related to different roles played by higher education systems.

In order to explore the variety of roles played by higher education at different stages of industrial development, four sets of countries were included in the chapter:

(a) the US, which has held a leading position in both industries from their birth;
(b) Japan and Finland which entered the global competition in high tech products based on significant industrial capability that already existed;
(c) a group of late-developers including Taiwan and Korea which nonetheless were building industrial capabilities around the time when these industries were born; and
(d) a group of countries which developed high tech industry from a much less developed industrial base (Ireland, Israel, China and India).

The Framework for Understanding Different Institutional Characteristics

What are the key dimensions that differentiate higher education institutions meaningfully? In this section, a framework for differentiating institutions is proposed using three different dimensions that measure institutional characteristics: responsiveness, basic science orientation, and selectivity (Fig. 13.1). The first dimension, responsiveness, distinguishes institutions in terms of their ability and inclination to respond to changing practical and industrial needs. The second dimension, basic science orientation, distinguishes institutions in terms of the level of commitment to fundamental science. The third dimension has to do with the level of selectivity with which students and staff are recruited into the institution, and distinguishes elite institutions with those that are open to the greater mass.

DIFFERENT ROLES PLAYED BY DIFFERENT TYPES OF INSTITUTIONS

This section describes the roles played by the different types of institutions in the development of high tech industry, drawing on the experiences of the countries listed above. No single type of institutions appears to be necessary for the development of high tech industry. Rather, different countries have seen different types of institutions playing different roles. The footprints of university roles are sometimes visible in the shape and nature of the resulting industry, but at other times industry developed incorporating university contributions in a way that became almost invisible.

It is well established that some American research universities played critical roles in the birth and development of biotechnology and computer industry. For instance, fundamental scientific discoveries in university labouratories and resulting patents (such as Cohen and Boyer's discovery of the recombinant DNA technique) led to the development of biotechnology as a whole new industry with strong linkages with academic scientific research (Henderson, Orsenigo and Pisano, 1999). The early evolution of the biotechnology industry was characterized by a number of new firms, many of which were academic spinoffs—usually with academics working in conjunction with professional managers, backed by venture capital. The early academic inventors were labelled as 'star scientists' as they were key players both in basic science and in their applications and had a special role mainly because of the significant amount of tacit knowledge associated with the original scientific discoveries (Zucker and Darby, 1996; Zucker *et al.*, 1998; Zucker *et al.*, 2002). The norms in American universities that permitted academics to get deeply engaged in commercialization, which had developed early given their value for being useful, played a key role in this process (Henderson, Orsenigo and Pisano, 1999; Eskowitz, 2002).

American universities also played key roles in the development of the computer hardware and software industry, though their visibility varied over time (Bresnahan and Malerba, 1999; Mowery, 1999; Rosenberg and Nelson, 1994). For instance, universities were actively engaged in the early development of computers in the 1940s (and indeed during this period, European universities such as Manchester, Cambridge and Berlin were as active as American universities). They also played a critical role in the development of microcomputers as exemplified by spinoffs from MIT, Stanford and University of Texas (only Cambridge University in the UK played a similar role in microcomputers in Europe).

There is evidence that industry values the less 'visible' contributions made by universities. One survey found that industry saw general research findings or instrumentation and techniques developed through research as more important university contributions than prototypes (Cohen *et al.*, 2002). The same survey found that publications, meetings and conferences, informal interactions and consulting were more important than patents, as mechanisms through which industry gained access to university knowledge. Further, industry reported that university research was helpful in solving problems, rather than in inspiring and triggering new research. These results have to do with contributions made by the American universities more generally, which are likely include a whole range of institutions including basic research institutions. Nonetheless, it is important to note that what is valued is not so much 'application' capabilities in universities, but 'relevant' research capability.

There is also some evidence that the development of the software industry was greatly facilitated by an early establishment of computer science as a new discipline in universities (Mowery, 1999). Universities were thereby capable not only of contributing to key knowledge formation but also of organizing and delivering education programmes to supply updated skills. Indeed, the American universities' ability to create and legitimate computer science as a new field was unparalleled by European or Japanese universities (Mowery, 1999).

In Israel, universities played similar roles, by supplying highly skilled human resources and in being a source of leading technologies not only in ICT but also in biotechnology and agriculture related research (de Fontenay and Carmel, 2004; Breznitz, 2007). Soon after its formation, the Israeli government made significant public investments in application oriented scientific research in universities, public research institutions and in the military. Their universities became well established scientific centres early, and today has world's highest publication record in volume per capita and in their citations. This did not stop them from becoming application-orientated also, as university-industry relationships had long been well established (Bresnitz, 2004), and as their unusually high patenting records show with three universities among the top six patent issuers in the country (Bresnitz, 2004; Trajtenberg, 2001). Israel became one of the first R&D sites abroad for US multinational companies with Motorola establishing a research unit in 1963 (de Fonteney and Carmel, 2004). Universities' contribution tends to be overshadowed by that of the Military in the stories told about Israel's high tech industry, but they have contributed to the emergence of an entrepreneurial sector directly and indirectly, through spinoffs as well as science parks, some of which had been established as early as the 1960s (Roper and Grime, 2005).

It is no accident that the resulting high tech industry in Israel was highly R&D oriented, and had cutting edge technological content. This provides a sharp contrast to other emerging economies. While in Ireland or India, their software industry largely grew providing software services, Israel's software industry developed on the basis of niche software products with global applications. Israel's innovation capabilities as judged by its patenting performance, for instance, lags behind US or Japan, but is comparable to Finland or Taiwan (Trajtenberg, 2001). Israel's ICT industry has a marked concentration on upstream R&D, compared with the Finnish ICT industry which covers a wider value chain ranging from R&D, production to marketing and distribution, or the Irish case, which has hardly any R&D (Roper and Grime, 2005).

In summary, relevant research universities appear to contribute through:

- conducting basic research in fields relevant to the developments in industry, and disseminating such knowledge through a varieties of activities such as patenting and licensing, academic spinoffs, consulting and advising.
- providing updated skills in areas relevant to industry, both in undergraduate education and in advanced research training for masters and Ph.Ds.

Practically Oriented Institutions

Practically oriented institutions played a unique role in offering engineering and science skills which were more specialized and directly relevant to industrial needs. In Ireland and Finland, professional institutions were created as an alternative to conventional university education, which was seen to be unresponsive to industrial needs. The institutional responsiveness was particularly important when new disciplines such as computer science emerged, and appeared to give countries a competitive edge, as was clear in the case of Ireland.

In Ireland, the government led expansion of technically trained manpower in the 1970s and 1980s played a key role in attracting multinational companies (MNCs) including in ICT. The starting point was the consensus that emerged early among policy makers that technical education was critically needed, but that universities were overly academic and that different institutions were needed to provide the critically needed technical manpower (White, 2001). Thirteen Regional Technical Colleges and two National Institutes of Higher Education were established in the 1970s for this purpose, representing the bulk of expansion in the tertiary sector. They were established specifically to be responsive to economic needs, and are today known to have well-established practices, for instance, in assessing industrial needs or in obtaining industrial inputs in curricular content (Breznitz, 2007).

Finland also made a decisive move in creating a set of responsive institutions when they established 29 polytechnics in the 1990s. By 2000, nearly 60 per cent of entrants to higher education were going to polytechnics. Though it is early to understand the full impact of polytechnics in Finland, their performance reviews have been positive, with indications that their expansion coincided with the timing of major industrial needs, particularly in telecommunications (OECD, 2003). In one survey of high tech industry in Northern Finland, 47 per cent of the companies said that polytechnics were important, compared with 38 per cent which thought a university with a known regional orientation to be important and 10-20 per cent that found other universities in Finland important (Juahiainen, 2006).

Teaching-focused Institutions

In the early stage of high tech industry development, companies often recruited generic science and engineering graduates who were not necessarily trained in a specialization relevant to the industry. Their provision was a role predominantly played by teaching institutions in Japan, Korea, Taiwan, China, and India, mainly because many institutions simply had not yet developed research capacity. In all cases, governments emphasized science and engineering. Beyond such a general statement, there is a significant divergence in terms of what happened.

In Japan, the government aggressively promoted science and engineering undergraduate programmes in response to growing industrial demand in the late 1950s through the early 1960s, not only in national universities, but also in private universities which were largely teaching oriented (Nakayama, 1995). Most private universities in Japan were teaching focused institutions with limited resources to undertake sciences or engineering or research. It was through special government subsidies for science and engineering, which provided up to half of undergraduate student costs and two-thirds of associated investment costs, that they managed to establish science and engineering programmes (Nakayama, 1995). This push no doubt helped Japan obtain a large number of scientists and engineers so that they were 27-28 per cent of all undergraduates in the late 1960s through the 1980s.

Korea and Taiwan made earlier moves in emphasizing science and engineering relative to their industrial development—as they both had met massive brain drains in early days. In Korea, More than a third of undergraduate enrolments were in science and engineering by the mid 1960s, and the proportion went up further to over 40 per cent in the subsequent period in spite of the massive expansion of the higher education sector that was taking place. Korea today has one of the highest tertiary enrolment ratios in the world of 91 per cent, with one of the highest proportions of science and engineering. In Taiwan, the proportion of science and engineering enrolments was about a quarter through the early 1970s, and gradually increased from the mid 1970s through the 1990s to over 40 per cent. In contrast, even in 2005, India's engineers comprised only 6 per cent of total tertiary enrolments, and even when combined with scientists, the proportion is significantly lower than others at 20 per cent. There is no magic number in terms of the share of science and engineering.

One factor whose influence appears to go well beyond that of 'numbers' is selectivity. Japan, Korea, Taiwan, China and India share a common characteristic in having highly selective institutions which recruited high calibre students into engineering nationally, and which have set quality standards in engineering schools more generally. Further, these institutions invariably had a significant share of their institutional profile in engineering, and in that sense, their origins were closer to "practically-oriented" institutions than generic teaching-focused institutions. At the time of the take off, graduates from these selective schools were not in high demand in the labour market; they represented cheap high calibre resources with training in science and technology.

Different Roles Revisited

In this section, six different roles played by higher education institutions are summarized, mainly to highlight the fact that the nature of these roles depends both on the institutional characteristics and the industrial contexts.

Education Roles

Different types of institutions have played different educational roles towards high tech industry development. Generic teaching institutions and basic research universities contributed to the production of generic scientists and engineers, and left the companies to take the responsibility for developing specialized knowledge and skills. This role was particularly pronounced when there was government intervention in preferentially expanding science and engineering programmes. Professionally oriented institutions played a more proactive role in keeping up with changing industrial skills needs and in supplying specialist knowledge and skills as industry evolved. Relevant research universities were able to play the similar proactive role at a higher level—in their research training.

Research Roles

Similarly, different types of institutions played different research roles as well. Academics in relevant research universities played the most proactive role in conducting research and in working directly with its applications, helped by universities' organizational capacity to promote and support consulting, patenting/licensing as well as spinoffs. Basic research oriented universities played a less active role in furthering industries' commercialization goals, but helped companies acquire better understanding of new scientific fields, provided advice and conducted joint research, albeit more often on universities' own terms. Other institutions such as government research institutions or professionally oriented universities helped industry to acquire existing technologies through application oriented research.

Spinoffs

University 'spinoffs' appeared to play a visible role when there was a significant capacity/knowledge gap between universities and surrounding industries but the nature of this capacity/knowledge gap could be very different, as demonstrated by the case of biotechnology in the US and ICT in China.

In biotechnology in the US, the knowledge gap had to do with fundamental scientific discoveries with significant related tacit knowledge. In China, the nature of the knowledge gap in ICT appears to have been about old technology which was nonetheless new in China. The capacity gap may also have arisen because of the highly selective nature of universities; universities may have been better positioned to assemble a group of high calibre individuals to lead and work in new ventures.

There were significant examples of academic spinoffs associated with universities with relevant research capabilities. Thus, in biotechnology in the US, academics from research universities got directly involved in spin-offs, and there were similar stories in different fields in Israel. In Ireland, where universities did not develop research capacity until late, owing to the lack of government funding (Sands, 2005), academic spinoffs were generally not frequent. However, one computer science department developed an early research capacity with European funding, and became known for its academic spinoffs (Breznitz, 2007).

A very different experience was found in China, where universities had become active in creating enterprises since the late 1980s, even when they had little research capability. Though they are sometimes described as 'spin-offs,' they are significantly different from the normal practice in that they are owned and managed by universities (Eun *et al.*, 2006). Some of these companies have been spectacularly successful, and include three of the most successful PC companies, Lenovo, Founder and Tongfang, which were enterprises created by the Chinese Academy of Sciences, Beijing University and Tsinghua University respectively. Some 40 university enterprises are already listed in stock markets in China and Hong Kong (*Ibid.*).

Interestingly, the knowledge content in these companies did not derive from significant scientific research, rather, it was the mechanisms through which skilled personnel moved from universities to the commercial sector (Chen and Kenney, 2007). These enterprises were one simple mechanism through which universities could contribute to industrial capabilities in an environment of very limited industrial capability (Eun *et al.*, 2006). They are closer to Japanese university start ups in the early phase of industrial development (Odagiri and Goto, 1996) where academics could behave as arbitragers of Western technology and were in a good position to create companies, given an under-developed Japanese industrial context.

It is not clear how long this practice of university enterprise will continue in China. Both the government and many universities may be going through a re-thinking process, as many enterprises have not been successful and managerial responsibilities are increasingly demanding (Ma, 2007; Kroll and Leifner, 2008). It is likely that China's university enterprise experience was a phenomenon dictated by the specific context of underdeveloped industry and a high concentration of talents in universities.

Science Parks

Taiwan provides the most visible example of a highly successful science park, which played a critical role in the development of its semi-conductor industry. However, universities were not the main feature of the Science Park. In 1980, the Taiwanese government established a science park in Hsinchu, close to two of Taiwan's best technical universities, and relocated ERSO to the park (Saxenian, 2004). There was a certain division of labour in that applied and relevant basic research were undertaken by ERSO, while the universities appeared largely to supply graduates as manpower to the park.

In China, many high tech zones, industrial and science parks have been established close to universities by the Central Government, local authorities, as well as the universities. The nature of their dynamic evolution is only beginning to be documented, though the diversity in approach is already evident (Chen and Kenny, 2007). The one established by the local authorities in Zhongguancun in Beijing, close to the Chinese Academy of Science as well as to Beijing and Tsinghua Universities, is considered one of the most successful in attracting MNC R&D facilities. Another well known example is the one established by Tsinghua University on its campus, which has many MNC R&D units as well as spin-offs from the university. An interesting variant is Shenzhen whose High-Tech Industrial Park has been used to attract established universities to create a virtual campus.

Licensing

This is one function that seems to be linked strongly to relevant research capacity in universities. However, its effectiveness depends also on the level of development of intellectual property related institutions in the country. In the celebrated case of the US, the patenting practice evolved as one of many mechanisms for technology transfer from universities, predicated upon huge government funding in relevant scientific research (Mowery *et al.*, 2004; Rosenberg and Nelson, 1994). However, it is increasingly clear that for most universities in the US, patenting/licensing is a net drain rather than a source of additional income (Thursby and Thursby, 2007).

The wider acceptance of WTO and other international regimes related to intellectual property will undoubtedly have consequences for the paths that future developing economies can take in catching up. While it is important for developing countries and their universities to increase their understanding about intellectual property, indiscriminate opening of technology transfer offices in universities with a view to patenting their inventions may be unwarranted.

Brain Drain/Circulation

Brain drain turned into brain circulation appears to play an increasingly important role in the introduction of high tech industry in developing countries. This undoubtedly reflects the increasingly global nature of the labour markets in developed countries, many of which are actively recruiting professionals from developing countries in areas of key skills shortages such as ICT. Such a brain drain can turn into brain circulation, once appropriate domestic conditions are developed for industrial development, when 'brains' that are enriched with international experience can return to their home countries.

Indeed, one feature of Taiwan's high tech development which distinguishes it from those of Japan or Korea, is the visible role played by their diaspora of engineers, particularly in Silicon Valley, and how their 'brain drain' turned into 'brain circulation' linked directly to the birth of high tech industry (Saxenian, 1999, 2002, 2004, 2006). Almost eighty per cent of the Taiwanese diaspora professionals in Silicon Valley had gone to the US to study and remained there for work (Saxenian, 2002). Early generations of the diaspora were instrumental in informing the Taiwanese government about Silicon Valley and its unusual dynamism, the reason why the Taiwanese had an early policy for building a cluster rather like Silicon Valley (Saxenian, 2004). In 1980, they invested in a science park in Hsinchu, close to two of Taiwan's best technical universities, and relocated ERSO (Saxenian, 2004). The science park became an active recipient of the returning diaspora with 40 per cent of companies there started by returnees (Wade, 1990; Saxenian, 2004).

It is well known that Taiwan suffered from a massive brain drain which started in the 1950s and lasted until the 1990s. Interestingly, this did not stop the government from organizing programmes of overseas study to complement Taiwan's own education system. In 1975, there were 2300 students studying under government auspices; in 1986, 7000 were in such a programme (Wade, 1990). This was happening in the midst of the massive brain drain, which was estimated as 20 per cent of the all engineering graduates in the late 1970s (Hou and Gee, 1993). Instead of stopping to send people, the Taiwanese government simply stepped up efforts to keep in touch with the diaspora community (Wade, 1990), the benefit of which was finally felt in the 1990s when the brains started to return.

China and India followed Taiwanese experience in brain drain to the Silicon Valley. In the survey of Silicon Valley professionals, over half of Indians and nearly 80 per cent of mainland Chinese had originally come to the US for their education (Saxenian, 2002). China was able to benefit doubly from diasporas, as Hsinchu-Silicon Valley-Shanghai increasingly became connected to broadly defined overseas Chinese engineering including those originally from Taiwan (Saxenian, 2006). In the early 2000s, the Chinese Government also stepped up effort to recruit back the overseas Chinese. For India, the dominance of Indian entrepreneurs not only in Silicon Valley but more broadly in US high tech companies is well documented (Saxenian, 2002, Wadha *et al.*, 2007).

Conclusion

This chapter has argued that higher education institutions can play a variety of roles in supporting high tech industry. The roles they play in turn can influence the shape and nature of high tech industry. This chapter also argued that not all higher education institutions or systems can or need to play the same set of roles. Rather, the roles they play would be determined by the characteristics that the institutions have developed over the years in terms of their responsiveness, their basic science orientation and their selectivity. Governments can play a critical role in influencing the orientations of institutions—through subtle or not so subtle means.

The production of scientists and engineers of high standards and in sufficient numbers has been one common element across all countries. While some countries depended on the large production of generic scientists and engineers, others benefited from sizable investments in specialist training with an emphasis on practical skills. However, in those countries with only generic training in science and engineering, selectivity of institutions appeared to play a key additional role in enabling industry to recruit appropriate manpower.

For a high tech industry needed to develop with high technological content, it was important to have sufficient research capacity in universities to provide advanced scientific skills in the labour force. While proactive industries could do wonders in extracting key scientific capacity and training from any universities with scientific research capacity, as the Japanese case showed, it is more helpful for industry if there was 'responsiveness' on the part of universities. It is perhaps no accident that in countries with proactive and relevant research universities such as the US and Israel, new industries or new strands of industries emerged and grew readily.

Even from universities with limited research capacity, high tech industry did benefit—but often predicated upon cheap high calibre labour and production advantages rather than on technological content. Ireland benefited much from specialist training as provided by practically oriented institutions, while China or India emerged as high tech centres even without such training capabilities. Perhaps in countries such as Ireland where labour costs cannot be as cheap as in China or India, it was important that their labour force provided the value added through additional skills.

Overall, institutions in the right hand cells of Fig. 14.22 appear to contribute more dynamically and directly than those in the left hand cells. Responsiveness is a key dimension for developing countries to encourage in their higher education institutions.

Responsiveness does not appear to emerge naturally. Rather, all the cases examined had some specific interventions—usually from government. There are standard practices that can be used to introduce a more scientific orientation in higher education systems, such as peer review or competitive research funding processes, and developing countries have an option to make use of the international infrastructures such as overseas Ph.D. training or international journals. In contrast, there is no simple way to encourage institutions to become responsive. The 'demand' to which institutions must be responsive is often local, intangible and ill-defined. Governments may require institutions to provide new educational programmes or to expand them, but simply following such a top-down requirement does not make them responsive. The Korean Government's central requirement to keep up the quota for engineering programmes may not have led institutions to become responsive. Indeed, it is possible that the more frequently a government interferes through regulations or even through financial incentives, the less institutions learn to be creative and strategic about what they do. In Ireland and Finland, new groups of institutions had to be established from scratch in order to build responsiveness into the system.

Without such concerted efforts, universities appear to drift towards the left-hand side of Fig. 13.2, as a result of peer pressures and academic norms, towards becoming basic research universities or academically oriented teaching institutions. To the extent that most countries do not have sufficient human or monetary resources to establish research oriented institutions at the outset (one exception being Israel), it appears essential for a country to have a strategy that promotes developments upwards and to the right in Fig. 13.2 so that at least some institutions become relevant research institutions.

Founding ethos does seem to matter, as shown by the Land Grant Colleges in the US or some institutions with technological and regional development missions in Finland. Equally, public statements and expectations that universities should be relevant can also help. The American Government's expectation that universities must be useful for Agriculture was a starting point in their funding of agricultural extension activities in universities. The Chinese Government's explicit demands that universities play a key role in technological upgrading of the society no doubt provided a powerful starting point for them to work with industry; the fact that 'funding' for such activities had to be sought from individual enterprises rather than some central agency was probably helpful as universities had to learn to work with a variety of 'stakeholders'. On the whole, there appear to be more examples of institutions which developed responsiveness first, then followed with fundamental science orientation (one good example being Massachusetts Institute of Technology—*see* Etzkowitz, 2002); it is probably easier to develop in that way rather than to attempt it the other way around.

Today, economic responsiveness of universities has become a global mantra. The last decade has seen an ever increasing number of government policies trying to push universities to develop such a dimension, leading to some changes in academic values. For instance, it would be unusual to meet an academic in any OECD country who would refute the need for a university to be economically relevant. Notwithstanding such a dynamic change taking place, most institutions have a long way to go to develop a full set of internal and external mechanisms to be responsive and proactive. As seen from the example of Japanese national universities, which are as collabourative with industry as are US institutions, they still substantively lag in proactive technology transfer metrics such as licensing and spinoffs. Indeed, in order for them to become truly 'proactive,' a whole new set of relationships are likely to be needed, not only with industry but also with as other players ranging from venture capital to proactive research funding bodies. It takes a full eco-system to help nurture responsive universities. One advantage that developing countries have over old economies may be the potential to develop new institutions that together can make up such a complete system.

Fundamental research orientation is something that requires serious commitment and investment, usually from government. Investments are needed not only in human capital in terms of advanced research training, but also in infrastructure such as libraries and labouratories, and direct expenses associated with research. It is an orientation that cannot be developed overnight. However, it is also an orientation that is hard to change once introduced, as Ph.D. trained academics usually gravitate towards research rather than teaching, and there is often a sense of elitism associated with being research-oriented—and the more 'basic' the more elite.

'Selectivity' is one dimension of higher education institutions which often emerges naturally as the demand for higher education expands and the competition for places increases. Such selectivity needs to be underpinned by robust selection systems that are fair but also provide good learning incentives for future students. This is not easy, but worth considerable attention, as selection systems can influence directly the reputation hierarchy of institutions as well as learning incentives of students for years to come. Some examinations inadvertently encourage students to become tactical rather than learning oriented. Equally, some scoring systems give spurious impression of accuracy.

The fact that all three dimensions are important in enabling institutions to play key roles does not mean that all institutions must be the same. On the contrary, as the case of the US or Finland show, there is a strong case for requisite variety—or diversification within a country. Indeed, it is reasonable for a national system of higher education to seek to have as much diversity as possible in terms of types of institutions.

Nehru, the first post-independence leader in India, the Indian Institutes of Technology would never have received the extraordinary technical assistance from the US, Soviet Union and Germany to develop the high standards that they did. Without the commitment of Deng Xiaoping, the Chinese government would not have committed as many resources to science and technology, which in turn helped attract the best and the brightest to the field. Such visible support of science and technology at the highest levels probably helped to foster commitment to science and technology within the society such that students more readily choose to study science and engineering.

Such national championship is not easy to maintain over time. Science is expensive and it takes a long time before its impact can be felt. It is easy for commitment to science to give way to fiscal pressures, particularly given that it is never clear how much is needed. It is also not easy to cultivate a high level of interest within the society to induce students to choose science and engineering. Many OECD countries, such as the US, UK and Japan are increasingly concerned about the level of interest among their students in science. Even in India, there is an emerging concern that fewer students are taking a science track.

One final point for reflection is the role of governance arrangements at both institutional and national levels. Quality assurance considerations often lead government bodies to become overly prescriptive about inputs as well as outputs. This is a significant dilemma in developing countries, where there is little tradition and culture about the quality of higher education. Attempts by governments to 'control' quality on the basis of inputs can lead to institutions becoming similar to each other and to being passive in defining what they are. To make the matters worse, some dimensions are easier to measure than others: publications and citations are often used to evaluate the quality of scientific research, but there are no established metrics that look at responsiveness. Metrics used to 'control' or 'guide' are often themselves skewed.

Tight regulatory control by government can also be a serious impediment when institutions need to respond to the changing needs of the nation. And yet the desire to 'respond' to national needs both from labour markets and from future students, particularly in dynamically developing countries, often pushes governments to centralize key decisions about the size and directions of the higher education system.

An institutional capacity to 'respond' to complex demands is unlikely to develop if institutions are not allowed to make strategic decisions. Managerial autonomy and academic autonomy to decide what to teach and research are critical elements for fostering responsiveness in institutions. At the same time, institutions are unlikely to be able to make good strategic decisions without governance arrangements which allow appropriate structures and processes to develop internally. The key for the future is to put in place governance arrangements at both institutional and system levels which meet the balance of such competing concerns and which guide evolving higher education systems effectively for the needs of the nation.

References

Agarwal, Pawan (2007). "Higher Education and Labour Market in India". Paper presented at the World Bank ABCDE conference.

Athreye, Suma S. (2005). "The Indian Software Industry." In Ashish Arora and Alfonso Gambardella eds., *From Underdogs to Tigers: The Rise and Growth of the Software Industry in Brazil, China, India, Ireland, and Israel*. Oxford: Oxford University Press.

Baba, Y., S. Takai, and Y. Mizuta (1996). "The user driven evolution of the Japanese software industry: the case of customized software for mainframes." In D.C. Mowery, ed. *The International Computer Software Industry: A Comparative Study of Industry Evolution and Structure*. New York: Oxford University Press.

Bartholomew, James R. (1989). *The Formation of Science in Japan*, New Haven and London: Yale University Press.

Basant, Rakesh and Pankaj Chandra (2007). "Role of educational and R&D institutions in city clusters: an exploratory study of Bangalore and Pune regions in India." *World Development*, 35(6): 1037-1055

Bresnahan, Timothy F., and Franco Malerba (1999) "Industrial dynamics and the evolution of firms' and nations' competitive capabilities in the world computer industry." In David C. Mowery and Richard R. Nelson, (eds.), *Sources of Industrial Leadership: Studies of Seven Industries*. Cambridge: Cambridge University Press.

Breznitz, Dan (2004). "The Israeli Software Industry." In Ashish Arora and Alfonso Gambardella eds., *From Underdogs to Tigers: The Rise and Growth of the Software Industry in Brazil, China, India, Ireland, and Israel*. Oxford: Oxford University Press.

Breznitz, Dan (2007). *Innovation and the State: Political Choice and Strategies for Growth in Israel, Taiwan and Ireland*. New Haven and London: Yale University Press.

Chun, Kun and Martin Kenney (2007). "Universities/research institutes and regional innovation systems: the cases of Beijing and Schenzhen." *World Development*, 35(6): 1056-1074.

Clark, Burton R. (1995). *Places of Inquiry: Research and Advanced Education in Modern Universities*. Berkeley, Los Angeles and London: University of California Press.

Cohen, W.M., R.R. Nelson and J.P. Walsh (2002). Links and Impact: The Influence of Public Research on Industrial R&D. *Management Science*, 48(1): 1-23.

Dahlman, Carl, Jorma Routti, and Pekka Yla-Anttila (2007). *Finland as a Knowledge Economy: Elements of Success and Lessons Learned*. Washington: World Bank Institute. Physical Health Education.

Media Reports, Press Releases, Press Information Bureau, RNCOS Report, Department of Industrial Policy and Promotion (DIPP), Union Budget 2016-17.

https://pib.nic.in/feature/fe0199/f0501991.html

https://www.cisco.com/c/en_in/about/thought-leadership/higher-education.html

https://www.ibef.org/industry/education-sector-india.aspx

https://www.weforum.org/agenda/2016/01/what-role-will-education-play-in-the-fourth-industrial-revolution/

14
Physical Health Education
A Comparative Study

Shahnawaz Ahmad

Introduction

More than 1 billion people live in ecological hotspots, many of which are remote areas of critically important biodiversity under intense pressure from human activity. Conservation work is usually located in these remote areas to protect the remaining biodiversity. In the developing world, the communities in these remote areas often suffer from ill health because of limited access to health services or family planning. These communities also tend to suffer from poor nutrition, water supplies or sanitation. Inadequate health care in these communities is usually because of economic struggles. Livelihoods in the rural communities depend on natural resources and small-scale agriculture, which can force people to use natural resources unsustainably because of pressures such as rapid population growth or health issues. This can be damaging to ecosystems and the biodiversity in these rural areas.

Conversely, people's health relies on the health of their environment. Their surrounding ecosystem provides them with goods and services such as water, food, medicine, fuel wood, building materials, and other resources. Damage or disruption of these natural goods and services can have severe consequences for human health.

Projects that take the PHE approach work to create healthier communities and ecosystems. These projects aim to bring better health services to remote communities to improve participation in conservation efforts. PHE projects also promote family planning services to help slow population growth that can put pressure on natural resources. That means PHE approaches strive to simultaneously improve access to health services while helping communities manage their natural resources in ways that improve their health and livelihood even as they protect the environment. Beyond this, the PHE approach also targets synergies between human health and ecosystem health by including a wide spectrum of development and conservation targets such as the sustainable management of natural resources, improving livelihoods, food security and nutrition, and by maintaining or restoring habitats and ecosystem functions. By focusing on the synergy between communities and their environment, the PHE approach conserves biodiversity while at the same time improving environmental health conditions for the local people. PHE is effective at achieving a wide range of positive results over multiple sectors.

In the late 1980s conservation organizations and practitioners began to realize the benefits of improving the quality of life for people by managing biodiversity and natural resources. These projects were initially called integrated conservation and development projects (ICDP) and addressed a wide variety of community development needs. At the end of the 1990s it was realized that ICDPs were not achieving conservation or development goals as successfully as anticipated. This was because the scope of ICDPs was often too broad. One of the lessons learned from ICDP attempts was that the success of the projects depended on the ability to focus on key interventions and avoid excessive complexity. From the lessons learned from early ICDPs the conservation sector gave birth to the PHE approach with a new generation of integrated projects.

Programme designers began to realize that efforts to conserve biological diversity (biodiversity) in developing countries was most successful in long-term indicators when local people perceived their efforts as serving their economic and cultural interests. This gave birth to the integrated development approach. To achieve success it was found that ICDPs had to consider the linkage between conservation and development objectives in every unique place that the project was implemented. The first step to determining the linkages is to consider where the conservation and economic development goals intersect. Development interventions should then be introduced where this intersection occurs.

One of the most important lessons learned from ICDPs in the last 20 years was the failure to equitably involve projected beneficiaries as partners in all phases of project implementation, from design through evaluation, has led to consistently disappointing project results. It must be recognized that local participants are not a homogenous group of community members but differ widely in terms of access and dependency of resources, economic positions and their sensitivity to environmental changes. These lessons learned from past ICDPs has led the design of the stakeholder analysis where individuals or groups vested in the project are identified and incorporated into all stages of project design and implementation.

Credentialing

Credentialing is the process by which the qualifications of licensed professionals, organizational members or an organization are determined by assessing the individuals or group background and legitimacy through a standardized process. Accreditation, license, or certifications are all forms of credentialing.

In 1978, Helen Cleary, the president of the Society for Public Health Education (SOPHE) started the process of certification of health educators. Prior to this, there was no certification for individual health educators, with exception to the licensing for school health educators. The only accreditation available in this field was for school health and public health professional preparation programmes.

Her initial response was to incorporate experts in the field and to promote funding for the process. The director if the Division of Associated Health Professions in the Bureau of Health Manpower of the Department of Health, Education, and Welfare, Thomas Hatch, became interested in the project. To ensure that the commonalities between health educators across the spectrum of professions would be sufficient enough to create a set of standards, Dr. Cleary spent a great amount of time to create the first conference called the Bethesda Conference. In attendance were interested professionals who covered the possibility of creating credentialing within the profession.

With the success of the conference and the consensus that the standardization of the profession was vital, those who organized the conference created the National Task Force in the Preparation and Practice of Health Educators. Funding for this endeavour became available in January 1979, and role delineation became a realistic vision for the future. They presented the framework for the system in 1981 and published entry-level criteria in 1983. Seven areas of responsibility, 29 areas of competency and 79 sub-competencies were required of health education professionals for approximately 20 years for entry-level educators.

In 1986 a second conference was held in Bethesda, Maryland to further the credentialing process. In June 1988, the National Task Force in the Preparation and Practice of Health Educators became the National Commission for Health Education Credentialing, Inc. (NCHEC). Their mission was to improve development of the field by promoting, preparing and certifying health education specialists. The NCHEC has three division boards that included preparation, professional development and certification of health educator professionals. The third board, which is called the Division Board of Certification of Health Education Specialist (DBCHES), has the responsibility of developing and administering the CHES examination. An initial certification process allowed 1,558 individuals to be chartered into the programme through a recommendation and application process. The first examination was given in 1990.

In order for a candidate to sit for an examination they must have either a bachelor's, master's, or doctoral degree from an accredited institution, and an official transcript that shows a major in health education, Community Health Education, Public Health Education, or School Health Education etc. The transcript will be accepted if it reflects 25 semester hours or 37 quarter hours in health education preparation and covers the 7 responsibilities covered in the framework.

In 1998 a project called the Competencies Update Project (CUP) began. The purpose of the CUP project was to up-date entry-level requirements and to develop advanced-level competences. Through research the CUP project created the requirements for three levels, which included entry-level, Advanced I and Advanced II educators.

Recently the Master Certified Health Education Specialist (MCHES) was created. The MCHES examination measures the knowledge of the advanced levels and sub-levels of the Seven Areas of Responsibilities. The first MCHES examination was given in October 2011.

In order to be eligible to take the MCHES examination you must have at least a master's degree in health education or related discipline along with a least 25 credit hours related to health education. In addition, five years of documented information of practice in health education and two recommendations of past/present supervisors must be provided. A vitae/resume must also be submitted.

The Competency Update Project (CUP), 1998-2004 revealed that there were higher levels of health education practitioners, which is the reasoning for the advancements for the MCHES. Many health educators felt that the current CHES credential was an entry-level examination.

Teaching

In the United States some forty states require the teaching of health education. A comprehensive health education curriculum consists of planned learning experiences which will help students achieve desirable attitudes and practices related to critical health issues. Some of these are: emotional health and a positive self-image; appreciation, respect for, and care of the human body and its vital organs; physical fitness; health issues of alcohol, tobacco, drug use and abuse; health misconceptions and myths; effects of exercise on the body systems and on general well being; nutrition and weight control; sexual relationships and sexuality, the scientific, social, and economic aspects of community and ecological health: communicable and degenerative diseases including sexually transmitted diseases; disaster preparedness; safety and driver education; factors in the environment and how those factors affect an individual's or population's Environmental health (for example air quality, water quality, food, sanitation); life skills; choosing professional medical and health services; and choices of health careers.

The National Centre for Education Statistics share that 99 per cent of public schools conduct some type of nutrition education. For each grade from kindergarten through eighth, 50 per cent or more of all schools have district or state requirements for students to receive nutrition education. However, only 40 per cent have these requirements for ninth and tenth grades; and about 20 per cent for eleventh and twelfth grades. The issue still lies with the content and thoroughness that is being taught. Topics taught in a most all of the schools are: the relationship between diet and health, finding and choosing healthy foods, nutrients and their food sources, the Food Guide Pyramid, and the Dietary Guidelines and goals. However, with the exception of the Food Guide Pyramid, less than half of schools cover these topics thoroughly. Overall, schools focus on increasing students' knowledge about what is meant by good nutrition, with less emphasis on influencing students' motivation, attitudes, and eating behaviours. Four of the five topics covered by more than 90 per cent of all schools are related to knowledge. With the exception of finding and choosing healthy foods, less than one-third of schools provide thorough coverage of topics related to motivation, attitudes, and eating behaviours. Not often are there teachers specific for nutrition. Most of the time the nutrition content is taught by the primary teacher.

Health Education Code of Ethics

Preamble

The Health Education profession is dedicated to excellence in the practice of promoting individual, family, organizational, and community health. The Code of Ethics provides a framework of shared values within which Health Education is practiced. The responsibility of each Health Educator is to aspire to the highest possible standards of conduct and to encourage the ethical behaviour of all those with whom they work.

Article I: Responsibility to the Public—A Health Educator's ultimate responsibility is to educate people for the purpose of promoting, maintaining, and improving individual, family, and community health. When a conflict of issues arises among individuals, groups, organizations, agencies or institutions, health educators must consider all issues and give priority to those that promote wellness and quality of living through principles of self-determination and freedom of choice for the individual.

Article II: Responsibility to the Profession—Health Educators are responsible for their professional behaviour, for the reputation of their profession, and for promoting ethical conduct among their colleagues.

Article III: Responsibility to Employers—Health Educators recognize the boundaries of their professional competence and are accountable for their professional activities and actions.

Article IV: Responsibility in the Delivery of Health Education—Health Educators promote integrity in the delivery of health education. They respect the rights, dignity, confidentiality, and worth of all people by adapting strategies and methods to the needs of diverse populations and communities.

Article V: Responsibility in Research and Evaluation—Health Educators contribute to the health of the population and to the profession through research and evaluation activities. When planning and conducting research or evaluation, health educators do so in accordance with federal and state laws and regulations, organizational and institutional policies, and professional standards.

Article VI: Responsibility in Professional Preparation—Those involved in the preparation and training of Health Educators have an obligation to accord learners the same respect and treatment given other groups by providing quality education that benefits the profession and the public.

Trends

Physical Education (PE) trends have developed recently to incorporate a greater variety of activities besides typical sports. Introducing students to activities like bowling, walking/hiking, or frisbee at an early age can help students develop good activity habits that will continue into adulthood. Some teachers have even begun to incorporate stress-reduction techniques such as *yoga*, deep-breathing and *tai chi*. *Tai chi*, an ancient martial arts form focused on slow meditative movements is a relaxation activity with many benefits for students. Studies have shown that *tai chi* enhances muscular strength and endurance, cardiovascular endurance, and provides many other physical benefits. It also provides psychological benefits such as improving general mental health, concentration, awareness and positive mood.[1] It can be taught to any age student with little or no equipment making it ideal for mixed ability and age classes. *Tai chi* can easily be incorporated into a holistic learning body and mind unit.[2] Teaching non-traditional sports to students may also provide the necessary motivation for students to increase their activity, and can help students learn about different cultures. For example, while teaching a unit about lacrosse in, for example, the Southwestern United States, students can also learn about the Native American cultures of the Northeastern United States and Eastern Canada, where lacrosse originated. Teaching non-traditional (or non-native) sports provides a great opportunity to integrate academic concepts from other subjects as well (social studies from the example above), which may now be required of many PE teachers. The four aspects of PE are physical, mental, social, and emotional.

PE is very important to students health and overall well-being. The Centres for Disease Control and Prevention stated that over the past three years obesity in children (ages 2-5) and adolescents (ages 12-19) has doubled because of lack of activity and diet. Quality Physical Education (PE) programmes will benefit the lifestyle of young people and in many cases already has. Good Physical Education programmes Provide Structure for students to improve students fitness, positive choices, and setting and reaching goals.[3]

SHAPE America's National Standards and Grade-Level Outcomes for K-12 Physical Education define what a student should know and be able to do as result of a highly effective physical education programme.[4]

Another trend is the incorporation of health and nutrition to the physical education curriculum. The Child Nutrition and WIC Reauthorization Act of 2004 required that all school districts with a federally funded school meal programme develop wellness policies that address nutrition and physical activity.[5] While teaching students sports and movement skills, PE teachers are now incorporating short health and nutrition lessons into the curriculum. This is more prevalent at the elementary school level, where students do not have a specific Health class. Recently, most elementary schools have specific health classes for students as well as physical education class. With the recent outbreaks of diseases, such as swine flu, school districts are making it mandatory for students to learn about practicing good hygiene along with other health topics. Today many states require Physical Education teachers to be certified to teach Health courses. Many colleges and Universities offer both Physical Education and Health as one certification. This push towards health education is beginning in the intermediate level, including lessons on bullying, self-esteem and stress and anger management.

Research has shown that there is a positive correlation between brain development and exercising.[6]

Incorporating local indigenous knowledge into physical education can lead to many meaningful experiences and a way of learning about other cultures. For example, by incorporating traditional knowledge from varying indigenous groups from across Canada students can be exposed to many concepts such as holistic learning and the medicine wheel. A unit could be focused on connecting to a place or feeling while outdoors, participating in traditional games, or outdoor environmental education. These types of lesson can easily be integrated into other parts of the curriculum and give Aboriginal students a chance to incorporate their culture in the local school community.[7]

Studies have been done in how physical education can help improve academic achievement. In a 2007 article, researchers found a profound gain in student's English Arts standardized testing students who had 56 hours of physical education in a year compared to like students who had 28 hours of physical education a year.[8]

In Brazil, the physical education curriculum is designed to allow school pupils a full range of modern opportunities, including sports. They said they offer martial arts classes, like wrestling in the United States, and PencakSilat in France, Indonesia, and Malaysia, are taught to teach children self-defence and to feel good about themselves. The physical education curriculum is designed to allow students to experience at least a minimum exposure to the following categories of activities: aquatics, conditioning activities, gymnastics, individual/dual sports, team sports, rhythms, and dance.

In these areas, a planned sequence of learning experiences is designed to support a progression of student development. This allows kids through 6th grade to be introduced to sports, fitness, and teamwork in order to be better prepared for the middle and high school age. In 1975, the United

States House of Representatives voted to require school physical education classes include both genders.[9] Some high school and some middle school PE classes are single-sex. Requiring individuals to participate in physical education activities, such as dodge ball, flag football, and other competitive sports remains a controversial subject because of the social impact these have cases physical education programmes have been cut.

Technology Use in Physical Education

New technology in education is playing a big role in classes. One of the most affordable and effective is a simple video recorder. With the use of a video recorder students can see the mistakes they are making in things such as a throwing motion or swinging form.[10] Studies show that students find this more effective than having someone try to explain what they are doing wrong, and then trying to correct it.[11] Educators also found the use of other technologies such as pedometers and heart rate monitors very successful, using them to make step and heart rate goals for students.[12]

Other technologies that can be used in a Physical Education setting would include video projectors, GPS and even gaming systems such as Kinect, Wii Fit and Dance Revolution. Projectors can be used to show students things such as proper form or how to play certain games. GPS systems can be used to get students active in an outdoor setting and active exergames can be used by teachers to show students a good way to stay fit in and out of the classroom setting.[13]

Another type of technology that is commonly used in Physical Education is the use of pedometers. Pedometers do not necessarily track how far a person is going, but it lets them know the number of steps they are making. It will let them know how many steps on average they are making.[14]

Health Education Career Opportunities

The terms Public Health Educator, Community Health Educator or Health Educator are all used inter-changeable to describe an individual who plans implements and evaluates health education and promotion programmes. These individuals play a crucial role in many organizations in various settings to improve our nations health. Just as a Community health educator works work toward population health, a school Health Educator generally teaches in our schools. A community health educator is typically focused on their immediate community striving to serve the public.

Health Care Settings: These include hospitals (for-profit and public), medical care clinics, home health agencies, HMOs and PPOs. Here, a health educator teaches employees how to be healthy. Patient education positions are far and few between because insurance companies do not cover the costs.[15]

Public Health Agencies: There official, tax funded, government agencies. They provide police protection, educational systems, as well as clean air and water. Public health departments provide health services and are organized by a city, county, state, or Federal Government.[16]

School Health Education: It involves all strategies, activities, and services offered by, in, or in association with schools that are designed to promote students' physical, emotional, and social development. School health involves teaching students about health and health related behaviours. Curriculum and programmes are based on the school's expectations and health.[17]

Non-Profit Voluntary Health Agencies: These are created by concerned citizens to deal with health needs not met by governmental agencies. Missions include public education, professional education, patient education, research, direct services and support to or for people directly affected by a specific health or medical problem. Usually funded by such means as private donations, grants, and fund-raisers.[18]

Higher Education: Typically two types of positions health educators hold including academic, or faculty or health educator in a student health service or wellness centre. As a faculty member, the health educator typically has three major responsibilities: teaching, community and professional service, and scholarly research. As a health educator in a university health service or wellness centre, the major responsibility is to plan, implement, and evaluate health promotion and education programmes for programme participants.[19]

Work-site Health Promotion: This is a combination of educational, organizational and environmental activities designed to improve the health and safety of employees and their families. These work site wellness programmes offer an additional setting for health educators and allow them to reach segments of the population that are not easily reached through traditional community health programmes. Some work site health promotion activities include: smoking cessation, stress management, bulletin boards, newsletters, and much more.[20]

Independent Consulting and Government Contracting: International, national, regional, state, and local organizations contract with independent consultants for many reasons. They may be hired to assess individual and community needs for health education; plan, implement, administer and evaluate health education strategies; conduct research; serve as health education resource person; and or communicate about and advocate for health and health education. Government contractors are often behind national health education programmes, government reports, public information web sites and telephone lines, media campaigns, conferences, and health education materials.[21]

Conclusion

Within the limitations and delimitations of this study, the following conclusions were arrived at:

1. Comparison of physical fitness variable agility between Visva Bharati University, Kalyani University and Bangladesh proved that there was significant differences between the physical education students and the students of Visva Bharati was significantly better than other two university students.
2. Though there was mean differences between the groups in explosive power, the mean difference was not statistically significant and it was concluded that there was no significant differences.
3. The mean difference between the physical education students of Visva Bharati University, Kalyani University and Bangladesh was statistically significant in cardio vascular endurance. It was concluded that Visva Bharati University students were significantly better than other two university students.

Notes

1. "Tai Chi for Mental Health | Psych Central News". *Psych Central News.* 24 May, 2010.
2. Lu C. (2007).
3. The Importance of Physical Education. (n.d.). Retrieved April 1, 2016, from http://www.veanea.org/home/1000.html
4. http://www.shapeamerica.org/standards/pe/
5. Pangrazi, Robert (2007) "*Dynamic Physical Education for Elementary School Children*", 15th ed. San Francisco, Calif. Harlow : Benjamin Cummings.
6. Reynolds, Gretchen. "Phys Ed: Can Exercise Make Kids Smarter?". *The New York Times.* Retrieved 18 April, 2013.

7. Lowen, G. (2009).
8. Tremarche, Pamela V.; Robinson, Ellyn M.; Graham, Louise B. (2007). "Physical Education and Its Effect on Elementary Testing Results". *Physical Educator.* 64 (2): 58–64.
9. "Physical Education—July 18, 1975–NBC–TV news: Vanderbilt Television News Archive". Tvnews.vanderbilt.edu. 1975-07-18. Retrieved 2015-08-13.
10. Wang, L., Myers, D., and Yanes, M. (2010). Creating student-centered learning experience through the assistance of high-end technology in physical education. *Journal of Instructional Psychology*, 37(4): 352–356.
11. Woods, M., Karp, G., Goc, H., and Perlman, D. (2008). Physical educators' usage. *Physical Educator*, 65(2): 82-99.
12. Grimes, G. (2011, November 21). Interview by M. Massey [Personal Interview].
13. "Using pedometers to assess physical activity participation levels". Humankinetics.com. 2010-04-01. Retrieved 2015-08-13.
14. "*PEC: Pedometer Lesson Activities*". Pecentral.org. Retrieved 2015-08 13.
15. McKenzie, J., Neiger, B., Thackeray, R. (2009). Health education can also Boone seen as preventive medicine (marcus 2012). Health Education and Health Promotion. *Planning, Implementing, and Evaluating Health Promotion Programmes*. (pp. 3-4). 5th edition. San Francisco, CA: Pearson Education, Inc.
16. Donatelle, R. (2009). Promoting Healthy Behaviour Change. *Health: The Basics*. (p. 4). 8th edition. San Francisco, CA: Pearson Education, Inc.
17. Joint Committee on Terminology (2001). "Report of the 2000 Joint Committee on Health Education and Promotion Terminology". *American Journal of Health Education*. 32 (2): 89-103.
18. World Health Organization (1998). List of Basic Terms. *Health Promotion Glossary*. (p. 4). Retrieved May 1, 2009, from https://www.who.int/hpr/NPHj/ddoocs/hp_glossary_en.pdf.
19. Cottrell, Girvan, and McKenzie, 2009.
20. Washington State Department of Health.
21. Bundy D., Guya, H.L. (1996). "Schools for health, education and the school-age child". *Parasitology Today.* 12 (8): 1-16. doi:10.1016/0169-4758(96)30011-2.

15

e-Governance in India: A Focus on Higher Education

R. Uma Rani

Introduction

E-Governance is the public sector's use of information and communication technologies with the aim of improving information and service delivery, encouraging citizen participation in the decision-making process and making government more accountable, transparent and effective. E-Governance involves new styles of leadership, new ways of debating and deciding policy and investment, new ways of accessing education, new ways of listening to citizens and new ways of organising and delivering information and services. E-governance may be understood as the performance of this governance via the electronic medium in order to facilitate an efficient, speedy and transparent process of disseminating information to the public, and other agencies, and for performing government administration activities. E-governance can bring forth new concepts of citizenship, both in terms of citizen needs and responsibilities. Its objective is to engage, enable and empower the citizen.

Change has been happening at an uneven pace in any growth-oriented industry, and the education sector is no exception. Rapid growth in the field of education has made governance in academic sector a very complex task. The 21st century has witnessed tremendous advancements intechnology which has led to far-reaching developments in the administrative system. Cost-effective technology combined with the flexibility in learning and administrative activities is essential to enhance efficiency.Computers can be used extensively for educational administration. There are some of the areas where computers can be used for effective educational administration—

- General Administration,
- Pay Rolland Financial Accounting,
- Administration of Student Data,
- Inventory Management,
- Personnel Records Maintenance, and
- Library System.

Information and Communication Technology (ICT) plays a vital role in supporting powerful, efficient management and administration in education sector. It is specified that technology can be used right from student administration to various resource administration in an education institution. The various administrative challenges for Indian education system of the 21st century are given below:

- Global and local challenges,
- Universal and individual challenges,
- Competition and equity challenges, and
- Extraordinary expansion of knowledge.

Moreover, many studies revealed the need for ICT integration into administrative activities of higher education institutions. The various ways of introducing technology in education institution administration are the following:

- Sending e-mail notices and agendas to staff, rather than printing and distributing them.
- Submission of lesson plans through e-mail.
- Foster technology growth by asking parents to write e-mail addresses on medical forms.
- Insist that all teachers create a class Web page.
- Attend technology conferences to see what other institutes are doing, what other teachers are doing to integrate technology, and what principals are doing to encourage the use of technology in their institutes and classrooms.
- Admissions through web-enabled services.
- All day-to-day activities of the institution (General Administration).
- Staff administration.
- Single Window System for students.[1]

E-Governance in Higher Education

India has one of the largest higher education systems in the world. Despite having the largest higher education system, the quality of education, ingeneral, cannot be claimed to be the best. Technical and vocational Education in India has seen enormous growth in recent years with a large increase in total number of institutes imparting higher education.On one hand, this growth promises to produce more skilled youth to fulfil needs of evergrowing Indian industry and on the otherhand it poses a huge challenge for the governing bodies like UGC, AICTE, NCVT, NCTE, PCI, MCI, INC, DCI etc. and state technical education boards to maintain and improve the quality of education being imparted through these new and existing Technical and Vocational institutes. But as has been reported by NASSCOM (National Association of Software and Service Companies) in its 2004 report, out of 3 million graduates and post-graduates added to the workforce in India every year only 25 per cent of technical and 10-15 per cent of non-technical graduates are employable by growing IT, and other sector, points to is a very serious situation. This lack of knowledge, qualities and skills desired by the employers, from the youth, may lead to the problems like unemployment/underemployment, which detain will lead to their disapproval and hence their offense that will be reflected in terms of an increase in crime and other antisocial activities.[2]

Necessity of e-Governance in Higher Education

If the quality of our higher education system has to be improved to make these institutes really word class, then there is no alternative to the introduction of e-governance in this sphere at the fastest possible pace. Implementation of e-governance in technical and vocational institutes will enable their effective and real time monitoring by Government/the regulatory bodies and other stakeholders their own managements, parents of the students and the society, thereby forcing them to maintain quality and become more responsible. E-governance process brings transparency in the system, so e-governance initiatives in the field of higher education will help reduce the corruption up to a large extent.[3] The introduction of e-governance in higher education is one such concept that can empower the governing bodies to administer the progress of the education plan in the whole country and serves various stakeholders in a much better ways. E-Governance is becoming a global phenomenon, that is increasingly attracting the attention of community citizens including politicians, economists, decision and policy-makers amongst others. An effective e-governance satisfies these following needs:

- Providing greater access to government information;
- Promoting public engagement by enabling the public to interact with government officials;
- Making government more accountable by making its operations more obvious and thus reducing the opportunities for corruption; and
- Providing development opportunities, especially benefiting rural and traditionally underserved communities.

E-Governance in higher education system will enable various stakeholders to control the improved operational efficiency in various key processes like grants, utilization certificates, approval processes, feedback mechanism etc. With deeper visibility and increased operational efficiency the Indian higher education system (IHS) would be implemented not only to satisfy the needs of students by making them more employable but also combat possible competition from foreign universities.[4]

In order to remove the copying of procedures, there should be consolidated information about each university and college to track their performance. The tools of e-governance may enable the universities or colleges to submit the documents online for approval. All agencies should internally co-ordinate to carry the details from common pool. This would greatly reduce the unnecessary duplication of work in the university. Apart from this there may be a number of other services that can be provided with the introduction of such type of governance.

Benefits of e-Governance in Higher Education

The benefits of e-governance in an educational sector are improved efficiency, increase in transparency and accountability of educational administrative activities convenient and faster access to services, and lower costs for administrative services. The multi-faceted benefits of e-governance can be described as under these points[5]:

- **Benefits to university**
  - Centralized information access from anywhere.
  - Increase in student enrolment ratio.
  - Provide quality e-services, e-participation.

- Increase clearness.
- Inventive teaching tools.
- Improved decision making, Private Public Participation.
- Less paper work.

- **Benefits to students**
    - Increase participation in education affairs.
    - Personalized login for each students.
    - Extensive saving in time cost and efforts.
    - Information and transaction services.
    - Job opportunities.
    - Social connectivity for collaboration.
    - Students can access virtual lectures and seminars.
    - Students can solve their problems like—examination queries, result verification etc.
    - Students can submit feedback to university.
- **Benefits to colleges**
    - Data can access easily.
    - Electronic data exchange with university.
    - Saving of hidden operational cost.
    - Instant statistical report generation.
    - Helpful for NAAC accreditation.
- **Overall education system**
    - Long term impact on organization goals.
    - Improve education system.
    - Empowerment of faculties, students and encouragement of their participation in governance.

Suggestions and Recommendations

The online methods enable more effective education and offer significant advantages over traditional services.

Provide E-Services—After the implementation e-governance, we improve the delivery of services to students, faculty by providing services like enrolment, examination, result, feedback, requests for documents, requests for certificates, issuing admit cards and ID cards, employment etc. The system provide timely alert to colleges through SMS/Emails. E-governance in education provides new ways of communicating to the students, imparting education and organizing and delivering information and services.

Improved Education System—E-governance in education sectors allows use of information and communication technologies with the aim of improving education, improve information, service delivery, encourage student participation in the decision making process, making administration transparent and effective and give universities a new channel of educational unemployment. Also, the system can obtain feedback from industry and students to modify course curriculum if deemed appropriate by the authorities. This will allow all the lesser performing colleges to reduce the gap with better performing institutes. It will be help in the betterment of the higher education in the country and increase the number of employable students.

Innovative Teaching Tools—The new technologies offer vast opportunities for progress in all walks of life with the introduction of new technological initiatives the structure of higher educational institutions has changed. The changing role of lecturers, the changeable learning environment and the design of e-Learning facilities all contribute to a potentially more flexible organizational structure of higher education in rural area. The future delivery of education will be based through e-Learning technology providing lecturers with superior teaching tools. The online methods enable more effective education and offer significant advantages over traditional teaching methods. This has been possible by technological implementation based environments such as boards, virtual lectures and e-Libraries and video conferencing. In e-learning environment can support communication with classmates and lecturers.[6]

Private Public Participation—Almost all e-government projects have found it convenient to involve different private agencies for different tasks through public-private-partnership (PPP) arrangements. These tasks include design and development of application software, population of data and content in the regional language, procurement and installation of networking and computer systems, deployment of software and delivery of services.[7]

Centralized Information—E-Governance has provided electronic information infrastructure to simplify service delivery, reduce duplication, and improve the level and speed of service at a lower cost. The centralized information approach of e-Governance keeps all information at one place in electronic form. This approach of making information secure prevents it against any theft or leakage.[8]

Use of Intranet—Intranet-based training provides a low cost and knock-on savings, is that it can be a virtual two-way system, with students connected to mentors and teachers receiving real-time feedback and support. Managers with employees scattered among sites and locations, particularly if they are so far-flung that they are in different areas, need a cheap and effective way to communicate them. ICT is already proven as the way to access knowledge based information from anywhere to anytime but a limitation of the university that they can not communicate with other colleges.[9]

With the help of above benefits and suggestions it is possible to design a system that is student centric and can provide a variety of services—*informative, interactive, and transactional* and integrated system across the entire spectrum of the education sector. Central Universities, State Universities, Autonomous Institutes, Deemed and Private universities and affiliated colleges will enter the data and cater the need of MIS of regulating and coordinating bodies[10].

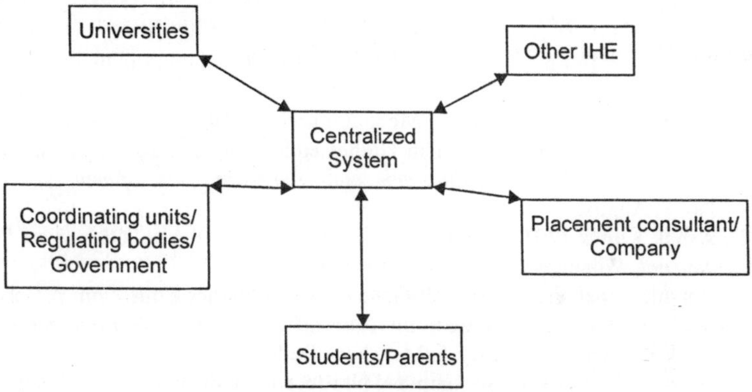

Fig. 15.1: Use of E-governance in Higher Education.
Source: Self-constructed.

Conclusion

The planning for efficient administration of higher educational institutions, increasing Global communication skill, to achieve the world class standard it is necessary to have a improved collaboration and access to information available in all the parts of the world are possible only by introducing IT in Educational Sector with e-governance as a security for maintaining standard. The e-governance needs security for smooth information flow, best practice database and enhanced capacity for information analysis etc. Government should support by enacting favorable legislations and updated amendments for maintaining standards in the educational process and improvements in the related field. It requires completely new infrastructure, procedures, policies and working skills for producing and collecting online information. With the advent of ICT, electronic governance is an emerging trend to re-invent the way the government works, becoming a new model of governance. Such a comprehensive and integrated system can also enable authorities to analyze the performance of one of the best performing institutes and compare it with other schools and colleges to identify the gaps. Through e-governance we improve the quality of higher education system in India. E-governance can create the transparency between the universities, colleges and students. It will bring forth, new concepts of governance, both in terms of needs and responsibilities. Many problems of higher education system can be solved by the Public Private Partnership model and e-governance.

Notes

1. Dr. R. Krishnaveni and J. Meenakumari (2010), Usage of ICT for Information Administration in Higher education Institutions—A study, *International Journal of Environmental Science and Development*, Vol. 1, No. 3, August.
2. Ashok Kumar (2012), E-Governance in Education Sector, *Gian Jyoti E-Journal*, Volume 1, Issue 2, January-March.
3. Harshita Bhatnagar (2013), E-Governance in Higher Education: A Case Study of IGNOU, *International Journal of Scientific & Engineering Research*, Volume 4, Issue 5, May, New Delhi.
4. Jatinder Garg, Sonu Bala Garg and Navdeep Choudhary (2011), Effective Implementation of E-Governance in Technical Institutions in India using ICT to Make them World Class, *Research Cell: An International Journal of Engineering Sciences*. Issue September, Vol. 4.
5. Ranjeeta Kapoor and Nishtha Kelkar (2013), E-Governance: Higher Education in Rural Area, National Conference on New Horizons in IT-NCNHIT.
6. Prateek Bhanti, Dr. S. Lehri, Dr. Narendra Kumar (2012), E-Governance: An Approach towards the Integration of Higher Education System in India, *International Journal of Emerging Technology and Advanced Engineering*. Volume 2, Issue 8, August.
7. Mr. Sanjeet Kumar Tiwari, Mr. Jubraj Khamari, Anjali Singh (2013), Promoting E- Governance Culture in Higher Education Institutions, *IOSR Journal of Research & Method in Education*. Volume 2, Issue 3, Jul.-Aug.
8. Sebahat Bartýn Orman Fakültesi Peyzaj Mimarlýðý Bölümü (2007), Importance of e-education and e-governance: Case of zonguldakkaraelmas university, Department of Landscape Architecture.
9. Sudip Suklabaidya, Angshu Maan Sen, (2013), Challenges and Prospects of E-governance in Education, *International Journal of Emerging Trends & Technology in Computer Science*. Volume 2, Issue 3, May-June.
10. Report of the Working group on Higher Education for the Twelfth Five Year Plan, September 2011.

16
Information Technology
A Development within the Space of Post-Colonial Era

Sanjeev Kumar Dey

Introduction

The crucial breakthrough in Information Technology in Education is that, in the post-colonial era, a variety of knowledge materials can be accessed instantaneously, by Learners as well as teachers, at their expediency. Learners can access the on-line libraries, articles, E-books and even aloofness knowledge is also made promising. Information technology has proved to be a noteworthy manager to all that. It works at the tip of one's fingers. The post-colonial space has, to the highest degree, multiplied the accessibility of knowledge, which hitherto cherished the native knowledge in their archives and libraries unlike the positioning of knowledge in the colonial period, where it was elusive.

Information Technology (IT) gives treatment to information. The acquisition, processing, storage and dissemination of vocal, pictorial, textual and numerical information by a microelectronics-based combination of computing and telecommunications are its main fields.[1] The central matter seems to be the close relation of information technology in teaching in the educational system. It is expected that learners must become familiar with the information technology usage; the most important reason for this may be that all future jobs will rely heavily on it and information technology must be positively used in teaching to reinforce and improvise the quality of teaching learning process. The introduction has provided a colonial free space to teaching learning process. A learner could access any knowledge undermining the colonial power.

The term information technology in its modern sense first appeared in a 1958 article published in the *Harvard Business Review*, in which authors Leavitt and Whisler commented that "the new technology does not yet have a single established name. We shall call it information technology (IT)".[2] The rapid expansion of global communications, media and visual culture in this digital era has shaken the structure of societies globally and has radically altered the dissemination and production of information and knowledge.[3] Here globalisation could only spearhead only within the space, that was created, of post-colonial era. In fact the world turned out to be a global village. It virtually unchained not only the colonized people at the first instance but also created the space for people from below to gather information and knowledge at their will.

Need of the Study

This chapter seeks to look into two issues: first, the importance of Information Technology in Education and the effect of Information Technology to the people from below. It is interesting to note that Information Technology emerged within the space and time of post-colonial era. This has affected the learners as well as the marginalised people. However, the question lies whether the introduction of Information Technology is a gradual development of electronic telecommunication or a different form of colonization. During the colonial period knowledge has earned great importance and only the well-to-do could have an access to it whereas the marginalised never had a chance to access it. But in the post-Independent era, things got reversed and Information Technology became common even to the 'unknown' and 'unwanted personalities'. Hence, the study from this perspective would be interesting and greatly needed at this time to explain various desirable questions. The interesting facet of the chapter is the treatment of learner in the said era within the space and the response of the people from below within the created framework.

Objectives of the Study

The objectives of the study is:

(i) To highlight the importance of Information Technology as an aid to teaching and learning; and
(ii) To focus the post-colonial era as a boom of Information Technology to the people from below.

Methodology Adopted in the Study Area

For the study need base secondary data, electronic and printed, is collected from published and unpublished documents. Libraries and journals are also consulted as and when needed. The research is mainly descriptive in nature. However, an attempt is made to put information technology within the space of post-colonial era and its consequence to the people from below.

Information Technology within the Space of Post-Colonial Era

In the post-colonial era the important happening is the development of Information Technology, and it has provided a great boost to the teaching-learning process in various ways. It has served as a treasure to the people who needed it most, the people whose voice is not heard. However, the following given points will explain the importance or advantage of using Information Technology in Education:

(i) Access to variety of learning resources;
(ii) Imparting knowledge without keeping place and time bound is made possible by computers and web networks;
(iii) Anywhere learning;
(iv) Collaborative learning;
(v) Multimedia in educational sector;
(vi) The information and data which are available on the net is acceptable and up-to-date to many an extent;
(vii) Access to online libraries made easy; and
(viii) Boosted distance education.

Information Technology skills and Information Technology understanding are thus fundamentals for the individual, for both now and future perspective. Along with this the above mentioned points show a close connection to the understanding that people at a far-flung areas could come close to education. However, a person has to be literate to have access to this knowledge.

Information Technology has turned to be very useful in the field of Education. The use of media in education attracts student attention more than usual method followed since centuries. It saves time and the learning is more durable than the early teaching-learning process followed. They reduce verbalism or the meaningless use of words and phrases and contribute towards the clearness of perception and accuracy in learning. They break monotony and offer variety to the classroom technique, which is always attractive to the learners. The use of media is technically sound and scientifically advanced which is having the capacity to stimulate individual activity on the part of the learners. According to John Mander the teaching aids help to teach something more quickly and thoroughly so that the learners may retain the subject matter taught. This will result in 'covering more ground' in a given time, and thus gives a better chance of "getting through the syllabus" (Aggarwal, 1988). Traditionally, and in a formal setting, an aid is likely to be presented by the teacher to the whole class, at some selected time during a lesson or piece of teaching. The teacher uses aids as a means of illustrating or emphasizing important points. In this approach the aid ought to be large enough for the whole class to see at the same time, e.g. large wall charts or maps, or projection into a large screen (Wastnedg, 1990). It is a reflection on the rate of innovation in education that the phase 'new resources for learning' is normally considered to include aids such as films and slides (Mackenzie, Eraut and Jones, 1970).[4] It has also proved alongside to not only to the common people of the mainland but to the marginalised as well. And to the more marginalised who are known to be people from below. This post-colonial development in Information Technology sector has remarkably disseminated knowledge, which till date, is believed to be under the control of the colonizers and people from above. Information Technology abruptly changed the scenario of the global world to a greater extent.

Conclusions

Learner has without any doubt excelled the predecessors in the field of education with the development of IT. Our Learners have grown up in the digital age and they are comfortable with technology. Whatever the case is, there is always a sector which remains open for more knowledge, as it is an unending process. The more we equipped with, the more informative and compatible we become with Information Technology. Along with all this the development has greatly influenced the people from below. The post-colonial development in the form of Information Technology has boosted up the marginalised class also. However, it is justifiable to leave the situation with future researchers to judge the cause of this happening. Whether Information Technology is a colonial policy to colonise again in different forms through knowledge or not? Only time and space could give answers to this question.

Notes

1. Longley, Dennis and Shain, Michael (1985). *Dictionary of Information Technology* (2 ed.), Macmillan Press, p. 164.
2. Harold J. Leavitt and Thomas L. Whisler, "Management in the 1980's", *Harvard Business Review*, 1958-2011.
3. Goldfarb, Brian (2002). *Visual Pedagogy: Media Cultures in and Beyond the Classroom*. Durham, NC: Duke University Press, p. 1.
4. As Cited in Hemanta Kr. Nath (ed.) (2009). Higher Education in the North-East: A Perspective, in Hazarika, Dr. A.S., *Need of Teaching Media*, Purbanchal Prakash, Guwahati, pp. 121-122.

17

Role of Educational Institutions in the Entrepreneurial Ecosystem

Shabana A. Memon

> "Education in India today has to be not only national but nation making."
> — *Nivedita*

> "It is time for a new generation of leadership to cope with new world problems and opportunities, for there is a new world to be won."
> — *John F. Kennedy*

Introduction

> "Education is not filling a bucket, but lighting a fire."
> — *William Keats*

Education is undisputedly considered as the bedrock of any meaningful development, be it economic, social or political. Education forms basis and essential ingredient to foster genuine economic growth and development. Including entrepreneurship in academic curriculum and providing practical exposure are important steps for building innovative and entrepreneurial individuals and firms which, in turn will fuel innovation by developing new products, improving existing products, services or processes, create jobs and promote economic growth.

Entrepreneurship can help in creating a level playing field between developed and developing countries. Thus in order to materialize India's dream of becoming super power in terms of growth, development and talent, it has a lot to prove to the world. The answer to the above doubt can be cleared by one single word, that is 'Entrepreneurship'.

Definition of Entrepreneurship and Entrepreneur

The term "Entrepreneurship" comes from the French verb "Entreprendre" and the German word "unternehmen", both means to "undertake". The necessity of entrepreneurship for production was first formally recognized by Alfred Marshall in 1890 in his famous book 'Principles of Economics'. Bygrave and Hofer in 1891 defined the entrepreneurial process as "involving all the actions and activities associated with perceiving of opportunities and creation of organizations". In 1934, Joseph Schumpeter introduced the modern definition of entrepreneurship, according to him "the carrying out of new combinations we call 'enterprise'," and "the individuals whose function it is to carry them out we call 'entrepreneurs'." Schumpeter associated entrepreneurship to the creation of five basic new combinations namely: introduction of a new product, introduction of a new method of production, opening of a new market, the conquest of a new source of supply and carrying out of a new organization of industry. Peter Drucker (1985) proposed that "entrepreneurship" is a practice.

One school of thought on entrepreneurship suggests that role of the entrepreneur is that of a risk-bearer in the face of uncertainty and imperfect information. Modern school of thought claims that the role of the entrepreneur is that of an innovator. Leibenstein (1966) claims that the dominant, necessary characteristics of entrepreneurs are that they are gap-fillers, they have the ability to perceive where market fails and develop new goods or services that the market demands. Thus, entrepreneurs have the special ability to connect different markets and make up for market failures and deficiencies. Gallup (Gallup 2011 data) defines an entrepreneur as an individual who proactively seeks to generate value through expansion of economic activity and who creatively responds to challenges and needs encountered in the process of accomplishing this outcome.

Entrepreneurship and Education

India's Higher Education System generates a large number of graduates every year. However, its economy is not in a position to absorb all the graduates passing out, leading to an increase in the educated unemployed. According to Labour Bureau's "Third Annual Employment and Unemployment Survey 2012-13" the unemployment amongst the graduate youth that happened to be at 19.4 per cent in 2011-2012 increased to 32 per cent during 2012-2013.

India's large growing population will further worsen the employment situation, so in order to keep up with the pace of developed countries, India needs to create many entrepreneurs by promoting entrepreneurship. If the school/university students with high entrepreneurial potentials get proper exposure in this area, there are more chances of them becoming "real" entrepreneurs.

Entrepreneurship Education can help to develop skills in, identifying current trends and market gaps, develop new competencies, creativity and leadership. Thus more must be done to ensure that both entrepreneurial and technology-based skills' training is provided to students at all levels of the education process. Entrepreneurship education should focus on 'Intrapreneurs' as well as entrepreneurs, as most of the students may use their entrepreneurial skills within companies or public institutions.

Review of Literature

Curley, M. and Formica P. (August 2012) in their paper "University Ecosystem and Entrepreneurial University" says that The university ecosystem approach can unleash the potential energy in university with graduates not just emerging in a state of readiness to be employee, but often as highly motivated entrepreneurs with business or social innovation. Thus entrepreneurial university will result in a harmonic coupling between scientific and academic entrepreneurship. Garba, A. (2010) in his paper "Refocusing Education System Towards Entrepreneurship Development in Nigeria: A Tool for Poverty Eradication" emphasizes the need and importance of entrepreneurship education, which will serve as a panacea to some social economic problems which call for different strategies and action. Refocusing education system will immensely contribute in developing the spirit and culture of entrepreneurship in country. Kathyccheng (2011) in the article "Universities: An Entrepreneur's Ecosystem" explains how Universities provide significant amounts of intellectual capital that spans the various disciplines required for businesses to succeed. If university ecosystems are strengthened, it might serve as a grassroots approach to stimulating national entrepreneurship. Kwong C., *et al.* (2012) in their paper "The role of environment in fostering conductive entrepreneurial learning Teaching the 'art' of entrepreneurship in boot camps" say that the numbers of university entrepreneurship courses have increased rapidly, but the importance of entrepreneurial skills appears to have been overlooked with a heavy concentration on teaching about entrepreneurship rather than for entrepreneurship. Liyan, Z. (2010)

"Entrepreneurship Education within India's Higher Education System" Higher education system should, satisfy the need for entrepreneurship by: selecting + motivating + training + supporting. Unfortunately, the present Entrepreneurship Education in India just concentrates on related courses. Moreover, the so-called entrepreneurship courses are similar to the general business courses. But, general business management education has no significant influence on entrepreneurial propensity.

Change in Government's Policy and Outlook Towards Entrepreneurship Education

Government policies on entrepreneurship education are needed as a government not only provide funds, but also plays a key role in the quality and promotion of Entrepreneurship Education. Government policies can help ensure that entrepreneurship becomes a part of the formal educational system and aim to facilitate the creation of an entrepreneurial culture, which will help budding entrepreneurs to identify and pursue opportunities. The new welcome initiative of the Central and State Government under RUSA [Rashtriya Uchchatar Shiksha Abhiyan (National Higher Education Mission)] approved by the Cabinet Committee on Economic Affairs on 3 October, 2013 provides a unique opportunity for fostering innovation eco-system in Higher Education.

India Budget 2014: A Boost to Entrepreneurship

An entrepreneurship-oriented budget was announced by the Government of India in July 2014. This had greatly excited the country's entrepreneurial community. Several proposals announced by the Finance Minister suggest that the government is serious about unlocking India's entrepreneurial power to fuel desperately-needed jobs and economic growth. It is strongly believe that if the ideas and proposals announced by the minister materialize, this could, indeed, turn out to be a momentous budget for India.

Highlight of the Announcements

1. In order to create a conducive eco-system for the venture capital in the MSME sector it is proposed to establish a 10,000 crore fund to act as a catalyst to attract private capital by way of providing equity, quasi equity, soft loans and other risk capital for start-up companies.

2. A nationwide "District level Incubation and Accelerator Programme" would be taken up for incubation of new ideas.
3. Provide necessary support for "Entrepreneur friendly legal bankruptcy framework for SMEs to enable easy exit."

Government of India's Policy Initiatives for Promoting Innovation for Entrepreneurship Development

In spite of having a large publicly funded science and technology infrastructure and a sizeable education base, India has not been able to realize its innovative potential due to a fragmented innovation ecosystem. India is a country with over 1.2 billion people, 379 million (31%) of which are between the ages of 18 and 35 (Census of India, 2011). Many of these young people are unemployed despite being educated. For example, only one among every four urban males under 29 years is employed even though they hold at least a certificate or diploma (National Sample Survey Office, 2013). The aim of the government is to create employment opportunities for youth while focusing on rapid economic growth. Entrepreneurship development is one of the mechanisms adopted by the Government of India towards the creation of job opportunities. The government's assumption is that support for innovation will enhance entrepreneurship development, which will in turn accelerate economic growth.

The Indian Government has taken many initiatives towards strengthening the innovation ecosystem, the most important of which are:

(1) The establishment of the National Innovation Council, whose mandate is to coordinate various innovation-related activities, and
(2) The new Science, Technology and Innovation Policy 2013, which is intended to promote entrepreneurship and science-led solutions for sustainable and inclusive growth.

Changing Role of Education in Facilitating Entrepreneurial Ecosystem

Education system should contribute in developing the culture of entrepreneurship in the country by—

- Educational Institutions need to develop learning content, pedagogy, curricula and examination system that encourage critical and creative thinking.

- Apart from theory the curriculum should include entrepreneurial experiences ranging from working on projects to researching and evaluating the commercial potential of ideas, to working on problems faced by local entrepreneurs.
- Student's success and efforts should be aptly rewarded to motivate them and encourage entrepreneurial behaviour among them.
- Apart from just focusing on education and research, an equally important role of value creation needs to be addressed.
- Our education system needs to equip students with personal competencies such as creativity, determination, integrity and self-challenge apart from just business skills.
- Incorporate case studies of real life situations in teaching learning process and bridge the gap between theory and practice.
- Create platform for networking, peer appreciation and felicitate budding entrepreneurs, this would provide motivation to others.

Entrepreneurship education can help in changing the students' mindset and offer business creation as an alternative career option. This has a clear advantage of—

> Seeking the Budding Entrepreneurs rather than Waiting for Them to seek it.

Current Status of Entrepreneurship Education in India

In India, many entrepreneurship centres have been established to coordinate the different programmes, activities and resources within the educational institutions.

Some of the institutes offering entrepreneurship courses are—

- **Narsee Monjee Institute of Management Studies (NMIMS)** conducts a two-year, full-time programme on Family Business Management. The course covers the managerial and legal aspects of entrepreneurship. The motivational aspect taught at NMIMS is very important, as it creates a desire and improves confidence level. This programme has armed students with the skills, knowledge and mind-set to run their family business.

- **Indian School of Business (ISB)** in Hyderabad affiliated to non-profit organization—Wadhwani Foundation (committed to promoting entrepreneurship), offers entrepreneurial and incubation assistance. ISB has experienced instructors equipped with business experience.
- The **NS Raghavan Centre for Entrepreneurial Learning in IIM, Bangalore (NSRCEL—IIMB)** undertakes international collaboration projects. The Global Entrepreneurship Monitor (GEM) Project with the London Business School, the Ewing Marion Kaufmann Foundation and Babson College has been a major project for the last three years.
- **IIM, Calcutta**, stresses on practical activities on innovation and entrepreneurship involving students, which are facilitated by the faculty members. The IIMC's entrepreneurship cell organizes one of the biggest business plan contest in Asia, i2I—ideas to implementation with Yale University's Yale Entrepreneurial Society (YES).
- Setting up of such centres and tie ups among various institutions are also happening in technical schools as well as in the business schools. Some prominent names include—
  - The Technology Business Incubation Unit, Delhi;
  - The SIDBI innovation and incubation centre in IIT, Kanpur; and
  - The Society for Innovation and Development (SID) at the Indian Institute of Science, Bangalore, is one of the oldest centres in India.
- **SID-IISc's** remarkable achievement is the project called SuTRA—Sustainable Transformation of Rural Areas—which uses non-edible oils from indigenous neem trees as a substitute for fuel generation. Ideas are now being focused on attacking on the problems of rural poverty, since "Innovation Is Getting Compassionate, too."
- B-schools are supporting the entrepreneurship trend wholeheartedly. They are going out of their way and taking hard efforts to promote entrepreneurship on their campuses. Many institutes like IIM-Ahmadabad, IIM-Bangalore, IIT- Bombay and SPJIMR, Mumbai have modified placement rules to offer 'Placement holidays' or 'Deferred placements' where students can try their hands at setting up their own businesses and if things

do not work out, they can come back to the campus for placements within two years of passing out.

- **Birla Institute of Technology and Science, Pilani** has launched the Entrepreneur in Residence Programme (EIR) to help its students and interested faculty with a unique opportunity to meet one-to-one with successful entrepreneurs. The aim of the programme is to provide real learning opportunities and interaction with experienced entrepreneurs, industry experts and venture capitalists; this help students to get insight about procedures for starting a business and also about trends in specific industries and markets. The programme is meant to be of special benefit for students interested in innovation and start-ups.

Embedding Entrepreneurship into Formal Education

The overall goal of entrepreneurship education is to give students the attitudes, knowledge and skills to act in an entrepreneurial way. In fact, the younger the people are when starting to learn these skills, the better it is. Entrepreneurial learning should be integrated into the curriculum, rather than only being offered as stand-alone courses. Entrepreneurship programmes should be developed across disciplines or sectors like science, engineering, technology, medicine and arts. The entrepreneurship education should also be promoted right from the school level. The broad dimensions of entrepreneurship education need to be broken down into various categories which will provide the framework for the wide range of specific learning outcomes.

At Primary School Level: Awareness and Inspiration

Since attitude takes considerable time to develop, it is essential that entrepreneurial attitude be incorporated into general education programme for the young people, i.e. at primary education level. Entrepreneurial attitudes like taking initiative and risk, critical thinking, creativity and problem solving along with focus on entrepreneurial skills of communication, presentation, planning as well as team work should be developed. Self-awareness and self-confidence should also be promoted. This will lead to discovering and trusting one's own abilities which allow individuals to turn their creative ideas into action.

In primary education, the adoption of school books, interactive games and exercises can help stimulating the brain, improving retention of ideas and increasing fun and learning. Activities like movie screenings, street plays, talks by entrepreneurs and contests like quizzes can be conducted. This would create a positive image about entrepreneurs, entrepreneurship and importance of enterprises for development of the society.

It is important to note that, at this level of education, learning outcomes cannot be linked to practical entrepreneurial skills. Entrepreneurship should not be taught as a separate subject at this level.

Secondary School Level: Basic Knowledge

At higher secondary level, entrepreneurship education may include the Introduction about Entrepreneurship and Charms of becoming an entrepreneur, changing entrepreneurial eco-system. Basic knowledge of some core concepts like idea generation, opportunity analysis can be imparted in short session. Other basic skills which form the important attribute of an 'Enterprising Self' need to be taught, like communication, negotiation, leadership initiative, risk taking, critical thinking, creativity and problem solving, entrepreneurial motivation, values and attitude.

At the secondary level, extracurricular activities, like 'Entrepreneurship Week', visits to work place of entrepreneurs, talks with entrepreneurs etc. will provide role models which will impact positively on students. Examples of business, corporate and social entrepreneurs like Ratan Tata, K.V. Kamat, Kiran Majumdar Shaw, Devi Prasad Shetty etc. can be presented so as to make them aware about the entrepreneurial activities in different fields.

At Junior College Level: Intermediate Knowledge

There can be a compulsory course on entrepreneurship, economic and financial literacy, specific knowledge of the environment can be applied to the entrepreneurship syllabus. Session on Business Idea Generation, Creativity, Creating Value Proposition, Delivering Value to Customers by Using Innovative Ideas, Evolving A Business Model should be conducted. These should be based on participative learning methods like, group work, simulation exercises, role play, case discussions. Workshops on entrepreneurship courses may include opportunity recognition, cases and experiential learning tools, introduction to preparing of a Business Plan, managing the SME, family-owned businesses and managing the transition from necessity to growth firms.

Here students can develop a plan but are not expected to implement the business. This will help develop in them the skill of being more focused on issues related to a firm's external environment and its internal workings. Also the various support systems (fund based and non-fund based) available for Entrepreneur should be introduced to them.

At Graduate Level and Post-Graduate Level

Practical Experience

Practical understanding of entrepreneurial opportunities should include the learning-by-doing method, including designing and implementing a business plan and running campus-based companies or running large-scale programmes in an E-Cell in which students have to raise funds. Issues relating to managing workplace diversity, corporate governance, corporate social responsibility, business ethics and conservation of natural environment should be the focus. These exercises will help build the student's understanding of what they have learned in theory.

Training in data storage and processing and using computing for financial calculations need to be taught to the aspiring entrepreneurs. The development of business plans teaches students to integrate accounting, economics, finance, marketing and other business disciplines. These will promote development of technology-based business plans and enhance technology transfer from the university to the market.

Real-World Experience

A practical intersection of education and enterprise is the business incubator, which can be based in an academic institution. Incubators can support firms that will become commercially viable, students can receive help and support as they enter the world outside their campuses. Business incubators may help to increase the success rate of start-ups.

Another key area to be addressed in entrepreneurship education is drafting curriculums that are tailored to the local environment; this will leverage existing resources by creating new local materials, case studies and examples of role models that entrepreneurs can relate to.

Note: This is just a suggestive outline. Implementation can be done according to the requirement of the Target Group.

Teachers are the Key to Entrepreneurship Education

Teachers have an important role, as they have a strong impact on the achievement of learners. They are facilitators of learning and multipliers of ideas. They shape learning processes and can help students to achieve entrepreneurial learning outcomes—concrete knowledge, skills and attitudes. Entrepreneurship education requires a way of teaching in which experiential learning and inspiration to students, to develop an enterprising attitude have a main role.

Teachers Role in Promotion of Entrepreneurship Education

Most of the teacher training institutes are at the higher education level. Much needs to be done at the primary and secondary levels. Entrepreneurship development training should be included in curriculums of teacher training institutes (D.Ed., B.Ed. and M.Ed.). Teaching methodology should promote "Experiential learning" and teaching-learning process be made interactive. This would expose the students to entrepreneurs, entrepreneurship and real business situations.

In order that learners benefit from entrepreneurship education in the curriculum, teachers should be trained to teach the following themes.

Entrepreneur as a Person: The following should be covered under this theme:

- *Entrepreneurial qualities*—For example, achievement motivation, creativity, decision making, initiative, innovation and risk taking.
- *Entrepreneurial skills*—For example, strategy formulation, leadership, planning and time management and financial concepts, communication and negotiation skills and self-knowledge.

Entrepreneurial Process: The following should be covered under this theme:

- *Economic education*—For example economic growth, unemployment, productivity, industry knowledge, tax, financial management and marketing.
- *Business idea*—For example sources of generation of ideas, creativity and innovation, opportunity identification and appraisal.

- *Writing a business plan*—For example visualizing all the aspects of starting a business and connecting the dots.
- *Starting a business*—The legal and government procedures for entry and exit to business.

Key Principles: For Enhancing Entrepreneurial Spirit in Teachers and Taught:

- '*Bird in the hand*'—realize that you do not need a blockbuster idea, or to run after 'fantastic' opportunities, just a solution to a simple problem.
- '*Affordable loss*'—consider how much time you can realistically invest, given that the venture might fail.
- '*Crazy quilt*'—as much as possible, form partnerships with other people and organizations.
- '*Lemonade*'—embrace surprises that arise from uncertain situations, remaining flexible rather than tethered to existing goals.
- '*Pilot in the Plane*'—focus on activities within your control; the future is neither found nor predicted, but made.

Conclusion

Entrepreneurship Education is a tool that can support young people to be more entrepreneurial. This is about how to develop a general set of competences applicable in all walks of life. It includes all forms of learning, education and training which contribute to entrepreneurial spirit, competence and behaviour and is not simply about learning how to run a business. Support for entrepreneurship has never been more important than it is now. Reinforcing entrepreneurial education in schools, vocational education institutions and universities will have a positive impact on the entrepreneurial dynamism of our economies. Apart from contributing to the creation of social enterprise and business start-ups, entrepreneurship education will make young people more employable and more 'intrapreneurial' in their work within existing organizations. Needless to say, the teachers and educators have a vital role to play in this. They shape learning processes and can help students to achieve entrepreneurial learning outcomes, concrete knowledge, skills and attitudes.

The development of entrepreneurship is not an automatic or spontaneous process. Concrete efforts by all stakeholders in the national economy led by an enlightened government are necessary to create the environment and conditions for value creation. This all is possible if we, as individuals, society, industry and a country lead the change by building an ecosystem of innovation, experimentation and ability to take risk, where entrepreneurship can thrive and prosper. Our education system, especially our schools and universities along with the industry must nurture the entrepreneurial ecosystem. We must appreciate this fundamental fact as we put our collective efforts behind the entrepreneurship vehicle, as this is the only vehicle that can create a Shining India.

References

Abubakar, S. (2010). "Refocusing Education System towards Entrepreneurship Development in Nigeria: A Tool for Poverty Eradication". *European Journal of Social Sciences,* Volume 15, Number 1, pp. 140-150.

Amuseghan, S. Adejimola and Tayo, O. Olufunmilayo (March 2009). "Spinning Off an Entrepreneurship Culture Among Nigerian University Students: Prospects and Challenges". *African Journal of Business Management,* Vol. 3(3): 80-88.

A Report of the Global Education Initiative at World Economic Forum, Switzerland, April (2009). *Educating the Next Wave of Entrepreneurs-Unlocking Entrepreneurial Capabilities to Meet the Global Challenges of 21st Century.*

Building a Culture of Entrepreneurship—Starting with Education. A report by Intel Global Challenge—A Joint project of Intel Foundation and UC Berkeley Lester Centre for entrepreneurship. (http://entrepreneurship.intel.com)

Caleb, C.Y. Kwong, Piers Thompson, Cherry W.M. Cheung, Humera Manzoor (2012). The Role of Environment in Fostering Conductive Entrepreneurial Learning Teaching the 'Art' of Entrepreneurship in Boot Camps. *Journal of General Management,* Vol. 38, No. 1, The Braybrooke Press Ltd.

Chien-Chi Tseng (2012). "Linking Entrepreneurial Infrastructures and New Business Development: Entrepreneurship Development in Taiwan," *The Journal of Entrepreneurship,* 21(1): 117-132, Sage Publications.

Curley, M. and Formica, P. (2012). University ecosystem and entrepreneurial University, *White paper* http://www.xconomy.com/boston/2008/02/25/universities-an-entrepreneurs-ecosystem.

Desai, V. (2010). *The Dynamics of Entrepreneurial Development and Management.* New Delhi: Himalaya Publishing House, Sixth Edition, ISBN: 978-93-5024-454-8

Economic Times, Power of ideas 11/11/12—In the article "Small companies in poor countries: Can the spirit of enterprise be taught?"

Goel, A. (2009). *Women Empowerment Myth or Reality,* New Delhi: Deep and Deep Publications, ISBN: 978-81-8450-182-7

Harvard Business Review on Succeeding as an Entrepreneur. (2011). Harvard Business Press, Boston, Massachusetts. ISBN: 975-1-4221-7224 7, pp. 19-30.

Holt, D. (2002). *Entrepreneurship,* New Venture Creation, New Delhi: Prentice Hall of India, Sixth Edition, ISBN 81-203-1281-3, pp. 101-109.

Inna, K. (2012). "Obstacles to the University-Industry Cooperation in the Domain of Entrepreneurship", *Journal of Business Management,* No. 6.

Isenberg, D. (June 2010). "How to Start an Entrepreneurial Revolution", *Harvard Business Review.*

Kathyccheng (2011) in the blog at wordpress.com-article "Universities: An Entrepreneur's Ecosystem". http://www.xconomy.com/boston/2008/02/25/universities-an-entrepreneurs-*ecosystem/*

Matthew, D., Regele and Heidi, M. Neck (2012). "Entrepreneurship Education Sub-Ecosystem in the United States: Opportunities to Increase Entrepreneurial Activities". *Journal of Business and Entrepreneurship,* 23(2), Winter 2012, pp. 25-47.

Venkataraman, S. and Sarasvathy, S. (2008) paper "The Fabric of Regional Entrepreneurship: Creating the Multiplier Effect", presented at the World Entrepreneurship Forum.

Zhang, L. (2010) "Entrepreneurship Education within India's Higher Education System". The globaljournals.com

Zoltan, A., (2006). "Entrepreneurship Good for Economic Growth", Innovation/ winter. pp. 97-107.

https://articles.economictimes.indiatimes.com/2012-08-01/news/32981433_1_indian-adults-entrepreneurship-gallup-world-poll

https://articles.timesofindia.indiatimes.com/2012-10-29/news/34797491_1_ecosystem-future-roadmap-world-entrepreneurship-forum

Section-IV
Emerging Trends and Future Prospects

18

Role of Women Education in Saudi Arabia

Challenges and Achievements

Sheeba

Introduction

Saudi Arabia is a country in South-East Asia with a population of approximately 19 million. The country was established in 1932 by King Abdul Aziz ibn Abdur Rahman al Saud. The country covers about 900,000 square miles. Arabic is the official language and Islam is the official religion. Saudi Arabia has a literacy rate of about 62 per cent, which is the lowest literary rate in the gulf nations. The first ever school for girls in Saudi Arabia, called the Dar al-Hanan school, opened in 1956, and until then, few girls had an opportunity to get an education of any kind. The reason the Department of Religious Guidance remained control of Education for women, was to ensure that women were educated in accordance with the principles of Islam as interpreted in Saudi Arabia, which traditionally espoused that women take roles that would be considered to be gender appropriate such as motherhood, housewifery, teaching or nursing. According to Natana Delonbas, the apparent oppression of women's education by contemporary Wahhabi regimes is due to the adherence to the interpretation of the Wahhabi Islam. Mona Almuijjed explains how within the last 40 years the government has built an educational programme that is succeeding in increasing school and university enrolment for women. Improvements in reducing illiteracy rates has also been a success in building the educational infrastructure in Saudi Arabia. Over the years basic education has been offered for children, both male and female, and has been of high quality education. Over the history for women's education in Saudi Arabia, women have received basic literacy and numeracy skills and have completed primary school on time.

Norms of Education

The government has put together system where women are second to men. Male guardians are responsible for making many decisions for women in Saudi Arabia. Women in Saudi Arabia need permission to study. The social norm of guardianship has eliminated many resources and materials that women cannot access for educational reasons. Many women have limited visiting times to public libraries, of which their male guardian would need to be present. Most of the time women are only allowed into libraries specific to women. This cause a huge gap in Educational materials women's are allowed to view and obtain.

Enrolment and Segregation in Education

The struggle for women's education is an ongoing battle in Saudi Arabia. There is no schooling that allows men and women to be in the same class. Segregation of men and women's education has been a part of Saudi Arab's culture for much of the 20th century. Abdul Aziz, the founder of the Saudi Kingdom, wanted and showed his support for women's education. Women have struggled to obtain equality at every level of education in Saudi Arabia. At the university level, women are allowed to view lectures given by a male professor through a monitor. These women can ask questions over the telephone also.

Political Participation

Saudi Arabia is governed by Sharia Law. With Sharia Law, it is open to many interpretations, but it does not usually encourage women to hold prominent positions. In 2005, Saudi Arabia held its first nationwide elections. Women who make up more than 50 per cent of the population did not participate. They were not permitted to vote or run as candidate in the elections. With the conclusion of the political participation, Abdul Aziz Al- Heis talks about how women will not be able to participate and find a platform to have their voice heard for equality and demands. There needs to be push forward and renewal of institutions for religious ideas so the political economy can include both men and women. Since 2015 women are allowed to vote and elect themselves as candidate for the country's municipal elections.

Social Status

A study of women and education in Saudi Arabia must take into account social and political events in recent years. Saudi Arabia was formally proclaimed a country only 70 years ago. In 1979, a Muslim extremist who was a former theology student led an attempt to seize the Holy Mosque in Mecca. He was attempting to officially put an end to what he called "Western Influence" in the country. In 1978, a year before the siege newspapers and magazines were publishing articles written by both men and women discussing women's rights to participate in public life. Issues such as women's right to drive, where women could and should work, and types of education appropriate for women were all hot topics (Doumato, 2000). However, some historians argued that Mecca siege was not all about women's freedom; it had a great deal to do with asserting the extremist's view on all aspects of life. Nevertheless, women issues became the focus in any discussion about progress. A woman's right to participate fully in the development of the nation was forbidden. In addition after that television stations were prohibited from broadcasting images of unveiled women. Women were also banned from conducting their own business with a male representative, preferably a family member. Nonetheless, a recent survey shows that approximately 16,390 businesses were owned by women and women own 40 per cent of the nation's wealth. According to Seddeka Arabia, in Islamic History, a 15 century old tradition shows many examples of independent Arab female entrepreneurs. These events significantly shaped the women's movement in Saudi Arabia for the next 20 years. Universities and colleges for women continued to be built throughout the nation. However, conservative religious scholars continued to pressure society to bend to their request, especially related to women. The general public also indicated that a Saudi women's place is in her home. The percentage of women working outside the home is not very good and all these women are in teaching and health sectors. Few women are recently gaining access to peruse professions other than teaching and medicine.

The Struggle for Women's Education: An Ongoing Battle

The advent of formal public schooling in Saudi Arabia dates back in the 1960s when the first official primary school for girls opened its doors in Riyadh (Al Munajjed, 1997). Prior to this, informal schooling took place for both boys and girls, the aim of which was to teach religious rituals.

The goal of education was to learn the Quran, the Hadith (prophet narrations), and Sunnah Prophet Mohammad's customary behaviour and opinion on various issues. Thus, education of both sexes in the Kingdom of Saudi Arabia first took place in the *kuttub* a class of Quran recitation for children, which was usually attached to the local mosque. The teaching of girls also took place in private tutorials, which occurred in the homes of professional male or female Quran readers. Education for girls stopped at puberty, "when strict seclusion at home began and veiling in public became mandatory" (Altorki,1986: 19). However, the first founder of the Saudi Kingdom, expressed his support for women's education. Abdul Aziz, the founder of the Saudi Kingdom expressed his support for women's education. But, education did not change the patriarchical nature of Saudi society. Women in every field are subordinate to men. But, the history of women initiatives to achieve education reaches back to as early as the 1940s. When the Ministry of Higher Education began sending a few bright young Saudi men to continue their studies abroad. A bright young woman by the name of Fatina Amina Shakir wanted to have the same opportunity. She applied for a Ministry of Higher Education grant to study abroad, but the Ministry rejected the application saying that it was immoral to allow young single woman to study abroad. Fatina and her father appealed to King Faisal, who was known to be the supporter of women's education. Fatina eventually became one of the very first Saudi woman to hold a Ph.D. Her thesis, which focused on the modernization of the Third World countries, features an interview with King Faisal, the man who had made her dreams comes true. (Arebi, 1994; Lacey, 1981).

Since women's education in Saudi Arabia officially began, educational levels have increased rapidly. The number of women's institutions has grown from 15 in the 1960s to 155 in the 1970s (Al Mohsen, 2000). Al Mohsen Points out that women's education started with arts and education, all other fields were available only to men. The first girls' college was established in 1970 in Riyadh and admitted those with secondary level schooling. Approximately, 10 similar colleges with the same requirements opened by the 1980s. Subjects included the Arts, Education, General Science and Sciences such as Biology, Mathematics, Religion, Arabic, Geography, History, English, Psychology and Home Economics. Library sciences were exclusively offered at Riyadh's College. (Al Malik, 1987). The first university that has a women's campus was Riyadh's King Saud University, which was opened in1979. In the 1980s, women's campuses at King Saud University added colleges for public administration, medicine, dentistry, nursing and education. The Jeddah campus of the University of King Abdul

Aziz admitted women to economics in 1967, and the Dammam city campus of the King Faisal University in 1978 opened a centre for women which included colleges of medicine, nursing, agriculture, nutrition, home economics and education. In 1971Umm Al-Qura University in Mecca admitted to women to all departments except Physical Education, the training of judges and Islamic Economics.

Despite the increased record of support, the Saudi government policy of sexual segregation has saddled women with facilities substantially inferior to those available to their male counterparts. Moreover, women do not receive the same quality of education as men, because teachers for men are better trained. More than 34 per cent of men teaching at men's universities hold doctorates compared to only three per cent of those who teach at women's universities and colleges. (Al Munajjed,1997). Saudi women are not able to enjoy the 200 public libraries mostly affiliated with schools, universities and religious institutions or the 70 public libraries except through a male relative liaison or restricted visiting hours. Libraries for women only are extremely small and often poorly equipped (Arebi, 1944)

List of Universities that Enroll Women

King Saud University, King Abdulaziz University, King Faisal University, Umm Al-Qura University, King Abdullah University of Science and Technology, Imam Muhammad Ibn Saud Islamic University, Institute of Public Administration, Taibah University, King Khalid University, Al Faisal University, Qassim University, Najran University, Jazan University, Majmaah University, Taif University, Princess Nora bint Abdulrahman University (Women only), University of Ha'il, King Saud bin Abdulaziz University for Health Sciences, Prince Sultan University, Salman bin Abdulaziz University, University of Dammam, Prince Mohammad Bin Fahd University, Al Jouf University, University of Tabuk, Shaqra University, Baha University, Effat University (Women only), Northern Borders University, University of Business and Technology, Dar Al-Uloom University, Al Yamamah University, Fahad Bin Sultan University, Dar Al-Hekma University, (Women only), Ibn Sina National College for Medical Studies, Riyadh College of Dentistry and Pharmacy and Batterjee Medical College.

Women and Education in Islamic Teaching

In discussing Islamic teaching with regards to women's education it is important to differentiate between the normative teachings of Islam and diverse cultural practices among Muslims. One of the most common criticism levied against Islam is that it treats women unjustly. Yet, in actually Islamic teachings express great respect towards women. Moreover, traditionally women have had a prominent role in society. "Women in Islamic societies have reached political heights unparalleled in the most advanced Western nations" (Ragab, n.d., p. 5). Arab history notes that one of the wives of the Prophet Mohammad, Aysha, led an army of 30,000 soldiers, cooked for them and helped medicate them. Aysha discussed and negotiated various issues and political matters with Prophet Mohammad, who freely acknowledged her wisdom. It is also noted in Islamic historical documents that one-sixth of the Hadith record Aysha as being part of the chain of transmission of the sayings and the traditions of the Prophet. This is greatly appreciated among Muslims today. As noted before, Khadija, the first of Prophet Mohammad's wives, managed a successful commercial endeavour and was the first prominent businesswoman in Islam (Badawi,1995). Fatima, Prophet Mohammad's daughter is cited in many historical documents as being politically active. Sukei'na, Prophet Mohammad's granddaughter, was a well known mathematician. More recently, Benazir Bhutto, a Muslim woman, was the Prime Minister of Pakistan. Nobel prize winner Sheerin Abadi from the Islamic Republic of Iran is also a Women's Lawyer and a Political Activist (Alsari, 2003a, 2003b). Many other examples in the history of Islam negate the claims of religious conservatives regarding women's education. Essential Islamic Teaching, however, strongly encourages the education of women in religious, economic, political and social domains. The Prophet Mohammad's views on education are evident in statements such as, "The search of knowledge is a duty for every Muslim male or female", and seek knowledge from the cradle to the grave (This phrase is attributed to Prophet Mohammad). Finally, progressive religious scholars must cooperate in presenting the essential liberating Islamic teachings regarding woman, especially as they relate to education.

Progress Achieved in Social Change for Women

Knowing the structure of Saudi Arabian Society and understanding the role of the tradition and religion is vital to understanding social change in the country, especially as it relates to women. The role of King Faisal and Iffat in the struggle for women's education challenges this belief. Today with the majority of Saudi women being educated and illiteracy declining uneducated women will soon be a small minority. However, the percentage of Saudi women in the workforce remains the same (Doumato, 2000) attributes the lower percentage of women in the workforce to segregation between the sexes. The main problem for many Saudi women especially businesswoman is tradition and above all conservative views on women's participation in nation building. Taking into consideration the religious background of Saudi society and the difficulty of implementing changes, the suggestion has been made to establish a Ministry of Women's Affairs to study in depth Saudi Society to determine its needs for future development. It is hoped that Ministry would also implement changes based on studies of educated, moderate Saudi women who appreciate the need for change.

Although the education of women is important, the dignity and value of being a wife and a mother should not be diminished by the concept of equality and educational opportunity. There is no either—or binary in Islam with regards to women's education and social participation. There is no contradiction between being a mother and a professional working outside the home. Women deserve to be able to make this choice. This means that women's education in Islam is not all contradictory to concepts such as chastity and dignity, which are highly esteemed and sacredly guarded in Islam (Jawad,1988). Education among Saudi women has been strongly encouraged by their illiterate mothers. In many cases it were these women who demanded classes in reading and writing for their children and adult literacy classes (Al Munnajjed, 1997: 80). Women's status in education in Saudi Arabia has been changing, and the Ministry of Higher Education has considered sending talented women abroad to finish their studies in high demand subjects. Moreover, recently the government supported the election of a Saudi woman, Thoraya Obaid, as an executive of the United Nations, Obaid, the first Saudi Arabian Executive Director of the United Nations' Population Fund (UNFPA), enjoys a reputation as a fighter and a pioneer for the education of women. In reading Saudi newspapers one is fascinated by the number of highly educated women participating in the public affairs and requesting more room for their initiatives. Newspapers published in both Arabic and English have a great number of female writers. Furthermore, Talal Ibn Abdul Aziz, the King's brother, continue effort to change the *status quo* and to support women's participation at all levels of Saudi Society. In the end Saudi Arabia will be ready for any global challenge.

Conclusion

It is practically impossible to discuss women's education in Saudi Arabia without introducing the social and political forces that have shaped women's status not only in education but in society in general. Women's role in Education in Saudi Arabia's conservative society, instead of serving as a tool for social change, serves as a force for conservation. Education entrenches and supports the prevailing class and gender structures and conforms to socio-economic and political expectations, and control mechanism. The Saudi education system and curricula needs to implement different strategies for looking at the other people with whom we disagree. On a macro level, recent changes in the international arena have opened the door to changes that were not attainable in the recent past. Space is allowed in the Saudi press for honest reflection as never before. Saudi columnists are able to constructively criticize the system's performance in the health, education, and women's rights sectors. This is of itself a great relief for both men and women who have long felt deprived of freedom of speech. Both women and men are hopeful for signs of slow but steady change occurring in the country.

The future developmental plans must be able to tackle problems of increased economic demands, segregation of the sexes, limitations of women's jobs and the cultural and religious heritage (Huyette, 1985). If the country plans to survive this globalised era women's education in all fields should be a priority. Educated open-minded individual's demands would bring changes and progress but to what extent? Is Saudi society ready for that change? Given the apparent variability in perspective of educated open-minded individuals who are seeking progress, and the attitudes of some conservative religious scholars and old traditions which resist any move forward it is difficult to predict. Until then women's issues will be at the centre of conflict between modernity and tradition.

References

Abo-Lughod, L. (1986). *Veiled Sentiments: Honour and Poetry in a Bedouin Society*. New York: University of California Press.

Afshar, H. (1993). *Women in the Middle East: Perceptions, Realities and Struggles for Liberation*. London: Macmillan.

Alghamdi, A. (2002). Brining a Global Education Perspective to Understand the 'Other': A Case Study of Western Myths of Muslim Women. Unpublished

Thesis Dissertation. Mount Saint Vincent University, Halifax, Nova Scotia: Canada.

Alireza, M. (1987). Women of Arabia. *National Geographic*, 172 (4): 423-453.

Al-Kotob (1975). *Perception of Female Students from the Countries of the Arab Gulf.*

Badawi, J. (1995). *Gender Equity in Islam: Basic Principles*. Plainfield, Indiana: American Trust Publications.

Boudy, A. (1999). *The relationship of age, gender, and economic statues to adult students attitudes towards becoming literate in Al-Ahssa Saudi Arabia.* Ph.D. Thesis Dissertation. Ohio State University, United States.

Doumato, E. (2000). *Getting God's Ear. Women, Islam, and Healing in Saudi Arabia and the Gulf.* United States: Columbia University Press.

Doumato, E. (2002). Women and Work in Saudi Arabia: How Flexible are Islamic Margins? *Middle East Journal*, 52 (2), Spring, 582.

Fakhro, M. (1996). Gulf Women and Islamic Law. In M. Yamani (Ed). *Feminism and Islam: Legal and Literary Perspectives*, pp. 251-262. New York: New York University Press.

Lacey, R. (1981). *The Kingdom: Arabia and the House of Sa'ud.* New York: Harcourt Brace Jovanovich.

Ragab, N. (n.d.). *The record set straight: Women in Islam have rights.* Submission. [Online] http://www.submission.org/noha.html [8 Dec., 2001]

Shukri, S. (1999). *Social Change and Women in the Middle East: State Policy, Education, Economic and Development*. Washington: Ashgate.

Smith, D. (1987). *The Everyday World as Problematic*. Toronto: Toronto University Press.

Texas International Education Consortium (n.d.) Middle East. [Online] http://www.tiec.org/mideast.html

Yamani, M. (1996). Some Observations on Women in Saudi Arabia. In M. Yamani (Ed). *Feminism and Islam: Legal and Literary Perspectives* (pp. 263-282). New York: New York University Press.

Zurbrigg, J. (1995). *Unveiling Portrayals of Muslim Women: Examining Western Texts on Saudi Women.* Unpublished thesis dissertation. University of Western Ontario, Canada.

19

Pedagogy in Teacher Education Course

Micheal M. Van Wyk

Introduction

The emergence of the Fourth Industrial Revolution (FIR) accelerated the transformation and use of the World Wide Web, in scope, velocity, and complexity (Warschauer & Matuchiak, 2010:180). The FIR brought several opportunities and challenges for the higher education sector by using and incorporating of different technologies into the classroom to change the traditional pedagogies employed by academics to include the digital natives in the process. The education sector, in particular Higher Education is not immune to this major globalized paradigm shift but need to embrace this opportunity and challenge to advance the knowledge economy. Education is currently experiencing rapid changes and challenges due to increase of technology based networked communities towards the FIR. In order for Higher Education sector to be relevant and compatible in this challenging society, universities are compelled to commit to the process of continuous change or become redundant (Bates, 2010:15). The higher education sector, in particular teacher education programmes started employing teaching—integrated technologies into pedagogy to change the traditional pedagogies employed by lecturers either residential or online classrooms to accommodate and include the digital natives in the learning process. In order for the teacher education programmes to be relevant and compatible in this challenging society, universities need to commit to the process of continuous change or become redundant. The Flipped Classroom Pedagogy (FCP) is a recent phenomenon used to support students learning. The current debate at faculties of education about the educational values of Flipped Classroom

Pedagogy (FCP) has been emerged as a powerful technology-integrated teaching strategy to enhance and to support student teachers to become competent teachers, in particular in online platforms.

Literature Review

Flipped Classroom Pedagogy (FCP) can be used to train future teachers as an imperative for self-directed and lifelong learning approaches. It is imperative that emancipating and transforming teacher education programmes for a quality education system needs creative and innovative strategies to empowering student teachers for the classroom of the future. Moreover, institutions of higher education are facing increased scrutiny to improve student learning and demonstrate programmeme effectiveness. Even though academics have access to numerous online teaching tools we know that teaching and learning is not all about the technology. Scholars advocated for more flexible, student-centred classroom teaching methods to promote "discovery" learning and "active" learning. According to Vaughan (2014) "opportunity exists through the use of innovative teaching models that capitalise on technology use, therefore teachers can seize the opportunity to arm preservice teachers with the pedagogical skills and strategies they will need to engage their own students" (p. 25). The author is of the view that we need to include and engage students by preparing them for world or work. One particular e-learning platform, Flipped Classroom Pedagogy (FCP), emerged as a technology-integrated teaching strategy as a means to support students in an open distance learning approach. In recent decades, the student-centred learning approach has shown significant learning gains and has reformed teaching styles in many higher educational institutions globally. In moving away from the lecture model to an instructional design involving interactive pedagogy and technology, many educators are paying attention to the Flipped Classroom Pedagogy. The flipped classroom promotes an environment which increases the interaction between the students and teachers and engages the students in learning through application and practice. The purpose of the FCP strategy is to promote a powerful learning environment which increases the constructive interaction between the students and teachers. It further collectively engages the students in learning through application and practice for ultimate self-directive learning. The FCP strategy is characterise by a student-centred approach. Moreover, Sams (2011) posits that this strategy places students at the centre of their student learning process meaning to develop self-directed learners. The student, is, therefore responsible for his/her learning and places more on the shoulders of students than teachers. This supports the view that students can experiment more with their learning through the FCP strategy. For example Bergmann and Sams (2013: 17-19) develop FCP instructional design, where students explore and make sense of their learning through active learning activities like inquiry learning, problem-based learning and peer collabouration (Sams, 2011). This creates the face-to-face time to have a "much deeper interaction" between the teacher and student as they engage and interact on case studies, and discuss particular problems (Leckhart & Cheshire, 2012; Gerstein, 2011). The learners are able to demonstrate what they have learned and to apply the material in a way that makes sense to them. As learners make sense of their learning, they create something that is individualized, and with application to the learners' everyday lives, it extends beyond the lesson. This is the highest level of learning under Bloom's Revised Taxonomy of Learning (Gerstein, 2011). Zappe, Leicht, Messner Litzinger, and Lee (2009) flipped a large undergraduate architectural engineering course and the students' evaluation of the course indicated that the flipped classroom had a positive impact on student learning as the students perceived the method of teaching as being more effective than lecturing and reported. It is important to realize that creating a flipped classroom is not just putting lectures on videos. Scholars of the FCP approach indicated several educational benefits of the FCP approach such as:

- Creating pod casts, videos and other technologies for students to revise anywhere, anytime and anyplace outside of class time;
- Providing technology-integrated learning activities for students to work collabouratively and collectively on task;
- Freeing up class time for students to work collabouratively and collectively on task;
- Increasing other learning activities to reinforce learning;
- Allowing the student to take responsibility for much of their learning;
- Increasing interaction and personalized content time between students; and
- Creating blended learning environments where students take responsibility for their own learning (Talley & Scherer, 2013; Steed, 2012; Leckhart & Cheshire, 2012; Gerstein, 2011; Stayer, 2012).

Moreover, in recent decades, this FCP student-centred learning approach has shown significant learning gains and has reformed teaching styles in many higher educational institutions globally. In moving away from the lecture model to an instructional design involving interactive pedagogy and technology, many educators are paying attention to the Flipped Classroom Pedagogy. This classroom approach promotes an environment which increases the interaction between the students and teachers and engages the students in learning through application and practice. With reference to this research, the latter educational benefits of the approach could be used for further exploration as a powerful technology-integrated teaching strategy to enhance and to support student teachers self-directed learning in an online platform (Sams & Bergmann, 2013; Talley & Scherer, 2013; Sams, 2011). On the other hand literature indicated that this approach is not just uploading videos, podcasts, using technology gadgets, setting up a classroom with no structure, students in class staring at a computer screen or students working in isolation. There are more to this approach (Sams & Bergmann, 2013; Leckhart & Cheshire, 2012; Zappe, Leicht, Messner, Litzinger & Lee, 2009).

Theoretical Frame

In view of the previous section on Flipped Classroom Pedagogy, this section of this chapter focuses on how the interrelatedness of theories for this study to enhance a student teacher self-directed learning in a teacher education course is explored to underpin the investigation.

Connectivity as a social networked e-learning theory: The motivation why a social networked theory foregrounds this study is to examine Economics student teachers views compiling evidence in an e-Portfolio through a Flipped Classroom Pedagogy to enhance self-directed learning within an open distance learning teacher education course. In this particular space specific interrelationships among students are framed during the Flipped Classroom Pedagogy. In the context of this study, the researcher explores the concepts of social network theory that underlie the power and popularity of a Flipped Classroom Pedagogy as an e-learning facilitation strategy during teaching practice placements for post-graduate certificate of education students in an ODL context. The researcher is of the opinion that lecturers often see new technologies as threatening their scholarly authority, precisely because these technologies require a re-thinking of roles, but this threat only materializes if we stay locked in a binary framework of lecturer *versus* student-teacher.

Andragogy as a self-directed learning theory: This concept is an overarching concept related to a learning-oriented and performance achievement-oriented approach. This theory focuses on numerous learning processes related to outcomes-driven, self-controlled learning behaviour (Zimmerman, 2000; Paris & Paris, 2001). Knowles (1975), the father of self-directed learning (SDL), defines self-directed learning as: a process in which individuals take the initiative, with or without the help of others, in diagnosing their learning needs, formulating learning goals, identifying human and material resources for learning, choosing and implementing appropriate learning strategies, and evaluating learning outcome (p. 15). Moreover, Zimmerman (2000) concurred with Knowles captures the idea that this phenomenon "... refers to self-generated thoughts, feelings, and actions that are planned and cyclically adapted to the attainment of personal goals" (p. 14). Moreover, the goals of self-directed learning include helping learners develop the capacity for self-direction, supporting transformational learning, and promoting "emancipatory learning and social action" (Merriam, 2001: 9). There are different views on the concept of self-directed learning (SDL). Scholars of the SDL view this phenomenon as a process of autonomy of students (Harrison, 1978), as a personal attribute (Guglielmino, 1977), as a moral, emotional, and intellectual autonomy (Candy, 1991). Emanating from these earlier findings, several frameworks have been emerged to understand SDL models developed by Mocker and Spear's Two Dimensional Model and Garrison's Three Dimensional Model. Paris and Paris (2001) describe the self-regulated learning (SRL) theory as autonomy and control by the individual who monitors, directs, and regulates actions towards goals of information acquisition, expanding expertise, and self-improvement.

Heutagogy as a self-determined learning theory: As indicated earlier, e-Portfolios as an empowering strategy can be used for the enhancement of SDL skills for personal growth and professional development. With reference to this study, the objective of the module SDEC00N Subject methodology for Postgraduate Certificate in Education (PGCE) and Baccaluareus Education is (B.Ed.) (Senior and Further Education and Training phase) Economics students is to equip students with subject content knowledge, pedagogical content knowledge skills, values, principles, methods and procedures to understand and explain orally and in writing the relevant theory of teaching in an problem-based education environment by using the Curriculum and Assessment Policy Statement (CAPS) to become competent Economics teachers for grades 10-12 (Department of Basic Education, 2011: 5). In planning, developing and compiling multiple pieces in the e-Portfolios, Economics education students take full responsibility for own learning. They become directly involve of what, how and why, they are learning specific content. After the completion of all multiple pieces, student showcase how they apply in practice pedagogical knowledge to teach, apply various teaching methods, develop competence in assessment practices, understand the principles of organising and implementing the Economics curriculum within the PGCE/B.Ed. learning programme, understand the curriculum theory and enlarge their capacity and ability to think critically and holistically as self-directed learners to advance quality education in South African schools.

This chapter explores the use of Flipped Classroom Pedagogy (FCP) as an e-learning tool in supporting Post Graduate Certificate of Education (PGCE) students, who were learning to teach economics education in open distance e-learning (ODeL) environment. For the purpose to conduct this study, the following research question: To what extent does a Flipped Classroom Pedagogy enhance student-teachers' learning to teach a teacher education course at an open distance learning university?

Context of Introducing the Flipped Class Pedagogy

This study was conducted in the College of Education, at the University in South Africa by starting the alternative assessment pilot project. The 2015 project was implemented for most undergraduate modules led by lectures that were willing to innovate and experiment in the alternative assessment approach. The module Economics subject teaching methodology (SDEC00N) was identified as part of the alternative assessment project of the University. As part of the project, different types of alternative assessment activities such as take-home assessments, e-portfolios, peer review assessment and continuous assessment were mandatory for the purpose of the alternative assessment pilot project. For SDEC00N, a flipped classroom pedagogy was planned and implemented through a learning management system (LMS) was linked to the web-based online platform, Mahara (http://mahara.org). This web-based tool integrated easy with the University's Sakai learning management system. The primary course lecturer and student teachers had access to Mahara by login with a username and password. The Flipped Class Pedagogy was introduced to the students in the tutorial letter as well in the recommended textbook, Teaching economics and management sciences (EMS) in the senior phase. The primary lecturer uploaded during the course of the year several types of content, namely: (1) examples of three written assignments; (2) examples of two different research projects; (3) four specific lesson plans with applicable activities; (4) three podcasts with specific topics; (5) PowerPoint presentations; (6) digital video clippings (DVCs) of classroom lessons; (7) multiple choice questions (MCQ); (8) related articles on contemporary economic issues (unemployment, poverty and inflation); (9) an example of grade 12 final year examination paper with memorandum; and (10) economic cartoons for students to be studied to complete activities to be included in their respective e-Portfolios. The ten different types of pieces were used in the FCP strategy that guided student teachers to design or develop similar original pieces as part of their ePortfolios for alternative assessment artefacts. In the tutorial letter a specific due date for the online e-Portfolio submission is provided. Student teachers submitted their final e-Portfolios by login to the online learning management platform. The Subject Methodology Economics module (SDEC00N) is an exit level module for final year PGCE/B.Ed. (Senior and Further Education and Training Phase) qualification.

Research Design and Methodology

Before this study commences, the online survey, Flipped Classroom Pedagogy Questionnaire (FCPQ) for collecting data was send to the Department of Statistics. A reliability test, Cronbach alpha coefficient ($\alpha = 0.7$) was run by using the Social Science Package for Statistical (SPSS) analysis. The overall reliability test computed was 0.89 for the online survey. The final FCPQ survey was send to ICT for uploading on LMS for the registered SDEC00N student teachers to be completed after completion of course. It is mandatory of University's ethical clearance policy that before any study or research project starts, the researcher is compel to apply for ethical clearance to their respective college committees for approval. For this research project, entitled, *e-Portfolios as an alternative assessment strategy in enhancing self-directed learning in a teacher education course,* ethical clearance was applied for to conduct research when using registered students' or data for research purposes. This study ethical clearance was granted (*see* Certificate ref. 2016/05/18/90178912/30/MC) and therefore, adheres to the Policy on Research Ethics of University. This project and in particular the contents of the data analysis process is a true and accurate reflection of the methodological and ethical implications of the findings of this study. All protocol observed in the study in strict accordance with the requirements for conducting the research project. Data analysis was computed by ICT unit at the university. Furthermore, this study was conducted in accordance with research ethics review committee of the College of Education requirements for research purposes.

This study used an explanatory quantitative research design. A closed structured questionnaire, Flipped Classroom Pedagogy Questionnaire (FCPQ), using a four point Likert scale was used to collect data. A purposive sampling of Post Graduate Certificate of Education (PGCE) and Baccaluareus Education is (B.Ed.) (Senior and Further Education and Training phase) student teachers (n = 371), who were learning to teach economics education in open distance learning (ODL) environments were selected and participated in this study. Descriptive and inferential data analysis was computed to explore student teachers' learning to teach an economics education course at a teacher education course.

Results

Sampling consisted of two hundred and fourteen (n = 214) Post-graduate Certificate in Education (PGCE) and one hundred and fifty seven (n = 157) Baccaluareus Education is (B.Ed.) (Senior and Further Education and Training phase) student teachers. Twenty nine per cent was male students (n = 109) and seventy one per cent was female (n = 262). Only PGCE (Senior Phase/Further Education and Training) and Bed SDEC00N students (N = 371) which were registered students per module on LMS participated in the study. Student teachers were assessed what they thought about their Flipped Class experiences, and whether the Flipped Class should be continued as a method of instruction. In this section of the study, students were asked about their experiences regarding the functionality of Flipped Classroom Pedagogy when compiling their ePortfolios in the subject. Results indicated in Table 19.1.

As reported in Table 19.1, ninety one per cent of student teachers strongly agree (Mean = 3.92; SD = 1.911) that the FCP strategy is a student-centred approach which increases student learning in an online platform. Additionally, respondents view the functionality of the FCP strategy as an e-learning tool for careful planning and preparation of activities to be effective. Furthermore, student teachers agree that it promotes, increase classroom interaction amongst students, helping students to engage by applying knowledge and skills meaningful. Moreover, respondents agree that it places students at the centred of the

Table 19.1: Students' views of the functionality of a FCP teaching strategy (n = 371)

To what extent do you agree or disagree that the functionality of the Flipped Class Pedagogy is important/not important to enhancing self-directed learning?	Mean	Std. Dev.	SA	A	D	SD
It promotes an environment which increases the interaction between the students and teachers out-of-class.	3.67	1.189	69%	31%	–	–
It engages the students in learning through application and practice of learned content.	3.89	1.334	89%	11%	–	–
It uses a Student-centred approach as it focuses on increases student learning.	3.92	1.911	91%	9%	–	–
It places the responsibility for learning more on the shoulders of students than teachers while giving them a greater impetus to experiment.	3.54	1.328	68%	29%	3%	–
It enhances active learning activities like inquiry learning, problem-based learning and peer collaboration to achieve learning outcomes.	3.59	1.799	72%	27%	1%	–
It creates something that is individualized, and with application to the learners' everyday lives, it extends beyond the lesson.	3.50	1.651	30%	58%	2%	–
It requires careful preparation and there is concern regarding the amount of time and effort the instructor has to put in.	3.49	1.981	23%	75%	2%	–
The process to implement FCP is time-consuming and creates additional work and may require new skills for the teacher.	2.58	1.881	23%	70%	7%	–

Likert scale: SA—Strongly Agree; A = Agree; D = disagree; SD = Strongly disagree.

learning process, which stresses that students must take full responsibility of their own learning. Furthermore, it enhances problem-solving, creative and critical thinking skills for challenges of the 21st century and beyond. Finally, overall student-teachers viewed FCP as a strategy that supports self-directed learning in an ODL environment. It emerged that student-teachers agreed that the Flipped Classroom Pedagogy created a positive lived experience and therefore, should be continued as a student-centred approach towards self-directed learning. Nonetheless, student-teachers views the FCP as time-consuming which creates additional work and may require new skills for them to implement the approach successfully (Mean = 2.58; SD = 1.881).

Student teachers were asked how they perceived the role the teacher in the Flipped Classroom Pedagogy should play in ensuring student learning.

Table 19.2: Teacher's role in a Flipped Class Pedagogy (n=371)

To what extent do you agree or disagree that the teacher play a crucial role in ensuring that the Flipped Class could be used to improve student learning?	**Mean**	**Std. Dev.**	**SA**	**A**	**D**	**SD**
The teacher can covers more material and allow students to see how the material can be used in authentic, problem-solving activities.	2.87	1.189	29%	44%	27%	–
The teacher provides students with simulations and hands-on activities.	3.06	1.334	34%	53%	13%	–
The teacher circulates and assists students who are struggling while correcting misconceptions, providing one-on-one tutoring.	2.61	0.911	4%	52%	44%	–
The teacher becomes a facilitator of learning, making him/her available to assist and support students throughout the process.	2.79	1.328	46%	51%	3%	–
The teacher plan out of class activities for in class that can be student-led to enhance learning.	3.41	1.181	28%	72%	–	–
The teacher must design FCP process to develop high-level, engaging questions that serve to deepen students' thinking and to address misconceptions in the lesson.	3.52	1.251	34%	76%	–	–
The teacher to decide what out-of-class and in-class elements that should be carefully integrated for students to understand the strategy and be motivated to prepare for the class.	3.77	1.381	29%	81%	–	–

Likert scale: SA = Strongly Agree; A = Agree; D = disagree; SD = Strongly disagree.

As indicated in Table 19.2, eighty one per cent of student-teachers strongly agree (Mean = 3.77; SD = 1.381) that the teacher played an important role regarding decision-making to what out-of-class and in-class activities should be carefully integrated for students to understand the strategy and be motivated to prepare for the class. This is the make or break of any FCP to be successful to achieve specific outcomes with the strategy. On the other hand, student teachers were less in agreement (Mean = 2.61; SD = 0.911) to the role that teachers play regarding the circulation and assistance to students who are struggling while correcting misconceptions, and providing one-on-one tutoring in the FCP strategy.

Student-teachers were asked to what extend the Flipped Classroom Pedagogy could enhanced student learning.

Table 19.3: Flipped Class Pedagogy enhancing student learning process (n = 371)

To what extent do you agree or disagree that the Flipped Classroom could be use to improve student learning?	Mean	Std. Dev.	SA	A	D	SD
It enhances students to entering into dialogue and reflective practice on how they experience course.	3.01	1.289	35%	63%	2%	–
It compels students may stop or repeat the lesson without stigma from peers.	3.11	1.334	54%	45%	1%	–
It helps students to develop individual strategies for how to learn and effectively find, evaluate, and use information to achieve outcomes.	3.65	1.011	29%	64%	7%	–
It forces students to take responsible for their own learning.	3.73	1.328	3%	97%	3%	–
It using meta-reflective thinking, students must discern whether or not they have mastered the concepts.	2.33	1.281	9%	90%	1%	–
It helps when students are confused about part of the lesson, they can revisit the course content at any time and any place.	3.55	1.451	34%	66%	–	–
It promotes interactive relation-ships amongst student communi-ties, and the teacher.	3.23	1.981	29%	69%	2%	–
It directs students to get more information and gain deeper insights into the material out-of-class.	2.05	0.671	33%	56%	1%	–

(Contd.)

To what extent do you agree or disagree that the Flipped Classroom could be use to improve student learning?	Mean	Std. Dev.	SA	A	D	SD
It supports students to move through the content faster with additional time to engage in independent research about the topic.	2.50	0.881	15%	69%	26%	-
It creates a space for communication among students to become the determining dynamic of a session devoted to learning through hands-on work.	3.12	1.322	20%	76%	4%	-
It help students to demonstrate what they have learned and to apply the material in a way that makes sense to them.	2.33	1.111	33%	61%	6%	-
It increases more students enjoy the class activities and benefit from watching the lecture videos outside of class.	2.45	0.983	30%	63%	7%	-

Likert scale: SA = Strongly Agree; A = Agree; D = disagree; SD = Strongly disagree

As shown in Table 19.3, ninety-seven per cent of student teachers agree (Mean = 3.73; SD = 1.328) that FCP forces students to take responsible for their own learning. It further help students to develop individual strategies for how to learn effectively, how to evaluate, and use information to achieve outcomes respectively (Mean = 3.65; SD = 1.011). These two items strongly correlated to increase student self-regulated learning process in the subject. Further, student teacher responded that FCP as an e-learning teaching strategy promoted interactive relationships amongst student communities, supporting by exchanging ideas and information on teaching practice, provide opportunities to interact, entering into dialogue and reflective practice on how they experience teaching practice placements. On the negative side, it directs students to get more information and gain deeper insights into the material out-of-class.

Discussion of Findings

Warschauer and Matuchiak (2010:180) argue that the emergence of the Fourth Industrial Revolution (FIR) which is multifaceted in scope, compelled higher education sector to rethink and reimagine how to be relevant in the 21st century. For this reason, several opportunities emerged to incorporating different technologies into the classroom to change the traditional pedagogies employed by academics. Scholars argue that institutions of higher learning are compelled to deliver quality education programmes to prepare millenniums with 21st century skills [problem solving, critical thinking, socialization, computer literacy, linguistic competence, collabourative skills) for demands of a dynamically transforming society (Chan, 2010; Gut, 2011). If higher education sector to be relevant, universities are compelled to commit to the process of continuous change or become redundant (Bates, 2010:15). Yet, in spite of 21st century challenges, the higher education sector, in particular teacher education programmes started employing technology-integrated pedagogies such as the Flipped Classroom Pedagogy (FCP), to accommodate the millenniums either residential or online classrooms, in the learning process. The FCP is a recent phenomenon used to support students learning either in a traditional face to face contact sessions or online classrooms. The FCP is more than just a pedagogical strategy for teachers; it is also a structured system for teaching students how to facilitate their own learning and engage in reflection on course content. There is no doubt the functionality of a FCP teaching strategy as important approach in support towards self-directed learning. Kong (2014:172) conducted a study on the functionality of FCP and results indicated that digital classrooms do enhance students' competency and critical thinking skills. While flipping the classroom requires careful planning and preparation in advance, the benefits of choosing this pedagogical approach have lasting impacts on students and teachers. This phenomenon promotes, increases classroom interaction amongst students and lecturers, by helping students to engage by applying knowledge and skills meaningful. Moreover, FCP positions student teachers at the centred of the learning process which stresses that students must take full responsibility of their own learning. Furthermore, it enhances problem-solving, creative and critical thinking skills for challenges of the 21st century and beyond (Kim, Sharma, Land, & Furlong, 2013; McMahon, 2009 and Yang and Wu, 2012) with students at tertiary education level. In this investigation, teacher's role in a Flipped Class Pedagogy is of vital importance to advances the FCP for optimal learning experiences for student teachers in the course. Furthermore, findings support the need for teacher preparation programmes to reflect on the job what they are doing in preparing preservice teachers for today's classrooms. A primary reflection from this inquiry relates to the classroom management strategies applied to the implementation of the flipped model. Some previous uses of the flipped model in higher education have resulted in student confusion (Strayer, 2012) and it is worth noting that teacher educators in colleges of education have a large amount of background in pedagogy and classroom management which may support the implementation of new instructional models. According to Sams (2011), FCP places students at the centre of their student learning process meaning student teachers take responsibility own learning. Similarly, several educational benefits are stated by scholars of the FCP as pedagogical phenomenon, creates a process of moral, personal and emotional autonomy for student learning (Harrison, 1978; Guglielmino, 1977; Candy, 1991; Larcara, 2014). Again, scholars posit that the Flipped Class Pedagogy promotes as a student centredness approach further enhances students' learning process in the course in an online platform (Steed, 2012; Sams & Bergmann, 2013; Talley & Scherer, 2013; Keengwe *et al.*, 2014).

Finally, this model integrates technology in ways that are meaningful to students and that elicit inquiry-based, discovery learning rather than rote memorization. Overall, preliminary findings in this chapter indicated the flipped classroom model addresses the common concerns of teacher time and efficiency in the classroom while providing an interactive learning experience for students. Emanating from the preliminary findings specific issues in relation to FCP as an educational tool are recommended for further research. This study focused on student perceptions of the Flipped Classroom experience. The summary of the preliminary research concludes that the majority of students enjoyed the Flipped Classroom and believed it supported their learning. The study had a limited number of participants due to the fact that there were only a few classes that were participating in the Flipped Classroom at this school.

Conclusion

Literature concludes that the FCP approach is online e-learning tool created through an online learning management system by lecturer to support student-teachers to demonstrate authentic learning experiences, performances, and achievements as evidence of achieved learning outcomes over time. Therefore, this study confirms earlier work by scholars who reported that FCP as student-centredness teaching as an approach do empowered students to become competent teachers, well-grounded in the knowledge, skills, values, principles, methods and procedures relevant to teaching at an open distance learning university.This finding confirmed and extended what is revealed by earlier research studies regarding the debate on the usefulness of FCP approach as powerful technology-integrated teaching design in teacher education courses. The flipped classroom is more than just a pedagogical strategy for teachers; it is also a structured system for teaching students how to facilitate their own learning and engage in reflection on course content. Student teachers agree that the FCP strategy is a student-centred approach, which needs careful planning and preparation of activities for students to take responsibility for their own learning and that the teacher played a crucial role in decision making to out-of-class and in-class activities to enhance self-directed learning. To accomplish self-directed learning teachers must ensure to support and motivate students to come prepare for the class for optimal learning. Clearly, this research study has shown that the student teachers perceived that a FCP approach in an online platform could be used as an empowering tool which impacts on the functionality, the role the lecturer should played in creating a positive lived experience and therefore, should be continued as a student-centred approach toward self-directed learning during the course. Finally, the findings of this investigation could not be generalised because only a small sample was employed in a teacher education course. Further investigation is needed regarding comparing other similar modules for the PGCE/BEd (Senior and FET phase) programmes over a longer inquiry period in the college. Further research should be explored in a mixed methods approach how student teachers perceived the different pieces compiled and used in the FCP strategy towards self-directed learning.

References

Bates, T. (2010). *New Challenges for Universities: Why they must Change*? In u-D. ehlers, 7 D.

Schneckernberg (Eds.) *Changing Cultures in Higher Education. Moving Ahead to Future Learning* (pp.15-25). Heidelberg: Springer.

Bergmann, J., and Sams, A. (2014). Flipped learning: Gateway to student engagement. *Learning & Leading with Technology,* 41(7): 18–23.

Brunsell, E. and Horejsi, M. (2013). Science 2.0: Flipping your classroom in one "take". *The Science Teacher,* 80(3): 8.

Chan, T.W. (2010). How East Asian classrooms may change over the next 20 years. *Journal of Computer Assisted Learning*, 26(1): 28-52.

Gerstein, J. (2011). The Flipped Classroom Model: A Full Picture. http://usergeneratededucation.wordpress.com/2011/06/13/ the-flipped-classroommodel-a-full-picture. Retrieved January 15, 2016.

Gut, D.M. (2011). Integrating 21st century skills into the curriculum. In G. Wan, and D.M. Gut (Eds.), *Bringing Schools into the 21st Century* (pp. 137-157). Dordrecht, New York: Springer.

Keengwe, J., Onchwari, G., & Oigara, J. (2014). *Promoting Active Learning Through the Flipped Classroom Model.* Hershey, PA: IGI Global.

Kong, S.G. (2014). Developing information literacy and critical thinking skills through domain knowledge learning in digital classrooms: An experience of practicing flipped classroom strategy. *Computers and Education,* 78(2):160-173, Retrieved January 15, 2016, from: http://dx.doi.org/10.1016/j.compedu.2014.05.009

Larcara, M. (2014). Benefits of the flipped classroom model. In J. Keengwe, G. Onchwari, and J. Oigara (Eds.), *Advances in Educational Technologies and Instructional Design: Promoting Active Learning through the Flipped Classroom Model* (pp. 132-144). Hershey, PA: IGI Global.

Leckhart, S. and Cheshire, T. (2012). University Just Got Flipped: How Online Video is Opening Up Knowledge to the World. *The Wire*. Retrieved January 15, 2016, from: http://www.wired.co.uk/magazine/archive/2012/05/features/university-just-got-flipped.

Prensky, M. (2001). Digital natives, digital immigrants. *On the Horizon,* 9(5): 1-6.

Roehl, A., Reddy, A.L., and Shannon, G.J. (2013). The flipped classroom: An opportunity to engage millennial students through active learning strategies. *Journal of Family & Consumer Science,* 105(2): 44-49.

Sams, A. and Bergmann, J. (2013). Flip your students' learning. *Educational Leadership,* 70(6): 16-20.

Stayer, J.F. (2012). How learning in an inverted classroom influences cooperation, innovation and task orientation. *Learning Environments Research,* 15: 171-193. doi:10.1007/s10984-012-9108-4

Steed, A. (2012). The flipped classroom. *Teaching Business and Economics,* 16(3): 9-11.

Talley, C.P. and Scherer, S. (2013). The enhanced flipped classroom: Increasing academic performance with student-recorded lectures and practices testing in a "flipped" STEM course. *The Journal of Negro Education,* 82(3): 339-347.

Tucker, B. (2012). The flipped classroom. *Education Next,* 12(1): 82-83.

Vaughan, M. (2014). Flipping the Learning: An Investigation into the use of the Flipped Classroom Model in an Introductory Teaching Course. *Education Research and Perspective: an International Journal*, 41(2): 25-41.

Warschauer, M. and Matuchiak, T. (2010). New technology and digital worlds: Analysing evidence of equity in access, use, and outcomes. *Review of Research in Education*. 34, 179-224. Doi:10.31202/0091732x09349791

Zappe, S., Leicht, R., Messner, J., Litzinger, T., and Lee, H.W. (2009). Flipping the classroom to explore active learning in a large undergraduate course. *American Society for Engineering Education*. American Society for Engineering Fducation.

20

Towards Quality in Higher Education for Sustainable Development in India

An Overview

Subhankar Ghosh

"Education is a human right with immense power to transform. On its foundation rest the cornerstones of freedom, democracy and sustainable development."

—*Kofi Annan* (*Former Secretary General, UN*)

Introduction

Higher Education in India has acquired special significance since independence. This is to be gauged in terms of what the society expects from it and the fulfilment of these expectations in terms of its requirements. Referring to the 21st century, which has been acknowledged worldwide as the Knowledge Society, every nation now finds itself operating in an increasingly competitive and globalized international environment where the information infrastructure, research and innovation systems, education and lifelong learning and regulatory framework are crucial variables. Higher education is regarded as a facilitator for growth for any society. According to UNESCO Report in the 21st century "*higher education is the mandate to bridge the knowledge gap between countries and communities enriching dialogues between people, culture, international living and networking of ideas, research and technologies.*" The institutions where post 10+2 education is provided are generally regarded as higher educational institutions. University Grants Commission and statutory bodies for professional disciplines work as the collective control mechanisms for higher education in India. These are regarded as policy formulators as well as the regulatory bodies in regard to higher education.

Higher Education: Historical Perspective

Education is the most vital input for the growth and prosperity of a nation. It has the power to transform human beings into human resource. We cannot build a sustainable and prosperous nation without human resource development which mainly depends on the health and vitality of higher education. Higher education has special value in the contemporary knowledge society which contributes both directly and indirectly to the wealth of a nation (Report to the People on Education, 2010-11). The objective of higher education was to provide specific skills. During the medieval age, emphasis of higher education was laid on liberal arts and study of religion. In the late 17th and 18th century, with the industrial revolution there was a need for education in science and technology. However, during the 20th century, education started acquiring an open character. With a 'knowledge force' becoming an essential requirement for national development, there was an increased demand for professional education. In the 21st century, with the impact of globalization, due to increased trade investments and mobility of people across borders, there has been a need to adopt higher education to the changed global reality. Thereafter may individuals in higher education question the need for a renewed focus on quality in higher education or the appropriateness of applying the concepts of total quality in higher education?

Present Scenario of Higher Education

In last one decade the higher education of India has expanded with a high speed. Today the higher education in India is a demanding, highly diverse, complex and competitive reality, operating at different levels. The system has undertaken a series of reformatory measures after globalization. Higher education sector has witnessed a tremendous increase in its institutional capacity in the year's science independence. As we all know that, India's higher education system is the third largest in the world, after China and United States. The private education market in India is merely 5 per cent, despite of growing the investment of education, 25 per cent of its population is still illiterate; only 15 per cent of Indian students reach high school, and 7 per cent are graduates. The Twelfth Five Year Plan includes setting up of 30 medical and engineering colleges as well.

On the other side of technical education 8 new IITs, 20 NITs, 20 IITs, 3 IISERs, 7 IIMs, and 2 SPAs are being organized.

Table 20.1: Higher Education Institutions in India

Types and Number of Institution	*Central*	*State*	*Private*	*Total*
University and University Level Institution	152	316	191	659
Colleges	669	13,024	19,930	33,623
Diploma Awarding institution	0	3,207	9,541	12,748
Percentage	2.6	38.6	58.9	100

Source: Twelfth Five Year Plan, Government of India.

While Government has made this impressive expansion in the field of higher education, people somehow seem to lag behind in 'Quality' and in international standards with the expectation of a high quality institution with future sustainability.

Quality Concern in Higher Education

Indian higher education system is in a state of change and flux due to the increasing needs of expanding access to higher education, impact of technology on the delivery of education, increasing private participation and the impact of globalization (Mangnale and Potluri, 2011). Indian higher education system is the world's third largest in terms of students, next to China, and United States. Over the past decade numerous books, reports, and commentaries have been expressed an increasing dissatisfaction with the performance of our higher education system. A focus on quality, on the other hand, complements and enhances the rich heritage.

- It recognizes the need for continuous development of the people who are part of the higher education system, whether students, faculty, or administrators.
- It involves principles applicable to institutional administration and class-room teaching, thus providing a bridge between traditionally separated parts of the system.
- It helps us meet the challenges of the 1990s and build effective universities and colleges of the twenty-first century.
- It builds on the tradition of concern for quality that has characterized higher education throughout the world.

Table 20.2: NAAC Quality Indicators

Criteria	*Key Aspects*
1. Curricular Aspects	• Curricular design and development • Curricular Planning and Implementation • Academic Flexibility • Curriculum Enrichment • Feedback System
2. Teaching-Learning and Evaluation	• Student Enrolment and Profile • Catering to Student Diversity • Teaching-Learning Process • Teacher Quality • Evaluation Process and Reforms • Student Performance and Learning Outcomes
3. Research, Consultancy and Extension	• Promotion of Research • Resource Mobilization for Research • Research Facilities • Research Publications and Awards • Consultancy • Extension Activities and Institutional Social Responsibility • Collaborations
4. Infrastructure and Learning Resource	• Physical facilities • Library as a Learning Resource • IT Infrastructure • Maintenance of Campus Facilities
5. Student Support and Progression	• Student Mentoring and Support • Student Progression • Student Participation and Activities
6. Governance, Leadership and Management	• Institution Vision and Leadership • Strategy Development and Deployment • Faculty Empowerment Strategies • Financial Management and Resource Mobilisation • Internal Quality Assurance System
7. Innovative and Best Practices	• Environment Consciousness • Innovations • Best Practices

Source: www.naac.gov.in/weightages.asp

If ranking and grading are any indications of institutions of quality, Indian institutions of higher learning have a long way to go both locally and globally. The performances have been less than satisfactory in terms of access, equity and quality.

Higher Education: Where We Stand Now

Education is essentially meant to ensure improvement in quality of life. The quality of life in Third World developing countries is in a race to reach the level set for the developed countries. Thus, the excellence in higher education has a direct dependency on the quality of education available at the institution [*see* Tables 20.3(a) and 20.3(b)].

Higher Education and Sustainable Development

Human development programmes, including Education for Sustainable Development (ESD) must consider three things for sustainability—Economy, Environment, and Society. ESD is based on few ideas and principles, i.e. gender equity, poverty alleviation, social tolerance, environmental preservation and restoration, peaceable societies. Sustainable Development (SD) is popularly described as "development that meets the needs of the present without compromising the ability of the future generations to meet their own needs" (Brundtland, 1987:19). Therefore, achieving SD will require educational balancing among these three for consideration in the pursuit of development and an improved quality of life (*see* Fig. 20.1).

Both the government and privately funded institution are engaged in knowledge creation and its transfer from their research programmes and production of quality graduates to participate in socio-economic development of the country. In this process, some institution are proactive in solving societal problems, enterprising and creating a dynamic learning and research environment, that benefits youth, region and contributes in sustainable national growth. Excellence in higher education through teaching learning and research needs funding, academic flexibility, academic accountability and proactive governance. It is right that development in this new century be even more conscious of its long-term impact. This implies a great challenge but also has considerable potential to enhance innovative developments in higher education. Hence higher education refers to the ability to contribute in a reflective and responsible manner to the developing of society for a sustainable future (*see* Table 20.1).

Table 20.3(a): Scenario of Higher Education in India (Graduate)

Level: Graduate

Sl. No.	Faculty	Total (Men + Women)			Total (Women)		
		Appeared	Passed	Pass %	Appeared	Passed	Pass %
1.	Arts	24,91,892	16,52,898	66.33	12,63,364	8,81,836	69.80
2.	Science	8,61,456	5,26,578	61.13	3,92,810	2,68,415	68.33
3.	Commerce/Management	10,64,796	6,79,184	63.79	4,41,126	3,04,374	69.00
4.	Education	5,40,787	4,40,807	81.51	3,35,751	2,73,454	81.45
5.	Engineering/Technology	8,56,801	6,39,992	74.70	2,51,929	2,09,031	82.97
6.	Medicine	1,60,577	1,26,333	78.67	82,483	69,975	84.84
7.	Agriculture	15,125	11,496	76.01	4,095	3,251	79.39
8.	Veterinary Sciences	2,853	2,649	92.85	791	691	87.36
9.	Law	87,965	49,621	56.41	26,751	15,871	59.33
10.	Others	50,322	36,910	73.35	20,280	14,810	73.03
	Total	**61,32,574**	**41,66,468**	**67.94**	**28,19,380**	**20,41,708**	**72.42**

Source: UGC, New Delhi (2015), *University Department of India: Basics Facts and Figures; Examination Results-2012*, p. 3.

Table 20.3(b): Scenario of Higher Education in India (Post-Graduate)

Level: Post- Graduate

Sl. No.	*Faculty*	*Total (Men+ Women)*			*Total (Women)*		
		Appeared	*Passed*	*Pass %*	*Appeared*	*Passed*	*Pass %*
1.	Arts	6,30,071	4,37,712	69.47	3,32,958	2,39,814	72.03
2.	Science	2,60,110	1,86,902	71.85	1,27,857	95,709	74.86
3.	Commerce/Management	3,58,949	255,188	71.09	1,28,824	99,321	77.10
4.	Education	25,265	19,864	78.62	15,234	12,510	82.12
5.	Engineering/Technology	58,149	48,274	83.02	19,099	16,888	88.42
6.	Medicine	33,772	30,503	90.32	13,971	12,831	91.84
7.	Agriculture	6,242	5,268	84.40	1,774	1,447	81.57
8.	Veterinary Sciences	1,510	1,369	90.66	441	401	90.93
9.	Law	8,814	4,858	55.12	3,593	2,209	61.48
10.	Others	36,304	27,662	76.20	16,897	12,959	76.69
	Total	**14,19,186**	**10,17,600**	**71.70**	**6,60,648**	**4,94,089**	**74.79**

Source: UGC, New Delhi (2015), *University Department of India: Basics Facts and Figures; Examination Results-2012*, p. 4.

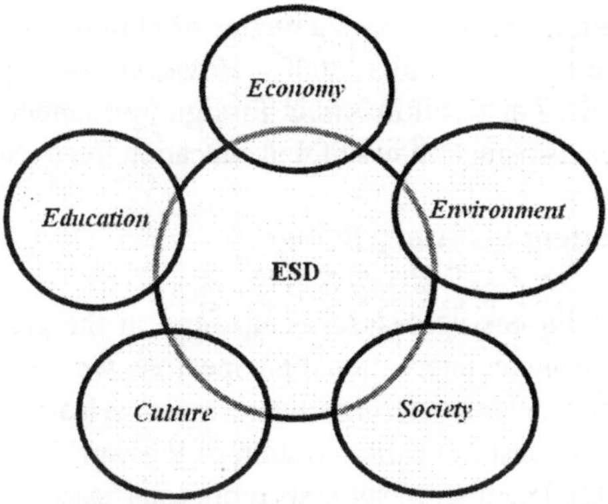

Fig. 20.1: Major Aspects of ESD

Table 20.4: Recognized Institution and Student Enrolment in Higher Education

Years	*Universities*	*Colleges*	*Enrolment of Students (in Lakhs)*
2014-15	757	38056	333
2013-14	723	36636	323
2012-13	665	35829	296
2011-12	642	34852	292
2010-11	621	32974	275
2009-10	436	25938	207
2008-09	440	27882	185
2007-08	406	23099	172
2006-07	371	19812	156
2005-06	350	16982	143
2000-01	254	10152	86
1990-91	184	5748	49
1980-81	110	6963	48
1970-71	82	3277	33
1960-61	45	1819	10
1950-51	27	578	4

Sources: (i) Statistics of Higher Education (2013-14).
(ii) AISHE Portal (www.aishe.gov.in).

Notable Educational Policies

In India education has always been governed by the tenets of accessibility, quality and social inclusion. In other words to low tuition fee, accreditation by government authorities and reservation quotas on caste basis. In India where the number of higher education institutions is so scarce, the common student finds himself at a loss due to the quota system, as qualifying for these examination becomes more a matter of elimination than selection (MHRD, Government of India, 2000). However, the supporters of the draconian regulations to allow direct foreign investment in India insist that no developed country allows FDI in education freely (*see* Table 20.5).

Higher Education: Statutory Bodies

Independent India has witnessed an upsurge in the growth of higher education. Yet from an international perspective, we are relatively slow, despite being steady in registering advancements in learning. Today India has the second largest education system in the world, next only to the USA. Yet, the total number of students represents hardly 6 per cent of the relevant age group, i.e. 18-23 years, which is much below the average of developed countries which is about 47 per cent. The gap is glaring. Hence, the phenomenal challenge. The journey from being 'Good' to being 'Great' appears to be long and arduous. The institutions imparting higher education at different levels are regulated by the bodies shown in Table 20.6.

Thrust Areas on Higher Education: Five Year Plans

In the knowledge economy, the objectives of a society changes from fulfilling the basic needs of all round development to empowerment. The education system instead of going by text-book teaching will be promoted by reactive, interactive self-learning, both formal and informal, with focus on values, merit and quality. The world is now like a global village, and continuous international interaction has become an essential component of human survival.

First Five-Year Plan[1]

The first Indian Prime Minister, Jawaharlal Nehru presented the First Five Year Plan to the Parliament of India on 8th December, 1951.

- During the First Five Year Plan, five Indian Institutes of Technology (IITs) were started as major technical institutions.
- University Grants Commission (UGC) was set up to take care of funding and take measures to strengthen the higher education in the country.

Table 20.5: Government Initiatives Pre- and Post-Independence

Sl. No.	*Years*	*Initiatives*
1.	Secular Buddhist Institutions (200 BCE to 400 CE)	These institutions systematically imparted knowledge and attracted a number of foreign students to study topics such as logic, grammar, medicine, metaphysics, arts and crafts.
2.	Islamic Scholar Alberuni (973-1048 CE)	India already had a sophisticated system of mathematics and science in place, and had made a number of inventions and discoveries.
3.	Indian Universities (1857)	Inception of universities in the three Presidency towns like Madras, Bombay and Calcutta.
4.	British Period (1867-1941)	A class of Westernized elite was versed in the Western system of education which the British had introduced.
5.	Maulana Azad, India's First Education Minister (1947)	Throughout the country a uniform educational system. However, given the cultural and linguistic diversity of India, it was only the higher education dealing with science and technology that came under the jurisdiction of the Central Government.
6.	University Grants Commission (UGC) 1953	The Government initiated a planned development of higher education in the country.
7.	The University Grants Commission (UGC) existence in 1953 to 1956	Promotion and coordination of university education and for determination and maintenance of standards of teaching, examination and research in universities.
8.	The University Education Commission (1948-49)	The foundations of the future of Indian Higher Education.
9.	Education Commission (1964-66)	Symbolized the symbiotic relationship between education and national development.
10.	The Central Advisory Board of Education (CABE) 1921	The Central Government to play an effective role in education, based on consensus among the representatives of the then Provincial Governments.
11.	The National Policy on Education (NPE) 1986	The five main goals for higher education, which include Greater Access, Equal Access (or Equity), Quality and Excellence, Relevance and Value Based Education.
12.	The National Policy on Education (NPE) 1992	To improve the quality through strengthening academic and physical infrastructure. To promote excellence in those institutions which have exhibited potential for excellence, and to develop curriculum to inculcate right values among the youth.

Source: World Bank, 2003 and MHRD, Government of India.

Table 20.6: Different Statutory Bodies in India

Sl. No.	*Years*	*Organisations*
1.	1911	Indian Council for Medical Research (ICMR)
2.	1929	Indian Council for Agricultural Research (ICAR)
3.	1942	Council for Scientific and Industrial Research (CSIR)
4.	1947	Indian Nursing Council (INC)
5.	1948	Dentists Council of India (DCI)
6.	1948	Pharmacy Council of India (PCI)
7.	1956	Medical Council of India (MCI)
8.	1956	University Grants Commission (UGC)
9.	1961	Bar Council of India (BCI)
10.	1969	Indian Council for Social Science Research (ICSSR)
11.	1970	Central Council for Indian Medicine (CCIM)
12.	1972	Council of Architecture (COA)
13.	1973	Association of Indian Universities (AIU)
14.	1973	Central Council of Homoeopathy (CCH)
15.	1985	Distance Education Council (DEC)
16.	1985	Ministry of Human Resource Development (MHRD)
17.	1987	All-India Council of Technical Education (AICTE)
18.	1992	Rehabilitation Council of India (RCI)
19.	1993	National Council for Teacher Education (NCTE)
20.	1994	National Assessment and Accreditation Council (NAAC)
21.	1995	National Council for Rural Institutes (NCRI)

Source: Various Government of India's web-Portal.

Second Five-Year Plan[2]

- The Second Five-Year Plan focused on industry.
- The plan attempted to determine the optimal allocation of investment between productive sectors in order to maximize long-run economic growth.
- It used the prevalent state-of-art techniques of operations research and optimization as well as the novel applications of statistical models developed at the Indian Statistical Institute.
- The plan assumed a closed economy in which the main trading activity would be centred on importing capital goods.
- The Atomic Energy Commission was formed in 1958 with Homi J. Bhabha as the first chairman.
- The Tata Institute of Fundamental Research was established as a research institute.
- In 1957 a talent search and scholarship programme was begun to find talented young students to train for work in nuclear power.

Third Five-Year Plan[3]

- During the Third Five Year Plan, many primary schools were started in rural areas.
- In an effort to bring democracy to the Grassroots Level, Panchayat Raj elections were started and the states were given more development responsibilities.
- State electricity boards and state secondary education boards were formed. States were made responsible for secondary and higher education.
- In the Third Five Year Plan larger facilities provided for diverting students to vocational and technological education.

Fourth Five Year Plan[4]

- The enrolment in Arts, Science, Commerce and Law courses in universities and colleges increased.
- Students provided education through correspondence courses, evening colleges and part-time classes.
- The correspondence courses were confined to humanities only.
- The main emphasis was on consolidation and improvement of higher education through the strengthening of staff and library and laboratory facilities.
- Assistance for fuller development given to a few colleges selected on the basis of their achievements, existing facilities and potentialities.

Fifth Five Year Plan[5]

- Construction of academic buildings, library, staff quarters, teachers' hostel, students' hostel, study homes, non-resident students' centre.
- Purchase of books, journals, equipment.
- Appointment of additional teaching staff, technical supporting staff etc.

Sixth Five Year Plan[6]

- Improvement of standards.
- Regulation of admission.

- Restructuring of courses for practical orientation and greater relevance.
- Centralization of instrumentation and repair facilities.
- Make extension as an integral part of education.
- Low priority was given to expansion of educational facilities by way of new universities, centres for post-graduate studies, new departments and to construction/extension of buildings.

Seventh Five Year Plan[7]

- Creation of research and other centralized facilities at selected centres for the benefit of a group of institutions in the region/country.
- Encouragement of academic mobility and cross-fertilization of ideas with a view to inculcating the feeling of national integration by providing special assistance for faculty housing/complex and hostels.
- Restructuring courses at first degree level so that they become relevant to the local needs and environment and increase the area of employability of graduates.
- Prioritization of programmes intended to achieve the national objectives.
- Development of Centres of Excellence.
- Optimization of use of the existing facilities in the universities/colleges especially physical facilities.

Eighth Five Year Plan[8]

- Strengthening of existing post-graduate departments in terms of laboratories, workshops and library services.
- Opening of new specialized courses and departments. In case of developed, with an inter-disciplinary approach provided they could be sustained by existing facilities.
- In case of developing universities, new departments and courses only if the need is justified.
- Viability of courses, departments etc. so that those courses that have lost their relevance or are outdated could be dispensed with and teachers in such subjects could be retrained.

Ninth Five Year Plan[9]

- Career development by encouraging the relevant courses with professional focus.
- Modification in traditional courses to make them application oriented.
- Encouragement to universities to develop basic theoretical understanding of discipline to ensure that the theory and practice are blended and integrated.
- Focus on hands on experience.
- Addressing the public concerns about downslide in the quality of education by focusing on the quality of education rather than on quantitative expansion.
- Access and Equity: Paying special attention to institutions of higher education in backward areas, hill areas and border areas in order to remove regional imbalances.
- Addressing the higher education needs of under-represented social groups including the SC/STs, women, handicapped and the minorities.
- Focus not only on quantitative expansion but also on qualitative development of institutions of higher education in the areas catering to the above groups.
- University and Social Change: Encouragement to universities to develop a greater emphasis on non-degree programmes in order to meet the expectations arising out of changes that are taking place in the society.
- These activities to be made the responsibility of every department; while the departments of adult and continuing education would be the focal point for social change function.
- Major thrust to be given to programme development for women studies and centre for women studies shall be essentially interdisciplinary.
- Management of Education: Support for streaming the university management system.
- Assistance for academic, administrative and financial decentralization.
- Autonomy of the Departments.
- Autonomy of the affiliated colleges and institutions.
- Developing in-house training facilities for non-teaching staff, rationalization of posts; increasing use of information technology in management.

- Establishment of College Development Council, workshops for College Principals, and improvement in backward and forward linkages.
- Resource Mobilization: Focus on planning for internal and external resource mobilization.
- Differential fee structure.
- Enhancement in fees for foreign studies.
- Generation of revenue through increased university-industry linkages.

Tenth Five Year Plan[10]

- The main objective in the Tenth Five Year Plan was to raise the enrolment in higher education of the 18-23 years age group from the present 6 per cent to 10 per cent by the end of the Plan period.
- Increasing access, quality, adoption of state-specific strategies and the liberalization of the higher education system.
- Emphasis has also been laid on the relevance of the curriculum, vocationalization, and networking on the use of information technology.
- Focuses on distance education, convergence of formal, non-formal, distance and IT education institutions, increased private participation in the management of colleges and deemed to be universities; research in frontier areas of knowledge and meeting challenges in the area of Internationalization of Indian education.
- To promote quality and relevance in higher education in the Tenth Plan by initiating complementary skill-oriented courses. The career development of students was promoted through courses with a professional focus.
- New courses, including vocational courses, relating emerging areas such as information technology, biotechnology, biomedicine, genetic engineering, applied psychology, tourism and travel, physical education and sports were introduced in more and more universities.
- The Administrative Staff Colleges (ASCs) proved to be good instruments for teacher training and orientation. Efforts were made to widen and enhance the range and scope of ASCs and set up more ASCs to achieve a uniform regional spread.
- Focus on increasing intake; quality of education, including

research in technology. Other issues include: faculty development; optimal utilization of resources through networking; development of information technology education; modernization of the curriculum; international benchmarking; developing capacity in new and emerging technology areas; strategic planning and management of the technical education system and developing the informal sector.

Elevent Five Year Plan[11]

- Expansion, inclusion and rapid movement in quality by enhancing public spending, encouraging private initiatives and initiating the long overdue major institutional and policy reforms.
- Quantitative Expansion through establishment of new government and private funded institutions and increased intake in existing institutions.
- Reduce disparities based on gender, caste, region etc. through differential support.
- Establish 30 new Central Universities, 16 in States where they do not exist and 14 as World Class Universities.
- Establish 8 new IITs, 7 new IIMs, 10 new NITs, 3 IISERs, 20 IIITs and 2 new SPAs.
- Provide flexibility to universities to raise fees accompanied by scholarships, fellowships and student loans.
- Establish a National Science and Engineering Research Board for rejuvenation of research in Universities.
- Launch a national Mission in education through ICT coverage in all the Universities and colleges; broadband connectivity through National Knowledge Network and requisite nodes within institutions.
- Strengthen Open Universities and reform statutory bodies, scale up SAKSHAT as the education portal for people.

Twelfth Five Year Plan[12]

- Growing youth aspirations and massive expansion of schooling is creating a huge demand for higher education.
- Higher education is also essential to build a workforce capable of underpinning a modern, competitive economy.
- The process of broadening access, making higher education

inclusive, and promoting excellence initiated during the Eleventh Plan must be consolidated and expanded further during the Twelfth Plan.

- A proper accreditation structure, quick redressed of disputes through educational tribunals and prevention of malpractices and establishment of a national level apex body, that is, National Commission on Higher Education and Research (NCHER) to ensure autonomy of institutions and enhancement of standards and provision for entry of foreign education providers.
- There must be a strategic shift from mere expansion of enrolment to improvement in quality higher education.
- New institutions may be set up to bridge regional imbalances and disparities across disciplines and to address special economic, social and technological needs of the country.
- Traditional education should be supplemented with skill-based studies and institutional differentiation should be encouraged so that institutions grow along their own growth trajectories without being clones of each other.
- The concept of Meta University aimed at collaborative and multi-disciplinary learning that redefines knowledge-creation and knowledge-sharing in the twenty-first century, could also be explored.
- There is an urgent need to step up both public and private investment in higher education (including technical), and increase in the efficiency of its utilization.
- The scale and reach of scholarship schemes and student loans need to be enhanced. Government guarantees for student loans could be considered.
- There is a need for a clear focus on improving the employability of graduates. Indian higher education is organized into 'General' and 'Professional' streams.
- For both 'General' and 'Professional' education streams, integrated curriculum with greater flexibility in choice of subjects and innovative pedagogic practices are needed to improve the quality and hence employability. Graduates now require the skills beyond the basics of reading, writing and arithmetic (the '3Rs').
- Skills such as critical thinking, communication, collaboration and creativity (the '4Cs') are now important in more and more jobs. Accordingly, there is need to focus on the '4Cs'. Special emphasis on verbal and written communication skills, especially

in English would go a long way in improving the employability of the large and growing mass of disempowered youth.

- Collaborative research, setting up industry incubation parks in Universities and institutions providing more research fellowships, promoting innovation through interdisciplinary research in new and emerging fields, strengthening Inter-University centres etc., need to be emphasized in the Twelfth Plan.
- A complete overhaul of the Academic Staff Colleges that are used to provide refresher courses for teachers is also necessary.
- Initiatives to improve the quality and availability of teachers in higher education need to be launched in a mission mode.
- Universities and colleges should be encouraged to engage more intensively than before with wider society and contribute to the local and regional development and provide intellectual leadership to society.
- ICTs should be harnessed to enrich teaching learning experience, to extend and diversify delivery, improve research quality and collaboration by making knowledge and information widely available, and ensure effective governance both at the institutional and systemic level. Student services needs to be significantly improved and admissions should be streamlined.
- Given the historical advantage in higher education (particularly among emerging market economies) the widespread use of English language and low cost living, India can potentially become a global hub for higher education.

Challenges Ahead

In this 21st century the quality of higher education is benignly neglected because of unbridled commercialization of higher education. Educational reform should not mean only the privatization *per se*, but genuine quality improvement. The educational dualism is becoming more pronounced in India. The success of Higher Education System (HES) thrives on social opposition. It does not give to due weightage to the quality of education. There are many basic problems facing higher education in India today. These include:

- Large vacancies in faculty positions and poor faculty;
- Outmoded teaching methods;

- Declining research standards;
- Low student enrolment rate;
- Inadequate infrastructure and facilities;
- Widespread geographic, income, gender, and ethnic imbalances; and
- Inadequate and diminishing finical support for higher education.

The higher education is not sustainable because its present success is not based upon the quality but upon a powerful educational dualism which manifests in difference employability, gender inequality and economic marginalization and inequality. The educated professionals are more insensitive and isolated from the society.

Measures for Improving QHE

Presently, the Indian higher education is expected to be informative and knowledge-based in the globalized world to stay competitive. The increasing number of higher education institution in recent times has brought positive changes in our social phenomenon but has also put a premium on their Quality of Education for Sustainable Development (QESD). Looking into various reports, policies and literature reviews of higher education these has been pointed out to strengthen the QHE:

- Implement the Plan into Action;
- Towards a learning society with New Vision;
- Need based job-oriented course;
- Innovative practices;
- Privatization, globalization of higher education;
- Quality in research;
- Mobilization of resources;
- Dynamic Methods of teaching; and
- ICT facilities in libraries and resources.

Conclusion

In general, more and more universities are involved in learning and change for sustainability in higher education and the improvement of quality has become the focus of current work. Compared with education at school level, higher education can play a more decisive role in the promotion of ESD, in addressing the complex problems of sustainability through academic research and university education. It also educates students in all professions, trains future government leaders and thus influences future policy development. Despite these achievements emerging within India, collaboration with the rest of the world and other developed countries has played a very important role in the creation of Indian SD policies and their implementation. It can be concluded that clear and substantial policies, well-planned priority programmes, and systematic distribution through regional centres, can provide substantial support to assist progress in large countries undergoing rapid growth. In order to sustain that rate of growth, there is need to increase the number of institutes and also the quality of higher education in India. We need an educational system that is in modern India, liberal, and can adapt to the changing needs of a changing society, a changing economy and the changing world. To reach and achieve the future requirements there is an urgent need to relook at the financial resources, access and equality, quality standards, relevance and the end the representativeness. In the future, further innovation from expert personnel, using localized theories and techniques, should result in improvements that align with the aims of the DESD to develop education and learning that will support the growth of more sustainable societies.

Notes

1. Five Year Plan, Planning Commission of India, GoI, New Delhi, 1951-1956.
2. Five Year Plan, Planning Commission of India, GoI, New Delhi, 1956-1961.
3. Five Year Plan, Planning Commission of India, GoI, New Delhi, 1961-1966.
4. Five Year Plan, Planning Commission of India, GoI, New Delhi, 1969-1974.
5. Five Year Plan, Planning Commission of India, GoI, New Delhi, 1974-1979.
6. Five Year Plan, Planning Commission of India, GoI, New Delhi, 1980-1985.
7. Five Year Plan, Planning Commission of India, GoI, New Delhi, 1985-1990.
8. Five Year Plan, Planning Commission of India, GoI, New Delhi, 1992-1997.
9. Five Year Plan, Planning Commission of India, GoI, New Delhi, 1997-2002.
10. Five Year Plan, Planning Commission of India, GoI, New Delhi, 2002-2007.
11. Five Year Plan, Planning Commission of India, GoI, New Delhi, 2007-2012.
12. Five Year Plan, Planning Commission of India, GoI, New Delhi, 2012-2017.

References

Babiuk, G. (2008). The Holistic Nature of Education for Sustainability. *The Holistic Educator*, 19(1): 2-5.

GCSP (2002). *Sustainable Pathways Toolkit for Universities and Colleges: Indicators for Campuses*. Augene: Good Company.

Mangnale and Potluri (2011). Quality Management in Indian Higher Education System: Role of Internal Quality Assurance Cell. *Asian Journal of Business Management*, 3(4): 251-256. Retrieved on 4th November, 2014, from http://maxwellsci.com/print/ajbm/v3-251-256.pdf

MHRD. (2012). *Report to the People in Higher Education*, 2001-12, MHRD, GOI, New Delhi.

Murnane, G. (1987). *Total Quality Management in Higher Education: An International Perspective*. Buckingham: Open University Press.

Planning Commission (2001). *Faster, Sustainable and More Inclusive Growth—An Approach to the Twelfth Five Year Plan*. Government of India.

Power, K.B. (2005). *Quality in Higher Education*. New Delhi: EDUPRO Publishers.

Sen, Amartya. (1970). *The Crisis in Indian Education*. Lal Bahadur Sastry Memorial Lectures, 10-11, March.

UN Full Report of the Open Working Group of the General Assembly on '*Sustainable Development Goal*', Retrieved on 5.10.2015, available at http://undocs.org/A/68/970

UNESCO (2008). *Education for sustainable development/education/objectives*. Retrieved from http://portal.unesco.org/education/en/ev.php

United Nations (2011). *The Millennium Development Goals Report-2011*. New York: UNO.

World Commission on Environment and Development (1987). *Our Common Future*. New York: Oxford University Press.

Webliography

Agenda 21, United Nations conference on environment and development, Conches, Ch. 36. Retrieved October 18, 2014 from: http://sedac.ciesin.org/entri/texts/a21/a21-36-education.html.

Chandra, Rakesh, *Women empowerment in India – Milestones and challenges*, available at: www.empowerpoor.org/downloads/women empowerment.pdf retrieved on 06.04.2014.

UNESCO (1999). *Statistical Yearbook*. Paris and Lanham, MD: UNESCO and Bernam Press. Retrieved October 25, 2013, from: http://www.virtualref.com/abs/82.html

United Nations Division for Sustainable Development (UNDSD) (2009). Agenda/21. Retrieved on Nov 22, 2014, from http://www.un.org/esa/dsd/agenda21/res_agenda21_36.shtml.

World Development Report, 2003: Sustainable Development in a Dynamic World: Transforming Institutions, Growth and Quality of Life, World Bank, retrieved on January 20, 2014, from https://openknowledge.worldbank.org/handle/10986/5985

www.censusindia.gov.in

www.naac.gov.in/weightages.asp

Transformation of Higher Education System of India

21

Transformation of Higher Education System of India

A Critical Appraisal

Shazli Hasan Khan

Introduction

Education is the most important instrument for social and economic change. Today's demand is the requirement of well educated population so that the growth in the higher education sector becomes inclusive, as it is the educated and skilled person who benefits most from the employment opportunities which development provides. All the issues related to higher education have to be addressed with utmost commitment and integrity so as to ensure quality, excellence and social welfare. It is the responsibility of the government alone to deliver services in this sector.

Since Independence, education has always been given the topmost priority which is essential for developing competent and sufficient manpower needed in building the nation. Education guarantees social and economic development to its citizens as investment in education is investment in human capital. According to 2011 Census, however, India's average literacy rate is 74.04 per cent. It is really quite appreciable that despite large disparities in literacy, overall access, and education infrastructure exist among the states; India succeeded in making its three-fourth of its population literate. Therefore, it makes good sense for government to prioritize education for social investment.

Although our economy is growing at 7 to 8 per cent per annum, there is no significant increase in the allocation of public resources to higher education. Keeping in pace with time the Government of India has expanded higher education in formal, professional and technical sectors, however, mere expansion is not going to help. The institutes imparting higher education are confronted with serious challenges in terms of equity, access and quality, despite initiating numerous steps to increase enrolment levels and provide budgetary support. Though the country has met the target of Gross Enrolment Ratio (GER) of 17 per cent in higher education, still it would require a Herculean effort to meet the target of GER of 30 per cent by 2020. In 2006, there were about 330 universities, both public and private, in India. By the end of 2012, the number shot up to 660 and now presently there are now more than 850 Universities. Thus almost 400 new universities have been established in the country within a span of ten years. The National Knowledge Commission has anticipated that in the era of knowledge economy, there is a need for 1,500 universities in the country if India wants to find its rightful place as an emerging power. By 2030, close to 400 million youth would be seeking college education and every year 10 million young adults will be entering the job market between now and 2020. Our GER will be 30 per cent by 2020 and by 2030 close to 400 million people will be going to universities. Our public universities are facing challenges like lack of teaching and research resources, large class sizes, a work culture that lacks accountability, politicization of educational institutions, outdated curricula and bureaucratic procedures that adversely affect quality of education.

The inability of public sector to absorb the growing number of students has given rise to private universities. Like public universities, few Private Higher Educational Institutions (HEIs) are research-oriented, knowledge-producing institutions. Moreover, most private HEIs offer a narrow range of market-focused professional programmes. Although, the private sector accounts for 91 per cent of seats in engineering, 64 per cent in management studies, 95 per cent in pharmaceutical studies, 93 per cent in physiotherapy, 50 per cent in medicine and 94 per cent in hotel management, its role is still viewed suspiciously by many in the country.

The existence of more modern and job-relevant curricula, better interaction with industry, international collaborations, greater emphasis on accountability and consequent reduction of the financial burden on the state make participation of the private sector in higher education a viable option. The Ministry of Human Resource Development (MHRD) has proposed that states should set up autonomous State Higher Education Councils (SHECs) in order to regulate Higher Educational Institutions. However, there is no mention of the division of responsibilities between the UGC, other regulatory bodies and SHECs.

It is being suggested that organizations similar to the National Assessment Accreditation Council (NAAC) should be set up at the state level. As it is, the states that have set up Regulatory Commissions for private HEIs are struggling to find amicable persons to be part of teams deputed to inspect private Higher Educational Institutions (HEIs). There is a need for a clearly formulated and regulatory framework for HEIs. Such a framework should create conditions, where private HEIs can operate effectively and efficiently, while at the same time maintaining quality in education standards. The Indian Higher Education System has a plethora of issues of concern at present like financing and management including access, equity and relevance, reorientation of programmes by laying emphasis on health consciousness, values and ethics and quality of higher education together with the assessment of institutions and their accreditation.

Recognizing the fact that the universities have to perform multiple roles, like creating new knowledge, acquiring new capabilities and producing an intelligent human resource pool, through quality teaching, research and extension activities so as to balance both the need and the demand, the University Grants Commission (UGC) had initiated nation-wide discussion on the said issues during its Golden Jubilee Year, 2003. Eleven Universities located in different regions were assigned the task of conducting seminars on topical subjects, addressing different issues and concerns of higher education in India.

Need and Importance of the Study

The Eleventh and Twelfth Five Year Plans envisage increase in the Gross Enrolment Ratio (GER) in Higher Education to 15 per cent to 20 per cent of the population in the age group of 18-24 years by 2011-12 and 2017-18 respectively. This requires a substantial increase in the number of institutions and consequently would require an adequate number of teachers for imparting education. Failure to redress the faculty shortage would hamper the achievement of the targets for increase in GER set out by government. The overall scenario of higher education in India presents a dismal picture. Hence, there is enough justification for an increased assessment of the quality of the country's educational institutions. Traditionally, these institutions assumed that quality could be determined by their internal resources, viz. faculty with an impressive set of degrees and experience detailed at the end of the institutes' admission brochure, number of books and journals in the library, an ultra-modern campus and size of the endowment etc., or by its definable and assessable outputs, viz. efficient use of resources producing uniquely educated, highly satisfied and employable graduates. Keeping this in view, the government has constituted a National Knowledge Commission to suggest measures to alleviate the problems that higher education sector is plagued with

National Knowledge Commission Recommendations in Context of Higher Education

The National Knowledge Commission (NKC) proposed establishment of Independent Regulatory Authority for Higher Education (IRAHE) so as to facilitate setting up of new universities especially by private investors and through public-private partnership.

One of the key objectives of IRAHE was to minimize conflicts of interest and to decrease the confusing and overlapping mandates due to multiplicity of regulatory agencies. This was conceptualized as a single window licensing authority for according degree granting power to higher education institutions and for settling disputes and monitoring standards. The body would apply exactly the same norms to public and private institutions. IRAHE shall consist of a Chairperson, a distinguished academic personality appointed by the Prime Minister based on the recommendations of a Search Committee. IRAHE shall also include six other members who are distinguished academicians in different disciplines, along with some part-time members of outstanding merit.

The functions of IRAHE, as given by National Knowledge Commission, are:

1. To determine eligibility for setting up new institutions based on transparent criteria.
2. To apply the same norms to private, public and international institutions.
3. Granting powers to higher education institutions to award degrees.
4. To monitor standards and settle disputes.
5. To determine the authority for licensing accrediting agencies.

NKC has also suggested curtailing the functions of regulatory agencies like All India Council of Technical Education (AICTE) and Medical Council of India (MCI). IRAHE was to have a highly centralized role with great responsibility. IRAHE would be free from political and functional constraints as there may be increased scope for politicization and high-level corruption.

Earlier the NPE (1986) has also recommended a coordinating body at the state level for decentralization of power and for better coordination at the state level. According to it, "State level planning and coordination of higher education will be done through councils of higher education. The UGC and these councils will develop coordinated methods to keep a watch on standards."

Growth and Trends in Higher Education in India

According to Agarwal (2006), the growth of higher education in India can be divided into three phases: (i) Period 1947 to 1980 can be termed as first phase; (ii) second phase is from 1980 to 2000; and (iii) the third phase from the year 2000 onwards. At the time of Independence in 1947, there were 20 universities and several hundred affiliated colleges (Agarwal, 2009).

The growth of Higher Education was largely confined to arts, science and commerce. Government not only supported higher education by setting up universities and colleges, but also took over the responsibility of running the institutions set up through private sector, which were known as grant-in-aid institutions or private aided colleges/institutions. Their number increased very quickly until the 1980s. By 1980, there were 132 universities and 4,738 colleges in the country, enrolling around 5 per cent of the eligible age group in higher education. Almost one-third of all colleges were private aided colleges. In such institutions, though the private sector financed a major part of the capital costs, public subsidies were provided to them to meet a part of the recurrent costs and occasionally for some capital works. Public funding was accompanied with considerable regulation of private institutions by the government (World Bank, 2003).

In the second phase, there has been a considerable increase in the population in the middle and higher income groups, which could afford to pay higher tuition fees. Due to this, there was first-time demand for quality Higher Education. Faced with such a situation, the rising demand of higher education from the growing middle and higher income groups accelerated the pace of growth of private higher education in the country.

In general, post-1980 period saw the emergence of new types of providers of Higher Education in India. The private institutions proliferated, the distance education programmes gained wider acceptance, the public universities and colleges started self-financing programmes, and foreign institutions started offering programmes either by themselves or in partnership with Indian institutions and the non-university sector grew rapidly.

The last phase starts from 2000 onwards with opening of *deemed to be university route* by private as well as by government institutions to award degree. Over the last few years, there has been sudden jump in the number of deemed universities. Manipal University—a pioneer in private higher education—became the first totally self-financed institution to be declared as a deemed university in 1976. After 2000, when the provision for conferring the demand to be university status to a *de novo* institution was introduced, there was sudden spurt in the growth of deemed to be universities in the private sector. Between 2000 and 2005, 26 private sponsored institutions got the deemed university status. This intensified the competition in higher education in the country.

Therefore, higher education sector was under control of government till about 1980. After that there has been a rapid proliferation of private higher education institutions. The growth has been phenomenal in institutions offering professional courses. Since 1976, education—comprising pre-primary, primary, middle, secondary and higher levels—has been in the concurrent list of the Constitution of India which implies that both the Union and Provincial governments exercise joint responsibilities in this sphere (Das, 2007).

The structure of Higher Education in India consists of universities, research institutions, deemed universities which are at the highest level of higher education institutions. At the next level, it is the colleges in disciplines such as arts, science, commerce, engineering, management, medical, agriculture and law colleges. In 2008-09, there were 15,852 arts, fine arts, social work, science and commerce colleges, 12,030 professional colleges, 2385 engineering, technology and architecture colleges, 2336 medical colleges and 3750 teacher education/training colleges in the country (Statistics of Higher and Technical Education, 2008-09).

The types of universities include central universities, state universities, institutions of national importance, deemed universities, private universities, open universities and women universities etc. Two major types of universities exist in India: (a) unitary university offering graduate and post-graduate courses; and (b) affiliating university, offering post-graduate courses prescribe to the affiliated colleges the course of study. These affiliated colleges are run either by State Governments or private agencies (Tilak, 2007a).

The educational institutions in India and in states are of three basic types based on funding and provision: (i) Government provision and financing of higher educational institutions; (iii) private provision and government financing; and (iii) private provision and financing referred to as self-financing institutions (Rani, 2004). In the country, university-level institutions widely differ in terms of their structure and coverage (UGC, 2011-12). Table 21.1 show that in India university-level institutions were sub-divided into six broad groups.

Table 21.1: Types of Universities/University Level institutions in 2014-15

Sl. No.	*Type of Universities/University Level Institutions*	*Total Number*
1.	Central Universities	46
2.	State Universities	290
3.	Private Universities	174
4.	Institutions established under State legislations Acts	25
5.	Institutions deemed to be Universities	274
6.	Institutes of National Importance	74
7.	Total Number of Institutions	883
8.	Number of Colleges	33,724

Source: UGC Annual Report, 2014-15.

In 2014-15, there were 46 Central Universities, 290 State Universities, 174 Private Universities, 274 Deemed Universities. Higher Education is coordinated by several agencies. While general universities and general education colleges come under the purview of the UGC, technical and professional institutions of higher education are coordinated by several National agencies. Some of these are the All India Council for Technical Education (AICTE), Medical Council of India and Indian Council of Medical Research (ICMR), Bar Council of India, Indian Council of Agricultural Research (ICAR), Association of Indian Universities (AIU) etc. can also be added to the above list. It is at best advisory agency, and the nodal university institution for dissemination of information (Ahmad, 2002).

Growth of Higher Education in India

India inherited a poor educational infrastructure from the colonial masters and the colonial policy neither focused on mass education nor on higher education. As a consequence, the country had to begin from scratch soon after its Independence (Rani, 2004). Since independence, higher education in India has expanded very fast. Several initiatives were taken including the setting up of the University Grants Commission, an autonomous body for the development and maintenance of standards in higher education, and establishment of several other institutions of technical and scientific excellence. The policy and action plan of higher education in independent India are largely based on two landmark reports called the University Education Commission (otherwise known as Radhakrishnan Commission) Report (1948-49) and Education Commission (Also known as Kothari Commission, 1964-66).

In 1986, a National Policy on Education was enunciated to prepare the Indian Education System for the 21st century (Statistics of Technical and Higher Education, 2008-09). The main aim of this policy is to transform a static society into a vibrant one with a commitment for development and change. Placing importance on higher education, the policy states that, "*higher education provides people with an opportunity to reflect on the critical, social, economic, cultural, moral and spiritual issues facing humanity and contributes to National development through dissemination of specialized knowledge and skills*" (Statistics of Technical and Higher Education, 2008-09).

There has been a spectacular growth in the higher education sector, in the post-Independence period in terms of the three indicators, viz. (i) number of educational institutions (universities and colleges), (ii) number of teachers, and (iii) number of students. The number of universities in India increased by almost 35 times from 20 in 1947-48 to about 833 in 2015-16. The number of colleges has registered almost 70 times increased from 496 in 1948 to 33,724 in 2014-15. The number of teachers has also gone up from around 24,000 in 1950-51 to 12,00,000 in 2015-16 depicting more than 35 fold increase. Similarly, the student enrolment increased by 170 times, from a tiny base of 1,00,000 to a whooping level of 2,89,74,883 over the said period (Agarwal, 2006, 2009). Table 21.2 indicates a very encouraging scenario on the expansion of higher education in India.

An analysis of growth trends in higher education since 1950-51 reveals that annual average growth rates of institutions, enrolment and teachers was very high during 1950s and 1960s. In 1970s growth of institutions of higher learning was relatively slow (Prakash, 2015) (*see* Fig. 21.1).

Annual average growth rate of higher education institutions, teachers and enrolment during the period 1980-81 to 2010-11 is given in Fig. 21.1. This figure shows that during the period 1980s, annual average growth

Table 21.2: Higher Education Institutions and Their Intake Capacity in India (1980-81 to 2010-11)

Sl. No.	*Years*	*No. of Universities*	*No. of Colleges*	*Total HEI*	*Student Enrolment*	*No. of Teachers ('000)*
1.	1980-81	133	4722	4855	2752437	193
2.	1981-82	141	4886	5027	2952066	199
3.	1982-83	143	5039	5182	3133093	209
4.	1983-84	149	5246	5395	3307649	216
5.	1984-85	150	5590	5740	3404096	220
6.	1985-86	159	5816	5975	3605029	226
7.	1986-87	165	6512	6677	3757158	234
8.	1987-88	175	6685	6860	4020159	241
9.	1988-89	182	6756	6938	4285489	249
10.	1989-90	186	7115	7301	4602680	257
11.	1990-91	190	7346	7536	4924868	263
12.	1991-92	193	7761	7954	5265886	270
13.	1992-93	198	7993	8191	5534966	278
14.	1993-94	207	8441	8648	5817249	286
15.	1994-95	214	9019	9233	6113929	301
16.	1995-96	219	9252	9471	6425624	310
17.	1996-97	225	9940	10165	6842598	321
18.	1997-98	232	10678	10910	7260418	331
19.	1998-99	238	11397	11635	7705520	342
20.	1999-00	247	11865	12112	8050607	351
21.	2000-01	256	12806	13062	8399443	395
22.	2001-02	272	13150	13422	8821095	427
23.	2002-03	300	15343	15643	9516773	436
24.	2003-04	320	16885	17205	10116330	457
25.	2004-05	343	17625	17968	10763775	472
26.	2005-06	355	18064	18419	11506475	488
27.	2006-07	369	19000	19369	11612505	488
28.	2007-08	416	20677	21093	13321817	505
29.	2008-09	471	22064	22535	14467493	521
30.	2009-10	504	25951	26455	15635360	589
31.	2010-11	564	33023	33587	16974883	699

Note: Total HEI = Universities + Colleges.

Source: (i) UGC Annual Reports, Various Issues.
(ii) Higher Education in India at a Glance (2012). UGC, New Delhi.

rates of universities were 3.6 per cent which came down to 3 per cent in the period of 1990s, but during the 2002-11 periods, it grows to a rate of 8.3 per cent.

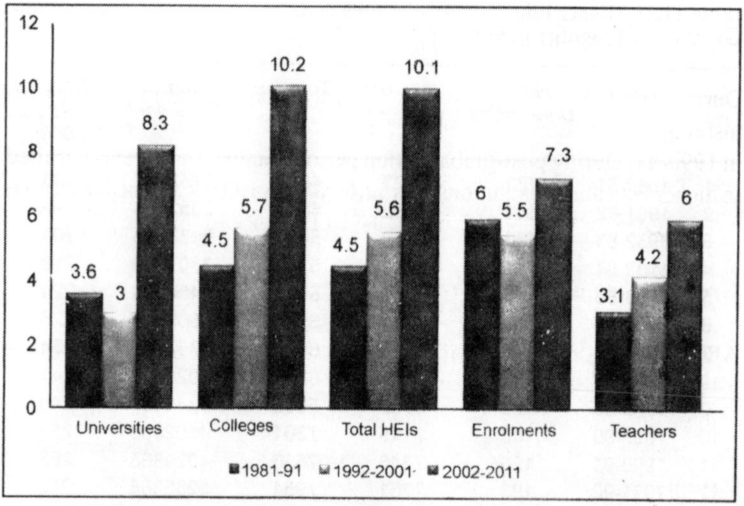

Fig. 21.1: Average Annual Growth Rate of Higher Education Institutions, Teachers and Enrolment in India, 1980-81 to 2010-11.

Source: Computed on the basis of data given in Table 21.2.

Growth of Universities

India has one of the largest higher education systems in the world with respect to number of institutions. In 2010-11, India has 33,587 university level institutions, as compared to 6,742 in USA and 4297 in China (Ernst and Young/FICCI, 2011). An analysis of Table 2.0 reveals that during pre-globalization period, the number of universities in India increased from 133 in 1980-81 to 190 in 1990-91. The decadal growth of universities depict that there has been 1.4 times increase in number of universities. During post-globalization period, the number of universities in 1991-92 was 193 which increased substantially by 2.9 times to a level of 564 in 2011-11. However, growth of universities has been very rapid and explosive during the post-globalization period.

Growth of Colleges

During pre-globalization period, number of colleges went up from 4722 in 1980-81 to 7346 in 1990-91, registering 1.5 times increase. During post-globalization period, number of colleges was 7761 in 1991-92 which increased by 4.2 times to a level of 33023 in 2010-11 (Table 21.2).

Growth of Enrolments

During pre-globalization period, enrolment of students in higher education institutions increased by 1.8 times from 27,52,437 in 1980-81 to 49,24,868 in 1990-91. During post-globalization period, number of students enrolled in higher education institutions was 52,65,886 in 1991-92, which increased by 3.2 times to 1,69,74,883 in 2010-11 (Table 21.2).

Growth Enrolment Ratio (GER) in Higher Education

After assessing the growth of higher education institutions, we now take a look into a very important parameter, that of students enrolment in India in the context of GER. The access to higher education is measured in terms of GER, which is a ratio of persons enrolled in higher education institutions to total population of the persons in the age groups of 18 to 23 years. GER in higher education increased from 0.7 per cent in 1950-51 to 1.4 per cent in 1960-61 (Sreeramamurthy *et al.*, 2012) to 5 per cent in 1980, 6 per cent in 1990 to about 10 per cent in 2000. It further increased to 12 per cent in 2007 to about 17.9 per cent in 2011-12 (Ernst and Young/ FICCI, 2012). Thus, accessibility to higher education in India has increased over the past few years.

The world average of the GER in higher education is around 26.7 per cent, the average of the developed countries is approximately 57.7 per cent and that of the developing countries is 13 per cent and the Government of India wants to increase this to 21 per cent by the end of Twelfth Five Year Plan (MHRD, 2010). Even though our higher education system is one of the largest in the world, the GER is far below the world average. Enrolment ratio is also relatively low, when compared with most developed (USA) and developing countries (i.e. China) (Ernst and Young, 2012). Besides low GER, there exists demand-supply gap in higher education in India.

The National target was to increase the GER to 15 per cent by the end of Eleventh Five Year Plan period (2011-12), which has been achieved, and 30 per cent by 2020. While this goal requires higher capacity for intake, improvement in access to higher education across gender and different social groups, and to bridge the rural-urban divide in order to ensure more equitable outcomes in educational participation (ASHE, 2016).

The overall demand for higher education in India is increasing but there are large variations in GER across States and Union Territories. In

2008-09, GER at the higher education level ranges from as low as 2.3 per cent in Daman and Diu to as high as 41.5 per cent in Chandigarh. The GER is above National average of 13.7 per cent in 18 States and UTs which includes Andhra Pradesh, Goa, Gujarat, Haryana, Maharashtra, Sikkim, Tamil Nadu, Uttarakhand, Chandigarh etc., and less that the National average of 13.7 per cent in 17 States and UTs that include Bihar, Chhattisgarh, Jharkhand, Madhya Pradesh, Odisha, Rajansthan, Uttar Pradesh and West Bengal etc., (Statistics of Higher and Technical Education, 2008-09). Delhi, Chandigarh and Pondicherry, which attract large number of students from outside states, have GER 30 and exceeding 30 per cent while States like Bihar, Assam, Rajasthan, Odisha and West Bengal have significantly lower GER. This shows that there are wide inter-state variations. This suggests a need for state specific strategies in addressing issues of expansion of higher education during the twelfth plan period (Ernst and Young/FICCI, 2012). Inequalities in access to higher education by gender, caste and religion increased and inter-institutional variations in quality of higher education became strikingly visible (Tilak, 2005b).

Table 21.3: Distribution of Stage-wise Enrolment in Higher Education in India (1980-81 to 2010-11)

Sl. No.	Years	Graduate	Post-Graduate	Research	Diploma/ Certificate
1.	1980-81	24,01,485 (87.2)	2,73,337 (9.9)	32,171 (1.2)	45,444 (1.7)
2.	1985-86	31,78,897 (88.2)	3,37,679 (9.4)	40,346 (1.1)	48,107 (1.3)
3.	1990-91	38,98,643 (88.1)	4,20,398 (9.5)	48,678 (1.1)	57,528 (1.3)
4.	1995-96	56,67,400 (88.2)	6,04,009 (9.4)	70,682 (1.1)	83,533 (1.3)
5.	2001-02	78,62,588 (89.13)	8,16,335 (9.25)	60,516 (0.69)	81,656 (0.93)
6.	2006-07	1,03,25,839 (88.92)	10,94,060 (9.42)	74,320 (0.64)	1,18,286 (1.02)
7.	2010-11	1,46,16,473 (86.11)	20,49,124 (12.07)	1,37,668 (0.81)	1,71,618 (1.01)

Note: Figures in brackets show percentage of student enrolment to total enrolments in higher education.

Source: (a) (UGC) New Delhi, 1984.
(b) UGC Annual Reports, Various Issues.

Stage-wise Enrolment in Higher Education

During the period of unprecedented expansion of higher education, the graduate sector witnessed a greater increase in its share. It can be seen from Table 21.3 that in 1980-81, about 87.2 per cent of students were enrolled at graduate level and only 9.9 per cent are enrolled at post-graduate level. Diploma and certificate education has a meager 1.7 per cent enrolment as it is considered as a last option for those who are not be able to make it in the mainstream of higher education.

The share of graduate enrolment to the total enrolment has gone up from 88.2 per cent in 1985-86 to 89.13 per cent in 2001-02. In 2010-11, the share of graduate enrolment declined to 86.11 per cent. On the other hand, the share of post-graduate enrolment remained almost constant over the years except in 2010-11, in which its share has increased to 12 per cent. The share of enrolment at research level has however shown marginal decline from 1.1 per cent in 1985-86 to 0.64 per cent in 2006-07. In 2010-11, the share of student enrolment at research level was 0.81 per cent. Thus, the analysis shows that majority of students were enrolled at graduate courses.

Graduate enrolments increased by 6 times from 24,01,485 in 1980-81 to 1,46,16,473 in 2010-11 while enrolment at post-graduate level went up 7.5 times from 2,73,337 to 20,49,124, during the same period.

Faculty-wise Enrolment in Higher Education

The distribution of students, across various disciplines is an important aspect of higher education is given in Table 21.4.

The enrolments in Arts Faculty continue to have a dominant share in total enrolment. It recorded a high of 40.5 per cent in 1980-81, reached to a maximum level of 46.13 per cent in 2001-02, since then it share has been consistently declining. The share of science faculty enrolment remains almost stable from 1980-81 to 2001-02, i.e. from 19.4 per cent to 19.8 per cent. In 2006-07, the share of student enrolment in this faculty has slightly increased to 20.45 per cent but further it decline to 18.42 per cent in 2010-11. The share of enrolment in Commerce Department has gone down from 20.1 per cent in 1980-81 to 17.87 per cent in 2001-02. Its share has slightly increased to 18.01 per cent in 2006-07 and again it came down to 17.11 per cent in 2010-11. The share of enrolment in engineering and technology is intrinsically linked with industrial base of the economy. It share has increased from 4.7 per cent in 1980-81 to 6.87

Table 21.4: Distribution of Enrolment by Faculties in India (1980-81 to 2010-11)

Sl. No. Faculty / Years	1980-81	1985-86	1990-91	1995-96	2001-02	2006-07	2010-11
1. Arts	11,14,417 (40.5)	14,66,295 (40.7)	17,89,48 (40.4)	25,92,925 (40.4)	40,69,632 (46.13)	52,40,727 (45.13)	61,77,730 (36.39)
2. Science	5,33,859 (19.4)	7,00,991 (19.4)	8,69,119 (19.6)	12,60,200 (19.6)	17,54,110 (19.88)	23,74,758 (20.45)	31,27,042 (18.42)
3. Commerce	5,54,253 (20.1)	7,82,068 (21.7)	9,69,882 (21.9)	14,10,119 (21.9)	15,75,940 (17.87)	20,91,411 (18.01)	29,04,752 (17.11)
4. Engg/Tech	1,28,937 (4.7)	1,76,540 (4.9)	2,16,837 (4.9)	3,15,720 (4.9)	6,05,597 (6.87)	8,37,261 (7.21)	28,62,439 (16.86)
5. Medicine	1,10,020 (4.0)	1,23,057 (3.4)	1,50,458 (3.4)	2,19,918 (3.4)	2,75,943 (3.13)	3,66,954 (3.16)	65,25,33 (3.85)
6. Education	71.204 (2.6)	82,636 (2.3)	99,613 (2.3)	1,47,720 (2.3)	1,14,678 (1.30)	16,95,42 (1.46)	56,99,61 (3.36)
7. Agriculture	39,231 (1.4)	41,901 (1.2)	46,908 (1.1)	67,990 (1.1)	52,833 (0.60)	67,352 (0.58)	93,166 (0.55)
8. Law	1,74,374 (6.3)	1,96,106 (5.4)	2,34,538 (5.3)	3,42,440 (5.3)	2,80,449 (3.18)	3,54,183 (3.05)	3,27,146 (1.93)
9. Vet. Sc.	7,648 (0.3)	9,486 (0.3)	11,063 (0.3)	16,201 (0.3)	14,270 (0.16)	17,418 (0.15)	27,423 (0.16)
10. Others	18,494 (0.7)	25,949 (0.7)	37,349 (0.8)	52,401 (0.8)	77,643 (0.88)	92,899 (0.80)	2,32691 (1.37)
11. All Faculties	**27,52,437 (100.0)**	**36,05,029 (100.0)**	**44,25,247 (100.0)**	**64,25,624 (100.0)**	**88,21,095 (100.0)**	**11,612,505 (100.0)**	**16,974,883 (100.0)**

Note: Figures in brackets are percentages.

Source: (a) University Development in India: Facts and Figures 1977-78 to 1981-82, (UGC), New Delhi,

(b) UGC Annual Reports, Various Issues.

per cent in 2001-02. In 2006-07 its share was 7.21 per cent which gradually increased to 16.86 per cent in 2010-11.

In 1981, the share of enrolment in the faculty of medicine was four per cent and after that its share remained almost constant over the period (i.e. around three per cent). Enrolment in the Faculty of Law has shown a continuous decline over the period 1980-81 to 2010-11. The share of education faculty in total enrolment has declined from 2.6 per cent in 1980-81 to 1.46 per cent in 2006-07. But, in 2010-11, its share reached to a maximum level of 3.36 per cent. There has been an extremely low share of enrolment in agriculture and veterinary science disciplines. The enrolment in agriculture courses has come down to 0.55 per cent in 2010-11 from 1.4 per cent in 1980-81. The share of enrolment in veterinary science remains almost stable; it is miniscule 0.16 per cent in 2010-11.

Status of Women in Higher Education

Since Independence, there has been a phenomenal growth in women's enrolment in higher education. Women's enrolment was less than 10 per cent of the total enrolment on the eve of independence has risen to 41.5 per cent in 2010-11 (Table 21.5). The rise of women enrolment is not confined to a particular stage, but it is consistently rising at all stages namely; graduate, post-graduate and research (Agarwal, 1995).

Table 21.5: Women's Colleges and Women's Enrolment in India (1980-81 to 2010-11)

Sl. No.	*Years*	*Women's Colleges*	*Women's Enrolment*
1.	1980-81	609	748525
2.	1985-86	741	1067484
3.	1990-91	874	1556258
4.	1995-96	1146	2363607
5.	2000-01	1578	3306410
6.	2005-06	2071	4466348
7.	2010-11	3982	7048688

Source: UGC Annual Reports, Various Issues.

Growth in the Number of Teachers

It can been seen from Table 21.2 that during pre-globalization period, teachers' strength in higher education institutions increased by 1.36 times from 1,93,000 in 1980-81 to 2,63,000 in 1990-91. During post-globalization period, number of teachers grew by 2.6 times from 2,70,000 in 1991-92 to 6,99,000 in 2010-11. In spite of increase in teachers in university and colleges, the reports of teacher's strength from each quarter of higher education had shown inadequacy in the staff strength. According to Ernst and Young (2012) report, there were 40 per cent and 35 per cent shortage of faculty in State and Central universities respectively.

There has been rapid and explosive growth in number of institutions (universities + colleges), teachers and students enrolment during post-globalization period. Thus, from the analysis of data, we can say that globalization has affected the growth of higher education system in India.

Private Sector and its Role in Higher Education

In recent years, there has been increasing trend both in the number of private higher education institutions and in enrolments. According to a study (Anandakrishanan, 2006) in 2000-01, private unaided institutions constituted 42.6 per cent of the total number of higher education institutions and 32.9 per cent of the total enrolment. This enrolment increased to 51.53 per cent in 2005-06. Now, more than 60 per cent of the higher education institutions in India comprised private institutions, mostly unaided.

Between 2007 and 2012, the number of private institutions grew faster than the number of Government institutions. About 64 per cent of the total higher education institutions are private unaided institutions in 2011-12 (Table 21.6). The share of unaided private institutions in the total number of institutions is up from 40 per cent a decade ago (Ernst & Young/FICCI, 2012). Thus, non-public sector accounts for a higher share than public sector.

Table 21.6: Unaided Private Higher Education Institutions as a per cent of Total Institutions in India

Sl. No.	*Year*	*Unaided Private Higher Education Institutions (%)*
1.	2001	42.5
2.	2007	61.8
3.	2012	63.9
4.	2015	67.8

Source: Twelfth Five Year Plan: Social Sector, 2012-2017.

Enrolment in public and private institutions is given in Table 21.7. In 2006-07 enrolment in public institutions was 63.38 lakh which increased to 89.63 lakh in 2011-12 while enrolment in private institutions increased at a rapid rate, i.e. from 75.12 lakh to 128.23 lakh over the same period and in 2014-15 it was 104.18 lakh in public institutions while it was 143.24 lakh enrolment in private institutions. Enrolment in private institutions has increased as a compound annual growth rate (CAGR) of 11 per cent over the last five years from 2007 to 2012, as compared to 7 per cent in Government institutions over the same period.

Table 21.7: Growth of Enrolment by Public and Private Institutions

(*Rs. in Lakhs*)

Sl. No.	*Category*	*2006-07*	*2011-12*	*2014-15*
1.	Government	63.38	89.63	104.18
2.	Private	75.12	128.23	143.24

Source: Twelfth Five Year Plan: Social Sector, 2012-17.

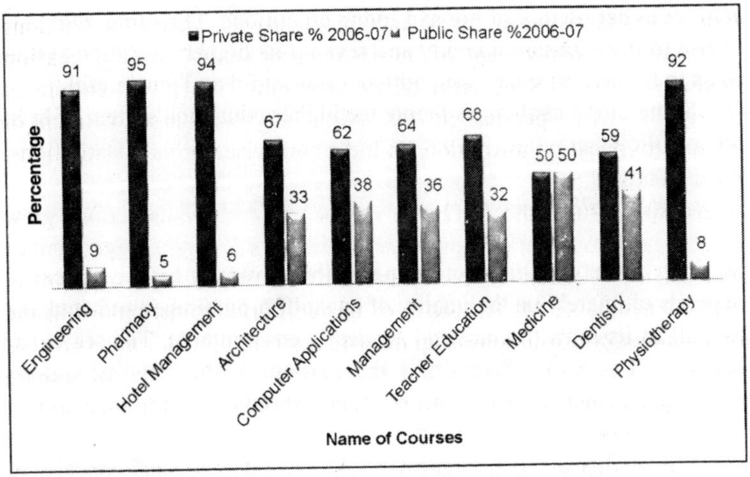

Fig. 21.2: Share of Public and Private Institutions in Selected Professional Courses in India

Source: Earnst & Young, 2011.

Figure 21.2 shows the growth of professional higher education in recent years (Ernst & Young, 2011).

This Figure 21.2 reveals that majority of institutions offering programmes in professional disciplines such as engineering, pharmacy and hotel management have been established by the private sector. In 2006-07, private sector participation ranged from 50 to 95 per cent of the total number of institutions for various professional courses while public sector participation ranged from 5 per cent to 50 per cent. Thus, data shows dominant share of unaided private higher education institutions in professional courses.

Challenges in Contemporary Indian Higher Education

In the present scenario, the major challenge of the country at the beginning of the twenty first century is to become a developed society by the year 2020, which requires a vibrant economy driven by knowledge. With the explosive growth of knowledge in the past century and with the development of information ad communication technologies as well as of other scientific innovations, competition has become fierce all over the world. As a result, knowledge has become the sole driver of Indian economy and has permeated into all the strata of Indian society so as to achieve better quality of life and living conditions. Therefore, India has to rise to the occasion urgently and revamp its higher education system so as to become vibrant, competitive, meaningful and purposeful.

Some of the challenges facing the higher education system of India are as following:

I. Quality Challenges

Meeting society's needs and expectations towards higher education depends ultimately on the quality of its staff, programmes and students, as well as its infrastructure and academic environment. The search for 'quality' has many facets and the principal objective of quality enhancement measures in higher education should be institutional as well as system-wise improvement.

The quality of higher education is a multidimensional concept. As stressed by Donal Ekong, one approach is through the composite concept of "quality assurance", which implies that "all the polices, systems and processes are directed to ensuring the maintenance and enhancement of the quality of educational provision within an institution. A quality assurance system is the means by which an institution confirms to itself and to others that the conditions are in place for students to achieve the standards that the institution has set."

The concept of quality assurance implies that quality can be understood as adaptation to what is required by the institution, i.e. that the set goals have been reached in a consistent and with fixed quality criteria. Thus, it is has led to the conclusion that quality is not centered exclusively on products but also on the processes initiated by the system when it operated and a coherent whole in order to ensure this social relevance.

II. Challenges of Staff Development

The chief wealth of high profile lies in the quality of their human capital. A quality assurance therefore is a means to identify the requisite skills and attitude profiles.

A quality assurance policy implies policies to develop "well articulated policies. Remove gender inequity in education and, more importantly promote the advancement of women in the entire society. This should include measures implemented by the institutions of higher education themselves. We suggest that meaningful affirmative action be taken in all possible directions. Women's associations and networks should be fully supported. A systematic and coherent policy of gender research and case studies should be implemented and their findings widely published...." (Dakar, para 45).

In many developing countries, the burden of teaching and supervision are sometimes so high that quality research is impossible and researcher status is an empty word. In the more developed countries, the problems are different: some teachers divest themselves of their teaching duties because research is better for their career and because scientific criteria are the main factors in appointments and promotions. Others have chosen to invest first and foremost in teaching for reasons of personal preference or because of difficulties in doing research, depending on the case. If such an investment is not properly recognized by the establishment in its career management, the establishment will find that it is harbouring a great many frustrated individuals could have a negative effect on a high quality research policy. The quality of the staff in these higher education institutions is central to their effectiveness.

For administrative and support staff there is equally rapid changes in management processes, techniques and technology. In considering any strategy for developing human resources an institution must consider all its staff; administrative and support personnel which can play crucial roles in helping students to learn, and in enabling and facilitating an environment that favours learning. In no country are higher education institutions immune from severe pressures and challenges. Among the principal challenges which affect human resources development are the following:

1. The growth in demand for higher education is a world-wide phenomenon whether one approaches it form the standpoint of an age participation ratio of 35 per cent or of 5 per cent. UNESCO has charted the expansion in student enrolments from 13 million in 1960 to 65 million in 1991 and to 115 million in 2011. In many countries the rate of expansion has exceeded that of the economy, while the reluctance of some countries to contemplate cost sharing has posed a major problem for their public sector financing.

2. Financial constraints in all countries mean that governments can no longer fund higher education to the same extent as they have been doing previously. Apart from asking students and their parents to share the cost, their response has been call for continued efficiency savings (or simple cuts) in institutional budgets, which has led throughout the world to more severe staff student ratios and heavier workloads for academic staff. Another government response is to expect institutions to generate more of their income from non-governmental sources such as industry or commerce. This places new demands on academic staff that is expected to master entrepreneurial skills in converting their specialist knowledge into market-oriented services. In many countries the reduction in funding for state institutions is leading to a growth in higher education provision by the private sector.

3. The government and public expectation of University and other tertiary institutions are that they will be able to serve wider audiences of students, at different levels, in different ways. Thus, among the new expectations will be: an ability to handle a growing proportion or part-time students (usually meaning longer hours for staff); willingness to teach a greater number of mature students; the assumptions that an institution can serve regional population using links to associated colleges or providers; an ability to offer distance learning and face-to-face tuition in "dual mode", an expectation that institutions can instill a set of "general transferable skills" in all their employable graduates.

4. A concern for quality of the product has accompanied the expansion in numbers and the reduction in funding. There is an inevitable fear that "more means worse" and quality will suffer as mass higher education becomes a reality. Governments, parents and students are asking questions about the teaching/learning process and are expecting institutions and funding bodies to monitor the quality of the processes and their outcomes.

5. Technological change affects all disciplines and expects staff members to be ready to handle the latest innovations in teaching method and research support. In the developing country the gulf between "technology haves" and "technology have-nots" has to be bridged. Access to the Internet will eventually enable developing country universities to remedy some of the deficiencies in the library and information services.

6. The importance of increasing women's participation among staff and students. As regards students this will affect their admission strategies, their student support services and sometimes their teaching practices. Thus, several categories of staff may need to be involved in the solution. A harder challenge faces those seeking to achieve a higher involvement of women in the higher ranks of teachers, researchers or institutional management. Whether the blockages to change in these two areas are in attitudes or processes, the problem requires a strategic review and firm action, if it is to be resolved.

7. The demands of the labour market are changing dramatically and inevitably affecting those institutions who are seeking more to be responsive to national or regional demand. One should not ignore global or regional perspectives in the curricula in any of the courses which aim to serve these industries. Patterns of employment are also changing; courses which once met National needs have now become obsolete. New offerings are required in areas such as telecommunications, tourism, health care, financial services, food technology and transportation studies. Students facing unemployment after graduation are now turning to more vocational and relevant courses which increase their chances of employment.

8. Effective management demands new skills within institutions which may not always be present among those who traditionally lead at either central or faculty level. There are widespread complaints within institutions about "new managerial cultures" driving out the old academic collegial spirit, yet the very complexity of the demands on senior institutional managers makes it essential for them to be fully professional. The technical skills needed by today's institutional managers call into questions some of the traditional management structures and job specifications.

9. Roles of people in higher educational institutions: These daunting challenges are likely to have a considerable impact on the work and role of each of the main participants in institution. All persons in higher educational institutions are affected by a number of common challenges and trends. They are:

(i) To be responsive and able to change:
(ii) Greater awareness of international perspectives in the context of curricula;
(iii) Demand for relevance in the curriculum from employers, governments and students;
(iv) Need for more inter-institutional cooperation, in some cases with burgeoning private sector;
(v) Awareness of the institution's role in society and its contribution to National development or the local community;
(vi) More emphasis on quality teaching then on research as a career goal for academic staff; and
(vii) The increase in demand for postgraduate provision, particularly in those countries that have relatively high participation rate in higher education.

Leadership skills would be essential as will communication and persuasive skills in convincing academic colleagues of the need for changes to long established habits. Thus, the key roles for such leaders will include:

- Providing strategic guidance and a vision of where the institution should be going;
- Persuading external bodies such as businesses men, donors and alumni to contribute funds so as to replace those which government has withdrawn;
- Encouraging innovation and an entrepreneurial culture; and
- Maintaining commitment to institutional goals in a community.

Institutional managers such as deans and heads of departments will share in the turmoil of managing institutions in transition and they will be in need of having more tangible competencies. Among them will be the following:

- People management skills, such as team building and helping staff to develop themselves academically and professionally;
- Numeracy and understanding of financial and cost issues;
- Sensitivity to new developments in the external environment;
- Customer consciousness and strategic awareness of the institution's position; and
- Understanding of how to use institutional decision making process in a collegial environment.

Academic staff faces probably the biggest set of challenges in higher working patterns. They bear the ultimate burden of having to "do more with less", as student numbers increase without matching funding. Their accountabilities are being sharpened and made explicit, as quality reviews and assessments examine what they do. In this harsh environment a model teaching staff member would have the following competencies:

- Awareness and understanding of the different ways in which students learn;
- Knowledge, skills and attitudes requirements in order to help students learn;
- Commitment to scholarship in the discipline;
- Sensitivity to external "Market signals";

- Mastery of new developments in teaching and learning;
- Customer awareness, as regards the views and aspirations of stakeholders;
- Ability to teach a diverse range of students, from different age groups; and
- Skills in handling larger numbers of students in formal lectures, seminars or workshops.

For academic support staff in libraries, resource and computer centres there are matching demands. The new technologies require mastery of new techniques and software in searching for information and a changed role in supporting users of these supports services. UK's Dearing Report endorsed this finding, "where communications and information technology has changed the nature of learning and teaching, there is a need to review and redefine the roles of academic and support staff within institutions."

For administrative staff new competencies required: information technology skills and tackling of financial pressures. In small states there are unique staff development problems arising from the small size of higher education institutions. Limited human resource capacity in the country makes senior staff very dependent on external partnerships for advice and information. Multi-skilling within institutions unavoidable and there are inevitable shortage of specialist staff.

III. Administrative Issues and Challenges

(i) Governance

Indian higher education is over-regulated and under-governed. Rigidity of the system and the bureaucratic controls over it has made the system more or less dysfunctional. The archaic rules and regulations have failed to ensure any accountability either. The static and rigid nature of the system has left very little scope for innovations or improvement. In the emerging International scenario, the higher education institutions require more flexibility and autonomy to perform effectively.

Administrative and governance reforms are imperative for quality enhancement in the higher education sector of the country. Too much political interference is there in appointments. Granting more autonomy for the universities and colleges is a prerequisite for overcoming the rigidity of the system. National Knowledge Commission has also suggested for granting more academic autonomy and greater accountability. With the increasing privatization of the higher education sector, instances of malpractices and exploitation of the student community have also become rampant. The policy makers should think of starting more institutions under the public-private partnership mode so as to achieve the targets set for higher GER.

There exists several other regulatory bodies in the higher education structure of the country which regulate and monitor their functioning. They include Bar Council of India (BCI); Central Council of Homoeopathy (CCH); Central Council of Indian Medicine (CCIM); Council of Agriculture (CoA); Distance Education Council (DEC); Indian Council of Agriculture (ICAR); Medical Council of India (MCI); National Council for Teacher Education (NCTE), State Councils of Higher Education (SCHEs) and Veterinary Council of India (VCI). On the basis of the recommendation of the *Committee on Renovation and Rejuvenation of Higher Education*, headed by Prof. Yahspal, the Ministry of Human Resource Development has put forward a proposal to set up National Commission for Higher Education and Research (NCHER) to replace the existing regulatory bodies and to act as the apex regulatory body in the field of higher education in India. The primary task of the proposed NCHER will be to evolve norms and standards for various aspects of higher education, including assessment and accreditation.

(ii) Burden of Affiliation

The system of affiliation was started in India much earlier to independence. This system of Affiliation has been able to provide access to a large number of students at relatively low cost.

In India, about 87 per cent of the total students in higher education institutions are enrolled in affiliated colleges. As shown in Table 21.3, 90 per cent of the under-graduate students and over 70 per cent of the post-graduate students in the country are studying in affiliated colleges. Under the affiliating system, several colleges, usually belonging to a particular geographical area are affiliated to the parent university. An affiliating university exercise rigid control over the colleges under its jurisdiction with regard to courses, syllabi examinations, etc. As the university treats all the affiliated colleges in the same way, there exists hardly any incentive or opportunity for better colleges to improve.

Under the system of affiliation, all the important decisions are taken by the parent university and as a result, affiliated colleges do not have much accountability. Both the National Knowledge Commission and the

Yashpal Committee have strongly recommended in bringing about a reform in the prevailing affiliation system.

(iii) Financing Higher Education

One of the important problems plaguing Indian Higher Education is the shortage of funds. With inadequate funding, there would not be any substantial increase in the GER. The government has all along been playing a crucial role in the financing of higher education in India. The Central and State Governments continue to be the chief sources for funding of the higher education sector. The Central Government established the UGC (University Grants Commission) in 1953 for the planned development of higher education in India through allocating and disbursing grants to eligible higher education institutions. Universities and colleges which are included under Section 2(f) and declared fit to receive Central assistance under Section 12(B) of the UGC Act, 1956 are eligible for financial assistance from the UGC under various schemes. Such institutions are eligible to receive UGC grants for both plan and non-plan schemes. The UGC provides funds for the purpose of upgradation of the existing facilities and their expansion to Central, State and Deemed universities. But, financial assistance for the maintenance of the existing facilities is given only to the centrally established institutions.

In order to realize 18 per cent of GER by the end of the Twelfth Five Year Plan, the Central Government had increased the allocation to higher education from Rs. 3,294 crore during the Tenth Five Year Plan to Rs. 46,449 crore in the Eleventh Five Year Plan. By making such a substantial increase, the allocation to higher education increased from about 0.40 per cent during the Tenth Five Year Plan to almost 1.0 per cent of the GDP during the Eleventh Five Year Plan.

Table 21.8: UGC grants given to Universities and Colleges during 2005-06 to 2010-11

(Rs. in lakhs)

Sl. No.	*Years*	*Total*	*Non-Plan*	*Plan*
1.	2005-06	216,411.94	1,35,691.46	80,720.48
2.	2006-07	283,723.49	1,58,778.69	124,944.80
3.	2007-08	384,990.44	158,778.69	124,944.80
4.	2008-09	587,921.33	272,287.92	315,633.41
5.	2009-10	774,157.75	391,787.32	382,370.43
6.	2010-11	970,141.89	493,867.32	476,274.57

Source: UGC Annual Report, 2010-11.

It can be seen from Table 21.3 that in the financial year 2010-11, a total amount of Rs. 9,701,41.89 lakhs were given to the universities and colleges out of which 50.6 per cent (4,93,867.32) was non-plan grant and 49.4 per cent (4,76,274.57) plan grant. The Non-Plan (maintenance) grants are provided chiefly to maintain higher education institutions. Plan (development) grants are provided to improve infrastructure facilities and for expansion. It is evident from Table 21.8 that, both Plan and non-Plan grants have been grossly inadequate to meet the growing financial requirements of the higher education sector. The higher education sector in India continues to be under-funded and the per student expenditure has been declining over the years with the growing student enrolment (Tilak, 2004).

Out of the 33,023 colleges in the country 2011, only19.4 per cent (6,417) of the colleges were eligible to receive grants from the UGC under Section 12(B) of the UGC Act. Like that, among the total 274 Deemed universities in the country during 2011, the UGC has been providing both Plan and Non-Plan grants to just 10 deemed universities whereas 24 deemed universities have been receiving only the development grants (UGC, 2011). Moreover, about 85 per cent of the total central funding to higher education (including technical education) goes to support just 3 per cent of the students enrolled in about 130 higher education institutions in India (Agarwal, 2010).

National Knowledge Commission suggested that at least 1.5 per cent of the GDP should be earmarked for higher education as against the present allocation of less than 1 per cent. The Central Government accounts for 40 per cent of the total development expenditure for higher education and the State Governments contribute about 60 per cent of the total expenditure. Therefore, central government also needs to increase their allocation for the expansion of the higher education sector.

The amount provided for the maintenance of library, laboratory and other physical infrastructure facilities is grossly inadequate. This has serious adverse implications on any substantial quantitative or qualitative improvement in the higher education sector. Therefore, the Governmental efforts in this regard needs to be supplemented in order to make any substantial difference in the system. Adequate funding for higher education by both public and private sectors in the country is absolutely essential if India has to sustain its economic growth.

IV. Challenges of Curriculum Development

An increasing number of factors have a profound impact on the need to modify curricula: the knowledge explosion and the burgeoning demand of new disciplines; the increasing need to adopt a multi- and trans-disciplinary approach; diversification and regionalization of education courses; and the desire for greater social relevance in a changing world. These pressures compel higher education to adopt three major types of qualitative change in their curricula: changes in goals, in methods and in the structure of curricula as they relate to one another.

Basic training must not be viewed simply a short accumulation of knowledge but must be directed at acquiring skills such as ability to mobilize their knowledge and related skills in order to analyse complex situations, resolve the problems they pose, be capable of teamwork, be capable of providing logical justification of their choices and show foresight.

While the quality of curricula is contingent on the quality of goals, it is highly dependent on the quality of teaching methods. As a result of mass education... higher education faces the temptation to make greater use of transmissive teaching in large groups, which it is difficult to reconcile with the goals set out above. To meet crucial challenge which is "to respond to the mass phenomenon and not diminish, and even increase quality", means a big effort on part of imagination by higher education. Methods which involve students more deeply in the management of their learning and the use of certain facilities offered by IT, whether in real time or at a distance, are routes which should be explored and cross-fertilized through exchanges of experience.

The curricula will have to adapt teaching methods according to the characteristics of the population concerned. The increasing openness towards greater flexibility and lifelong learning schemes is leading, and will increasingly lead, higher education institutions to carry out a fundamental reconsideration of their curriculum structures so as to create a linkage, or an "*inter-structuring*" of curricula.

V. Challenges of Higher Education Research

Higher education is now regarded as an institution not only for developing knowledge and training young minds, but for disseminating and plying such knowledge as well.

The current triumphs of research are due in large measure to the provision of adequate financial support from government, from the private sector and from international agencies. The success of the newly emerging economies in South East Asia... the present economic crisis notwithstanding... provide sufficient evidence that in a science and technology-driven economy, it is the university that must be the powerhouse of the "*knowledge economy*".

However, there is a price to pay for this. The injection of public funds into the University for research requires accountability that may be directed by an outside body and not by reliance upon the university's own evaluative procedures. This may impact negatively on a tenet the university holds so dear: respect for academic freedom and autonomy of choice in conducting one's own research.

There is also the problem of research being conducted outside the university. The total government expenditure for research is often shared between the university and other specialized national research institutes or centres, while multinational industries have their own laboratories for research. The conduct of advanced research is no longer solely the preserve of the university. Research results contained in national research institutes as well as industry may be classified and so may remain unknown to the research public, sometimes until two or more decades have passed. No longer is all knowledge readily disseminated to all those capable of benefiting from it.

National agencies used to support basic research principally for its potential applications in the military and in commerce. But now they are least investing in it. Yet everyone recognizes the economic and social benefits of basic research: it produces background knowledge, it develops research skills, new techniques, instruments and methods that in turn yield economic benefits power a much broader range of production sectors. Thus, inadequate funding for basic research has an immediate deteriorating effect not only on higher educational institutions themselves but on national economies. Higher educational institutions should ensure that the education of the researcher includes training in both the natural and social sciences. International organizations including International Council for Science Union (ICSU) and the International School Science Council (ISSC), must prepare guidelines for their members concerning the ethics and responsibility in the conduct of their research.

Information Technology has proven to be a powerful aid to the researcher. Its recent forays into the Higher Education Industry, through the establishment of the '*Virtual University*', has led some to forecast the demise of the traditional university structure as it is presently constituted. This is because of the several advantages the '*Virtual University*'. It encourages collaboration between universities and staff in distant locations; it affords the ready availability of first class libraries to students in varied institutions; and it is an excellent tool for cutting down costs. In this way, it enlarges the research community to include those outside one's physical neighbourhood.

ICSU has created a Committee on Responsibility and Ethics in Science, with the duty of helping to find solutions to problems concerning ethics and responsibility in the conduct of science. ICSU aims to ensure that the contributions science makes to humanity will be for humane social progress. It is the challenge to the researcher so as to ensure that the two values of freedom and responsibility in the conduct of research are kept in their proper perspective.

Most governments of the developing countries are now capable of providing a reasonable percentage of their GNP for the promotion of quality higher education and capacity-building in research. The advanced countries can also equip researchers of the developing world for full participation in knowledge-based socio-economic development.

Issues and Concerns in Higher Education

Although, higher education has expanded several times since independence, issues of access, equity and quality still continue to be the burning areas of concern.

1. Access

For higher education. GER has risen from 0.7 per cent in 1950-51 to 1.4 per cent in 1960-61 and 8 per cent in early 2000. The current GER which is about 12 per cent stands very low when compared to the world average of 23.4 per cent, and an average of 54.6 per cent for developed countries ands 11.3 per cent of developing countries. In view of the projected population in the age groups of 18-24 years for 2011-12 which is 144.287 million (Tables 21.3 and 21.4) the access to higher education for all eligible in the country will be a major issue before the policy-makers.

2. Equity

Due to regional disparity in economic development and uneven distribution of institutions of higher education, the higher education is not equally available to the different sections of the society.

3. Quality

The higher educational institutions suffer from large quality variation;

NASSCOM Report-2005 has said that not more than 15 per cent of graduates of general education and 25-30 per cent of technical education are fit for employment. The various regulatory bodies have constituted an autonomous body for monitoring quality standards in the institutions under their purview such as National Assessment Accreditation Council (NAAC) by UGC, National Board of Accreditation (NBA) by AICTE, Accreditation Board (AB) by ICAR, Distance Education Council (DEC) by NCTE etc. Though, there exist autonomous bodies for assessment and monitoring quality standards in the institutions of higher education, but still they suffer from two major deficiencies. First, the quality norms of such councils are not comparable with international stranded. Secondly, the enforcement process is not stringent. Further, political interference and corruption dilute the impact of these institutions.

4. Lack of Competency and Research

The volume of knowledge doubles now every five years. New skills and knowledge are required to be updated. Unlike in the West, the contribution of our Universities to Science, Arts or Literature is very meagre. Research facilities do not exist in many colleges. University teachers do very little research work; college teachers do even less; many teachers are content with their present qualification and record. Only a few voice their views on academic or national problems.

5. Defective Curriculum

The curricula of higher education are full of defects. The subjects of study are old and out of date. The curricula fail to fulfil the interests of different types of students and national aspirations.

6. Global Competition

India being a signatory of WTO is bound to open up its market for trade in services including education but it does not have a clear policy for strengthening its education sector to compete with the giants in the world. Lack of proper policy provisions in time, higher education sector in the country is adversely affected.

7. Autonomous Colleges

To keep up with the changes in higher education due to globalization, institutions which have infrastructure and other facilities should be given more functional autonomy. By the year 2005 there were 138 colleges functioning as autonomous colleges in the country.

8. Red-tapism

A large number of institutions are without having adequate infrastructure and offering sub-standard education are not only surviving but are increasingly flourishing and thriving under the nose of the government. Therefore, it is desirable to develop a professional transparent and efficient mechanism to ensure expansion of quality education.

9. Privatization

In India, both public and private institutions operate simultaneously. In the year 2000-01, out of 13,072 higher education institutions, 42 per cent were privately owned and run catering to about 37 per cent of students enrolled into higher education, that is approximately 3.1 million out of total of 8.4 million students. Approximately 50 per cent of the higher education in India is imparted through private institutions, mostly unaided involving high cost.

10. Cost of Education

Government funding on higher education has been diminishing on a yearly basis. In view of withdrawal of government support to finance higher education, private institutions have been allowed and the model self-financing and self-sustaining institutions have been introduced. The terms and conditions imposed by banks in terms of guarantee and criteria of minimum income of family restrict the talent coming from the poor families to go for higher education.

11. Caste-based Reservation

Successive governments have introduced caste-based reservations in higher education. At present, the caste-based reservation is applicable in only government funded institutions that amount to approximately 49 per cent of the total seats. Due to the caste-based reservation, better talent coming from non-reserved category is deprived of the admission in good institutions.

12. Shortage of Teachers

Higher education in India has been passing through transition and withdrawal of financial support from the government has been finding it difficult to attract adequate number of teachers to teaching jobs.

13. Declining Enrolment in Traditional Fields of Knowledge

Today a major chunk of youths opts for professional courses leading to early employment and faster growth. Therefore, the teaching and research in such facilities is able to attract the best of the talent leaving only a few for fundamental research in basic sciences, literature, art and languages. It, thus, poses the challenge to the sustenance and the development of these basic pillars of knowledge.

14. Vocationalization at the First Degree Level

A scheme to provide career orientation through education at the first degree level was launched in 1994-95. Under the scheme, a university/college could introduce one to three vocational courses in 35 identified subjects. As a result, a number of job oriented programmes lasting for approximately six months to one year have been introduced in the college/universities.

15. Lack of Guidance and Counselling

There is no provision for giving proper guidance and counseling to the students. Hence, the students select their courses either according to the own choice or with the advice of some inexperienced persons.

16. Defective System of Examination

The Indian University Commission in 1902 pointed out that, "*The greater evil form which university education in India suffers is, that teaching is subordinate to examination, and non examinations to teaching.*" The University Education Commission of 1949 also pointed out that, "*If we are to suggest one single reform in university education, it should be that of examinations.*"

17. Indiscipline

Prof. N.K. Siddhant, former Vice-Chancellor of Calcutta University, has mentioned the following types of activities coming within the purview of indiscipline: (1) Financial irregularity, (2) Minor misconduct, (3) Disorderly misconduct, (4) Theft and burglary, (5) Sexual misconduct, (6) Misuse of privilege, and (7) Cheating in examination. In his book *Indian University Administration*, Prof. N.K. Siddhant said, "The problem of maintaining discipline in the seats of higher education is assuming greater importance day by day."

18. Too Much Commercialization of Higher Education

Too much commercialization of education system has adversely affected the student community as well as world at large. This new commercial approach adapted by many educational institutions has done away with the basic essence of academics and is having a vicious affect on the society and the country and orientation towards excellence in academics has gone for a toss.

19. Lack of Investment India Faces Another Problem which is the Lack of Investment

Only about 10 per cent of the relevant age groups in India go to universities where as in many developing countries, the figure is between 20 and 25 per cent. Most of the funds that are allocated for education department are directed towards the primary education schemes. For higher education, fewer initiatives have been taken up by the Government of India. So, it is the fees which primarily act as investment in this sector. If India needs to establish a world class higher education system then more investment from government is required in order to provide world class infrastructure and facilities.

20. Lack of Appraisal

One of the weakest link in our education system has been lack of appraisal of college heads, college and university administrators and university and college teachers, even though we have long been aware of their importance for effective and efficient operation of our educational institutions. In many institutions administrators are being evaluated in a very unsystematic and unscientific manner and the most common mechanism used is the confidential report of any. The judgmental remarks are usually subjective and which are complex and difficult to evaluate.

This does not evaluate the individual in any constructive way. Any formal system of periodic appraisal for teachers is yet to be devised.

The time now is to modernize our education system so that our country can get much more technically graduated people which can help our country to become a developed state.

Suggestions to Ameliorate the Condition of Indian Higher Education

There are some suggestions which can metamorphose the present state of higher education into a better one:

1. Introduce Innovation in Curriculum

The syllabus of Indian higher education system is obsolete. An innovative curriculum is needed which is progressive in nature. Curriculum must contribute towards development of soft skills, logical and analytical skills. Curriculum should be more project oriented.

2. Privatization of Higher Education

In reality only 24 per cent of the population is educated in India. So, improved standard of education as first priority should be offered to the majority by the government authorities with sincere political will. Also, privatization of higher education is absolutely necessary in a vast country like India as government alone is helpless to do so.

3. Information, Communication and Technology (ICT)

The world has now entered into an information age and developments in ICT will open up new quality vistas and cost-effective approaches. Thus, there is need for continuing education so as to meet the demands of explosion of information, fast-changing nature of occupations, and lifelong education.

4. Enhance Government Funding

Out of an annual budget of 170bn USD, only 1.12 per cent is spent on higher education. There must be appropriate increment in the allocation of budget to higher education if India wants to achieve a desired target GER of 18 per cent. Government should also provide sufficient funds, annual schemes for unaided institution for enhancing overall support.

5. Student-Centred Education and Dynamic Methods

Methods of higher education also have to be updated and should be according to the needs of the learner. Student centred education and implementation of dynamic methods of teaching would require from teachers new attitudes and new skills. Methods of teaching through lectures will have to subordinate other methods that would stress on self-study, personal consultation between teachers and pupils and dynamic sessions of seminars and workshops.

6. Improve Teaching Faculty through Incentives

Major reason for poor quality of education is the poor quality of teachers in various government schools. Government schools are unable to attract good quality teachers due to inadequate teaching facilities and low salaries. The government currently spends only 3 per cent of its GDP on education which is inadequate.

7. Change in Reservation Policy

In the present world of competition, reservation on the basis of caste (SC/ST/OBC) seems to be quite unjustified. Instead reservation can be given on the basis of financial strata of the student and his/her family. For example: Below Poverty Line.

8. Provide Need-based Job-oriented Courses

Present day education is neither imparting true knowledge of life nor it is improving the talent of a student. So a combination of arts subjects and computer science and science and humanities or literature should be introduced. Meritorious students should be recognized through teaching assistantships with stipends over and above the research fellowships.

9. Status of Academic Research Studies

The number of researchers engaged in research and development activities as compared to other countries as was found to be only 119 researchers per million in India, whereas Japan has 5,287 and US has 4,484 researchers. Number of doctoral degrees awarded in all subjects are 16,602 out of which 6,774 are in Arts and 5,408 in Science and rest in others (professional subjects) (Ernst & Young, 2011). India has little over 6,000 doctorates in science and engineering, compared to 9,000 in China and 25,000 in the United States. In comparison, there has been a modest increase in India. National Science Foundation (NSF)—Science and Engineering Indicators (2002) shows that in the US, about 4 per cent of the science and engineering graduates finish their doctorates. This figure is about 7 per cent or Europe. In India this is not even 0.4 per cent. Data on doctorates particularly in science, engineering and medicine suggest that only a few institutions have real research focus.

10. Establishment of Navratna Universities

It is needed to establish more universities because, present number of universities is too less. On 13th June, 2005, Government of India constituted a high level advisory body known as National Knowledge Commission (NKC) to advise the Prime Minister about the status of education in India and measures needed to reform this sector and proposed to establish more than 1,500 universities by the end of Eleventh Five Year Plan.

11. Public-Private Partnership

Public-Private Partnership is very essential to bring in quality in the higher education. UGC and Ministry of HRD can bring a interface between the universities, industries and National Research Laboratories (NRLs) as a step towards PPP. Funding to NRLs by the government should ensure the involvement of institutions of higher education engaged in research activities to facilitate availability of latest sophisticated equipment. There is need to create a real partnership between government, educators and industry—partnership that can provide our high-tech industries with skilled workers who meet the standards of their industry.

12. Affordability of Higher Education

Private institutions, these days charge hefty sum of money as fees. The primary focus should be on making education affordable either through making available scholarship or soft loans to economically weaker students.

13. Modernization

The time now is to modernize our education system. There should be optimal use of audio visuals, information technology and internet networks. Teaching of skill development courses by practicing professionals in technologies is required.

Other suggestions which can alleviate the state of Indian Higher Education are:

1. Develop content, pedagogy and assessment systems that can support student-centred learning;
2. Revamp the existing structure of teaching in higher education institutions;
3. Train faculty in being good facilitators;
4. Encourage a liberal arts approach to education that focus on development of
   (i) Critical thinking skills, communication and creativity-related skills, conceptualization and problems-solving skills;
   (ii) The 'case study' method of teaching can be adopted to develop problem solving and critical thinking skills; and
   (iii) Instill in students the ability to apply knowledge and skills in real-world settings by: (a) adopting a project-based approach; (b) integrating industry internships into the curricula; and (c) Focusing on co-curricular activities to develop leadership and team-building skills;
5. Introduce multi-disciplinary courses to enable students to get broader exposure;
6. Launch specialized courses to cater the need for trained manpower in "*industries of the future*";
7. Introduce basic skill-based courses and enable flexibility/multiple points to enter and exit them;
8. Develop entrepreneurial ecosystems in institutions;
9. Promote lifelong learning for working professionals;
10. Promote blended learning using Massive Open Online Courses;
11. Adopt flipped classroom model and experiential learning to improve learning in the classroom;
12. Adopt a learner-centred paradigm of education;
13. Introduce multidisciplinary/industry-oriented entrepreneurship and skill-based courses;
14. Modify norms related to recruitment of faculty members;

15. Give adequate weightage to industry experience;
16. While recruiting faculty, encourage industry professionals to take up faculty positions;
17. Depute faculty to relevant industries for short tenures to gain practical exposure;
18. Ease norms for top-tier institutions to hire the best talent from overseas;
19. Introduce reforms in the selection process of faculty members;
20. Grant autonomy to nest-in-class institutions to devise their own mechanism to recruit faculty;
21. Develop a system of rewarding the best performing faculty members by providing performance linked monetary and non-monetary benefits by implementing:
    (i) Annual performance appraisals;
    (ii) Explicit promotion standards; and
    (iii) Performance-based remuneration system.
22. Proper evaluation of faculty through regular student feedback;
23. Provide significant weigthage to research while evaluating their performance;
24. Increase involvement of faculty in curricula design and decisions relating to pedagogy;
25. Ensure active participation by best-in-class faculty from top-tier institutions to be 'hubs' for training and development of junior and mid-level faculty members from other institutions;
26. Adopt mentor model to develop strong research capabilities at leading research institutions in India. In this model, a leading international university with strong research depth can mentor four to five research-focused institutions in India in order to develop their research capabilities, framework, policies, governance structures etc. This would provide Indian universities access to global knowledge and help them become world class research-focused institutions.
27. Identify areas that would be of mutual benefit to foreign and Indian institutions so as to forge research-based collaborations;
28. Provide adequate funding for the creation of centres of excellence;
29. Promote collaborative research within academia and between academic and research centres;
30. Promote the development of Inter-Institutions Centres (IICs) and Inter-University Consortium;

31. Develop platforms for interaction between higher education institutions and research centres in the country to establish research-based relationships;
32. Develop adequate infrastructure and the requisite environment for R&D;
33. Facilitate industry involvement in research activities at academic institutions;
34. Encourage research activity at academic institutions in areas relevant to industry;
35. Encourage live research projects that can be undertaken by higher education students;
36. Develop level playing-fields, forums, seminars, portals for industry-academia collaboration;
37. Provide adequate salaries and incentives to attract high quality faculty;
38. Limit the teaching load of faculty members so as to allow them to focus on research;
39. Provide scholarships and funds to best-in class faculty to carry out research activities;
40. Strengthen industry-academia linkages across all aspects of the education;
41. Encourage tie-ups between higher education institutions and providers of skill-based training;
42. Set up institutions that target socially relevant groups;
43. Incentivize selected private participants to establish high-quality institutions;
44. Allow high-quality foreign universities to open branch campuses in India;
45. Increase access to high-quality education through content-sharing;
46. Develop framework for procurement and development of e-content;
47. Widen access through virtual classrooms and Massive Open Online Courses;
48. Evaluation parameters should include a combination of the inputs required to conduct research and outcomes the institution has delivered over the evaluation period;
49. Devise a mechanism to evaluate the performance of a higher education institution in the field off research;
50. Appointment of an independent agency to assess the institution that is to receive research grants;

51. Ensure efficient and transparent disbursement of grants to eligible institutions;
52. Encourage endowments form industry by multiple means: (a) Direct funding: Provision of funds to higher education institutions to support research-based activities. (b) Indirect funding: Developing research facilities/centres of excellence at institutions including infrastructure, faculty training, industry mentoring, industrial visits etc.;
53. Promote individual-based funding *vis-à-vis* institutions-based funding;
54. Enforce mandatory disclosure of key financial and operational information by all institutions;
55. Provide a thrust to internationalization of leadership, separate ownership and management for effective governance;
56. Ensure accountability in thorough functioning of regulators and accreditation bodies;
57. Develop a centralized database to aggregate information from individual higher education institutions which can be accessed by all;
58. Undertake regular audits of the centralized database to check its accuracy; and
59. Ensure mandatory disclosure of key financial and operational details by all private and public higher education institutions.

Conclusion

The present chapter concluded that development of education and particularly higher education is one of the most important key factors in promoting socio-economic growth in India. In India concerted effort was made to expand the base of education. As a result, not only there has been substantial increase in the number of institutions but also in the enrolment of students. Since with the advent of globalization, the growth has been very impressive; the number of universities has increased by three times, the number of colleges by 4.2 times, teachers by 2.6 times and enrolment by 3.2 times from 1992-2015. Inspire of increase in teachers institutions of higher education, there remained dearth of teachers in these institutions.

India has the large number of higher education institutions in the world, with more than 850 universities. Due to the efforts made by the government and the University Grants Commission (UGC) over the years, women's education in India has also grown both in terms of number of women's colleges and women's enrolment. The analysis of quantitative growth of higher education in India reveals that there has been rapid and explosive growth in numbers of institutions, teachers and students enrolment during post globalization period comparison to pre-globalization period. It shows that globalization has affected the growth of higher education system in India which started with new economic reform policy. The primary objective of most higher education institutions in India is to teach as many people possible rather than to create a knowledge base or superior research facilities.

In India, GER in institutions of higher education is approximately 17.9 per cent of the age cohort in 2011-12, which is lower than the average of the world 26.7 per cent as well as average of the developed countries 57.7 per cent. In addition to this, there are wide regional disparities in the access parameter of higher education among States and Union territories in India. While the aggressiveness to achieve higher rates of GER still remains unfulfilled, it would be very challenging to create sufficient opportunities to assure access to every eligible candidate in the relevant age cohort. This might continue to smooth the process of increased role to be played by the private higher education sector *vis-à-vis* public sector struggling to meet ends on other priorities avenues of public expenditure. Equitable access may still be a misnomer for policy makers as there are complex challenges in assuring the same.

The period-wise analysis of Annual Average Growth Rate (AAGR) of Indian higher education system exhibits that during 1980s AAGR of universities was 3.6 per cent which came down to 3 per cent in the period of 1990s, but further it increased to 8.3 per cent in 2002-11. The hike in the annual average growth rate of institutions after 2001-02 could be attributed to the participation of the private sector particularly in professional education. The growth rate of colleges and total higher education institutions was lowest in the period of 1980s, i.e. 4.5 per cent for both. Thereafter, AAGR of colleges in total higher education institutions saw an increase from the 1990s and registered an upward trend after 2001-02. In 1981-91, growth rate of student enrolment in higher education was 6 per cent which declined to 5.5 per cent in 1992-2001. After that it increased to a relatively faster annual average growth rate of 7.2 per cent in 2002-11. The growth rate for teachers was lowest in the period of 1980s, and thereafter, it has been increasing consistently. The analysis shows that during post globalization period, growth of higher educations system was highest after 2001-02 onwards.

The data in respect of stage-wise enrolment shows that form 1981-2011, majority of students were enrolled for a variety of courses at the graduate level. Currently 86 per cent students were enrolled at graduate courses, 12 per cent of the total number of students were enrolled at post-graduate programmes. The lack of focus on research in India is reflected in the fact that only 0.81 per cent students were pursuing research in various areas. Only 1.01 per cent of the total number of students were enrolled in Diploma/Certificate courses. The data analysis shows wide-disparity between stage-wise enrolment, which is not beneficial for the sustainable growth and development of the economy. Thus, a policy is needed to balance this type of variation in the enrolment of students. The faculty-wise enrolment shows that during the period 1981-2011, maximum influx of students was in the faculty of arts. In spite of that its share is declining in recent years. Whereas there was only a meagre enrolment recorded in the Faculty of Engineering/Technology was around 5 per cent over the period 1981-96 but from 2002 onwards its share has increased sharply to almost 17 per cent in 2011. This shows that globalization is biased towards professional courses like engineering/ technology which has high market demand. The preference for professional courses and thereby enhanced enrolment is favoured by increased private providers and other stakeholders, who anticipate better job prospects. This likely to hamper the basic research output. Further, the share of enrolment in science has shown a declining trend in recent years. The enrolment in Commerce Faculty was 20 per cent in 1980-81 and remained 21 per cent from 1985-86 to 1995-96 after that its share has declined to 17 per cent in 2011. As far as enrolment in medicine is concerned, its share has also declined from 4 per cent in 1981 to around 3 per cent over the years. The faculty of Law has shown a maximum decline to 1.93 per cent in 2011 from 6.3 per cent in 1981. Thus from the analysis, it has been found that over the period, student enrolment across various faculties has been very uneven.

The share of unaided private higher education institutions in the country has grown significantly in the last few years, contributing to the growth in the higher education segment. The growth is also reflected in the dominant share of private institutes in professional courses. For India achieve its GER target of 30 per cent it is imperative to further involve the private sector by creating a conducive environment for their participation (Ersnt & Young/FICCI, 2011). Private sector should be encouraged to start professional institutions, but it must be ensured that their entry do not lead to commercialization.

There is an urgent need to relook at the financial resources, access, equity, accountability, affordability, quality standards, relevance and at the end responsiveness. To attain and sustain National, regional or International quality, certain components are particularly relevant, very importantly careful selection of staff and continuous staff development, in particular through the promotion of appropriate programmes for academic development including teaching/leanring methodology and mobility between countries.

The politicization of higher education is another area of concern. The effect of internal and external politics of higher education is counterproductive to the quality of higher education. The appointments of Vice-Chancellors to teachers to students are often influenced by the politics and politicians, as a result of which incompetent teachers are appointed which have led to deterioration in quality. The appointments should be fair and should only be based on merit. As pointed by UNESCO, the candidate's qualifications, aptitude and passion for the subject, course and the job must be given due consideration before appointments are made.

We are moving towards an era which would be defined by the parameters of knowledge and wisdom. The decisions that are going to be taken on these are likely to hold the key to India's future as a centre of knowledge production. We need highly educated persons who are skilled and one who can drive our economy forward. When India can provide skilled people to the outside world then only we can transform our country from a developing to a developed nation very easily and rapidly.

The authorities and policy makers should devise new strategies and programmes to rejuvenate and revamp the system to make it internationally competitive through quality enhancement and through an effective use of the Information and Communication Technology. To reap the benefits from the merging knowledge based world economy, India has to introduce the much needed academic and administrative reforms. We need an educational system that is modern, liberal and can adapt to the changing needs of a changing society, a changing economy and a changing world. The thrust of public policy for higher education in India has to be to address these challenges. India would enable to rise as a global economic power only by nurturing its huge human resource potential through providing access to quality higher education for the millions of young Indian. It is, therefore, what Prof. Amrik Singh has seems to be so apt under the prevailing circumstances, that "The single most important thing needed now is to get out of the rigidity of the system. In the rapidly changing world of today, one thing is certain; yesterday's education system will not meet today's need and even less so the need of tomorrow."

References

Agarwal, Pawan (2006). *Higher Education in India: The Need for Change.* ICRIER Working Paper No. 180. Retrieved from: www.icrier.org/pdf/ICRIER_WP180_Higher_Education_in_India_pdf.

Agarwal, Pawan (2009). *Indian Higher Education—Envisioning Future*, New Delhi: Sage Publications Pvt. Ltd.

Ahmad, Nighat (2002). *Economics of Higher Education in Uttar Pradesh.* AMU Press, Aligarh.

Anandakrishnan, M. (2006). *Privatization of Higher Education: Opportunities and Anomalies.* Paper presented at National Seminar on Privatization and Commercialization of Higher Education, May 2, NEUPA, New Delhi.

Das, S. (2007). The Higher Education in India and the Challenge of Globalization. *Social Scientist*, 35 (3/4): 47-67, March-April.

Ernst and Young/FICCI (2010). *New Realities, New Possibilities: The Changing Face of Indian Higher Education.* Ernst and Young Pvt. Ltd., Kolkata. Retrieved from www.evcp.berkeley.edu/sites/default/files/ISTF_Appendix_VII.pdf.

Ernst and Young/FICCI (2011a). *Private sector participation* in *Indian Higher Education.* www.ey.com/....higher education/..../Private_Sector_participation_in_Indin_higher_education.pdf

Ernst and Young/FICCI (2012). *Higher Education in India: Twelfth Five Year Plan (2012-2017) and beyond*...FICCI Higher Education Summit 2012. Retrieved from: www.ey.com/Publicaitons/VWLUAssets/Higher_Education_in_India/File/EY-FICCI_Higher_Education_Report_Nov12.pdf.

Ernst and Young-EDGE (2011). 40 Million By 2020: Preparing for a New Paradigm in Indian Higher Education. Ernst & Young Pvt. Ltd., India.

Geetha Rani, P. (2004). Economic Reforms and Financing Higher Education in India. *Indian Journal of Economics and Business*, 3(1): 1-30.

Ministry of Human Resource Development (1986). *National Policy on Education—1986*, New Delhi: Government of India.

MHRD (2010). *Report to the People on Education (2009-10).* July, NUEPA, MHRD, GOI, New Delhi.

National Knowledge Commission (NKC). (2007, 2008). *Report to the Nation 2006* and *Report to the Nation 2007*. New Delhi: Government of India.

Prakash, Ved (2015). Trends in Growth and Financing of Higher Education in India. *Economic and Political Weekly*, XLXI (31): 3549-3558, August 4-10, Sameeksha Trust Publication, Mumbai.

Statistics of Higher and Technical Education (2008-09). Government of India, Ministry of Human Resource Development, Bureau of Planning, Monitoring and Statistics, New Delhi, 2012.

Tilak, J.B.G (2003). Higher Education and Development in Asia. *Journal of Educational Planning and Administration*, 17 (2): 151-173, April, National Institute of Educational Planning and Administration (NIEPA), New Delhi.

Tilak, J.B.G (2003). *Public Subsidies in Education in India. Economic and Political Weekly*, XXXIX (4), January 24, pp. 343-59.

Tilak (2005b). Higher Education under Structural Adjustment. In Steve O. Michael and Mark A. Kretovics (Eds.), *Financing Higher Education in a Global Market*, New York: Algora Publishing, pp. 257-99.

Tilak, J.B.G (2007). Knowledge Commission and Higher Education. *Economic and Political Weekly*, 42 (8): 630-633, February 24. Sameeksha Trust Publication, Mumbai.

UGC (2012). *Higher Education in India at Glance*. UGC, New Delhi.

UGC Annual Reports (2012/13/14/15). MHRD, Various Issues, GOI, New Delhi.

UNDP. (1999). *Human Development Report*. New York: Oxford University Press.

World Bank (2003). *A policy note on the grant-in-aid system in Indian education.* South Asia Human Development Sector. Report No. 3. World Bank, New Delhi, November.

used to study at the same *Gurukula*. Their companionship sets an example for others. Years after leaving the *Gurukula* when Sudama was facing financial crisis, Krishna helped him. That is what the Indian Education System was all about. Students were imparted good values. They were taught the lessons of balance, humankind and helping one another. That was the real esteem based education framework and we ought to embrace such a framework in present times too.

However, selfishness and self-centredness can be smelt in the character of student these days. They are just concerned about their rights and are completely ignoring their duties towards their families, nation and society. They are also falling prey to curses like drugs, terrorism etc. There are many factors behind it. There is frustration in our youth due to unemployment and underemployment. We can see act of violence committed by youth all around the country. The crime rate is increasing day by day. The teenagers are becoming gangsters, murderers, rapists etc. Thus we have not been able to give our student values but also could not make them skilled to the extent that they get good jobs. The parents and teachers are likely to teach the kids as how to face various hardships in life. So we, parents and teachers, have failed on both the fronts.[3] India is the land of great personalities like Vivekananda, Mahatma Gandhi and so on. These people have made the nation proud and given it global recognition. Unfortunately we have taken wrong paths and forgot the importance of spirituality in one's life. Not only the environment (water, air etc.) around us is polluted now, but the minds of people have also got polluted. Values are the guiding forces in our life that enlighten our minds and souls. These values are universal in nature and produce same output irrespective of region, religion, community etc. They are essential for the growth in any nation. These values provide right directions to our thoughts and motivate us to take the right path.

Effect of Professional Education on Value System

Profession is defined as a number of people practising a definite technique specialised with the help of intellectual study and training.[4] The mere aim of which is to supply service or advice to others for a particular fee or salary. The major difference has been stated between the old and the new profession lies between their secular character, the system of payments and their outlook towards their jobs.[5] For being a good manager, a person must have three types of skills—technical skill, human skill and conceptual skill.[6] A technical skill refers to the ability of a person to apply his specialised knowledge related to his job to his work. We can also define it as expertise in performing one's job. Technical skills are learnt through education, training programmes, on-job training etc. A human skill is related to the ability to work with and cooperate others. It is concerned with team work and motivating others. It is essential for a manager to have ability to communicate, motivate, lead and cooperate others. A conceptual skill refers to the ability of a person to analyse and handle complex situations. So, it is clear that manager should have human skills besides having the technical and conceptual skilis. The institutions insist upon technical and conceptual skill only. They do not try to incorporate humanity and human skills in management students who are future managers of the country.

Education *vs.* Qualification

Education, which is a relatively broader concept, has got confined to very limited scope. The only aim of the educational institutes, teachers, students and parents is to get good results in the examinations and get good jobs. Thus we are making the minds materialistic instead of making them intellectual. The education just provides bookish knowledge and the aim is just to score good in the examinations instead of development and upliftment of the society. The Government is spending so much on education, still the students are losing morality.[7]

Education is called "*vidya*" in Hindi. "*Vidya*" comprises two words "*vid*" and '*ya*'. "*Vid*" implies light. "*Ya*" implies which. In this way, *Vidya* is which gives us light. Thus, education implies directing light which manages us all through our entire life. Thus education not only means qualification. It also consists of qualities for being a good human being. Institutions only lay stress on curriculum and book. They have forgotten the importance of qualities like being social, encouraging others and not feeling jealous of others, being tolerant and humble etc. William Coronon suggested 10 qualities of an educated person:[8]

1. Educated people know the importance of listening. They listen to others carefully and understand their words, emotions, tone etc.
2. They know how to read the words and interpret them to understand their meaning. They read for both joy and knowledge.
3. They can talk to every type of people according to the requirement of the situation.

4. They know the art of putting words together and express what they want to convey.
5. They have the ability to solve problems. They solve problems by decomposing it into sub-problems, solving each of the sub-problems and putting together the solution of sub-problems.
6. They are always ready to learn new things to enhance their knowledge.
7. Educated people are humble not arrogant. They are open to other's suggestions and perspectives.
8. They make effort to make the world a better place to live. They try to devote a small part of their lives to others.
9. They are social and understand that the success of others is also essential fro one's own success.
10. They encourage people to connect with each other.

An attempt has been made to compare the culture of Western countries and India.[9] He found out that the Western culture lays stress on knowledge about the physical world. At the same time, Indian culture put more emphasis on the knowledge about the social world as compared to physical world. Kochhar laid stress on the teaching of Indian history to students. He specified the following aims of teaching history to students:

- To upgrade the feeling of patriotism in them.
- To make them to show regard towards other individuals' sentiments, thoughts and convictions.
- To make them respect different religions and beliefs.
- To make them set up fellowship with individuals from other group.
- To offer them some assistance with learning to co-work with others in social and urban exercises.
- They figure out how to acknowledge social varieties.
- To fortify their faith in correspondence of man independent of religion caste and creed.
- To advance a comprehension of the procedure of progress and improvement through which human social orders have developed to the present stage.
- To advance a comprehension of basic foundations of human civic establishments and energy about essential solidarity of humankind.
- To foster understanding that common association of different societies is vital variable in the advancement of humankind.

Importance of Teachers

Guru means the person who deserves honour. In history of India, however the highest position was held by the King yet really the country was controlled by the '*Gurus*'. *Gurus* never went to Kings to request anything but Kings went to *Gurus* to look for their recommendation on urgent and general matters. The rulers never questioned the guidance given by the *Gurus* and had blind faith in them. They simply used to take after what the *Guru* had said. The great Mauryan Emperor, Chandragupta is renowned in the historical backdrop of India only because of his *Guru* Chanakya. Chanakya's words were his command. Chanakya used to add some poison in his food without his knowledge to make him immune to poison. One day Chandragupta gave some of his food to his wife to eat. His wife passed on subsequent to eating it. But, he never questioned his *Guru's* intentions.

One more illustration of the values of students in old India is that of Eklavya. Eklavya is a standout amongst the most sensible characters from the epic *Mahabharata*. He is a good example for the students today. He really comprehended the significance of a teacher. Only those students who regard their educators and obey them can succeed in life. Eklavya was a youthful sovereign of the Nishadha. He wanted to learn archery in the *Gurukula* of Dronacharya. Dronacharya was the master of Pandavas and Kauravas. He was considered one of the best teachers in archery and trained Arjuna in it. Dronacharya rejected Eklavya in light of the fact that he was a *shudra* and not a *kshatriya*. Eklavya got extremely baffled yet it did not influence his determination of taking in the specialty of bows and arrows. He made a mud statue of Drona and installed it close to his home. He started learning archery in front of statue and used to practice very hard. Before long he got to be master in it. He became a better archer than Arjuna.

One day Acharya Drona and Arjuna were going through the backwoods. They saw a dog barking. Then Eklavya sealed the dog's mouth with an arrow. Arjuna was extremely astounded to see it. Dronacharya let him know that this strategy is known as '*Shabda Bhedi*' in archery. He told Arjuna that he was still not competent enough to learn that technique. Dronacharya asked Eklavya about the person from whom he had learnt that technique. Eklavya said that the person behind his success was none other than his *Guru* Dronacharya. Dronacharya was extremely upbeat to know it yet he additionally recollected his guarantee of making Arjuna the best archer on the planet. Dronacharya realized that Eklavya was more gifted than Arjuna. He realized that Arjuna can not be the best bowman on the planet as long as Eklavya was there. In this way, he requested '*Guru Dakshina*' (Teaching expense) from Eklavya. Eklavya got ready to give anything Dronacharya would ask for. Dronacharya had seen that Eklavya used his right thumb in archery. So, he asked for his right hand thumb. Eklavya immediately cut the thumb of this right hand and gave it to Drona. In this way he fulfilled Drona's dream of making Arjuna the best archer in the world. The story of Eklavya is classic example of the value of teachers for their students in ancient times.

Role of Teachers

As far as value education is concerned, the teachers should apt the saying "Practice what you preach". In order to inculcate the values in student, first the teachers ought to reflect those values in their behaviour and attitude. Teachers need to set examples in front of their students and lead them from the front if they want to build a humanistic society. There is a strong need to train teachers for positive character formation.[10] Teachers can impart values implicitly by enforcing discipline, appreciating the humanitarian moves of students in classrooms, encouraging excellence, motivating students to give real reasons instead of excuses thus promoting truthfulness and many other means. It has been stated that the code of ethics should be there not only for students but also for the teachers[5]. As teachers are the ideals for students. So, they should set examples for students. Teachers should follow a strict code of conduct themselves only then they can tell the students to follow certain ethics. So, a teacher should lead by example. He specified a code of ethics for teachers which specify the following things:

Obligation Towards Students

- Help each individual student in achieving his/her maximum potential.
- Have some personal information about the student to protect him from being a victim of any situation.
- Never exploit students for any personal or professional interest.
- Encourage the students to be self-dependent.
- Avoid using obscene language.
- Avoid taking up tuitions. If you do so, it must be for betterment of students and not for monetary gains.

- Learn latest trends in your own area of specialization.
- Keep on learning and teaching new things.

Obligation Towards Community

- Be patriotic but at the same time secular.
- Have responsibility for equal educational opportunities for all sections of the community.
- Your civic responsibility should not hurt your professional code of conduct.
- Participate in formulation of educational policies.
- Use your skills to fulfil personnel needs of the community.

Obligation Towards the Profession

- Match individual behaviour with the code of ethical conduct.
- Cooperate and adjust with others working with you.
- Play vital role in implementation of educational policies.
- Do not let non-professional persons discharge professional functions.
- Keep confidential information secret.
- Utilize the vacations for professional growth.

The teachers must serve as role models for their students. The role of teachers is not limited only to teach the students but also provide them a caring and civil climate in the school and classrooms.[11] For teaching the students how to respect others, First of all the environment of the school should be such that where respect is practiced continuously.

Value Based Education: The Solution

Value based education can be defined as a type of education system which bestows various moral, ethical, cultural, social, spiritual values in students which would support their holistic development and make them good human beings. It includes physical as well as psychological well-being, etiquettes and social conduct and so forth. Each one of us is very much aware about significance of these qualities in our life yet we do not try to develop it in ourselves and in our students. Thus bringing about various behavioural and moral issues.[12]

Value education should not be considered as a separate subject which needs to be added into the curriculum, rather it is a philosophy which is inseparable part of real education system, a pedagogy of teaching-learning method, an approach to build the nation and a move towards promoting humanity. Institutes, that have embraced value based education system, have observed qualitative improvement in the behaviour and attitude of the students. Value education is a tool which not just gives us a profession to pursue for earning livelihood but also teach us how to live a decent life. The reason for our life is without a doubt to know oneself and act naturally. We can not do it unless we figure out how to distinguish ourselves with every one of that lives.[13]

Ignorance of value education, which is an inseparable part of an ideal education system, has given rise to incompetent, immoral and shallow learning. In order to preserve and cherish the inherited culture, the society needs to pass on the traditions, ethics and values to the generations to come. It is possible only if our education system is value based system. Education is a teaching-learning process which is meant to acquire knowledge and wisdom. Thus the teachers as well as students must come together to make the education system more effective and efficient. In real means, education builds the moral character of the younger generations and is the only answer to disastrous problems people are facing these days.[14]

The disintegration of values and expanding skepticism in the public arena has brought the requirement for rearrangements in the educational programmes keeping in mind the end goal to make training an instrument for development of social and good values.[15] Education should foster moral values. It should guide people towards unity and not divide them. Values will help in avoiding violence, communal riots, superstition etc. It will insulate human values in people. So, there is a strong need for adding teaching of values and morals in the curriculum for the students. Lickona laid great stress on the need on value education.[16] He said that value based education promotes ethical values and these values serve as a base of good character. So, value education will make the citizens of a country bearing good character. He defined character as a combination of thinking, feelings and behaviour. The value based education should be designed in such a way that it motivates the students to develop a good character first of all.

Most of the problems faced by Indian Universities and colleges are due to their inability to generate intellectual work of their own.[17] The teachers don't inherit scholarly traditions from their ancient counterparts. A plant can not flourish if it is not connected to its roots. He laid stress on the cultural roots and to discover the hidden treasure of India's rich culture and traditions. The value based education system will lead to love, respect, understanding and peace in our society.[18] At present social, moral and cultural values are degrading day by day. The evils like corruption, indiscipline and violence are dominating human beings. To fight with these evils, a value based education system is essential. Such an education system will help in cultural and moral development. It will help in resolving conflicts, cooperative living and maintaining harmony. So, value oriented education will help in developing a complete man with a sound mind and a good heart.

Education expenses have always been an important part of Union Budget of India. Additionally, wrong-doings are expanding step by step. So, two conflicting things are developing. Expansion of education should lead to decrease in crime. However, the situation is absolutely inverse. The reason behind this situation is that in place of giving education, institutes are giving just degrees to the students. Stress ought to be set down to show moral qualities to understudies alongside educating the educational modules. To save the world, to extra humankind it is fundamental to make the understudies great people along with making them great experts in the professional fields.

In old times, Krishna fiscally helped his adolescence companion Sudama. Presently days, siblings are quarrelling for cash and are ready to kill one another. Eklavya gave his educator Dronacharya his thumb cheerfully. These days, an understudy would not dither notwithstanding for a brief moment before cutting his educator's thumb. These things demonstrate that individuals were better than average on the most fundamental level in old India since they were taught moral values from the very beginning. That is where present students slack in. So the conclusion of this research is that there is a solid need of conferring value based education to students alongside other subjects.

Notes

1. Meglino, B.M. and Ravlin, E.C. (1998). Individual values in organizations: concepts. controversies and research. *Journal of Management*, *24*(3): 351-389.
2. Kochhar, S.K. (1992). *Teaching of History.* New Delhi: Sterling Publishers Pvt. Ltd., pp. 31-35.
3. Jayaram, N. (2015). *Sociology of Education in India*, Rawat Publications, New Delhi.

4. Stinnett, T.M. (1965). *The Profession of Teaching.* Sydney: Prentice-Hall, p. 3
5. Singh, R.P. (1984). *The Teachers in India.* New Delhi: National Publishing House, p. 8.
6. Robbins, S.P. (2003). *Organizational Behaviour.* (10th ed.). Sydney: Prentice-Hall.
7. Divine Vision by Sri Sathya Sai Institute of Higher Learning, Prasanthi Nilyam, Andhra Pradesh, November, 2006.
8. William Cronon (1992). *Uncommon Ground: Rethinking the Human Place in Nature and Nature's,* Metropolis, Chicago.
9. Gardner, H. (1993). *Frames of Mind: the Theory of Multiple Intelligences* (10th Ed.). Basic Books, New York.
10. Narvaez, D., and Lapsley, D.K. (2008). Teaching moral character: Two alternatives for teacher education. *The Teacher Educator*, 43(2): 156-172.
11. Williams, M.M. (2000). Models of character education. *Journal of Humanistic Counseling, Education and Development*, *39*(1): 32-40.
12. Awasthi, D. (2014). Value based Education is the only Solution to the Problem of Crisis of Moral Values among the Youth of India, *GJRA— Global journal for Research Analysis*, 9(3): 4-5.
13. Borah, A.K. (2014). A comparative study on Need for Value Based Education an Opinion Survey among School Teachers, *International Journal of Humanities and Social Science Studies*, 1(1): 42-51.
14. Iyer, R.B., and Ranjani, D. (2013). Value-Based Education: Professional Development vital towards effective integration. *IOSR Journal of Research and Method in Education*, 1: 17-20.
15. Rao, D.B. (1996). *National Policy on Education.* New Delhi: Anmol Publication Ltd., p. 140.
16. Lickona, T. (1992). *Educating for Character. How Our Schools Can Teach Respect and Responsibility.* New York: Bantam Doubleday.
17. Shils, E. (1974). *The Higher Learning in India.* New Delhi: Vikas Publishing House Pvt. Ltd., p. 205.
18. Walia, J.S. (2000). *Philosophical and Sociological Bases of Education.* Jalandhar: Paul Publishers.

Index